ALSO BY ANDREW NAGORSKI

Last Stop Vienna

The Birth of Freedom:
Shaping Lives and Societies in the New Eastern Europe

Reluctant Farewell:
An American Reporter's Candid Look Inside the Soviet Union

THE

GREATEST

Andrew Nagorski

BATTLE

Stalin, Hitler, and the Desperate

Struggle for Moscow That Changed

the Course of World War II

SIMON & SCHUSTER   New York   London   Toronto   Sydney

SIMON & SCHUSTER
1230 Avenue of the Americas
New York, NY 10020

First Simon & Schuster hardcover edition September 2007.

SIMON & SCHUSTER and colophon are registered trademarks
of Simon & Schuster, Inc.

Images in the picture section are credited as follows:
Getty Images: 1, 3, 8, 9, 10, 13, 18, 19, 25
AP/Wide World Photos: 2, 5, 12
Polaris Images: 4, 6, 7
ITAR-TASS Photo Agency: 11, 20
Time-Life Pictures/Getty Images: 14, 16, 17, 21, 22, 23, 24
Franklin D. Roosevelt Library: 15

For information about special discounts for bulk purchases,
please contact Simon & Schuster Special Sales at
1-800-456-6798 or business@simonandschuster.com.

Designed by Jaime Putorti

Manufactured in the United States of America

10 9 8 7 6 5 4 3 2 1

Library of Congress Cataloging-in-Publication Data

Nagorski, Andrew.
The greatest battle : Stalin, Hitler, and the desperate struggle for Moscow
that changed the course of World War II / Andrew Nagorski.
     p. cm.
   Includes bibliographical references and index.
   1. Moscow, Battle of, Moscow, Russia, 1941–1942. 2. Stalin, Joseph,
1879–1953—Military leadership. 3. Hitler, Adolf, 1889–1945—Military
leadership. I. Title.
D764.3.M6N33 2007
940.54'214731—dc22   2007017053

ISBN-13: 978-0-7432-8110-2
ISBN-10:   0-7432-8110-1

For Stella,
the first of the next generation

And, as always,
for Krysia

We will break them soon, it's only a question of time . . . Moscow will be attacked and will fall, then we will have won the war.

—Hitler speaking to an aide in mid-September 1941

Are you sure we are going to be able to hold Moscow? I am asking with an aching heart.

—Stalin in a phone call to General Georgy Zhukov
in mid-November 1941

Contents

Contents

A Note on Transliteration

The transliteration system found in the body of this book is the one that is usually used by the American media. Although it is not always totally consistent, it is considered the simplest and most readable. The system used in the endnotes and bibliography, however, is the Library of Congress system, which is commonly employed by U.S. libraries. In the case of Russian works that have been translated previously into English, the spelling of the authors' names has been adopted as published.

Introduction

In the fall of 1941, two gargantuan armies fiercely fought each other on the northern, southern, and western approaches to Moscow. On both sides it wasn't so much the generals who were calling the shots as the tyrants Adolf Hitler and Joseph Stalin. Those two leaders issued everyone their orders, never hesitating to send millions to their death whether in combat or in prisons and the camps. Both demonstrated ruthless resolve and, at times, brilliant tactics, but they were also prone to strategic shortsightedness on a colossal scale.

Hitler dispatched his armies deep into Russia without winter clothing, since he was convinced they would triumph long before the first frosts arrived. Stalin sent many of his troops into battle without guns, since he hadn't prepared the nation for the German onslaught. This doomed countless thousands of Germans to death by freezing in the first winter of the Russian campaign and countless thousands of Red Army soldiers to instant death because they did not survive long enough to pick up whatever weapon they could find among the dead and the dying.

The battle for Moscow, which officially lasted from September 30, 1941, to April 20, 1942, but in reality spanned more than those

203 days of unremitting mass murder, marked the first time that Hitler's armies failed to triumph with their *Blitzkrieg* tactics. When those armies had crushed Poland, France and much of the rest of Europe with breathtaking speed, they had looked unstoppable. "This defeat, however, was more than just another lost battle," Fabian von Schlabrendorff, one of the German officers who later joined the conspiracy against Hitler, recalled in his memoirs. "With it went the myth of the invincibility of the German soldier. It was the beginning of the end. The German army never completely recovered from that defeat." True enough, but the German forces would continue to fight with astonishing tenacity, and their ultimate defeat was still a long way off, which is why such judgments have been rendered only with the benefit of hindsight.

The battle for Moscow was arguably the most important battle of World War II and inarguably the largest battle between two armies of all time. Combining the totals for both sides, approximately seven million troops were involved in some portion of this battle. Of those seven million, 2.5 million were killed, taken prisoner, missing or wounded badly enough to require hospitalization—with the losses far heavier on the Soviet than on the German side. According to Russian military records, 958,000 Soviet soldiers "perished," which included those killed, missing or taken prisoner. Given the treatment they received at the hands of their captors, most Soviet POWs were, in effect, condemned to death. Another 938,500 soldiers were hospitalized for their wounds, which brought overall Soviet losses to 1,896,500. The corresponding number for the German forces was 615,000.

By comparison, the losses for other epic battles, while horrific, never reached those kinds of figures. In the popular imagination, the battle for Stalingrad, from July 1942 to early February 1943, is generally considered the bloodiest of those struggles. It was huge but never approached the size of the battle for Moscow. About half the number of troops—3.6 million—were involved, and the combined losses of the two sides were 912,000 troops, as compared to the 2.5 million in the Moscow battle.

None of the other major battles of the two world wars come much closer to Moscow's tallies. In the battle of Gallipoli in 1915, for example, the combined losses of the Turkish and Allied troops were roughly 500,000; for the battle of the Somme, from July to October 1916, German, British and French losses totaled about 1.1 million. And just in terms of the numbers of troops involved in the fighting, many other legendary battles of World War II weren't even in the same league as the battle for Moscow. At the pivotal battle of El Alamein during the North African campaign, for example, the opposing armies totaled 310,000.

This was also a battle that was played out in front of a global audience, with the United States, Britain, Japan and others making key decisions based on their assessments of its likely outcome. There's no doubt that if the Germans hadn't been stopped at the outskirts of Moscow, the repercussions would have been felt around the world.

And yet the battle for Moscow is now largely forgotten. Historians have paid far more attention both to the battles of Stalingrad and the Kursk salient, which represented clear-cut victories over Hitler's forces, and to the searing human drama of the siege of Leningrad. By contrast, the battle for Moscow was marred by too many errors and miscalculations by Stalin and raised too many unsettling questions to be subject to the same level of attention. As a result, it was often hastily dealt with in the history books and has never attained the mythological status of the later victories. But it's precisely because of its crucial role in the early period of World War II and what it reveals about the nature of the totalitarian giants who faced off against each other that the real story of the battle for Moscow has to be told, elevating this battle to its proper place in the history of the war.

History always looks inevitable in retrospect, but the plain fact is that there's usually nothing inevitable about the cataclysmic events that shape our world. To the Soviet leadership in 1941, there was nothing inevitable about the outcome of the German assault on their country, despite the official rhetoric. In the confrontation between the two monstrous leaders of all time, Hitler and Stalin, it was the German who initially caught his Soviet counterpart off guard. Stalin had ignored a rising flood of intelligence warning him that the Germans were about to attack and expressly forbidden his generals to take the measures that would have given their armies a better chance of withstanding the invaders.

The result was that the Soviet forces were thrown into total dis-array during the early months of the war, and the Germans pushed deeper and deeper into the Soviet heartland, with Moscow clearly in their sights. On August 12, 1941, Wilhelm Keitel, Hitler's Chief of the High Command of the Armed Forces, outlined the main target of the German offensive. "The object of operations must then be to deprive the enemy, before the coming of winter, of his government, armament, and traffic center around Moscow, and thus prevent the rebuilding of his defeated forces and the orderly working of government control," he wrote in Directive 34a. In other words, Hitler's goal of a swift victory in the east, so he could then turn his attention back to the war against Britain, depended on his ability to surround and then seize the Soviet capital.

Soon enough, that looked like a very real possibility. While some Soviet troops fought heroically against overwhelming odds, others—and they numbered in the hundreds of thousands—sur-rendered as quickly as they could. Stalin, for his part, suffered a near psychological collapse as his country looked as though it might implode. Buoyed by their early swift progress, German sol-diers put up signposts proclaiming "To Moscow." As Hitler pre-pared for Operation Typhoon in September 1941, which was supposed to culminate in the collapse of the Soviet capital, he told his subordinates, "In a few weeks we shall be in Moscow." Then, he added, "I will raze that damned city and in its place construct an artificial lake with central lighting. The name of Moscow will disap-pear for ever." Whether or not he meant the last part literally or was carried away by the emotion of the moment, his boasts accu-rately reflected the growing sense that the Soviet capital wouldn't be able to mount an effective defense against the forces preparing to launch a massive assault.

And what would the seizure of Moscow signify for the entire war effort? When foreign invaders had seized the city twice before— the Poles in the early seventeenth century and Napoleon in 1812— those victories had proven to be short-lived. In Napoleon's case, the breakthrough to Moscow only set the stage for the catastrophic defeat and retreat of his *Grande Armée*. But Moscow in those earlier times wasn't nearly the prize it was in 1941. By then, it was not only the political but also the strategic and industrial center of the country and its transportation hub. Its seizure would have been a devastating blow for the Soviet Union—and for all those seeking to thwart Hitler's war aims.

Boris Nevzorov, a Russian military historian who has spent his life studying the battle for Moscow, argues that the Germans' failure there was the key event that determined the outcome of the war. "If they had taken Moscow, the war would have ended with a German victory," he maintains. Other historians and some of the surviving participants dispute that claim, insisting that the Soviet Union would have eventually rebounded even from the loss of its capital. Neither side can prove its case, of course; history doesn't provide definitive answers to "what if" questions. But Nevzorov is on indisputably firm ground when he characterizes the battle for Moscow as "our first great victory and the first great loss for Nazi Germany."

Soviet accounts of the battle solemnly mention the danger the country faced as German troops closed in on the capital in the fall of 1941. "It was the lowest point reached throughout the war," notes the five-volume official *History of the Great Patriotic War of the Soviet Union,* which was published in the early 1960s. But those accounts don't dwell on the significance of the German failure to complete the push to take the city. This is no accident, *nye sluchaino,* as the Russians say. The early Soviet histories of the period had plenty of reasons to dispose of the battle for Moscow quickly.

First of all, the disastrous series of events associated with the battle raised all sorts of questions about Stalin and his incessant use of terror as a weapon against his own people—a practice he continued throughout the war. It was his mistakes that allowed the Germans to get as close as they did, and the subsequent scenes of panic in the city as people rushed to escape belied the myth that everyone had an unshakable faith in victory from the beginning.

Then there was the sheer scale of the Soviet losses. Boris Vidensky was a cadet at the Podolsk Artillery Academy when the war started and was among the lucky few of his class who survived when they were thrown—thoroughly unprepared—against the advancing Germans. He went on to become a senior researcher at the Military History Institute in Moscow. In retirement, he recounted that after the war, Marshal Georgy Zhukov, the legendary Red

Army architect of the Soviet victory, decided to try to estimate the losses of his troops near Moscow. In the postwar period, Zhukov served as defense minister, and he ordered his deputy to make some rough calculations. When the deputy showed him the figure he had come up with, Zhukov quickly barked out an order. "Hide it and don't show it to anybody!"

Even when the German drive to take the capital was repulsed, the battle for Moscow proved to be an incomplete victory. Just as it was preceded by Stalin's huge miscalculations, it was followed by more of them. Stalin's insistence, over the opposition of his generals, that they now hurl their exhausted forces into an all-out offensive against the Germans produced a series of costly defeats and sent casualty counts skyrocketing. The Germans stubbornly hung on to pockets of territory, notably around the town of Rzhev, northwest of Moscow, for nearly a year after the battle for the capital was officially declared over. The initial relief that Moscow was saved was quickly replaced by bitter disappointment.

In other words, despite the genuine courage and heroism of Moscow's defenders, this huge battle was marked by humiliations and defeats from its earliest days all the way through to its lengthy aftermath. Both sides came to realize that they were in for a long war, the bloodiest fighting in human history. And it was even bloodier than necessary because of Stalin's and Hitler's miscalculations and unremitting ruthlessness. For Stalin, the human toll was the least of his concerns. As he would tell Chinese Premier Zhou Enlai during the Korean War, the North Koreans could keep fighting because they "lose nothing, *except for their men.*" He maintained the same attitude toward his own country's losses as they mounted at a dizzying pace.

To be fair, Stalin also inspired many of his countrymen, and it was his decision to stay in Moscow when he had already ordered the evacuation of other top officials and both military and civilian installations that proved, in retrospect, to be a key turning point in the battle for Moscow. If Stalin was living proof of Machiavelli's dictum that for a ruler it is much safer to be feared than loved, he also at times came close to the Florentine's ideal "that one ought to be both feared and loved." The war was one of those times. Many of his countrymen were genuinely willing to sacrifice their lives for their country and for Stalin, convinced that they were one and the same.

This book draws upon a broad range of sources, some tapped for the first time. Among them: large numbers of newly declassified documents from the archives of the NKVD, as the KGB was then called; first-hand accounts from survivors, some of whom only now feel free to talk about the full range of their experiences, often contradicting the sanitized version of events presented by Soviet and even some Western writers; interviews with the children of such key figures as Marshal Georgy Zhukov, Politburo member Anastas Mikoyan, and top NKVD leaders responsible for planning for resistance and sabotage in a German-controlled Moscow; published and unpublished diaries, letters and memoirs from a variety of Russians and foreigners.

All of this evidence makes clear that the battle for Moscow wasn't just the largest single battle of the war but also its earliest turning point. To be sure, the battle of Britain had already demonstrated that the German military machine wasn't unstoppable, but that was an air battle. Wherever Hitler's armies could march, they had continued to win victories—that is, until the battle for Moscow.

At a rally in Berlin's Sportpalast on October 3, 1941, Hitler told his cheering supporters that the drive to Moscow, which appeared to be in its final stages, was "the greatest battle in the history of the world." Once the Soviet dragon was slain, it "would never rise again," he predicted. While keenly aware of the precedent set by Napoleon, Hitler was convinced—and managed to convince his armies—that they didn't have to fear defeat in the snows of Russia. But he was soon to be proven wrong in all his predictions. He was right only in his claim that the battle for Moscow was the greatest battle ever—but from his perspective, for all the wrong reasons.

How Stalin eventually turned what looked like a rout into a victory, the human price of that victory, and how it set the stage for so much that followed—both in terms of the fighting and the early diplomatic wrangling between Stalin and the West about the future of a postwar Europe—is the subject of this book. For even as Moscow's fate hung in the balance, Stalin was already laying the groundwork for the expansion of his empire, and the United States and Britain were struggling to find an effective counterstrategy. If Moscow had fallen, none of this would have mattered. Yet Moscow survived, even if just barely, and that was enough to make all the difference.

Finally, a personal note. As someone who was stationed in Moscow twice as a foreign correspondent, I thought I had a general idea about the significance and scale of the fighting there. Now that I've spent the past few years digging out what I can about that subject, I realize I couldn't have been more wrong. Like everyone who flies in and out of Sheremetyevo Airport in the Russian capital, I have passed the battle monument on the airport road—three oversized hedgehogs representing the anti-tank barriers that were strewn about the city in anticipation of a German assault—on each of those occasions. But my knowledge of what really happened was extremely limited. I knew the Germans had come close, perhaps right up to where the monument now stands in the Khimki district on the outskirts of the city, a mere half-hour drive from the Kremlin when the road isn't jammed with traffic. Nonetheless, like most Westerners and even most Russians, I was oblivious to so much of Moscow's story. This book is my attempt to fill in this gaping hole in the history books and the popular imagination.

1

"Hitler will not attack us in 1941"

For a time, it seemed, they were natural allies, two dictators who mirrored each other in so many ways that they seemed like a perfectly matched couple in their cynicism, cunning and staggering brutality. When Hitler and Stalin concluded their infamous nonaggression pact, signed by their foreign ministers, Joachim von Ribbentrop and Vyacheslav Molotov, on August 23, 1939, they both knew this was the signal for World War II to begin, allowing the Germans to invade Poland from the west on September 1 and the Red Army to attack from the east on September 17 to divide the spoils. But it may have been precisely because Hitler and Stalin were so much alike that they had to become enemies, that even at a time when they were acting in concert, the next act would be a life and death struggle pitting one against the other. Maybe it was true that the world wasn't big enough for two such monsters.

Just how alike were they? Valeria Prokhorova, a Muscovite who was a student during the uneasy Nazi-Soviet alliance and then witnessed the battle for Moscow, calls Hitler and Stalin "spiritual brothers." Like many of her generation, she has plenty of reasons to feel that way: the memory of family members and friends who perished in Stalin's successive waves of terror in the 1930s and, after the war, her arrest on trumped-up charges that led to six years in the hell of the Gulag. The main difference between the two men, she maintains, was one of style. "Stalin reminds me of a murderer who comes with flowers and candy, while Hitler stands there with a knife and a pistol."

There is a long list of uncanny similarities in their life stories, some trivial and coincidental, others more significant and telling. Prokhorova notwithstanding, there are also major differences, not just of style, which would ultimately play a decisive role in the outcome of their showdown. But these were and are less immediately evident.

The parallels begin with their childhood. Both men were born far from the political center of the countries they would come to rule: Hitler in Upper Austria, then part of the Hapsburg empire, and Stalin in Georgia, an impoverished southern region of the Russian empire. It's hardly surprising that both of them had a father who believed in harsh discipline, which, particularly in Stalin's case, translated into frequent beatings. Stalin's parents were serfs, who were freed in 1864, only fourteen or fifteen years before Joseph was born (his official year of birth is listed as 1879, but his birth certificate is dated a year earlier). His father was a cobbler, probably illiterate. He undoubtedly shaped his son's character. "Undeserved and severe beatings made the boy as hard and heartless as the father was," recalled a friend of the young Stalin, or Joseph Dzhugashvili as he was originally called. "Since all people in authority over others seemed to him to be like his father, there soon arose in him a vengeful feeling against all people standing above him."

Hitler, who was born a decade later, in 1889, had a father who had risen higher in society than his peasant ancestors, enjoying a relatively comfortable life as a customs official. But he, too, was a stern, authoritarian figure. To be sure, in those days in both cultures this was more the rule than the exception, and plenty of boys with similar fathers grew up to lead reasonably normal lives. And in Hitler's case, his failure to gain admission to the Vienna Academy of Arts after his father's death and his years of drift and frustration in the Hapsburg capital probably played a more significant role in stoking his sense of grievance than the beatings he received as a child. But without overindulging in armchair diagnosis, it's fair to say that in both men's lives the stern father was an essential component of their early development.

General Dmitri Volkogonov, the former propaganda chief of the Red Army, who in the glasnost era wrote one of the most thorough and devastating biographies of Stalin, offered this description of his subject. "His contempt for normal human values had long been evident. He despised pity, sympathy, mercy. He valued only strong features. His spiritual miserliness, which grew into exceptional harshness and later into pitilessness, cost his wife her life and ruined his children's lives." Except for the part about his wife and children, this could have described Hitler as well as Stalin. So, too, could the credo of the nineteenth-century Russian anarchist Mikhail Bakunin, which Stalin underlined in his book: "Don't waste time on doubting yourself, because this is the biggest waste of time invented by man."

Both men built their career by appealing to a collective sense of grievance, which they magnified and exploited. Hitler was famous for his virulent denunciations of Jews, communists, the Weimar government and everyone else whom he blamed for Germany's defeat in World War I, the humiliating terms of the Versailles Treaty and the economic misery and political unrest that followed—all of which were elements in his stab in the back theory, which he elevated to the status of popular gospel. Although no match as an orator, Stalin, too, launched his political career by claiming to represent the little people, all those who were oppressed by the tsarist system for any reason, even in direct contradiction to Marxist ideology.

In a 1901 essay, Stalin ponderously evoked the oppression of national and religious minorities. "Groaning are the oppressed nationalities and the religions in Russia, among them the Poles and the Finns driven from their native lands and injured in their most sacred feelings," he wrote. "Groaning are the many millions of members of Russian religious sects who want to worship according to the dictates of their own conscience rather than to those of the Orthodox priests." In hindsight, this reads like the theater of the absurd, but it highlights the yawning chasm between Stalin's words and his deeds that would exist throughout his entire gruesome passage through the world. As with Hitler, that chasm never gave him the slightest pause; in fact, it felt perfectly natural.

Both men suffered early setbacks, resulting in imprisonment and, in Stalin's case, exile to Siberia. Those episodes provided grist for the "struggle" sections of the biographies-hagiographies that would be churned out once they emerged victorious. Of course, none of those accounts noted the obvious: the penal conditions they experienced as inmates were laughable compared to the concentration camp systems under their leadership. Isaac Deutscher, one of the early Stalin biographers, pointed out that the future Soviet leader "spent nearly seven years in prisons, on the way to Siberia, in Siberian banishment, and in escapes from the places of his deportation." Offering nothing like the cozy conditions Hitler experienced during his less than a year in Landsberg prison after the aborted Beer Hall putsch of 1923, tsarist prisons and banishment were Spartan, even harsh. But as measured against the horrors that would soon replace them, they were hardly draconian. And the fact that Stalin, like many early revolutionaries, easily escaped on numerous occasions is the clearest proof of that.

When it came to women, Stalin appeared to be the more "normal" of the dictators. He enjoyed the company of women and—unlike Hitler, whose sexual abilities and proclivities are still the subject of endless speculation—he was married twice and had three children. As a young man, he married Yekatarina Svanidze, the sister of a fellow student at the Georgian seminary where he would switch his allegiance from religion to revolution. Yekatarina bore him a son, Yakov, but she died in 1907 of tuberculosis. Although Stalin had been largely an absent husband, he told a friend at her funeral, "This creature softened my heart of stone. She died and with her died my last warm feelings for people."

Hitler, by contrast, only married Eva Braun shortly before they committed suicide together in his bunker in Berlin as Soviet troops were taking the city. In his early days as a rising political leader, he demonstrated an ability to charm older women and solicit their financial backing for the Nazi movement. But he was visibly ill at ease with women his age, and he was drawn to teenage girls—although the nature of any physical relationship is far from clear. This is particularly true when it comes to his long affair, if that's what it was, with his vivacious niece Geli Raubal, who came to live in Munich as a teenager and soon moved into his spacious new apartment, which was funded by his supporters. There were rumors of angry, jealous fights, and in 1931, at the age of 23, Geli was found shot dead in his apartment, with an unfinished letter on the table that gave no indication of what had transpired. The death was ruled a suicide, but even the strong-arm methods of the Brown-shirts couldn't quell the rumors that Hitler had subjected her to humiliating sexual practices.

The story of Stalin's second marriage to Nadezhda Alliluyeva, which took place in 1918, looks more prosaic at first. Twenty-two years younger than her husband, she bore him a boy, Vasily, and a girl, Svetlana; they also took in Yakov, Stalin's son by his first marriage. As Stalin consolidated his grip on power, the Ukraine suffered a massive man-made famine, the result of forced collectiv-ization, and Nadezhda almost certainly heard about the ghoulish sightings of starving peasants from relatives who traveled or lived there. This, combined with the rising tensions within Stalin's court as the first cycle of terror started and Stalin's frequent crude bully-ing of his young wife, took a cumulative psychological toll. Nade-zhda began suffering from chronic migraine headaches and depression. One night, after attending dinner with her husband, she committed suicide. The date was November 8, 1932, just a little over a year after Geli had been found dead in Hitler's apartment in Munich. The eerie similarity doesn't end there. In both cases, a Walther pistol was the death weapon.

Death stalked Stalin's and Hitler's early rivals as well. In each man's case, there were those within their party who questioned their rapid rise. Most famously, a dying Lenin warned in the politi-cal testament that he dictated on December 24, 1922: "Comrade Stalin, having become general secretary, has boundless power con-centrated in his hands, and I am not sure whether he will always be capable of using that power with sufficient caution." In an adden-dum dictated on January 4, 1923, he spoke more bluntly. "Stalin is too crude, and this defect, although quite tolerable in our own midst and in dealings with us Communists, becomes intolerable in a general secretary. That is why I suggest that the comrades think about a way of removing Stalin from that post." To take his place,

Lenin urged, they should find someone who is "more tolerant, more loyal, more polite, and more considerate to the comrades, less capricious, etc."

By the time Lenin's widow delivered this letter after his death a year later, it was too late. Stalin's rivals and anyone perceived as a potential rival—a long list beginning with Leon Trotsky and Nikolai Bukharin—would pay with their lives. After fleeing Russia, Trotsky ended up as an exile in Mexico, where he was finally murdered in 1940. Bukharin was one of the stars of the show trials of 1938, which inevitably ended with guilty verdicts and prompt executions.

Hitler's only serious potential rival was Gregor Strasser, who represented the socialist wing of the Nazi party. He was also one of the first of a long line of people who made the mistake of thinking they could harness Hitler's "magnetic quality" for their own purposes. Strasser's younger brother Otto, a propagandist for the Nazis who later broke with Hitler and fled into exile, tried to persuade Gregor to follow his lead. Earlier than most, he understood the danger of Hitler's appeal. "Hitler responds to the vibration of the human heart with the delicacy of a seismograph, or perhaps of a wireless receiving set, enabling him, with a certainty with which no conscious gift could endow him, to act as a loudspeaker proclaiming the most secret desires, the least admissible instincts, the sufferings and personal revolts of a whole nation," he wrote. "But his very principle is negative. He only knows what he wants to destroy."

Instead, Gregor dissociated himself from Otto, only to lose out completely in a power struggle in 1932, the year before Hitler became chancellor. On June 30, 1934, he was among the scores of victims murdered in the Night of the Long Knives, which would give a foretaste of Hitler's reign of terror. Neither Strasser nor Bukharin possessed enough cunning and ruthlessness to have a chance against Hitler or Stalin. But the fact that they were perceived as rivals was enough to seal their fate.

While both dictators used highly suspicious but convenient pretexts—the Reichstag fire in Hitler's case, the assassination of the Leningrad Party boss Sergei Kirov in Stalin's case—to sweep away any restraints on their power, they also carefully nurtured their image as brilliant statesman, benevolent father figure, and heroic

savior. It's no accident that many of the propaganda trappings—
the giant portraits, lavishly orchestrated public gatherings, fawning
tributes—looked so similar in Germany and the Soviet Union. Or
that each dictator produced a turgid book that became the bible of
his country, which all his subjects were supposed to study as the
fount of all wisdom: *Mein Kampf* and *History of the All-Union Communist Party: A Short Course.* While Hitler dictated all of *Mein Kampf,*
Stalin only wrote one chapter of *Short Course,* but he edited the full
text five times.

Valentin Berezhkov, who served as Stalin's interpreter for his
meetings with German and then Allied leaders during the war, vividly recalled his emotions when he witnessed Hitler arriving at the
opera in Berlin in June 1940—the frenzied crowd, the shouts of
"Sieg Heil!" "Heil Hitler!" and *"Heil Führer!"* "As I am watching all
that, I am thinking to myself—and the thought scares me—how
much there is in common between this and our congresses and
conferences when Stalin makes his entry into the hall," he wrote.
"The same thunderous, never-ending standing ovation. Almost the
same hysterical shouts of 'Glory to Stalin!' 'Glory to our leader!'"

Less known, or more quickly forgotten, is the way both leaders
could turn on the charm and convey the sense that they were focused on the welfare of others and embarrassed by the adulation
they routinely demanded. Even in the midst of the war, Hitler
could put a nervous young woman, Traudl Junge, at ease when she
tried out for the job of his personal secretary. Her story, which she
told in the revealing 2002 documentary *Blind Spot—Hitler's Secretary,* paints a picture of a man who could keep those around him
totally blind to his true nature.

Stalin would go to great lengths to make sure a colleague received a comfortable dacha or was sent on a well-deserved vaca-
tion, and he loved carefully orchestrated references to his modesty.
At a Party meeting in February 1937, when his terror was reaching
new heights, Lev Mekhlis, one of his most loyal henchmen, rose to
read a note Stalin had written in 1930 opposing the use of such
terms as "leader of the party" in describing his role. "I think such
laudatory embellishments can only do harm," Mekhlis quoted his
boss as writing. Of course, such passages were written precisely so
that they could leak out in this manner.

Hans von Herwarth, a German diplomat who served in Moscow in the early 1930s, offered this comparison of the two leaders. "Stalin struck me then as exuberant, not without charm, and with a pronounced capacity for enjoying himself. What a contrast he seemed to make with Hitler, who had so little zest for pleasure! As a distant observer, I was also left with the strong impression that Stalin, again in contrast to Hitler, had a sense of humor. Stated simply, Stalin was quite appealing in his way, while Hitler was thoroughly unattractive." But the diplomat, whose dislike of his own leader may have led him to heighten the contrast, also was struck "by the feline quality in which he [Stalin] moved." He added, "It was easy to think of him as a lynx or a tiger"—in other words, as a dangerous yet appealing animal.

Most telling of all was the mutual if grudging admiration the two leaders occasionally voiced for each other, their subordinates sometimes echoing them. Stalin took immediate notice of his counterpart's Night of the Long Knives. "Hitler, what a great man!" he declared. "This is the way to deal with your political opponents." Hitler was just as impressed by Stalin's reign of terror, and during the war, once declared, "After the victory over Russia it would be a good idea to get Stalin to run the country, with German oversight, of course. He knows better than anyone else how to handle the Russians." Even if this was less a recommendation than an ironical aside, the sentiment behind that remark was genuine. Later in the war, Hitler would complain that he should have followed Stalin's example and purged his military brass. And Ronald Freisler, the president of the notorious Nazi People's Court, saw his Soviet counterpart, Andrei Vyshinsky, as his role model. Vyshinsky presided over the worst of the purge trials of the late 1920s and 1930s, dispatching his victims with the command "Shoot the mad dogs!"

That admiration hardly made up for the wariness the two leaders felt as they monitored each other's rhetoric and actions. Hitler's notions about what the Bolshevik Revolution represented were clearly spelled out in *Mein Kampf*. "Never forget that the rulers of present-day Russia are common blood-stained criminals; that they are the scum of humanity. . . . Furthermore, do not forget that these rulers belong to a race which combines, in a rare mixture, bestial cruelty and an inconceivable gift for lying, and which today more than ever is conscious of a mission to impose its bloody oppression on the whole world." And Stalin had carefully read the passages of *Mein Kampf* where Hitler spelled out his intention to conquer and enslave Russia, treating it as *Lebensraum* for the German people. He also had read Conrad Heyden's *The History of German Fascism,* which left no doubt about Hitler's tactics: "His promises cannot be regarded as those of a reliable partner. He breaks them when it is in his interest to do so."

Both sides professed their good intentions as they prepared their nonaggression pact. During his visit to Moscow that culminated in the signing of the agreement, Ribbentrop insisted that his country was directing its efforts against the West, not the Soviet Union. Stalin raised a glass of champagne and declared: "I know how much the German nation loves its Führer; I should therefore like to drink to his health." But Stalin clearly hadn't forgotten Hitler's track record. When Ribbentrop proposed a flowery preamble to the pact, Stalin would have none of it. "The Soviet Union could not possibly present to the Soviet people in good faith assurances of friendship with Germany when, for six years, the Nazi government has showered the Soviet government with buckets of shit," he retorted. During the actual signing of the pact, Stalin added, "Of course, we are not forgetting that your ultimate aim is to attack us."

Nonetheless, both leaders were elated by the agreement. Hitler had obtained the guarantee of Soviet nonintervention he needed to be able simultaneously to conquer Poland and prepare for a war with Great Britain and France, the European powers that had pledged themselves to defend that doomed country. And Stalin was convinced he had outsmarted both the Western powers and his German counterpart, while setting up his grab not only of eastern Poland but the Baltic states as well. "Hitler wants to trick us, but I think we've got the better of him," he told Nikita Khrushchev.

In the long run, Stalin did get the better of Hitler. He proved to be more coldly calculating, less blinded by fanatical messianic goals than his German counterpart. But in the immediate period that followed—right up until Hitler launched Operation Barbarossa, the invasion of the Soviet Union less than two years later, and right through the battle for Moscow—Stalin's boast that he had outsmarted Hitler would ring hollow. The events unleashed by the nonaggression pact would demonstrate that both leaders, wrapped in their respective cocoons of absolute power, had delusional tendencies that clouded their judgment, contributing to their misjudgment of each other. Their countrymen would soon begin paying the price for their enormous mistakes.

After Germany and the Soviet Union crushed Poland's forces, which were unable to stop the onslaught first from the west and then from the east, the victors hailed the dawn of a new era by signing the German-Soviet Agreement of Friendship and on the Frontier between the U.S.S.R. and Germany on September 29, 1939. The collapse and partition of the Polish state, the agreement claimed, had "laid the solid foundations for a lasting peace in Eastern Europe," and it was time for Britain and France to reconcile themselves to the new order rather than remain in a state of war with Germany.

A month later, Molotov left no doubt that the Soviet leadership had been engaged in far more than a tactical maneuver when it had decided to come to terms with Germany. In a speech to the Supreme Soviet on October 31, he expressed his delight that Poland had been wiped off the map and branded Britain and France aggressor nations. "A short blow at Poland from the German Army, followed by one from the Red Army, was enough to reduce to nothing this monster child of the Treaty of Versailles," he declared. "Now Germany stands for peace, while Britain and France are in favor of continuing the war. As you see, the roles have been reversed."

Then he added a rhetorical flourish that demonstrated just how far the Kremlin had gone in its embrace of its new ally. "One may like or dislike Hitlerism, but every sane person will understand that ideology cannot be destroyed by force," he said. "It is therefore not only nonsensical but also criminal to pursue a war 'for the destruction of Hitlerism' under the bogus banner of a struggle for 'democracy.'"

But in purely military terms, the Soviet Union wasn't nearly as ready as Germany to capitalize on the new conditions for "a lasting peace." It was one thing to "liberate" the western Ukraine and Belorussia from the Poles, who were reeling from the German invasion, and to begin applying the pressure on the tiny Baltic states that would soon lead to their occupation. It was quite another, Stalin quickly discovered, to project Soviet power against even a small country that had the resources and will to put up surprisingly stiff resistance. That country, of course, was Finland, which would exact a high price from the Soviet forces who attacked it, thus diminishing Stalin's standing in the eyes of the world, and especially in Hitler's.

When the Soviet Union demanded that Finland allow it to establish military bases on its territory and cede the Karelian Isthmus north of Leningrad, the Finns refused. Stalin then prepared for what Politburo member Anastas Mikoyan would later call the "shamefully conducted war with Finland." Working with Defense Commissar Kliment Voroshilov and other top officials, he mapped out the plans for a military strike that, he was convinced, would produce a quick victory and allow him to install an already prepared puppet government and turn Finland into the Karelo-Finnish Soviet Republic. "He was confident that everything would be done in two weeks," Mikoyan recalled.

Instead of accepting their fate, the Finns fought back with a ferocity that stunned the ill-prepared Soviet forces. "Most of our troops were ground up by the Finns," Khrushchev wrote later. That was hardly an overstatement. More than 125,000 Soviet troops perished in the Winter War, while Finnish losses totaled about 48,000. The Finns had also dealt the Kremlin a huge psychological blow. "The Germans could see that the U.S.S.R. was a giant with feet of clay," Khrushchev continued. "Hitler must have concluded that if the Finns could put up such resistance, then the mighty Germans would need only one powerful blow to topple the giant." With the benefit of hindsight, he added, "Stalin lost his nerve after the defeat of our troops in the war with Finland. He probably lost whatever confidence he had that our army could cope with Hitler." Although the Finns were finally forced to accept the Soviet terms that they had rejected earlier, this was a far cry from the outcome that Stalin had expected.

Stalin would later complain to Churchill and Roosevelt that

"the Red Army was good for nothing" in the Finnish campaign, and he would sack Voroshilov. In what would prove to be a foretaste of his behavior after every setback, he was eager to shift responsibility for everything that went wrong: the failure of Soviet intelligence to detect how heavily the Finns had fortified the Mannerheim line, the shortage of automatic weapons and winter clothing, the breakdown of supply lines, and all the other indicators that the campaign was a product of incompetent planning.

In stark contrast, Hitler soon proved that his Polish campaign was only the first in a string of victories. From April to June 1940, German forces took Norway and Denmark, swept through the Netherlands and Luxembourg to strike at Belgium, and bypassed the Maginot Line to storm into France, whose swift collapse left Stalin sputtering in frustration. Khrushchev was with Stalin when he heard about France's surrender. "He was racing around cursing like a cab driver," he recalled. "He cursed the French. He cursed the English. How could they allow Hitler to defeat them, to crush them?" Stalin also spelled out what this could mean for Russia, that it would allow Hitler "to beat our brains in."

As far as the German leader was concerned, the Soviet debacle in Finland and his own victories only proved that his original strategy could and would work. On August 11, 1939, shortly before Ribbentrop's trip to Moscow that would produce the nonaggression pact, he told Carl Burckhardt, the League of Nations Commissioner in Danzig, "Everything I undertake is directed against the Russians. If the West is too stupid and blind to grasp this, then I shall be compelled to come to an agreement with the Russians, beat the West and then after their defeat turn against the Soviet Union with all my forces. I need the Ukraine so that they can't starve us out, as happened in the last war."

There was just one problem: England stood in the way of Hitler completing the "beat the West" part of this plan. During the summer of 1940, Hitler was still hoping to lay the groundwork for Operation Sea Lion, the invasion of Britain. But when the Luftwaffe failed to best the Royal Air Force in the battle of Britain, he recognized that his forces weren't capable of mounting such an invasion anytime soon. On September 17, he postponed Operation Sea Lion indefinitely.

Hitler then talked himself into believing that the fastest road to defeating England was by turning on his Soviet ally. In his early writings, he had always posited the destruction of his eastern neighbor, and now he was convinced more than ever that this was the solution that would solve his other problems as well. "Britain's hope lies in Russia and the United States," he told his generals on July 31, 1940. "If Russia drops out of the picture, America, too, is lost for Britain, because elimination of Russia would tremendously increase Japan's power in the Far East. Russia is the Far Eastern sword of Britain and the United States pointed at Japan." With Russia defeated, he reasoned, the Japanese would tie down the U.S. in the Far East, restricting its ability to help Britain.

As for the European theater, Russia's defeat would be equally devastating for Britain, he continued. "With Russia smashed, Britain's last hope would be shattered. Germany then will be master of Europe and the Balkans." As General Franz Halder, the German Army Chief of Staff, noted, Hitler's conclusion was unambiguous. "Decision: Russia's destruction must therefore be made a part of this struggle. Spring 1941. The sooner Russia is crushed the better."

After his victory in France, Hitler had paid a visit to Paris, stopping at Les Invalides to visit Napoleon's tomb. But if he had any thoughts about the possible parallel between his own ambition to defeat Russia and the disastrous experience of the French emperor, he kept them to himself. Later, he would tell his generals, "I will not make the same mistake as Napoleon." It was far from clear, however, what particular mistake he thought he was avoiding. It certainly wasn't the mistake of taking on Russia in the first place. He was too deeply wedded to the idea that victory in the east would strengthen, not weaken, his drive for domination over the Western world.

According to General Henning von Tresckow, Hitler believed that Britain was able to keep resisting because of its alliance with the United States, which was a "hinterland" full of resources that would eventually wear down German might. To counteract this, Hitler needed to gain control of Russia's vast industrial and agricultural resources, along with its manpower. Some German officials were skeptical of this line of reasoning. The number two man in the Foreign Ministry, State Secretary Ernst von Weizsäcker, wrote to Ribbentrop that "to beat England in Russia—this is no program." But Ribbentrop wasn't the type of official who would stand up to his boss. As Hitler's interpreter Paul Schmidt, who also held the rank of ambassador in the foreign ministry, told U.S. Army psychiatrist Leon Goldensohn during his imprisonment in Nuremberg, "Ribbentrop was a complete imitator of Hitler—even to the design of his cap."

At the end of 1940, Hitler issued Directive 21, his secret order for Operation Barbarossa, as the planned attack on Russia was called. (The origin of the name hardly seems auspicious: Barbarossa was the nickname of Frederick I, the German emperor who drowned while trying to lead his troops to the Holy Land in 1190.) According to the order, "The German Armed Forces must be prepared, even before the conclusion of the war against England, to crush Soviet Russia in a rapid campaign." It outlined a strategy of "daring operations led by deeply penetrating armored spearheads" that would wipe out Soviet forces in western Russia. The object was to surround and destroy the major fighting units before they could retreat. "The final objective of the operation is to erect a barrier against Asiatic Russia on the general line Volga–Archangel," it stated. "The last surviving industrial area of Russia in the Urals can then, if necessary, be eliminated by the Air Force." In other words, Germany would be the master of the European part of the Soviet Union, with all its resources.

To achieve that result, the German assault would first need to destroy Soviet forces in the Baltic region and Leningrad. Afterward the order envisaged an attack "with the intention of occupying Moscow, an important center of communications and of the armaments industry." The capture of the Soviet capital, it added, "would represent a decisive political and economic success and would also bring about the capture of the most important railway junctions."

Hitler had clearly shoved aside not just historical misgivings based on Napoleon's Russian campaign but also those based on Germany's more recent experiences in World War I. As he had noted in *Mein Kampf*, "For three years these Germans had stormed the Russian front, at first it seemed without the slightest success.

The Allies almost laughed over this aimless undertaking; for in the end the Russian giant with his overwhelming number of men was sure to remain the victor while Germany would inevitably collapse from loss of blood." This time, however, his string of victories from Poland to France, coupled with the Red Army's humiliation in Finland, convinced him that his forces would triumph easily.

How easily? In December 1940, Hitler insisted that by the following spring his forces would be "visibly at their zenith" while Soviet forces would be at "an unmistakable nadir." "Since Russia has to be beaten in any case, it is better to do it now, when the Russian armed forces have no leaders and are poorly equipped," he added in early January. On another occasion, he told General Alfred Jodl, "We have only to kick in the door and the whole rotten structure will come crashing down." Propaganda chief Joseph Goebbels chimed in with a similar prediction. "Russia will collapse like a house of cards," he wrote in his diary.

Taking their cue from their Führer, some German generals grew increasingly euphoric in their predictions. General Günther Blumentritt suggested to his colleagues in April 1941 that "fourteen days of heavy fighting" might prove enough to achieve victory; other military estimates ranged from six to ten weeks. This only reinforced Hitler's own optimism, which looked almost cautious by comparison. He predicted a campaign that would last no more than four months, maybe three. With that in mind, he at first set May 15, 1941, as the date for the invasion. If he wanted to avoid Napoleon's mistake of getting caught in the Russian winter, then that date afforded him the time he needed to achieve victory before the first snows—even if victory would take the full four months.

If Hitler had stuck to this timetable, he would have launched the invasion of the Soviet Union about a month earlier than Napoleon did when he led his *Grande Armée* into Russia in late June 1812. It would have given him extra time to reach his key strategic objectives, especially Moscow, before summer weather gave way to fall rains that turned the country's roads into tracks of mud and then the fast approach of winter. It would have given him that extra margin of time that could have played a crucial role.

But with Hitler's confidence soaring while Stalin's was plummeting, the German leader felt free to address other problems in the broader war. And, thanks to his putative ally Benito Mussolini, he felt compelled to do so just when his focus should have been on final preparations for Operation Barbarossa, making sure that the military brass was able to stick to the original timetable.

Mussolini had chafed at the fact that Hitler's procession of surprise attacks and victories, which were often as much a surprise to Il Duce as to the victims, had left him looking like a marginal figure. In the fall of 1940, he decided to spring his own surprise and prove that he, too, could swiftly conquer. When Hitler came to meet him in Florence on October 28, Mussolini proudly announced, "Führer, we are on the march! Victorious Italian troops crossed the Greco-Albanian frontier at dawn today!"

Within a few days, the Italian troops were in retreat, and, as Hitler put it to his generals, Mussolini's action was proven to be a "regrettable blunder." It jeopardized German control of the Balkans. Even as he was preparing the plans for Operation Barbarossa, Hitler began drawing up plans for Marita, a German offensive in Albania and Greece to salvage the situation. Then he was enraged by another unexpected development. In March 1941, a coup in Belgrade overthrew the pliant Yugoslav government and produced a new challenge to German control over the region. The army and the Luftwaffe would exact revenge by attacking Yugoslavia and Greece in early April, taking special care to devastate Belgrade on his instructions. But in order to do so, Hitler issued a fateful order to his generals. "The beginning of the Barbarossa operation will have to be postponed up to four weeks," he told them.

"This postponement of the attack on Russia in order that the Nazi warlord might vent his personal spite against a small Balkan country which had dared to defy him was probably the most catastrophic single decision in Hitler's career," William Shirer wrote in *The Rise and Fall of The Third Reich*.

At the time, though, Hitler had no inkling of that. He wanted the Balkans tidied up before he dealt with Russia, and, looking eastward, he continued to believe that he still had enough time to triumph there, even if the margin for error in his calculations was narrowing. Instead of launching Operation Barbarossa more than a month earlier than Napoleon had done 129 years before, he would end up sending his armies eastward at exactly the same time in June as the French emperor.

So what was Stalin thinking? What did he know and when did he know it?

Hitler was blinded by his burning conviction that Germany had to defeat and subjugate the Soviet Union, a country that he contemptuously dismissed as "a Slavic-Tartar body" with "a Jewish head." But Stalin was suffering from a different kind of blindness, willful disbelief of the staggering amount of evidence that Hitler was about to unleash his forces against him. The fact that German troops would then get as close as they did to seizing Moscow was a direct consequence of the Soviet leader's refusal to see what he didn't want to see during the nearly two-year period of the Nazi-Soviet alliance.

There are no easy answers to the question of why Stalin behaved the way he did, ignoring warnings from his own intelligence agents and from the West, though there are some plausible, hotly contested theories. The record of those years shows that, without a doubt, Stalin had all the information he needed to reach the correct conclusion and prepare his country for the attack that was coming rather than assume that he still had time for a lengthy period of preparation or that the attack might not come at all. But again and again, Stalin would insist on his version of events, allowing his wishes to overcome his reason and, in his mind, to represent reality.

Curiously, it initially appeared that the Kremlin brass were more the realists than their German counterparts. At the time of the Munich Pact in 1938, Stalin had expressed his frustration with Britain's Neville Chamberlain for his refusal to recognize the folly of his policy of appeasement. "One day that madman Hitler will grab his umbrella and hit him with it. And Chamberlain will take it without complaining," he said. It wasn't just Stalin's contempt for Chamberlain that is revealing here; it's also his casual use of the term "madman." Along with occasional flashes of grudging admiration, that sort of disdain for Hitler and his entourage was commonplace in the Kremlin.

Lavrenty Beria, Stalin's fearsome secret police chief, mocked Ribbentrop by saying, "He struts around like a turkey puffed up with pride." While imprisoned in Nuremberg at the end of the war, Ribbentrop, for his part, declared, "I rather liked Stalin and Molotov, got along fine with them." In fact, several members of Hitler's inner circle expressed respect for Stone Bottom, as Molotov was known among his comrades because of his ability to sit working as long as the boss required. During his interrogation at Nuremberg, Hitler's translator Paul Schmidt offered this assessment of Molotov: "He reminded me of my old teacher of mathematics. He's the type of man who makes sure to cross his *t*'s and dot his *i*'s. He likes meticulousness. He is a legal expert, a hard worker, and rather stubborn. But I don't know if he has much imagination. Like all Russians he will obey Stalin's orders unwaveringly." In other words, Molotov and Ribbentrop were alike in their slavish devotion to their respective tyrants.

In assessing the British, Soviet officials certainly sounded more prescient than the Germans. When Ribbentrop visited Moscow to conclude the nonaggression pact, he held conversations with Stalin, who warned him, "England, despite its weakness, will wage war craftily and stubbornly." To be sure, Stalin would be proved wrong on another prediction: that the French would put up a stiff fight as well. But at least as far as the British were concerned, the Soviets exhibited a far more healthy respect for their determination and fighting abilities than the Germans did. In November 1940, Molotov was attending a banquet in his honor in Berlin when the RAF attacked the city, forcing his hosts to retreat with him to Ribbentrop's bunker. When the German foreign minister insisted that Britain was finished, the normally dour Molotov delivered his best riposte ever. "If that's so, then why are we in this shelter and whose bombs are those falling?" he asked.

But if Stalin and other top Soviet officials sometimes came out on top in their rhetorical sparring with the Germans, they acted as if they could really rely on their nonaggression pact and other agreements to keep the peace between the two countries—at least for a good long while. Stalin was determined to honor his trade commitments to Germany throughout the period of the pact, and his country provided huge amounts of oil, wood, copper, manganese ore, rubber, grain, and other supplies to keep the German military machine well stocked. The more warnings Stalin received that he was only strengthening a military power that was about to turn against him, the more he insisted on keeping those commitments, ensuring prompt deliveries so that Hitler wouldn't have any suspicion that Stalin might be suspicious of him. As Khrushchev put it, "So while those sparrows kept chirping, 'Look out for Hitler! Look out for Hitler!' Stalin was punctually sending the Germans trainload after trainload of grain and petroleum. He wanted to butter up Hitler by living up to the terms of the Molotov-Ribbentrop pact!"

Among the best "sparrows" were many of the Soviet Union's spies abroad. As early as June 1940, when Germany was moving swiftly through France, Colonel Ivan Dergachev, the Soviet military attaché in Bulgaria, sent a report from a source who predicted the conclusion of an armistice with France and then "within a month's time" a sudden attack on the Soviet Union. "The purpose would be to destroy communism in the Soviet Union and to create a fascist regime there," he wrote. On June 22, France was forced to conclude an armistice with Germany, and, while the actual invasion was still a year off, a month later Hitler was telling his generals to begin preparing for an attack on Russia.

The Soviet military intelligence service delivered a steady stream of reports from its sources that warned of war preparations. From Berlin, a source code-named Ariets reported on September 29, 1940, that Hitler intended to "resolve problems in the east in the spring of next year." On December 29, the same source predicted an attack in March 1941. In February 1941, he reported confirmation "that war has definitely been decided on for this year." Major General Vasily Tupikov, who as military attaché was in charge of this intelligence gathering, agreed with that assessment and noted that Germany was decreasing its troop deployments in the west and shifting them to the border with the Soviet Union. "The U.S.S.R. figures as the next enemy," he concluded. On May 9, he added details of a German war plan. As he summarized it, "Defeat of the Red Army will be complete in one or one and a half months with arrival of the German Army on the meridian of Moscow."

Other Soviet military missions delivered similar bad news. On March 13, 1941, Bucharest quoted a German major as saying, "We have completely changed our plan. We will move to the east against the U.S.S.R. We will obtain grain, coal, and oil from the U.S.S.R. and that will enable us to continue the war against England and America." According to one Bucharest source, "The German military are drunk with their successes and claim that war with the U.S.S.R. will begin in May." On March 26, Bucharest added that "the Romanian general staff has precise information that in two or three months Germany will attack the Ukraine." The report added that the attack also would be aimed at the Baltic states, and that Romania would participate in the war and be rewarded with Bessarabia, the border territory that Stalin had seized from it. The mission went on to report the four-week delay of German plans because of the action against Yugoslavia and Greece and the growing confidence of the German military that it would defeat the Soviet Union in a matter of weeks.

But Stalin's reaction—and increasingly that of the men he put in charge of sifting through this growing body of intelligence—was to dismiss it. First of all, Stalin rid himself of Ivan Proskurov, the head of Soviet military intelligence, who had consistently refused to buckle under the pressure to deliver better news. He replaced him with Filipp Golikov, who began relying on the reports of those of his officers who were clearly picking up German disinformation. In March 1941, for instance, the Soviet military attaché in Budapest, who had no credible sources, dismissed all talk of a German invasion as English propaganda. "Everyone considers that at the present time a German offensive against the U.S.S.R. is unthinkable before the defeat of England," he reported.

Golikov endorsed those conclusions. "Rumors and documents that speak of the inevitability of war against the U.S.S.R. this spring must be assessed as disinformation emanating from English and even perhaps from German intelligence," he maintained. There's little doubt why he was responding in this way. On April 17, when his Prague station sent a report predicting that "Hitler will attack the U.S.S.R. in the second half of June," Golikov dutifully sent it on to Stalin. Within three days, it landed back on Golikov's desk with Stalin's note in red ink: "English provocation! Investigate!"

But no one angered Stalin more than Richard Sorge, the Soviet master spy in Tokyo, who delivered report after report to his superiors in military intelligence that was right on target. Born in Baku of a Russian mother and a German father, Sorge was raised in Germany, recruited by the Comintern, and moved to Tokyo as the German correspondent of the *Frankfurter Zeitung*. To all appearances a dedicated Nazi, he ingratiated himself with the German ambassador and his staff and with senior Japanese officials. Taking advantage of this unrivaled access to inside information, he was among the first to report in late 1940 that an attack on the U.S.S.R. was likely, and he offered chapter and verse on German troop movements eastward. He warned that "the Germans could occupy territory on a line Kharkov, Moscow, Leningrad." But as he continued to provide more evidence for his claims, Golikov's main response was to cut back on his expenses, which Sorge correctly characterized as "a kind of punishment." When Sorge reported in May that an attack was imminent, Stalin dismissed him as "a little shit who has set himself up with some small factories and brothels in Japan."

The NKVD's foreign intelligence operatives encountered similar reactions when they produced reports that paralleled those of their military counterparts. One of their best sources was Harro Schulze-Boysen, code-named Starshina, who worked in the German Air Ministry. He consistently kept them up to date, in considerable detail, about preparations for the invasion. On June 17, he warned that everything was ready and that "the blow can be expected at any time." Stalin's response: Starshina should be sent back to "his fucking mother."

Stepan Mikoyan, a fighter pilot during the war and the son of Anastas, offers a straightforward explanation of Stalin's refusal to believe his agents. "Stalin's attitude to intelligence data reflected his extreme distrust of people. In his opinion everyone was capable of deceit or treason." In his memoirs, the younger Mikoyan mentions that Stalin ordered a recall of his resident agents from abroad so that, in Stalin's words, he could "grind them into dust in the camps."

Given Stalin's suspicions, it's hardly surprising that he also dismissed Western warnings that Hitler was about to turn against him.

In April 1941, both Laurence Steinhardt, the U.S. ambassador in Moscow, and Winston Churchill attempted to point this out—to no avail. Other attempts, particularly by the British, to alert the Kremlin to the significance of German troop movements in preparation for the invasion proved equally ineffective. As Stalin saw it, those warnings were all meant to sow discord between Moscow and Berlin, with the ultimate objective of turning one against the other. "They're playing us off against each other," he complained.

If Stalin's pathological distrust of his own agents and the West was hardly surprising, it's harder to explain his blindness to so many other signals of Hitler's intentions. As far back as August 14, 1940, Hitler dropped a clear hint by requesting a schedule of Soviet deliveries for the period "until the spring of 1941." And in the run-up to the invasion, the Germans were steadily recalling diplomats and their families from the embassy in Moscow. By the time of the attack, the German presence had been reduced to just over a hundred people. As Valentin Berezhkov, who was serving in the Soviet embassy in Berlin, pointed out, the equivalent number for the Soviet side was about a thousand people. "Stalin, concerned about making Hitler suspicious, had forbade us from reducing the numbers of our employees in Germany," he wrote.

Then there were all the signs of military preparations, easily observable, especially in the border regions. With increasing frequency, German planes flew into Soviet air space, clearly on reconnaissance missions. After several instances of Soviet border troops opening fire or Soviet planes attempting to scramble to intercept them, and even one incident in which five German planes landed in Soviet territory and claimed they had lost their way before running out of fuel, Stalin's impulse was to restrict the actions of his own troops. "In case of violations of the German-Soviet border by German aircraft or balloons, do not open fire," NKVD Directive 102 on March 29, 1940, ruled: "Limit yourselves to preparing a report on the violation of the state frontier." On April 5, another order from Beria informed the border troops that, in the case of any confrontations, they should "strictly see to it that bullets do not fall on German territory."

The Germans offered the lame explanation that the frequent overflights were a result of the fact that several military flight

schools were located near the border. As the number of such incidents kept growing (between April 19 and June 19, 1941, there
were 180 of them), the Soviet response became increasingly grovel-
ing. An official note assured the German government that border
troops had been instructed not to fire on its planes "so long as such
flights did not occur frequently." After he received one of the many
reports about German overflights, Stalin declared: "I'm not sure
Hitler knows about those flights."

Stalin's efforts to assure the Germans that, no matter what actions they took, he wanted to maintain good relations reached
almost comical proportions—if not for the fact that the stakes were
so high. On April 18, 1941, the Soviet leader was seeing off Japanese Foreign Minister Yosuke Matsuoka at a Moscow railway station, in itself an unusual event, when he practically begged the
German diplomats on the platform to believe his protestations of
eternal friendship. Spotting German ambassador Count Friedrich
Werner von der Schulenburg, he threw his arms around him and
proclaimed, "We must remain friends and you must now do everything to that end!" A little later when he saw Colonel Hans Krebs,
the German military attaché, he first checked that he indeed was
German and repeated his message: "We will remain friends with
you in any event."

Stalin's efforts impressed Schulenburg, an aristocrat who was
singularly unperceptive in his observations of both the Soviet
Union and the new leader of his own country. When he reassured
the wife of the American ambassador at a party in early 1941 that
Russia and Germany wouldn't go to war with each other, he almost
certainly believed it. Later he began to recognize that he had been
misreading the signals, but he kept trying to convince his superiors
in Berlin that they should take Stalin's appeals for continued cooperation seriously. "I honestly believe that in realizing how serious
the international situation is, Stalin has made himself personally
responsible for preserving the U.S.S.R. from a conflict with Germany," he argued.

But as Goebbels noted in his diary, the Nazi leaders intention-
ally kept Schulenburg in the dark about the war preparations and
were happy to have him still act as though there was a serious
chance of avoiding a military confrontation. Goebbels asserted that

the ambassador "hadn't the faintest idea that the Reich was determined to attack" while he kept pressing the campaign to keep Stalin an ally. "There is no doubt that one does best if one keeps the diplomats uninformed about the background of politics," the propaganda chief wrote. "They must sometimes play a role for which they don't have the necessary theatrical abilities, and even if they did possess them, they would undoubtedly act an appeasement role more convincingly and play the finer nuances more genuinely, if they themselves were believers in appeasement."

As for Stalin, he played *his* appeasement role so convincingly that the Turkish ambassador in Moscow sent a dispatch to his home office, which was intercepted by the Germans, portraying Stalin as willing to do almost anything to convince Hitler he genuinely wanted peace. "Stalin is about to become a blind tool of Germany," he reported. The question is whether Stalin was just playing a role or acting out of genuine conviction.

The standard defense of Stalin is that he did what he had to do, playing for time because of the weakness of the West and the need to prepare his own forces. According to that line of reasoning, the Soviet leader was under no illusions about Hitler's ultimate intentions. "To argue that we did not expect a German attack is just plain stupid, particularly coming from military people who were close to the general staff," Khrushchev maintained, certainly with more of an eye to protecting his own reputation as part of Stalin's inner circle than to protecting the boss himself. "No one with an ounce of political sense should buy the idea that we were fooled, that we were caught flat-footed by a treacherous surprise assault."

But the Kremlin leadership—and, as a result, many of its troops—were in fact caught flat-footed when the invasion started. Take the question of the country's defensive lines. In the 1930s, heavily fortified lines were built along the Soviet Union's western borders. But when those borders were moved further west as a result of the Nazi-Soviet pact, Stalin decided that the old fortifications should be largely abandoned and new ones should be constructed along the new dividing line between Germany and the Soviet Union.

This turned out to be a disastrous decision. Petro Grigorenko, who as a young soldier had helped build the original fortifications, recalled that in the spring of 1941 Stalin ordered the destruction of many of the old fortifications and "tens of thousands" of them were blown up. "I do not know how future historians will explain this crime against our people," the future general—who would become a dissident—wrote later. "No better gift could have been given to Hitler's Barbarossa plan. How could this have taken place? Stalin's justification must be that he was insane."

The worst thing about Stalin's orders was that building and equipping new fortifications lagged way behind the abandonment or destruction of the old ones. When the Germans attacked, most of the newly constructed concrete emplacements were short of artillery and otherwise inadequately prepared for the German onslaught. The result was that they were easily overrun or bypassed. If Stalin had had another couple of years to prepare them, perhaps this wouldn't have been the case, but time was a luxury he didn't have.

There's no question that Stalin was playing for time. Isaac Deutscher, one of his early biographers, claimed that Stalin was hoping to be as successful as Tsar Alexander I, who made peace with Napoleon, which provided him with four years to prepare for war. The problem is that the Soviet leader clearly convinced himself that his wishes represented reality, and his refusal to accept the evidence to the contrary amounted to a monumental failure of leadership. This meant that he not only failed to make the best use of the time he had to prepare his forces for the attack that was coming but also impeded many of the efforts to make such preparations. Instead of putting his troops on full alert, he ordered them to do nothing that the Germans might construe as hostile behavior. Instead of signaling the need for utmost vigilance, he encouraged a false sense of security.

As late as June 14, 1941, the Soviet news agency Tass dismissed rumors that the German troop build-up on the border meant that an invasion was imminent. "Germany is observing the terms of the nonaggression pact as scrupulously as the U.S.S.R., and therefore rumors of Germany's intention to violate the Pact and attack the U.S.S.R. are groundless, while the recent transfer of German forces from the Balkans to the eastern and northeastern areas of Germany must be assumed to be linked to other motives unconnected

with Soviet-German relations," it asserted. The impact of such statements was, as one Soviet officer put it, "to dull the forces' vigilance."

True, Stalin did take some actions that indicated he realized he
might be wrong in his calculations. He appeared to issue an indi-
rect warning to Hitler when he spoke to the graduates of the military academy on May 5. "Is the German Army invincible?" he asked.
"No. It is not invincible." He argued that the German leaders "are
beginning to suffer from dizziness" from their string of successes.
"It seems to them that there is nothing that they could not do," he
added. Then, repeating his point that the Germans weren't invincible, he concluded, "Napoleon, too, had great military success as
long as he was fighting for liberation from serfdom, but as soon as
he began a war for conquest, for the subjugation of other peoples,
his army began suffering defeats."

Leaving aside the irony of Stalin preaching about liberation
versus subjugation and the implied message that the German con-
quests were justified up to that point but wouldn't be if Hitler attacked the Soviet Union, the speech did signal some awareness of
the looming danger. A week later, the Soviet leader agreed to the
calling up of five hundred thousand reservists to strengthen border
defenses, but this was a classic case of too little too late. Many of
the fresh troops wouldn't be deployed in time. Besides, production
of new weapons had barely begun, and many existing military units
were woefully underequipped. In March 1941, Stalin received the
news that only 30 percent of tank and armored units could be ade-
quately supplied with the parts they needed to operate. "Fulfillment of the plan for the supply of the military technology the Red
Army needs so acutely is extremely unsatisfactory," his top generals
reported a month before the Germans attacked.

Some historians have argued that at one point Stalin was even
contemplating a preemptive attack against Germany, but a far
stronger case can be made that he deluded himself to the very end
that, at the very least, he could stall the Germans for another year.
And, given his preoccupation with imposing Soviet rule on eastern
Poland and the Baltic states—which meant full-scale terror in the
form of mass deportations and executions—there's even the possibility that he still believed that the ideal scenario would be one in

which the Soviet Union and Nazi Germany never went to war. In that situation, the Germans and the Allies would wear each other out in a long struggle, giving the Soviet Union all the breathing room it needed and possibly the chance of more territorial gains later.

Late in 1939, the French news agency Havas reported on a speech Stalin allegedly delivered on August 19 of that year, right before formalizing his agreement with Hitler. In it he argued that if the West defeated Germany in a long war, that country would be ripe for sovietization; but if Germany won in a long war, it would be too exhausted to threaten the Soviet Union and a communist take-over would be possible in France. Hence a win-win situation for the Soviet Union and his conclusion that "one must do everything to ensure that the war lasts as long as possible in order to exhaust both sides."

Stalin reacted to the Havas report by promptly branding it a total fabrication. But in his denial he insisted, "It was not Germany that attacked France and Britain but France and Britain that attacked Germany, thereby taking on themselves responsibility for the present war." Even if Stalin didn't make that speech, his protests were almost as revealing as the contested transcript. Besides, Stalin let slip similar comments on September 7, 1939, in the presence of several of his top aides. Discussing the war "between two groups of capitalist countries," as he characterized the Western powers and Germany, he concluded, "We see nothing wrong in their having a good fight and weakening each other."

Whatever Stalin had come to believe about German intentions by the spring of 1941, he continued to react with fury whenever he was confronted with more evidence that he had grossly miscalculated. His underlings knew that they had to couch all bad news in slavish praise of their boss. Just a day before the German invasion when Beria sent Stalin a report with the prediction of Vladimir Dekanozov, the Soviet ambassador in Berlin, that the attack was imminent, the secret police chief prefaced it with the declaration: "My people and I, Joseph Vissarionovich, firmly remember your wise prediction: Hitler will not attack us in 1941!"

By that time, the Germans were ready to strike. On the night of June 21, Soviet military commanders had reports from three separate German deserters from the front lines, who had crossed to the Soviet side to warn that the attack was coming at dawn. In each case, the news was relayed up the chain of command until it reached Stalin. But the Soviet leader kept insisting that the deserters had been sent over to provoke his troops. While he continued to maintain that Hitler wouldn't attack, he did belatedly agree to place border units on alert. At the same time, he issued an order to shoot the third German deserter—Alfred Liskov, a young communist from Berlin who had brought the "disinformation" that would prove Stalin wrong.

In Stalin's world, "shoot the messenger" wasn't a metaphor.

2

"Look how smart we are now"

Unlike many of his counterparts who commanded other military units on the Soviet Union's western border, General Georgy Miku-shev wasn't content to sit idly by while the German military machine geared up for its attack. His Forty-first Infantry Division, which consisted of fifteen thousand men, was deployed about six miles from the border of the western Ukraine, with seventy thousand German troops facing them on the other side. The Germans had about four hundred artillery pieces and mortars ready for the attack, twice the number possessed by Mikushev's regiment. The Soviet general may not have known the exact numbers of enemy troops and guns he was facing, but he wasn't impressed by the Kremlin's desperate insistence that nothing was amiss in the German-Soviet relationship, and he was determined to prepare for the worst—even if it meant defying his superiors.

On June 17, Mikushev quietly began calling back his units that had been dispatched on exercises or other assignments. At the base camp, the troops were ordered to make sure they were fully armed and ready. The artillerymen prepared their shells, machine gunners gathered up their rounds, and snipers filled their ammunition pouches with bullets. On the evening of Saturday, June 21,

Mikushev gathered his top officers, who assured him that their men were all on alert. They also reported growing anger in the ranks about the frequent overflights by German aircraft and the lack of retaliation against them.

Mikushev listened and then chose his words very carefully. "Since the regiment is near the border and we have specific missions, we must be ready for all kinds of developments," he told them. "I know how cunning the German army is from my experience in World War I. And, of course, the Fascists are even more cunning." As he wrapped up his talk, Mikushev ordered his officers to stay with their units, taking as little time off as possible. And he emphasized that they had to be ready to fight at very short notice. To maintain that state of readiness, the officers would need to pass those orders down the line. To deflect attention from the real motive for these preparations, Mikushev had his officers explain to their subordinates that the regiment was expecting a visit from senior brass, which meant everyone had to show themselves to be battle ready.

It was just after 3 A.M. the following day, June 22, that the German attack began. While many other regiments were caught completely by surprise and routed almost instantly, Mikushev's troops quickly sprang into action, firing back at the attackers and slowing their advance. But this was in direct contradiction of an order from the Kremlin sent out less than an hour earlier, instructing the border units to reach the stage of "full combat readiness" but at the same time warning them "to not respond to any provocative actions that might result in serious complications."

Although many units—including Mikushev's—didn't even receive this order before the German attack began, his immediate superior, Lieutenant General Ivan Muzichenko, was furious when he received a report from informers in the Forty-first Division that Mikushev had authorized his troops to open fire. By 7 A.M., with the battle raging around them, a young officer arrived carrying instructions from headquarters to dismiss and arrest Mikushev for issuing the order to shoot without permission from his superiors—in other words, for insubordination. Mikushev kept his cool, telling his aides, "I think this situation will not last for long. Presumably the order has already been rescinded." Even the NKVD agents in the unit who were supposed to arrest him looked stymied. Here they were supposed to arrest their commander who had had the foresight to prepare them for the German assault that was now in full swing. Mikushev told them they could arrest him and his men would go on fighting anyway.

But it wasn't an angry exchange. Mikushev had good relations with the senior NKVD officer in his regiment, and neither wanted to make the other look bad—and both men recognized the gravity of their predicament. Formally, Mikushev agreed to his arrest, and he retreated to a dugout where he would officially be held. But during the next three hours, his two top aides kept visiting him, getting his orders and relaying them to the troops so that nothing came directly from him. This maintained the pretence that he was under arrest and no longer in command.

At 10 A.M., as the German offensive intensified, the senior NKVD officer and an aide went into the dugout. After a brief conversation with the "prisoner," Mikushev emerged dressed in blue dungarees and a helmet and carrying an automatic weapon. Looking calm and in command, he took up a position in a cluster of pine trees outside the camp and started issuing orders directly to his troops again. Seeing his confident manner, they continued fighting, acquitting themselves well against the superior numbers and firepower of the German invader. In fact, they even pushed across the border a few kilometers into German-occupied Poland before they were driven back.

Mikushev's story was atypical for several reasons. Because of his foresight and initiative, his troops put up a more effective resistance than most of their compatriots elsewhere who also bore the brunt of the initial German attack. Because the senior NKVD officer in his unit was a reasonable man, he only went through the motions of an arrest without the normal consequences and then dropped the pretence altogether that Mikushev was a prisoner. And because Soviet defenses were collapsing so quickly and the Kremlin leadership had no idea what to do about it, Mikushev pulled off the virtually impossible feat of acting independently of his Stalinist masters and getting away with it.

True, as his troops kept fighting during that summer, he was nearly arrested again when he escaped with his men from a

German encirclement, ignoring the general orders not to retreat under any circumstances. But his evident courage and skill won the day in that case as well. On September 9, however, his luck ran out. A German machine gunner cut him down during a battle for control of a bridge. "Men like Mikushev fought till the last drop of blood," says retired Red Army colonel and military historian Nikolai Romanichev. But what was remarkable about Mikushev's heroism was that it was as much a product of his defiance of Stalin's willful blindness as of his courage in facing the Germans.

Far more typical, though, were the stories of German troops who were pleasantly surprised by the speed of their first victories and by the confusion and disarray of the Soviet defenders. Hans von Herwarth, who had served in the German embassy in Moscow in the 1930s, found himself crossing back into Soviet territory, this time as part of the army of would-be conquerors. Before dawn on June 22, his regiment's artillery let loose against the Red Army's positions for forty-five minutes, the firepower "making an awesome impression" against the dark sky. "For several hours the Soviets did not reply," he recalled. "We had caught them unprepared, and, as many Russians told us later, not even dressed for the day." This lack of preparation was more the norm than the exception. When German troops shelled the western Ukrainian city of Lvov, the local Soviet commander also failed to respond. After he was taken prisoner, he told his captors that he was initially convinced that German artillery must have been firing at his positions by mistake and that he was also acutely aware of the Kremlin's order to avoid overreacting to any "provocations."

As they crossed the Bug River into Soviet territory, Herwarth's regiment encountered strong resistance from NKVD border troops, some of whom were hidden in tree tops, allowing them to fire down at the invaders. But once they had overcome those fighters, the Germans discovered that the next part of their advance was remarkably easy. "The fighting spirit of the Soviet infantry could not have been lower," Herwarth wrote. "If they put up any stiff resistance it was only because of the difficulty of deserting at that particular moment, due, for example, to the temporary stabilization of the front line."

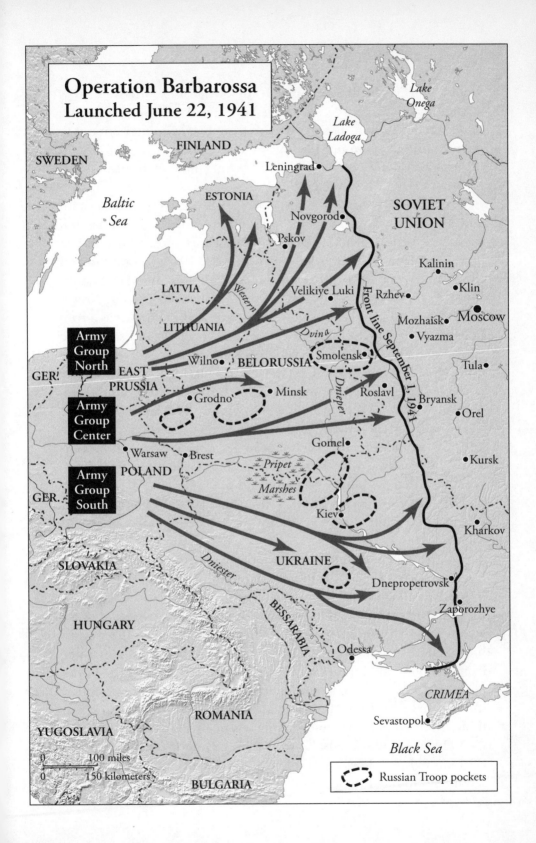

Operation Barbarossa
Launched June 22, 1941

SWEDEN

FINLAND

Baltic Sea

Lake Onega

Lake Ladoga

Leningrad

Novgorod

Pskov

ESTONIA

SOVIET UNION

Kalinin

Klin

LATVIA

Western

Velikiye Luki

Rzhev

Mozhaisk

Moscow

Vyazma

LITHUANIA

Dvina

Army Group North

Wilno

BELORUSSIA

Smolensk

GER.

EAST PRUSSIA

Tula

Grodno

Minsk

Dnieper

Roslavl

Bryansk

Army Group Center

Orel

Warsaw

Brest

Gomel

Pripet

GER.

POLAND

Marshes

Kursk

Army Group South

Kiev

SLOVAKIA

Dniester

UKRAINE

Kharkov

HUNGARY

Dnepropetrovsk

BESSARABIA

Zaporozhye

Odessa

Front line September 1, 1941

YUGOSLAVIA

CRIMEA

ROMANIA

Sevastopol

0   100 miles
0   150 kilometers

Black Sea

BULGARIA

- - - Russian Troop pockets

Once the Germans broke through the Soviet line, "the Red Army abandoned all resistance, throwing away their weapons, and waiting to be taken prisoner." Cavalry patrols from his regiment went out to round up their seemingly willing victims. "The prisoners followed without resistance, often trudging in long lines behind a single German soldier," he added.

From the tales of Red Army soldiers who survived the German assault, it's easy to understand why many of their comrades felt they were better off in captivity. Vyacheslav Dolgov, who had just graduated from military school on June 21, 1941, was dispatched to serve as a political officer for the 375th Regiment in Staraya Russa in the Novgorod region on the northwestern front. Now a retired general living in Moscow, Dolgov describes himself as a true believer in those days. "I honestly believed in the iron fist and the genius of Stalin." But he also vividly recalls the fear everyone in his unit felt about facing the Germans, particularly given how poorly equipped they were. "We asked our commander to give us weapons, since we were sent to fight without guns. We were told to seize weapons from the enemy and defeat them with their guns," he said. "We would sometimes manage to get some guns from the Germans, but that was why there were so many casualties. I saw fields covered with dead bodies." Dolgov and the regiment's commander had to urge their troops on with shouts of "Hurrah! For the motherland! For Stalin!" and lead the attack before anyone would follow.

Dolgov also recalled the sight of "cowards" surrendering in huge numbers. Once, he spotted a group of men wandering between two villages, waving white clothes. "These were desperate Russian soldiers who had taken off their white underwear and were waving it to surrender," he said. Other soldiers fled to the woods, hiding there and surviving by eating berries and scooping up water from the bogs and boiling it in their helmets after taking the lining out. During the battles around Staraya Russa, Dolgov was wounded for the first of several times during the war. Of the two to three thousand men in his regiment, only seventy-five survived.

As his comrades died all around him, Dolgov recalled, he saw German fighters downing the few Soviet air force planes that had scrambled to meet them. "I felt sorry for our pilots," he said. "The

Germans kept hitting our planes, and I remember seeing one of our pilots parachuting from his burning wreck. A German pilot shot him." The German pilots also dropped propaganda leaflets claiming that the whole Soviet front was collapsing, right up to and including Moscow. "Moscow has surrendered," they asserted. "Any further resistance is useless. Surrender to victorious Germany now." Despite the speed of the German advance, there was no way this could have been true at that point, but the leaflets convinced many of the frightened soldiers that they were already part of a defeated army.

Little wonder that they felt that way. The German strike proved devastating for the Soviet air force, many of whose planes stood in neat formation on airfields in the western districts, offering Luftwaffe pilots ideal targets. On the first day of the assault, the Germans destroyed almost all the planes of the Baltic military district before they ever had a chance to take off, and throughout the border regions, the scorecard for the first day totaled approximately twelve hundred Soviet aircraft. At the same time, the German planes were free to roam the skies, attacking panicked ground troops and civilians at will. Major General I. I. Kopets, the commander of the Western front's air force, had vowed to shoot himself if his planes were wiped out by a surprise attack. Seeing this happen on the first day of the German invasion, Kopets did exactly that.

During the first month, German troops would advance about 450 miles, a staggering pace that reflected the disarray they encountered in most of the areas under attack. Morale among the invaders rose in proportion to the confusion they encountered as they moved steadily deeper into Soviet territory. "I feel born anew," Lance Corporal Henry Nahler wrote in a letter home on June 26. Describing the initial assault four days earlier, he noted, "it seemed as if all the weapons along the front line were fired at the same time." As German bombers appeared in the skies, "people ran like mad along the roads with their belongings." He added that he found a bucket of fresh milk and two fresh eggs in a barn, which allowed him to drink and eat by way of celebration. "Generally speaking, everything was very cozy and festive," he concluded. "The Russians didn't direct their artillery against us."

His upbeat mood was echoed in other letters from soldiers. "We will send big Russia to hell," an NCO by the last name of Bering wrote on the same day. "If the Führer has decided to do something like this, he will certainly succeed." A Lance Corporal von Dirdelsen added, "We will defeat the country with the mad government and beat the Red Army. Our company first crossed the Bug, destroyed three bunkers and advanced 40 kilometers [twenty-five miles] during the first three days." While he conceded that many officers perished during that drive, he claimed that their bravery only inspired their men to keep moving forward. In other letters, soldiers described how they watched German planes shoot out of the skies the Soviet planes that managed to confront them. "Yes, our pilots are great fellows!" Nahler wrote. "I just saw one German fighter attack a group of enemy fighters, bringing down four Russian planes. It was unforgettable."

Back in Moscow, the average Soviet citizen had no idea just how bad things looked on the front lines. Georgy Kumanev, who was ten at the time, went with some friends to the mobilization office and listened to the crowd assembling there. Kumanev, who has been long ensconced in the Center for Military History in Moscow and has conducted interviews with many of the key figures of the wartime era, recalls that people were full of bravado. "We will knock Hitler's teeth out," they were saying. Others asked, "Have you heard? Our troops are approaching Königsberg," the East Prussian port city. Or "Have you heard that the Red Army is already in enemy territory?" Some of the young men were in a hurry to enlist to have a chance to take part in the war, because they were convinced that it would end very quickly and they might miss it if they didn't join up immediately.

Children chanted the new ditties that arose for the occasion. "Here and there—Hitler beware! Bet your boots—Hitler's *kaput*!" one of them went. But along with other Muscovites, the novelist Yuri Druzhnikov, who remembers reciting that line as an eight-year-old at the time of the invasion, saw that optimism quickly evaporate. His father, Ilya Druzhnikov, a book illustrator in his mid-forties, was immediately called up and sent to the front with other recruits in cattle cars. Once there, he found himself in a scene of "total chaos," where no one seemed to know what was going on.

As Ilya Druzhnikov would tell his son long after the war, there was only one rifle available for every ten men in his unit, which meant that unarmed men trailed behind each armed man. Whenever one of the armed men fell, the next man was expected to pick up his weapon. The officers, he pointed out, were ready to shoot any of their own men who dared move in the wrong direction— away from the fighting instead of right into it. Periodically, the order was issued for the recruits to go to the fields and strip the corpses of everything they could carry—weapons, ammunition, and clothing. One reason for these shortages was that the Germans had quickly captured or destroyed large stockpiles of Soviet weapons and other supplies near the western border, which Soviet planners had stored there apparently with no consideration of the possibility that this would make the job of the invaders all that much easier.

Druzhnikov was at the front for a very short time. During a period of heavy rains, he came down with a skin disease that army medics feared could be infectious. Sent back to Moscow, he recovered and was put to work, along with other artists, painting the roofs of the capital's buildings. Carting buckets of green, yellow, and brown paint, they tried to camouflage the buildings as best they could, making them look like a forest—at least to German bombers at a considerable distance.

Doing what he was told and keeping silent about what he had seen during his brief stint at the front came naturally to Druzhnikov. As an illustrator who also was skilled in retouching photographs, he knew that one slip of the tongue could cost him his life in Stalin's Russia. In the late 1930s, two NKVD agents had arrived at his apartment. They ordered Druzhnikov's wife to take young Yuri and his sister outside while they stayed behind with the terrified husband and father. Both Ilya and his wife were convinced he was about to be arrested. Instead, one of the agents pulled out a photograph of Stalin, a close-up of his face, which—unlike the face in every photo that had ever been published—was visibly pockmarked, probably from his childhood bout of smallpox. The agents asked if he could retouch the photograph to make the unsightly pockmarks disappear. Standing over him as he painstakingly did so, they watched the leader's cheeks become smoother and

smoother. When Druzhnikov was done, they handed him a document to sign. It stated that he was in possession of a state secret
that must never be revealed. The illustrator signed and only told
this story to his son Yuri long after Stalin died.

At the time, the disastrous rout of Soviet forces that were unprepared for the German onslaught was considered as big a secret as
Stalin's pockmarks. Ilya Druzhnikov was schooled enough in the
Soviet system to remain absolutely silent about both of his chilling
experiences, whether or not he had signed an oath of secrecy. He
was lucky to have survived each of those harrowing ordeals—and
he was acutely aware of that fact.

The leader who inspired such terror, who presided over a state
built on fear, suddenly looked paralyzed by his own fear when the
Germans invaded. He had persisted in his state of denial about
German intentions right up to the moment the enemy struck. On
June 20, two days before the invasion, the supervisor of the Baltic
port of Riga had called Politburo member Anastas Mikoyan with
news that could hardly be misinterpreted: the twenty-five German
cargo ships in the port at that moment had received instructions to
leave the next day, whether or not they had completed their loading and unloading of cargo. Mikoyan went straight to Stalin and
urged him to order that the German ships not be allowed to
depart. "It's going to be a provocation," the Soviet leader responded angrily. "We cannot do it. Instruct them not to impede
the ships and to let them go."

Even when the invasion started, Stalin's first instinct was to disbe-
lieve it. When General Georgy Zhukov, Chief of the General Staff,
called Stalin's dacha at 4 A.M. to wake the leader and inform him of
the reports of heavy German shelling and bombing raids coming in
from all across the western part of the Soviet Union, Stalin's first instructions were to avoid striking back. Arriving at the Kremlin a
short time later, he speculated that the German military might be
acting on its own. "Hitler surely doesn't know about it," he declared.
Then he ordered Molotov to meet with German Ambassador Schulenburg to find out what the reports from the border could mean—
as if there was still a chance that they could be wrong.

In fact, the German envoy had already requested a meeting with Molotov to deliver a clear-cut message from his government. When he arrived at 5:30 that morning, Schulenburg didn't hide his own disappointment about its contents, which undid all his efforts to keep the peace between their two countries. The statement explained that the threat posed by the growing number of Soviet forces on the border had compelled the German government "to take immediate military countermeasures." Incredibly, Molotov asked the ambassador what this statement could mean. As the Soviet note taker at the meeting dryly reported, "Schulenburg replied that in his opinion it meant the beginning of the war." Molotov protested that, in fact, there was no build-up of Soviet troops at the border and that the only military activity consisted of routine maneuvers. The ambassador said there was nothing he could add on the subject. Molotov went back to Stalin to relay the message that "the German government has declared war on us." The Soviet leader muttered, "Ribbentrop deceived us, the scoundrel!"

The German army that launched the attack numbered 3.05 million men and included 3,550 tanks, 2,770 aircraft, and about six hundred thousand horses; despite the Nazi military machine's modern equipment, horses were still essential for transporting weaponry and other supplies. Another half-million troops were provided by Finland and Romania, which were allied with Germany. This was the biggest military force ever assembled but only begins to suggest how large a conflict the Soviet-German war would prove to be. Over the next four years, on average about nine million troops were involved in this epic conflict at any one time.

The Germans divided their invasion force into three parts: Army Group North, Army Group Center, and Army Group South. Army Group North was to direct its assault through the Baltic states, with Leningrad as its ultimate target. Army Group South was to focus its efforts on reaching Kiev, the Ukrainian capital. But it was Army Group Center that was the most heavily equipped, boasting half of the German armored divisions and its most famous panzer units. Its assignment was to encircle and take Minsk and then continue the drive due east toward Moscow. As the fighting moved in that direction, the single largest concentration of troops would be involved in the battle for Moscow.

But with communications spotty—German saboteurs had cut telephone and telegraph wires wherever they could, and many Soviet divisions were overrun in the initial fighting—Stalin and his entourage in the Kremlin still had little idea of the power and size of the invading forces. Or just how unrealistic the Soviet leader's initial orders must have sounded to those who received them. True, many of the troops had been equally clueless. As General Ivan Fedyuninsky admitted later: "When the showdown came, the might of the German Army came as a complete surprise to many of our officers." But they quickly realized that they were up against an onslaught that their leaders hadn't prepared them to face.

The Kremlin leaders were still reluctant to concede the magnitude of their mistakes. As he was receiving reports from all over that the Luftwaffe was bombing and strafing military and civilian targets during the morning of the invasion, General Ivan Boldin, the deputy commander of the western military district, received a call at his headquarters in Minsk from defense commissar Semyon Timoshenko.

"Comrade Boldin, remember no action is to be taken against the Germans without our knowledge," Timoshenko told him. "Will you please tell [General Dmitry] Pavlov that Comrade Stalin has forbidden to open artillery fire against the Germans."

"But how is that possible?" Boldin yelled. "Our troops are in full retreat. Whole towns are in flames, people are being killed all over the place."

Timoshenko wasn't about to relent, since Stalin was still unwilling to believe what he was hearing. But within a few hours, Stalin could no longer doubt that the country was facing a full-scale invasion. He then started issuing orders that reflected even more ignorance. Frontier troops were instructed "to attack enemy forces with all the strength and means at their disposal, and to annihilate them wherever they had violated the Soviet border." The air force was ordered to strike "mighty blows" and "smash the main enemy troop concentrations and their aircraft on its airfields." Soviet bombers were supposed to hit Königsberg and Memel, and the Soviet forces in the southwestern region were supposed to capture Lublin, the Polish city thirty miles across the border. With much of the Soviet air force in the west already destroyed and whole armies disintegrating, Stalin could just as well have been ordering his generals to fly to the moon.

The orders were signed by Timoshenko, Zhukov and Georgy Malenkov, a member of the Kremlin inner circle—but not by Stalin, who undoubtedly understood that he was facing a situation that could reflect badly on him. In the early morning hours, Soviet radio had continued to air innocuous programming, ignoring the alarming news from the front. But the assembled political and military brass in the Kremlin realized they had to announce the fact that the war had started, and they urged Stalin to do so. "Let Molotov speak," he replied. His aides argued that the people would expect Stalin "at such a significant historical moment." To no avail, since Stalin wouldn't budge. "That was certainly a mistake," Mikoyan recalled later. "However, Stalin was so depressed that he didn't know what to tell the nation."

So Molotov spoke, delivering the radio address at noon that every Soviet citizen who was alive then still remembers. Stalin helped him draft his address, which reflected the leader's sense of shock that Hitler had turned against him. "This unheard-of attack on our country is an unparalleled act of perfidy in the history of civilized nations," Molotov declared. "This attack has been made despite the fact that there was a nonaggression pact between the Soviet Union and Germany, a pact the terms of which were scrupulously observed by the Soviet Union." Disregarding his country's acquiescence in German aggression up to that point, he denounced Germany's enslavement of "the French, the Czechs, the Poles, the Serbs, and the peoples of Norway, Denmark, Holland, Belgium, Greece and other countries." He vowed that the "arrogant Hitler" would meet the same fate as Napoleon in Russia. And, wrapping it up, he uttered the words that would stick in the minds of most of his listeners. "Our cause is just. The enemy will be crushed. Victory will be ours."

But the news from the front hardly justified such optimism. With the Kremlin still issuing senseless orders for Soviet troops to go on the offensive, German forces of Army Group Center, the troops assigned to drive straight east through Belorussia, were making rapid progress. On June 28, the Belorussian capital of Minsk fell to the invaders, trapping four hundred thousand Red Army troops. The city may not have been that significant a strategic target, but Stalin had been determined to defend it, and its collapse sent him into a psychological tailspin. The next day he informed his entourage, "Lenin left us a great inheritance and we, his heirs, have fucked it all up!"

As the news only got worse, the leader retreated to his dacha and didn't show up in the Kremlin the next day. Callers were told, "Comrade Stalin is not here and is unlikely to be here." For two days, the Politburo members wondered whether he was still in charge. Finally, a delegation of them nervously made their way to his dacha. When they entered, Stalin looked at them and asked, "What have you come for?" As Mikoyan recalled, "He had the strangest look on his face, and the question itself was pretty strange, too." The thought flashed through Mikoyan's mind that Stalin assumed they were about to arrest him.

Instead, Molotov told Stalin that there was a proposal to set up a State Defense Committee that would preside over the war effort. "With whom as its head?" the leader asked. Both Molotov and then secret police chief Beria promptly told him that he would be in charge. Stalin looked both surprised and relieved. "Fine," he said.

Stalin resumed his leadership role, but he hardly inspired confidence in his ability to lead his country out of its mortal crisis. To be sure, he had taken some sensible steps during the very first days of the invasion. On June 24, for example, he created the Council of Evacuation, charged with the task of transporting entire factories, their workers, and supplies to eastern regions of the country beyond the reach of the Germans. This was the start of a process that would eventually lead to the dismantling of thousands of factories, from small workshops to major enterprises, and their reassembly in their new locations.

But in those early days, Khrushchev observed that he was "a different Stalin, a bag of bones in a gray tunic." When Khrushchev told him that things were going badly because of the shortage of weapons, the leader offered a sardonic response. "Well, they talk about how smart Russians are. Look how smart we are now."

Khrushchev wasn't amused, especially when later he called from Kiev to ask for weapons for factory workers who were demanding them. He got Malenkov on the line. According to his account, that led to the following testy exchange:

"Tell me, where can we get rifles?" Khrushchev asked. "We've got factory workers here who want to join the ranks of the Red Army to fight the Germans and we don't have anything to arm them with."

"You'd better give up any thought of getting rifles from us," Malenkov replied. "The rifles in the civil defense organization here have all been sent to Leningrad."

"Then what are we supposed to fight with?"

"I don't know—pikes, swords, homemade weapons, anything you can make in the factories."

"You mean we should fight tanks with spears?"

"You'll have to do the best you can. You can make fire bombs out of bottles of gasoline or kerosene and throw them at the tanks."

Khrushchev felt "dismay and indignation." As he put it, "Here we were, trying to hold back an invasion without rifles and machine guns, not to mention artillery or mechanized weapons!"

The *Stavka,* or main command headquarters, may have been providing few satisfactory answers to such frantic appeals, but from the moment that Stalin returned to the Kremlin after his near breakdown, he was once again clearly in charge. On July 3, he finally addressed his countrymen. It was a remarkable performance on several levels. But the most important part of the speech was its opening. "Comrades! Brothers and sisters! Men of our army and navy! I am addressing you, my friends!" Stalin declared.

For the despot to address his people as "brothers and sisters" and "my friends" was unprecedented. His listeners knew something fundamental had changed. He was appealing to them as partners in the common struggle, not just as subjects. That was truly revolutionary, and his listeners felt it. This was different from Molotov speaking. The dual message was that Stalin was fully in charge and that he needed everyone's help in fighting back against the German invaders.

The rest of his speech was more predictable and contorted. He warned of the "grave danger" the country was facing, and praised "the heroic resistance of the Red Army," claiming that the Germans had already suffered terrible destruction of their "finest divisions and finest air force units." In the same breath, he admitted that "the enemy continues to push forward, hurling fresh forces into the attack." He had to reckon with the evident gains of the enemy, while reassuring his countrymen that these were only temporary. "History shows that there are no invincible armies and never have been," he declared, echoing his speech to the graduates of the military academy in May. "Napoleon's army was considered invincible, but it was beaten successfully by Russian, English, and German armies." He vowed that the Nazi invaders, like Napoleon, "will be smashed" on Soviet soil.

Reverting to form, he issued a direct warning to his own countrymen, vowing to wage "a ruthless fight against all disorganizers of the rear, deserters, panic-mongers" and to "exterminate spies, saboteurs, and enemy parachutists." Military tribunals would quickly mete out justice to anyone guilty of "panic-mongering and cowardice," he added. In cases where retreat was absolutely necessary, he ordered the evacuation of all equipment and supplies. "The enemy must not be left a single engine, a single railway car, not a single kilogram of grain or a liter of fuel." Anything that could not be taken, he concluded, "must be destroyed without fail."

But Stalin also felt compelled to give a convoluted justification for his decision to agree to a nonaggression pact with Hitler. He argued that it "secured our country peace for a year and a half and the opportunity of preparing its forces to repulse fascist Germany should she risk an attack on our country despite the pact." That begged the question why that time wasn't put to better use and why Soviet forces were so ill prepared for the invasion.

Stalin tried to explain away the initial setbacks. "As to part of our territory having nevertheless been seized by German fascist troops, this is chiefly due to the fact that the war of fascist Germany on the U.S.S.R. began under conditions favorable for the German forces and unfavorable for Soviet forces." He noted that the Germans were fully mobilized "whereas Soviet troops had still to effect mobilization and move up to the frontier." He insisted that the responsibility for that disparity lay with the Germans for "treacherously" violating the nonaggression pact—and, of course, there was not a hint of a *mea culpa* in any part of the speech.

The speech accomplished its purpose of showing that Stalin was indeed in control of the country and of holding out the hope of eventual victory. But on the battlefields, the Germans just kept coming. By July 16, German troops led by General Heinz Guderian, or *Schneller Heinz* as the famed tank commander was called, had reached Smolensk, the next big city to fall after Minsk on the march east. Once again, hundreds of thousands of Red Army troops found themselves encircled and killed or captured. It was only three weeks since Hitler had launched the invasion, and the successful drive to Smolensk meant that the invaders only had to keep going another 230 miles due east to reach Moscow. Stalin's assurances notwithstanding, the Red Army looked as though it wasn't capable of preventing the German forces from doing almost anything they pleased—including seizing the Soviet capital, if Hitler chose to make that their next goal. On July 21, German bombers attacked the Soviet capital for the first time. The prognosis was bad and still getting worse.

Like most dead men, Vladimir Ilyich Lenin hadn't traveled after he reached his resting place in 1924. Admittedly, he hadn't been exactly allowed to rest. The scientists who cared for his body, which remained on display in the mausoleum built for him on Red Square, were constantly fiddling with him, applying special fluids to his exposed face and hands at least a couple of times a week and every eighteen months or so soaking him in a bath of potassium acetate, glycerin, water, and enough quinine chloride to serve as a disinfectant. They had followed this procedure ever since their first frantic efforts to find a way indefinitely to preserve Lenin at Stalin's behest. The new Soviet leader was determined to keep his predecessor around as an object of worship, thereby solidifying the mythology of the Bolshevik Revolution and his own stranglehold on power. All of this elaborate maintenance took place in the mausoleum and its special lab in the basement, allowing Lenin to stay on the premises as he underwent his successive tune-ups.

That is, until July 3, 1941, when Lenin was sent on a long journey out of the Soviet capital for the first and only time since his death. Even before General Guderian's tanks reached Smolensk two weeks later, and even as he prepared to address his countrymen for the first time since the invasion started, Stalin recognized that Moscow was in mortal danger. Which meant that Lenin was also in danger. If the Germans seized the Soviet capital, it would be a humiliating defeat. But if they also seized the holiest of holies, Lenin, the defeat would be beyond humiliating. It would be a crushing psychological blow, representing the triumph of fascism over communism, the cult of Hitler over the cult of Lenin—and, by extension, of Stalin. So the Soviet leader ordered the evacuation of Lenin in total secrecy to Tyumen, a small city more than a thousand miles due east of the capital.

Ilya Zbarsky remembers that day, the ensuing train journey, and Lenin's stay in Tyumen, which would last nearly four years until the war was ending in March 1945. He remembers for one good reason: he is the sole survivor of the handful of caretakers who accompanied Lenin's body on that voyage. His father, Boris Zbarsky, was one of two men who had developed and carried out the original embalming work on Lenin, and he was in charge of the clandestine operation to move the body to safety. In 1934, he had persuaded his son Ilya, who was studying biochemistry at Moscow State University, to join the mausoleum's team of scientists whose task it was to ensure Lenin's preservation. For the next eighteen years, Ilya's work was focused on that one overarching goal.

Sitting in his modest two-room Moscow apartment in charcoal slacks, a light gray shirt, a red sleeveless sweater, and the slippers that are *de rigueur* in every Russian home, Zbarsky, with an elegant mane of white hair, looked a good deal younger than his ninety years when I visited him in early 2004. As his wife served us tea and generous slices of a creamy cake, he reminisced freely about his family history, his frequently tense relations with his father and a stepmother he detested, and, of course, the privileges and perils of serving as one of those entrusted with the care of a body that had been for all practical purposes deified by the Soviet state.

From his father, Ilya knew the story of how he and Professor Vladimir Vorobyov, head of the anatomy department at Kharkov University in the Ukraine, had worked with a team of assistants for four months to preserve Lenin's body—a feat that many of their colleagues thought was unlikely to succeed and, for that reason, politically and personally dangerous. Over the objections of Lenin's widow, Nadezhda Krupskaya, and Leon Trotsky, Stalin's rival and future victim, Lenin was subjected to an audacious, unprecedented embalming process. On Stalin's orders, his brain was removed so that scientists at a special institute could study it to find clues to his "genius." (Despite their best efforts, they never found any evidence that it had any unusual characteristics.) The team also removed his internal organs, such as lungs and liver. They made small cuts in the skin and soaked the body in innovative chemical baths that were designed to allow it to retain moisture and elasticity. Finally, Lenin's eyes were replaced with fake ones, and the mouth was stitched below the mustache to keep his lips closed.

The first time he participated in undressing Lenin to prepare him for one of his routine chemical baths, Ilya recalled, he found something "disagreeable" about handling him, although he'd worked with corpses before. Maybe it had something to do with the texture of the skin, he mused, but more likely it had to do with the thought that he was handling the corpse of someone who was the object of such intense glorification. Even from the perspective of the next century, he found it hard to analyze his feelings coolly.

And then there was the fear factor. This was the 1930s, a decade when Stalin unleashed wholesale terror against his own people, a period when purges, executions, and one-way trips to the Gulag were as common occurrences as today's weather reports. Thanks to his job, Boris Zbarsky and his family appeared to be protected from Stalin's machinery of terror. At one point, his son recalled, the NKVD—the secret police, which would later be renamed the KGB—raided thirty-four of the thirty-six apartments in the prestigious government building where they lived; the elder Zbarsky's was one of the only two left untouched. But they could not be sure that this would always be the case. Ilya never discussed politics with his father. "In my mind, I felt it was terror, an awful time," he said. "But it was dangerous to even think about it."

Boris Zbarsky lived a privileged life, with a lavish salary and access to ample food when others were starving, but he knew everything could change in a moment. His own background provided plenty of ammunition for the NKVD should they have cared to use it. He was, by the definition of the times, a "Jewish cosmopolitan." He had studied in Switzerland, spoke several languages, and counted people like the painter Leonid Pasternak and his son Boris, the future Noble Prize winning writer, among his friends. And, in fact, in 1952, Boris Zbarsky would discover that his service to Lenin—and, of course, by extension, to Stalin—didn't guarantee him indefinite protection. Arrested for allegedly working for the Germans, he was one of many scientists and doctors caught up in one of Stalin's final wave of purges, this one targeting Jews, before the dictator's death in March 1953. Released in December of that year, he died soon thereafter, a broken man.

But all that was in the future on July 3, 1941, when both Zbarskys accompanied Lenin to Tyumen.

On that morning, Boris told his son of the secret Politburo decision to evacuate Lenin, informing him that he and his family had better start packing their personal belongings for the train ride east. Ilya recalled that he didn't need to be convinced of the urgency; the German forces were advancing toward the capital, and there was little to indicate that they could be stopped. He heard Stalin's radio address that day and was startled by his sharp Georgian accent and his opening words, in which he greeted his countrymen as brothers, sisters, and friends. "It was the first time that Stalin spoke to his people as human beings, not just as 'comrades,'" Ilya noted. Only a truly dire situation could have prompted such a dramatic reversal.

"We knew that it was dangerous to stay in Moscow," Ilya added. Still, he felt upset by the order, which left him with a sense that he was abandoning Moscow at a time when it would need every defender it could muster.

In the evening, NKVD cars arrived to pick up Ilya and his family, along with another colleague from the mausoleum team, Professor Sergei Mardashev, and his family, depositing them at a siding of the Yaroslavsky Station. There, as NKVD guards looked on, they boarded a special train that would carry Lenin, the scientists, their families, and forty Kremlin guards. But for all the preparations, the train wasn't refrigerated, and the scientists had to work hard to protect the body, lying in a wooden coffin, from deterioration in the stifling summer heat. Ilya remembers putting curtains on the windows to block out the sun, switching shifts with his father and Mardashev, never leaving the body unattended during the four-day journey, and regularly dabbing it with fluids.

The train was well stocked with food, and its route was lined with an unending string of green signals. At stations along the way, guards and troops were stationed to block anyone hoping to board it. With the Germans moving closer and Luftwaffe air raids already striking deep into the Russian heartland, there were crowds of desperate people seeking any transport east. The special train left them all behind.

In Tyumen, the local authorities put a Tsarist-era, two-story building belonging to an agricultural college at the disposal of the guests from Moscow and their "secret object." Surrounded by a brick wall and isolated from the rest of the town, it had its own guards, who made sure no locals wandered in by mistake. Ilya and his wife lived in a two-room apartment on the first floor, but they had to share it with his wife's mother, sister, and two nephews, who had accompanied them on the journey. Ilya's father, stepmother, and their son occupied an apartment on the second floor, where Lenin's body was kept.

The building was refurbished, and it was well heated and well lit, unlike most other buildings during the war. But there were no refrigeration facilities, and huge amounts of distilled water were either flown in from Omsk or sent by train, along with the special chemicals needed to prepare Lenin's chemical baths. Before immersing him, Ilya and the other caretakers would wrap the body in special bandages made of India rubber that were produced in Leningrad for this exalted purpose. Ilya estimates that, unlike in Moscow, where Lenin was mostly on display, he was left soaking in his baths for about 70 percent of the wartime period in Tyumen. Since they had few other responsibilities, the caretakers regularly worked on whatever blemishes they found on the body. They never wrote any reports, but a special commission that arrived later in the war to check on how Lenin was holding up concluded, according to Ilya, "that the body was even in better condition than before the evacuation."

Along with the contingent of guards, the building had a full kitchen staff, and Ilya recalled that they lived very comfortably during a time when most Russians were struggling with even worse food shortages than usual. "They fed us well," he said. "It was a lot easier than in Moscow. There was tea, cake, cognac." They tuned in to Russian and German radio stations, and they were alarmed by the news that indicated that the Germans were still advancing and then particularly by the reports from Moscow in mid-October 1941. "It was clear that something terrible was happening," Ilya noted. He heard from friends of the panic as many Muscovites tried to flee the city, convinced that it was about to fall. He also heard about arrests of professors who taught German, professors he had known at Moscow State University. Later, the Tyumen residents learned more about the fighting from wounded soldiers arriving from the front.

Although Moscow would hold off the Germans, Stalin didn't permit Lenin's return to the capital until the war was ending in March 1945. Delighted with Lenin's "health," the government awarded Boris Zbarsky the Order of Lenin and the title Hero of Socialist Labor. It awarded his son Ilya the Order of the Red Banner of Labor. But when Boris was arrested in 1952, Ilya was fired from his job as well, and he never returned to work at the mausoleum.

Looking back at his life and the focus of so much of his attention, he finally was willing to voice his true feelings about Lenin. "He should be taken out of the Kremlin and buried somewhere else," he said. "He's more a symbol of terror than a hero." Yet Ilya still bristled at mention of newspaper accounts from the early 1990s that claimed that Lenin's body hasn't really been preserved, except for the hands and head. "This is all nonsense," he protested. "Everything is intact."

Whatever conclusions he had come to about the system Lenin built, Ilya was proud of the role he and his father played in keeping Lenin "alive" during those nightmare years of the war, when millions of their countrymen perished. If the Germans had captured Lenin, the symbolism would have been enormous. And, of course, it would have meant that they had captured Moscow. And if they had captured Moscow, the early war years would have taken a very different path, and the outcome of the conflict would have been far from certain.

But Lenin lived.

That summer of 1941, when Stalin was secretly dispatching Lenin to Tyumen, Hitler was increasingly confident that the Soviet

Union—with Moscow at its center and Lenin as its symbol—would soon be history. It was Hitler's confidence that allowed him to launch Operation Barbarossa in the first place, sweeping aside all reservations and banishing worries about unnerving precedents. And it was his recharged confidence that now prompted him to edge toward another major miscalculation, which would prove to be a key factor in the outcome both of the battle for Moscow, which was still just looming, and of the entire war on the Eastern front.

Hitler felt liberated by the attack on the Soviet Union. "Since I struggled through to this decision, I again feel spiritually free," he wrote to Mussolini. "I am now happy to be relieved of these mental agonies." And the initial German victories and the speed of their advance only seemed to confirm the Führer's wisdom. On July 3, the day that Stalin was trying to rally his countrymen, German Army Chief of Staff Franz Halder wrote, "It is thus probably no overstatement to say that the Russian Campaign has been won in the space of two weeks." But he cautioned that it wasn't over yet. "The sheer geographical vastness of the country and the stubbornness of the resistance, which is carried on by all means, will claim our efforts for many more weeks to come," he added.

It was clear that Halder was envisioning a mopping-up operation over many more weeks, not months. On July 8, he wrote the following passage in his war diary:

"It is the Führer's firm decision to level Moscow and Leningrad and make them uninhabitable, so as to relieve us of the necessity of having to feed the populations through the winter. The cities will be razed by air force. Tanks must not be used for the purpose. 'A national catastrophe which will deprive not only Bolshevism, but also Muscovite nationalism, of their centers.'"

Presumably the last sentence quotes Hitler directly. Over dinner with his entourage on July 27, the German dictator outlined his broader vision, not just for Moscow and Leningrad but for the entire territory he expected to conquer. His empire, he explained, would extend two to three hundred kilometers (124 to 186 miles) east of the Urals. The German overlords should be able to control that expanse "with 250,000 men plus a cadre of good administrators." As his inspiration, he pointed to the British empire. "Let's learn from the English, who, with 250,000 men in all, including 50,000 soldiers, govern 400 million Indians. This space in Russia must always be dominated by Germans." The conquered people would be subjugated mercilessly, and the overarching strategy would be "to Germanize this country by the immigration of Germans and to look upon the natives as Redskins . . . In this business I shall go ahead cold-bloodedly."

But for all the heady optimism of those early days, and despite the collapse of Soviet defenses in most key areas, there were signs even then that the Germans were up against more than they expected. German units quickly discovered that roads and other infrastructure, which may have looked good on their maps, were often virtually nonexistent. And from the very first day, some Soviet soldiers fought back fiercely, refusing to surrender no matter how doomed they were.

For example, the Germans expected to brush by the fortress at Brest, right across the border, but found themselves bogged down in several days of intense fighting. Soviet troops, along with their wives and children, held out under a steady barrage of German artillery and machine gun fire longer than seemed humanly possible. A few diehards kept fighting from the fort's tunnels and ramparts for up to a month. "Russians, surrender," the Germans appealed to them on loudspeakers. "German command guarantees your lives. Moscow has already capitulated." Ironically, Polish troops had resisted the German invaders at the same fortress in September 1939, when Brest still belonged to Poland. (One of its defenders who survived was this writer's father.) Later the Germans had handed over Brest to the Red Army, since the city was assigned to the Soviet Union in Hitler and Stalin's division of the spoils.

Field Marshal Fedor von Bock, the commander of Army Group Center, who observed the fighting in and around the fortress and then the battles nearby, recorded in his war diary on June 23, only a day into the invasion: "The Russians are defending themselves stubbornly. Women have often been seen in combat. According to statements made by prisoners, political commissars are spurring maximum resistance by reporting that we kill all prisoners! Here and there Russian officers have shot themselves to avoid being captured."

As he and the rest of the Soviet diplomats prepared to leave Berlin following the outbreak of hostilities, Valentin Berezhkov met with SS Senior Lieutenant Heineman, who was in charge of the guards around the embassy. Heineman proved to be far less of a committed Nazi than he first appeared, and he quickly informed Berezhkov that top German officials were extremely worried by the determined resistance they were encountering in some areas during the initial fighting, which was leading to heavy German casualties. "Some people in the Imperial Chancellery even wonder whether Germany should have started the war against the Soviet Union in the first place," he told Berezhkov.

The SS man, it turned out, was eager to be recruited for money, so he may have been overstating his case. For the most part, the initial successes of the German invaders buoyed the spirits of the Nazi leadership, convincing them that Hitler had been right to make his bold move against his eastern neighbor. But even Goebbels, while claiming in his diary on June 24 that "military developments in the East are excellent beyond all our expectations," tempered his optimism with grudging respect for his adversaries. In denouncing the "wild atrocity propaganda" of Moscow in response to the invasion, he noted on June 25 that "their propaganda is better than London's. Here we find ourselves facing a more practiced opponent." It was a theme he returned to again two days later. "The Bolsheviks are not Englishmen," he wrote. "They know a thing or two about subversive propaganda."

More significantly, his reports about German victories quickly were peppered with admissions that their opponents were often putting up serious resistance. On Friday, June 27, he noted: "The Russians are suffering huge losses in tanks and aircraft. But they are fighting well and have learned a great deal even since Sunday [the day of the invasion]." The next day he added, "The enemy is defending desperately and is also very well led. The situation presents no threat, but we have our hands full."

As the Kremlin began gearing up its defense of the Soviet capital, organizing the *opolchenie* or home guard units that quickly attracted 120,000 recruits following Stalin's speech, a note of hesitancy began to creep into the thinking of the German leadership about the targeting of Moscow. On July 4, Goebbels reported once again that the situation on the central front was "excellent" and that "the enemy is beginning to wilt." But he cautioned, "I ban any special emphasis on Moscow from German propaganda. We must beware of fixing the public gaze on this one fascinating goal."

Why the hesitancy when German troops were driving east at such speed? General Alfred Jodl, Hitler's chief of staff, provided at least a partial explanation. "The Führer has an instinctive aversion to treading the same path as Napoleon," he said. "Moscow gives him a sinister feeling. He fears that there might be a life and death struggle with Bolshevism."

But it was precisely that life or death struggle that Hitler triggered when he launched Operation Barbarossa. And there was no doubt that the Germans needed to conquer Moscow in order to have a chance of dealing a mortal blow to the Soviet state. And yet that summer, just when that goal appeared within reach, Hitler hesitated. Moscow's fate—and ultimately the fate of both totalitarian regimes—hung in the balance, and suddenly the normally bold Führer, much to the dismay of his generals, didn't seem to know what he wanted to do. His lingering optimism from the first stages of the invasion convinced him that he had enough time to pursue other targets of his eastern campaign first, especially victory in the Ukraine, while his underlying nervousness about Moscow convinced him this was also the safer course.

This would prove to be a major miscalculation, offering Stalin his first glimmer of hope. It was almost as if each despot was determined to match the other mistake for mistake.

3

The Price of Terror

When Germany invaded the Soviet Union on June 22, Ilya Vinitsky was a student at the Moscow Aviation Institute (MAI) and had just started a job as a summer trainee at a factory on the Volga. Raised in a Jewish family in Kiev, he had trained as a sniper while he was still in high school there. So he was ready—eager—to volunteer for military service when the war broke out. He rushed back to Moscow the very next day. The regional Party committee office assigned him to the First Special Communist Battalion of Moscow, a 307-man unit composed of a few other MAI students along with more experienced engineers and factory foremen, some of whom had gained combat experience in the Spanish Civil War.

At the first briefing of the new battalion that same evening, three Party officials in civilian clothes arrived and, after telling the military instructor to step outside, informed the volunteers that they were entrusted with a special mission. Many Soviet troops were fleeing the German attackers; the battalion's job was to stop them, the officials explained. They admitted that in the Baltic region many soldiers had dropped their guns, stripped down to their underwear, and swum across a river to escape; many others were simply waiting to surrender. The task of the new battalion, they continued, was to reimpose discipline and put an end to such behavior. "The Central Committee authorizes you to take whatever measures prove necessary—even executions," they declared.

Recalling those words as an octogenarian, Vinitsky found himself fighting back tears. Few memories are as painful to veterans of the Great Patriotic War, the official designation of World War II in Russia, as those of Soviet troops killing their own men. To this day, many veterans have suppressed everything to do with that particular memory—or at least have avoided talking about it. But the practice was started in the earliest period of the war and became frighteningly commonplace. Right from the beginning, Stalin acted on his core conviction, which was evident throughout every period of his reign, that he needed to wage a two-front war: one against the foreign invader and the other against those he and his armies of willing executioners deemed traitors or enemies within.

The terror of the 1930s morphed quickly into a new wartime terror campaign. And most of those who went to war in 1941 recognized—or soon came to recognize—that it wasn't only the Germans who threatened their lives; it was also their own comrades, superior officers, and NKVD enforcers. Even the most loyal soldier couldn't be sure that he wouldn't run afoul, sometimes unwittingly, of someone from his side on or off the battlefield.

As a young man who had just donned a uniform, Vinitsky wasn't put off by the instructions his unit received—quite the contrary. "We were proud we were assigned this special mission," he recalled. That mission also meant that they were all equipped with rifles and grenades at a time when many other units were given only minimal supplies. And since they were volunteers who hadn't gone through the mobilization office, their paperwork was different from that of most other recruits. Because of an oversight, they were allowed to keep their internal passports—the identification document all civilians were required to carry with them at all times—instead of turning them in for military ID cards, as almost everyone else was required to do. This bureaucratic slip-up would soon almost cost Vinitsky his life.

But first, along with his unit, he had to make it to the front. One of their military lecturers had told them about the soil of East Prussia, explaining why it would be difficult to dig trenches there—

as if it was really possible that they'd soon find themselves that far west, pushing the Germans back into their own territory. Instead, they boarded a train heading west that made it only as far as Velikiye Luki, a town 280 miles from Moscow. "That was it. There was no Soviet power any further," Vinitsky recalled.

The town and everything in it had been abandoned by Soviet troops, although no Germans were there yet either. Even the railway switches were locked. With the help of a local engineer, they managed to unlock them and pull out in the evening, only to find themselves under attack from German planes the next morning. Vinitsky and the others jumped off the train, but about thirty were killed or wounded before they could make it to the cover of nearby woods. "For the first time, I saw what 'a little blood' meant," he said, referring to the popular prewar boast of the Soviet authorities that they would defeat any enemy on his territory, spilling only "a little blood" of their own. The dead and dying were sprawled out everywhere. A bomb fragment had split open the head of one of his friends, killing him instantly, but his eyes were still open and seemed to be looking at Vinitsky and the other survivors "as if in reproach." Nothing of the train was left but a useless wreck.

Ordered to return to their main job of finding retreating units to force them back into battle, the survivors dispersed in the woods, usually in pairs. Vinitsky soon found himself alone, since his partner disappeared during the night. After walking several hours, he came upon a group of sixty to seventy Soviet soldiers sitting around a fire. Everything about them indicated that they had given up. Two senior officers, who were identifiable by the insignia they had torn off their uniforms, were clearly preparing to surrender to the Germans. Sitting listlessly by, their men were ready to follow their lead. Some had already burned their personal documents.

Facing them alone, Vinitsky asked who was in charge of their unit. No one answered. "Line up!" he ordered them, and, remarkably, the men obeyed. He told them he had full authorization from the Central Committee to take charge, and that he was also authorized to shoot any cowards. He then instructed them to follow him, and, once again, they obeyed. "They were happy to see anyone assuming any kind of responsibility," he said. "The men were encouraged since they believed I had confidence in what I was doing."

That was hardly surprising, since many of the soldiers had seen only incompetent officers. Vinitsky told the two officers of his plan to lead the men back to his unit so that they could be reconstituted as a fighting force. But when they looked at a map together to figure out what route to follow, he realized that the unit's political officer didn't even know how to read it. The reason was that the senior officers in that particular unit had all been purged less than a year before, and Party loyalists, who had no knowledge beyond Party slogans, had risen to take their place.

Although he could easily have done so, Vinitsky didn't shoot the officers or anyone else. He acknowledged that he had been tempted for a moment, particularly when he saw that the officers had torn off their insignia. But when he marched the men he had found back to the main unit, he heard that things had gone differently elsewhere. Some of his comrades freely admitted that they had executed soldiers to assert their authority. The special unit had rounded up about fifteen hundred soldiers in all, but Vinitsky didn't know how many they had killed in the process.

Vinitsky's battalion didn't hesitate to do whatever it took to survive, no matter who paid the price. They seized horses, grain, and any other food supplies they could find in the villages that weren't yet occupied by the Germans. Vinitsky claimed his men issued receipts for whatever they took, but the peasants knew they were worthless. "You are leaving us to the Germans and stealing from us—you bloody 'defenders,'" they'd shout at the soldiers.

At one point, Vinitsky's unit spotted a German automobile and ambushed it. Inside were a German general, a Russian nurse, and a driver. "We killed them all," Vinitsky noted. "We had to kill the nurse as well. There was no way for us to capture them. It wasn't practical. We could hardly find food for ourselves." He added, "The nurse was a defector. You would not believe how many traitors there were." Many of the men had already witnessed the destruction wrought by the Germans, sometimes on their hometowns, families, and neighbors. As a result, Vinitsky concluded, "We were furious and unmerciful."

Ironically, those charged with hunting down the "traitors," troops preparing to surrender, were just as likely to fall victim to others charged with the same mission. That, too, was commonplace in Stalin's system. The hunters could—and very often would—suddenly become the hunted.

When the summer was almost over, Vinitsky received orders to make his way back east to Rzhev, a fiercely contested town north-west of Moscow. He was supposed to help maintain the Soviet planes that were based there. On his way, he found himself with a day to kill while waiting for a train connection in a small town. "My legs were aching, I was hungry, I had no money with me, and I couldn't buy any food," he recalled. So he decided to go to a nearby lake, take off his boots, and soak his feet in the water, enjoying the rare peaceful view on a warm summer day. He was wearing a dirty uniform and carrying a German machine gun and binoculars that he had seized in battle. But worst of all, he was still carrying his internal passport, which normally would have indicated that he wasn't really a Soviet soldier, since soldiers were supposed to carry only military ID cards or dog tags. "I was like a gift for the counterintelligence service," he noted sardonically. "At that time, hunting for spies was in full swing."

Sure enough, he suddenly heard the order, "Get up! Hands up! Freeze!" A three-man patrol had crept up on him, and the three men had their guns pointed at Vinitsky. "Your papers!" they demanded. When Vinitsky pulled out his internal passport and his student ID card, they pushed him to the ground and tied his hands behind his back. Though he had a piece of paper assigning him to his battalion, they were convinced this was a German forgery. As far as they were concerned, they had nabbed a German spy.

The patrol marched Vinitsky back to the NKVD office in the town, where three other men began interrogating him and quickly dismissed his story as an obvious fraud. One of the men began working him over, punching him in the face. He paused for a moment as Vinitsky spat out some of his front teeth, and the captive managed to have the presence of mind to throw out another defense: he was Jewish. His tormenter then made him undress to prove he was circumcised. But that only convinced the trio that he was "a very well-camouflaged spy." The beating continued until the NKVD officer was tired. He then proposed they shoot Vinitsky on the spot.

But one of the other men, the local Party secretary, had continued to examine his documents and he concluded they weren't forged. Which could mean only one thing: he was an even more important spy than they had thought; and so he should be dispatched to the local NKVD headquarters in the bigger town of Kalinin, where they could "make this bastard tell the truth." Three armed men escorted him on the train ride to Kalinin, and, once there, he was thrown on the cement floor of a windowless cell in the NKVD headquarters, still tied up and with his mouth still bleeding.

Vinitsky didn't know it yet, but he was lucky to be there. His new interrogator, a young NKVD agent wearing civilian clothes, wrote down everything he said, including his protestations that it wasn't his fault that he was never issued a military ID card. Much to Vinitsky's surprise, the interrogator heeded his plea to call the director of MAI, who could testify to the veracity of his story that he was a student who had volunteered for military service. The interrogator asked him detailed questions about MAI, where the aviation institute was located in Moscow, and where its main lecture halls were situated inside the building. When Vinitsky answered everything accurately, he ordered a guard to untie him, allowed him to wash up, and offered him tea and dry bread. Vinitsky could only drink the tea since, after his beatings, he couldn't chew.

The interrogator freed Vinitsky, who would go on to do maintenance work on airplanes, though not in Rzhev. That town's plane facilities had already been destroyed in the fighting. Later, Vinitsky would learn about the fate of the rest of his unit. Of the 307 men, thirty-two survived. He was among those very few lucky ones, and, not all that unusually, his closest brush with death came when he was taken prisoner by his own side.

Censorship of private correspondence was routine in the Soviet Union before the German invasion, and the NKVD censors stepped up their work as soon as war broke out. They flagged anything that sounded seditious, and retribution was swift. On June 24, for instance, the censors' internal report quoted several letters.

Chervyakov, identified only by his last name and the description that he had served in the tsarist army, claimed that the Kremlin had made a mistake by allying itself with Germany instead of with

Britain and France and that the outbreak of the war was already revealing "great dissatisfaction in the army." The censors' report contained the final line: "Chervyakov was arrested."

An ethnic German "manufacturer" named Kuhn wrote, "The Soviet Union is totally responsible for the war," echoing German propaganda that Soviet troop deployments along the border amounted to a provocation. "Soviet power isn't the product of the will of the people," he added. "And now people will protest." Here, too, the final line was: "Kuhn was arrested."

Danilov, an employee of the road department of Moscow's Stalin district, erroneously reported that Hitler's armies had already captured five major cities, including Kiev and Odessa. "At last we shall breathe freely," he wrote. "In three days Hitler will be in Moscow and the intelligentsia will live the good life." There was no note about Danilov's fate, but it isn't hard to imagine.

Kurbanov, who worked for the construction department of Intourist, the state travel bureau, wrote, "It's questionable whether Soviet power will prevail in this war. In 1919–20 [referring to the Civil War] the people fought for liberty and their rights. Now they have nobody to die for. Soviet power has made people remarkably angry." Here, too, there was no word on his fate.

Finally, Mauritz, described only as another ethnic German, predicted that peasants would welcome the outbreak of the war. "It will free them from the Bolsheviks and the collective farms that they hate." The notation: "Mauritz was arrested."

In fact, many Ukrainians and others on the western periphery of the Soviet Union initially greeted the Germans as liberators, since they were convinced that the conquerors would put an end to the wholesale terror they had experienced under Stalin. The forced collectivization campaign of the 1930s, accompanied by mass starvation, arrests, and executions, had led to millions of deaths, and it was hard for the survivors to imagine that the Germans could treat them any worse than that. "The local population showed genuine kindness towards the German troops and pinned great hopes on our arrival," Hans von Herwarth, the German diplomat turned warrior wrote. "Everywhere we went we were greeted with bread and salt, the traditional Slav symbols of hospitality."

But if this behavior could be discounted because it was coming from the Ukrainians or other nationalities whose loyalty was suspect, the censors' classified reports on intercepted letters showed that the inhabitants of Moscow and other Russian cities weren't immune to such sentiments either during the earliest days of the fighting. While most rallied to the cause, the doubters—and those who unabashedly hoped for the defeat of the communist regime—weren't simply figments of the paranoid imagination of Stalin and his enforcers. They may have constituted a small minority, but there were enough of them to feed the regime's paranoia further. There were enough, too, to belie the propaganda line that the Soviet people were completely united in their resolve to defeat the German invaders.

Far more serious than the signs of civilian discontent was the situation on the battlefields as the Germans kept advancing. Stalin had plenty of reason to suspect that many of his demoralized troops were giving up all too willingly and that discipline was breaking down in major units all across the front. "It was not the German attack that took Stalin by surprise but the collapse of our troops," Sergo Beria, the son of the NKVD chief Lavrenty Beria, maintained in his account of the period. Although he was wrong in his contention that Stalin wasn't surprised by the attack itself, the younger Beria was right about the shock that the Soviet leader felt when he realized that his armies were, in many cases, disintegrating in the face of the German assault.

Faced with this avalanche of alarming news, Stalin reverted to form, issuing a series of draconian decrees that would play a key role in how the battle for Moscow would be fought and every other battle afterward. In essence, they amounted to a death sentence not only for those who fled or wavered but also for many brave soldiers who stood their ground.

On June 28, he authorized the first instructions that set out his attitude toward all those Soviet soldiers who were captured by the Germans. The "traitors who had fled abroad," as he called them, were to be immediately punished upon their return, and, in the meantime, their families were to be punished as well. A month later, he issued Order 227, known as Not a Step Backward. Forbidding Soviet soldiers to retreat, it warned that they would be shot if they disobeyed. The NKVD was also given the authority to shoot any Soviet soldiers who escaped from German captivity. To be captured by the Germans, the prisoners soon learned, amounted to a virtual death sentence. A German report dated February 19, 1942, indicated that nearly three million of the four million Soviet prisoners they had taken up to that point had perished. While the report almost certainly exaggerated the number of Soviet prisoners, the 75 percent death ratio was in all probability close to accurate. And Stalin's order meant that most were doomed even if they managed to escape.

Then, on August 16, Stalin issued his infamous Order 270, spelling out the specifics of his policy. "I order that (1) anyone who removes his insignia during battle and surrenders should be treated as a malicious deserter whose family is to be arrested as a family of a breaker of the oath and betrayer of the Motherland. Such deserters are to be shot on the spot. (2) Those falling into encirclement are to fight to the last and try to reach their own lines. And those who prefer to surrender are to be destroyed by any available means, while their families are to be deprived of all state allowances and assistance."

Stalin had already demonstrated that he meant every word of that. A month earlier, Yakov, Stalin's eldest son, a lieutenant in the Fourteenth Armored Division, found himself surrounded by German troops at Vitebsk. "I am Stalin's son and I won't allow my battery to retreat," he announced, trying to follow his father's instructions. But he was captured, which meant he hadn't followed them to the end. When the Germans trumpeted the capture of this high-profile prisoner, Stalin was furious. "The fool—he couldn't even shoot himself!" he exclaimed.

After Order 270 was announced, the NKVD arrested Yakov's wife—Stalin's daughter-in-law—Yulia, dispatching her to a camp for two years. The Germans would later offer to exchange Yakov for their famed Field Marshal Friedrich Paulus, who was captured at Stalingrad on January 31, 1943. Stalin refused, and, a few months later, his son carried out his father's wish. Stranded as a POW in Germany, Yakov committed suicide by throwing himself on the camp's fence.

Nothing could change Stalin's mind about those who fell into captivity. Early in the war, the Germans suggested that a postal system should be set up for POWs on both sides. "There are no Russian prisoners of war," Stalin responded. "The Russian soldier fights on till death. If he chooses to become a prisoner, he is automatically excluded from the Russian community. We are not interested in a postal service only for Germans."

That attitude meant that those Soviet POWs who managed to escape or to survive until the end of the war found themselves arrested if they were lucky and executed immediately if they weren't. Nikolai Pisarev, for example, was wounded and captured in July 1941 in the western Ukraine. By October, he was among the first group of prisoners dispatched to Auschwitz, where Soviet POWs were ordered to build the Birkenau section of the camp, which would become the site of the gas chambers. Almost all of those Soviet POWs perished, but Pisarev managed to escape while assigned to a work detail at the railroad station in the town. With the help of local Poles, he dodged his pursuers and then survived the war as a member of a Polish forced-labor brigade. When he returned to Moscow, NKVD interrogators imprisoned and tortured him for a month, beating him unconscious. He survived that ordeal, too, and a subsequent period of internal exile. That's what passed for luck in such cases.

As the Germans drove further east during the summer of 1941 and Moscow looked increasingly vulnerable, Stalin kept demanding more instant retribution anywhere that the Soviet lines were breaking—which was almost everywhere at first. On July 10, for instance, he had the *Stavka*, the main command headquarters, issue a declaration that it was "totally dissatisfied" with what was happening on the northwestern front. "The officers who did not carry out orders, abandoning their positions like traitors and leaving the defensive ridge without orders, have not yet been punished," it complained. And it ordered a prosecutor and NKVD officers "to go at once to forward units and deal with the traitors and cowards on the spot."

There was no doubt about what was meant by the command "to deal with the traitors." By September, just as the battle for Moscow was looming, "blocking units" began to appear. These were squads that took up positions behind Soviet troops going into battle, and their job was to mow down any of the men who tried to retreat. Hence the terrifying scenes of Soviet soldiers finding themselves driven back by the Germans only to be cut down by machine gunners from behind. "What can one think of an army in which one soldier is ordered to fire on the enemy and another is ordered to fire on his compatriots?" Sergo Beria, the son of Stalin's secret police chief, asked later. "There was something dirty and sticky there, like in Dostoevsky's books." While the blocking units weren't as well organized as they would be in later battles, such as Stalingrad, their origins can be traced to the build-up to the battle for Moscow.

In other respects, the Stalinist system of retribution was already fully operational during that period. The shooting of deserters had become commonplace. Sometimes this meant the shooting of hundreds of soldiers in a single unit. Some soldiers shot themselves in the left hand, thinking this would allow them to escape the fighting. General Konstantin Rokossovsky later wrote that he had encountered "a great number of instances of cowardice, panic, desertion, and self-mutilation" during the initial fighting. "At first, this so-called 'left-handedness' appeared when [they] shot themselves in the palms of their left hands or shot off one or several of their fingers," he reported. "Then we noted 'right-handedness' began to appear. Self-mutilation appeared by agreement: a pair of soldiers would mutually shoot one another in the hands." But the soldiers who resorted to such desperate measures were signing their own death warrant. NKVD units were ordered to shoot anyone suspected of self-mutilation. Even those who had really sustained such wounds in battle weren't believed. They, too, faced prompt execution.

As for other forms of "justice," they were equally swift and harsh. According to an NKVD report, 667,364 soldiers who had "escaped from the front" had been rounded up by October 10, 1941. Of those, 10,201 were shot, 25,878 were kept under arrest, and 632,486 were formed into new units—in many cases, penal battalions that were routinely sent on suicidal missions. During the course of the war, the ranks of the penal battalions were also filled with hundreds of thousands of prisoners from the Gulag. After all, they were considered perfect candidates for such tasks as marching through minefields ahead of the regular units. At the same time, Stalin continued supplying the Gulag with a steady flow of new prisoners, ensuring that those sent to the front were easily replaced with new slave laborers.

Stalin wasn't content with simply terrifying the masses of soldiers; he also wanted to drive the message home that their commanders were every bit as endangered by failure as they were. Besides, he needed at least a few scapegoats for the embarrassing string of early defeats. General Dmitry Pavlov, the commander of the Western front, whose forces were unable to stop the German invaders as they captured Minsk and kept moving east, and his top aides were quickly picked to serve that function. They were arrested and tortured until confessions were beaten out of them. Their alleged crime: participation in "an anti-Soviet military conspiracy." Approving their death sentences, which immediately followed, Stalin issued clear instructions to his aides. "No appeal. And then inform the fronts, so they know that defeatists will be punished without mercy."

The executions would also include those officers who were already under arrest when the war started. A few days before the German invasion, Pavel Rychagov, a pilot who had distinguished himself during the Spanish Civil War and had later become Deputy Commander of the Soviet Air Force, was arrested along with Yakov Smushkevich, another highly decorated veteran of the same conflict. On October 28, 1941, at a moment when the fighting around Moscow was at a crucial stage, they were among several top officers, along with Rychagov's wife, who was also an accomplished air force pilot, to face the firing squad.

As Stepan Mikoyan, who served as a fighter pilot in the war while his father remained in Stalin's inner circle, pointed out later, "A great war was on, our army was suffering severe losses and defeat, and in the meantime experienced battle commanders, instead of being relied upon for saving the situation, were hurriedly put to death. . . . It is painful to imagine the feelings of people who, at a time of acute danger to their country, were awaiting death at the hands of their own compatriots."

During the course of the entire war, an estimated 158,000 Soviet soldiers were sentenced to death. By contrast, German military tribunals sentenced a total of twenty-two thousand soldiers to death for desertion, not just on the Eastern front but everywhere they served. When it came to condemning the soldiers and officers in his armed forces, Stalin easily outdid Hitler. But that was hardly surprising. The Soviet leader had plenty of practice in executing his military men well before the war broke out. And that bloody track record proved to be a major factor in the appalling lack of preparedness of the Soviet armed forces when the Germans invaded. Stalin murdered early and often, and it wasn't only the direct victims who paid the price.

In the 1930s, when Stalin methodically extended his reign of terror to eliminate anyone he deemed an enemy or possible threat to his rule, no one and no institution was free from suspicion. One day in the middle part of that horrifying decade, Stalin was walking through the Kremlin corridors with Admiral Ivan Isakov. As usual, NKVD officers were standing guard at every corner. "Did you notice how many of them were there?" Stalin suddenly asked Isakov. "Every time I walk the corridors I think: Which one of them is it? If it's this one, he will shoot me in the back. But if I turn the corner, the next one can shoot me in the face."

Aside from the obvious targets of terror, such as the Ukrainian peasants and those intellectuals and aristocrats who hadn't been dealt with already, Stalin targeted the Communist Party, the NKVD, and, in 1937 and 1938, the armed forces. In each of those cases, many of the executioners would soon find themselves among those about to be executed. The logic of the purges and Stalin's insatiable demand for more victims meant that there was no way to stop or even to slow down what became known as the Great Terror. During 1937 and 1938, when the purges included the military, the NKVD rounded up about 1.5 million people, of which only about 200,000 were freed later. Many were dispatched to the Gulag, but even more—probably about 750,000 of that number—were simply shot. Their bodies were dumped in the execution pits that were dug near almost every city across the country.

Despite those staggering numbers, Stalin was often personally involved in the killing process. The NKVD had assembled albums with about 44,000 names of the more prominent proposed victims. "Stalin, a busy man, was expected to go through the list and tick off recommended sentences whenever he spotted a name he knew and had a preference for what should be done," writes his biographer Robert Service. Stalin also insisted on getting the approval of his Politburo members, and some were prone to add their own

comments to the death sentences as an expression of their enthusiasm. Molotov, for instance, liked to write beside a name, "Give the
dog a dog's death!"

When the military's turn came, the Soviet leader was engaged in
every major decision. He regarded the military as a priority target,
since, if a revolt were ever conceivable, they would have to lead it. For
someone who saw potential enemies everywhere, Stalin wasn't about
to overlook the institution that had the real firepower and knew how
to use it. Besides, among the top brass, there were plenty of officers
with evident vulnerabilities, whether because of their early experience in the tsarist army or later links with Leon Trotsky, who had been
the first People's Commissar for Military Affairs and had made many
of the appointments of the officers who were now serving Stalin.

At a Central Committee meeting on March 2, 1937, Kliment Voroshilov, the defense commissar, initially tried to avert a bloodbath
by explaining that the military had been methodically purging its
ranks ever since Trotsky had lost out in the power struggle and
been forced to flee. "Without any noise, we got rid of a lot of useless elements, including Trotsky's people and other suspicious
scum," he declared. He added that those actions had led to the
purging of "about 47,000 people."

But there were more recent activities that Stalin also now deemed
suspicious. During the period of close military cooperation between
the Soviet Union and Weimar Germany in the 1920s and early 1930s,
the military brass of both nations had the chance to evaluate each
other and to examine each other's arms build-ups. German pilots
and other officers were trained in the Soviet Union, and Soviet officers were invited to Germany to observe military maneuvers. That
meant there were personal contacts that, at least in theory, could
have served as cover for any kind of subversive activity.

Stalin's mind worked the same way when it came to those Soviet
fighters, such as the fighter pilots Pavel Rychagov and Yakov
Smushkevich, who had gone to Spain to fight the forces of Fran-
cisco Franco during the civil war there in the late 1930s. With
Hitler and Mussolini supporting Franco, this became a proxy war,
the first outright confrontation of the two ideologies, and Stalin
was just as engaged in supporting the other side. No matter. The
Soviet veterans of the conflict, who had fought alongside not just

Spanish Republicans but also the multinational army of volunteers who responded to the calls by leftist parties for help, were tainted by their association with so many ideologically suspect foreigners.

All of which meant that the interrogators and torturers had plenty of material to work with when it was time to concoct their cases against the military brass, signaling the start of a wholesale purge of the armed forces. Recognizing that his initial assurance that the military was already cleansed had failed to slow the build-up to the next wave of terror, Voroshilov abruptly changed his message. He pledged to the Central Committee that he would unveil a sinister plot that "will make even your steel-hard hearts shake." The writing was on the wall, and it would only take a short time for the bloodletting to start.

In June, the "plot" was revealed. Marshal Mikhail Tukhachevsky, the aristocrat turned Red Army commander who was widely admired at home and abroad, headed the first list of eight culprits. In the 1920s, he had presided over the transformation of the Red Army, which was still very much a product of the Bolshevik Revolution and the Civil War, into a modern fighting force. But he wasn't one to hide his opinions, and he had found himself at odds with Stalin on more than one occasion. In 1936, for instance, he had predicted that Germany might attack without warning and that the result would be a long, costly conflict. "What are you trying to do—frighten Soviet authority?" Stalin had responded angrily.

Tukhachevsky and the other top army officers were put on trial on June 11, 1937. A ninth "conspirator," Yan Gamarnik, the First Deputy Commissar for Defense, managed to commit suicide before the NKVD was able to seize him. By then, no one could have been under many illusions about the methods to be used to extract confessions. When Tukhachevsky's statements were sent to Stalin to edit, the bloodstains were clearly visible on the documents. Another legendary Soviet general, Vasily Blyukher, who was arrested in October 1938, was so badly tortured because of his refusal to confess that his wife, who was also imprisoned, recalled that he looked "as if he had been driven over by a tank." His tormenters continued to beat him, and blood flowed from one eye. "Stalin, do you hear how they're beating me?" he'd shout. He finally died from the unrelenting torture.

But for Tukhachevsky and the first group, nothing less than a quick trial and formal executions would do. The charge was treason. Shortly before the show trial, Stalin declared, "There was without a doubt a political-military plot against the Soviet regime, which was stimulated and financed by German fascists." As evidence, he noted that several of the accused had gone to Germany and met with their military counterparts there. The Soviet leader conveniently omitted any mention of the fact that they were traveling under official auspices during the period when the two countries were committed to a policy of military cooperation. He also never acknowledged that it was Tukhachevsky who had warned of the dangers of a German attack. "Spies, spies!" he insisted.

According to several Western accounts, Stalin may have not invented the charges on his own. The Germans reportedly leaked disinformation about plans for a military coup within the Soviet military to Czechoslovakia's President Edvard Beneš, who in turn passed them on to the Kremlin. No documents have surfaced to confirm this version of events, which makes some Russian historians doubtful of its accuracy. In any case, Stalin and his henchmen were fully capable of concocting their own phony evidence, and whether or not the Germans were involved, they were going to "prove" their case no matter what. Of course, that meant they'd mete out their version of justice. As Ivan Belov, one of the judges at the trial wrote, "When I saw the scoundrels in the courtroom, I was shivering. A beast was in me. I didn't want to judge them, but beat and beat them in a wild frenzy."

All the defendants had been beaten already, and some were promised leniency if they confessed, or at least leniency for their families. This was commonplace during the Great Terror, as was the casual way in which the authorities forgot those promises once they had extracted the confessions, implicating an ever-growing circle of future victims. But whether they confessed or not, the outcome was the same. Mercy was out of the question. When one of the defendants, General Jonah Yakir, sent in a particularly emotional appeal, Stalin wrote on it, "Swine and prostitute." Voroshilov dutifully added, "A perfectly precise definition," and Politburo member Lazar Kaganovich chimed in, "For a bastard, scum, and whore there is only one punishment—the death penalty." Tukhachevsky—who had tried to argue his innocence in the kangaroo court—and all the others were convicted on June 11. Stalin promptly authorized the death penalty. All eight were shot on June 12.

For the families of the victims, the ordeal was often just beginning. As British historian Robert Conquest notes, "wives of enemies of the people" was a penal category in Stalin's Soviet Union. Compared to others in that category—fifteen of whom were shot on August 28, 1938—Nina Tukhachevskaya and several other widows of the officers in that first trial got off relatively lightly at first. They were sentenced to eight years' imprisonment. But at the height of the battle for Moscow, in October 1941, the authorities changed their mind. Just as in the case of the pilots Rychagov and Smushkevich, who were executed at about the same time, it suddenly became a matter of urgency to finish them off, no matter that the capital looked as though it was ready to succumb to the German invaders at that very moment. The authorities hastily retried those widows and shot them as well.

The trial of Tukhachevsky and the others in June 1937 was a signal for the Great Terror to sweep through the armed forces with devastating results. On November 29, 1938, Voroshilov reported, "The purge was drastic and thorough. We purged everyone that it was necessary to purge, starting with the high positions and finishing with the low ones." He concluded that this accounted for the "impressive" final tally: the Red Army had been "cleansed of more than 40,000 men."

The impact is hard to exaggerate. Konstantin Rokossovsky, who was imprisoned for two years but managed to survive and even emerge as one of the top generals during the war, commented, "This is worse than when artillery fires on its own troops." The purges hit senior officers the hardest, including three of the five marshals, thirteen of the fifteen army commanders, eight of the nine fleet admirals and admirals grade 1, fifty of the fifty-seven corps commanders, 154 of the 186 divisional commanders, and so on down the chain of the command.

Although about thirteen thousand of the purged officers were reinstated between 1939 and 1941, Khrushchev argued that the toll of executions, arrests, and irreversible dismissals was one of the key reasons why the Soviet military was so poorly prepared to face the

Germans in 1941. "So many were executed that the high command as well as middle and lower echelons were devastated," he wrote. "As a result our army was deprived of the cadres who had gained experience in the civil war, and we faced a new enemy unprepared."

According to Stepan Mikoyan, his father, Anastas Mikoyan, agreed with that assessment—although, like Khrushchev, he never dared suggest that anything was wrong with these policies when he served Stalin. "I have repeatedly heard from my father that the loss of the experienced, well-educated and thinking commanders on the eve of the war, especially in its first days and weeks, produced the single most damaging effect on both the preparation for repelling Hitler's attack and the course of the war itself," Stepan recalled.

As a result of the purges, junior officers were quickly promoted, often solely on the basis of their political reliability. In countless cases, men with extremely limited military skills replaced seasoned veterans who were purged. These events didn't pass unnoticed. The Germans watched the bloodletting inside the Red Army with morbid fascination, concluding that this could only be "disastrous" for their future enemy. It was almost as if Stalin were trying to help Hitler. In his classic biography of Stalin, General Volkogonov, who served as propaganda chief of the Red Army, argued that the purges "forged the defeats of 1941 which were to bring millions of new victims." This was no overstatement.

Another early Stalin biographer, Isaac Deutscher, offered a radically different perspective on Stalin's military purges. "Let us imagine for a moment that the leaders of the opposition lived to witness the terrible defeats of the Red Army in 1941 and 1942, to see Hitler at the gates of Moscow, millions of Russian soldiers in captivity, a dangerous crisis in the morale of people such as had developed by the autumn of 1941, when the whole future of the Soviets hung by a thread and Stalin's moral authority was at its nadir," he wrote. "It is possible that they would have then attempted to overthrow Stalin. Stalin was determined not to allow things to come to this." This sounds like an appalling apologia. It seems to take for granted that there was at least a latent opposition in the army, not just tortured, terrified officers who were forced to confess to nonexistent crimes and traitorous plans.

But then Deutscher banished any suggestion that there might have been some truth to Stalin's charges against his victims. "Among all the documents of the Nuremberg trial of the Nazi leaders not a single one contains as much as a hint at the alleged Nazi fifth column in the Soviet government and army," he added, somewhat curiously, in a footnote. "Could there be a more eloquent refutation of the purge trials than that amazing gap in the otherwise abundant evidence of Hitler's preparations for the war?"

Deutscher also failed to ask the logical question that flows from his earlier speculation about how Tukhachevsky and the legions of murdered commanders would have reacted to the setbacks of 1941 and 1942. If they had survived and the purges hadn't happened, would those defeats have been anywhere near as devastating as they proved to be? Judging by the reflections of Rokossovsky, Khrushchev, Mikoyan, and so many others from that era, there's little doubt that the Red Army would have been a more effective force under those circumstances—even if, in all probability, it still would have been fighting a desperate battle for survival. But at least it would have been a battle for survival against the Germans, without the additional burden of the battle for survival in the face of the unremitting terror from within.

Wherever and whenever Stalin extended his power, terror followed against the civilian population as well. Once the Soviet Union invaded Poland from the east, dividing up the battered country with the Germans as spelled out in the Nazi-Soviet pact, both the German and Soviet occupiers launched terror campaigns against the local population in their respective occupied territories. In what had been eastern Poland, the Soviet authorities quickly organized special trains to deport an estimated two million of their new subjects between September 1939 and June 22, 1941. Hundreds of thousands died either in the horrific train convoys or at the remote destinations in the camps of northern Russia, Siberia, and Kazakhstan or in exile in regions where many froze or starved to death.

"At a time when the Germans were still refining their preparations for Auschwitz and Treblinka, the Soviets could accommodate a few million Polish and Western Ukrainian additions to the population of their 'Gulag archipelago' with relative ease," noted British historian Norman Davies. According to a saying that the Poles attributed to the Russians during that time, the occupiers divided the Polish population under their control among "those who were in prison, those who are in prison, and those who will be in prison."

And then there were the mass executions. Stalin was determined to wipe out those Poles who might one day still try to resist the subjugation of their country by the Soviet Union. In March 1940, the Kremlin decreed the "supreme punishment—execution by shooting" of 14,736 Polish army officers and officials, along with an additional 10,685 Poles held by the NKVD. The bodies of about four thousand Polish officers, each with a bullet hole in the head, were discovered by the Germans in the Katyn forest near Smolensk in 1943. Right up to the collapse of the Soviet Union, the Soviet authorities claimed that the Germans were trying to pin the blame for a German atrocity on the Kremlin. But even then, it was clear that the timing of the massacre, as evidenced by the belongings of the victims, could lead to only one conclusion: this was a Soviet massacre. In a goodwill gesture to Poland in 1992, Russian President Boris Yeltsin finally released the order from the Politburo that officially confirmed that grim fact.

In the Baltic states, where the Soviets took longer to establish full control, there was a similar preoccupation with targeting anyone who was classified as a potential enemy of the people. Along with such measures as the nationalization of commercial enterprises and the banning of books and other literature deemed as anti-Soviet or nationalist, the arrests began in earnest in Lithuania on the eve of the first elections under Soviet control. Two thousand people were rounded up on the night of July 11 to 12, 1940, and the arrests continued at the rate of two to three hundred a month until the end of the year.

If any further evidence was needed to demonstrate how preoccupied the Soviet authorities were with repression even as they were receiving daily signals from all over that Germany was preparing its invasion, the timing of the mass deportations from the Baltic states certainly provided it. As early as November 28, 1940, Lithuanian Interior Minister Aleksandras Guzevičius issued a list of no less than fourteen categories of people targeted for deportation. They included members of "leftist" and "nationalist" anti-Soviet parties, veterans of the tsarist or White armies, officers of the Lithuanian and Polish armies, "all political émigrés and unstable elements," Red Cross officials, clergymen, former noblemen, and merchants, among others. In effect, this amounted to a carte blanche to deport just about anyone. But it wasn't until the night of June 13 to 14, 1941, just one week before the Germans launched Operation Barbarossa, that the authorities undertook their major action.

While there are differing estimates of the numbers involved, approximately sixty thousand Estonians, thirty-five thousand Latvians, and thirty-four thousand Lithuanians were deported by the Soviet occupiers before the Germans struck, with by far the largest contingents rounded up and sent east in railroad boxcars on that horrific night in June and during the following few days. For such tiny states, those were staggering figures: in Estonia's case about 4 percent of its population, and for Lithuania and Latvia about 1.5 to 2 percent. If Stalin thought that he was ensuring loyalty by such draconian measures, he was, of course, mistaken. Little wonder that many Balts, like many Ukrainians, were initially convinced that the German invaders were liberating them from Stalin's reign of terror.

When the Germans attacked, the first instinct of the NKVD and its bosses was to accelerate its work in the occupied regions of Poland and the Baltic states that were about to change hands again. In the Stalinist mental scheme, all the "anti-Soviet" political prisoners who were still in custody in the border areas couldn't simply be abandoned. They had to be eliminated. Even if it meant assigning troops to this gruesome task rather than sending them to fight the Germans, this was considered perfectly logical. In Lvov— or Lwów, as it was known when it was part of Poland until 1939— the NKVD began executing prisoners right on June 22. A Ukrainian uprising briefly forced the NKVD to retreat, but it returned to slaughter the remaining prisoners in their cells. By the time the Soviet troops began to flee, they had killed about four thousand prisoners, leaving their machine-gunned bodies behind in thinly disguised mass graves.

The NKVD and Red Army troops engaged in similar killing sprees in other Polish and Baltic towns, shooting thousands more prisoners wherever they were held. In the end, some prisoners were abandoned or managed to escape, since the panicked Soviet executioners couldn't take care of them all. Further back from the border, though, other prisoners of the Gulag were subjected to forced evacuations eastward, usually on foot, because railroad transport was only rarely available. Some of the resulting scenes foreshadowed the death marches from the Nazi concentration camps at the end of the war when the German front was collapsing. "Those who can walk will walk," one Soviet guard told his prisoners. "Protest or not—all will walk. Those who can't walk we will shoot. We will leave no one for the Germans."

As the Germans continued their drive east beyond the border areas into Russian territory, the Kremlin's policy toward prisoners remained unchanged. NKVD chief Beria, whom Stalin called "our Himmler," issued order after order, with the full backing of his boss, to shoot prisoners in Russian cities such as Orel, where 154 were executed before the city fell to the Germans in early October. Even as the road to Moscow looked wide open, the rulers there continued to devote their attention to ordering more such executions.

Looking at such actions from the perspective of more than six decades later, Viktor Chernyavsky, who served in the NKVD during that period, still found it difficult to understand why these killings should be seen as troubling. "It was a practicality of life," he explained, referring to the execution of prisoners. "The situation on the front was terrible. Imagine: they had to think how to transport the prisoners and all that stuff. They would call Beria and ask his advice about what to do. The Germans were next door and it was dangerous, so the answer was to liquidate them. Thus, it was a practicality of life. Prisoners were a burden."

Even that twisted logic didn't apply in some cases. The authorities managed to evacuate about three thousand prisoners from Moscow's Butyrka prison to Kuibyshev, the city on the Volga where evacuees from the imperiled capital were supposed to regroup. But in the midst of all this, they took the time to execute 138 of the most prominent prisoners. In all, according to a recent Russian study, 42,776 prisoners were "lost for various reasons" during the German advance and hectic Soviet retreat and evacuation of towns they could not hold. Many were executed before they ever left their prisons or camps, while others died or were shot during the forced marches.

Gradually Stalin and Beria had to think more of replenishing the ranks of the army, given the staggering losses they suffered during the early months of the German invasion, and the pace of executions slowed. In a few cases, top military officers who looked as though they were doomed received sudden reprieves. This was the case with General Kirill Meretskov, who found himself arrested and tortured in the early days of the war, when Stalin was looking for scapegoats. Beaten mercilessly with rubber rods, Meretskov subsequently was allowed back into the inner circle, although this included a former colleague who had been his chief torturer. Unlike others in that kind of situation, he didn't hide his unease. "We used to meet on informal terms, but I'm afraid of you now," he told his tormenter. For his part, Stalin made a rare concession. Since Meretskov had been crippled by his brutal treatment, the Soviet leader allowed him to sit down while reporting to him.

Nothing was too surreal in Stalin's universe of terror. After General Rokossovsky was released from prison in 1940, Stalin noticed that the freed man had no fingernails and asked if he had been tortured. When Rokossovsky confirmed that he had been tortured, Stalin declared, "There're too many yes-men in this country." At other times, he'd ask about a particular individual and express surprise and disappointment that he had been executed, as if he had had nothing to do with such decisions.

Stalin's cohorts and defenders insist that his terror tactics both before and after the German invasion were justified. In particular, Molotov, who was the quintessential loyalist until his death in 1986, defended the military purges of 1937 to 1938: "Of course there were excesses, but all that was permissible, to my mind, for the sake of the main objective—keeping state power! . . . Our mistakes, including the crude mistakes, were justified." When it came to the first top military victims of the purges, such as General Tukhachevsky, he was equally unapologetic. "If trouble started, which side would he have been on? He was rather a dangerous man," he declared. "I doubted he would have been fully on our side when things got tough, because he was a right-winger. The right-wing danger was the main danger at the time. And many right-wingers didn't realize they were right-wingers, and were right-wingers in spite of themselves."

His arguments reflected a logic that only a true Stalinist could comprehend. You could trust no one; anyone could be an enemy of the people, even if he didn't know it yet. That was the logic of Stalin before the war, and it would continue to be his logic during the war, as the German advance continued. According to this reasoning, only terror and more terror—whether in the form of "blocking units" shooting at their own retreating troops or frenzied executions of prisoners who couldn't be evacuated—could ensure victory.

Sergo Beria, the son of Stalin's secret police chief, offered a very different perspective on the prewar terror, particularly the military purges of 1937 and 1938. "My father explained to me that if this policy of extermination of the elite had continued for another two years, the Germans would not have needed to invade us because the state would have collapsed by itself," he wrote. To be sure, this was part of a son's defense of the indefensible, a monstrous father, by a claim that his father was trying to mitigate the policies that he, in fact, was carrying out with brutal efficiency. But it's still a revealing commentary on the policy of wholesale slaughter of his own people that Stalin and his cronies pursued. That policy wreaked havoc on the Soviet armed forces and antagonized many of Stalin's subjects, particularly in the newly occupied regions between 1939 and 1941. It also left a climate of fear that paralyzed many of the military officers who survived, which hardly encouraged effective leadership when the moment of crisis came.

But luckily for Stalin, Hitler was intent on imposing his own rule of terror everywhere his forces advanced, which produced a more equal contest than initially appeared to be the case. It was also, not surprisingly, a contest that reflected the ruthlessness that flowed from the top of both regimes. As Robert Service wrote, "Warfare reverted to the colossal brutality last seen in the religious wars in the seventeenth century and Stalin was in his element." So was Hitler, but his forces were trying to navigate the terrain of a country they didn't know and were facing a people they didn't understand. To reach Moscow, they'd need to remedy those deficiencies fast and make all the right moves with little delay. The Führer had his window of opportunity, but it wouldn't remain open very long.

4

Hitler and His Generals

During those crucial summer months when German forces drove deeper and deeper into Soviet territory, Hitler and his generals often failed to see eye to eye on both tactics and strategy. This was hardly the first instance of such tensions. The generals had been hesitant in each previous case when Hitler had gambled and won—annexing Austria, dismembering Czechoslovakia, invading Poland and then conquering France and most of the rest of Continental Europe. And, of course, when Hitler launched Operation Barbarossa, some generals were dubious about his prediction that the Soviet Union would quickly collapse. Once the invasion took place, however, Hitler suddenly proved to be the hesitant one when it came to deciding when and how to attack Moscow, frustrating his generals in the field, who were convinced that only a swift, direct assault on the Soviet capital would provide the knockout blow that was so badly needed to ensure victory and the destruction of the Soviet Union.

At the same time, Hitler planted the seeds of resistance to the German invaders by pursuing his policy of terror against the inhabitants of the territories conquered by his armies. Many of his generals would later claim they had opposed those policies, too. But if they

did, they rarely did so openly. And it's unlikely that any of those misgivings were based on moral inhibitions. By serving Hitler as long as
they already had, they, in effect, had shelved their consciences.

Nonetheless, their subsequent protestations that they recognized that the brutality of German rule was quickly turning local
populations against them has a more convincing ring—at least in
some cases. In purely practical terms, they could see that Hitler's
determination to rule by full-scale terror could backfire, making
the subjugated peoples fear Hitler's reign of terror even more than
Stalin's reign of terror. Most important, it would give Stalin the ammunition he needed to mobilize his people against an unmistakably evil foe, making the job of Soviet propagandists remarkably
easy. Leading the pack was Ilya Ehrenburg, the poet who returned
to Moscow from his long exile in Paris in 1940. "Let us kill!" he
urged his countrymen. "If you haven't killed a German in the
course of a day, your day has been wasted."

As many German soldiers reported, their initial reception in
some parts of the western Soviet Union reflected a very different
mind-set. Hans von Herwarth, the former German diplomat in
Moscow who had returned as part of the invasion force, watched
with astonishment the reaction of villagers as they looked up at a
one-sided aerial battle between German and Soviet fighters. "All
the Soviet planes were shot down," he noted. "As each crashed to
the ground in flames, the villagers clapped their hands, shouting
that soon Stalin, too, would fall." He reported that peasants eagerly
asked if the Germans would now dissolve the collective farms, and
some brought lists of communist officials "against whom they
wanted us to take action."

But such early acceptance quickly gave way to suspicion and
then to fear and hatred. Captain Karl Haupt, whose 350th Infantry
Regiment was initially greeted by villagers with bread, salt, and
flowers in the western Ukraine, reported that by mid-July local attitudes had become "hostile through and through." He lamented
that "there is no place for trust, chumminess, or letting one's guard
down." And he would follow up those observations with orders to
his men to employ "the harshest, most ruthless measures" against
the inhabitants of villages that only a couple of weeks earlier had
looked so welcoming.

Many of the German invaders professed to be shocked by the first atrocities from the Soviet side that they witnessed, claiming that their own actions were mostly of a retaliatory nature. General Erich von Manstein, who was commander of the Fifty-sixth Panzer Corps at the beginning of Operation Barbarossa and who would soon attain the rank of field marshal, claimed that on the very first day of the fighting his men came across a German patrol that had been cut off by Soviet forces. "All its members were dead and gruesomely mutilated," he wrote in his memoirs. Upon seeing this, he recalled, he and his officers vowed "that we would never let an adversary like this capture us alive."

On another occasion, Manstein reported that his unit had recaptured a German field hospital where three of their officers and thirty men had been left behind during a battle. All thirty-three had been killed, he wrote, and "their mutilations were indescribable." He also complained that there were several cases of Soviet soldiers throwing up their hands as if in surrender and then opening fire, and other incidents in which Soviet soldiers pretended to be dead "and then fired on our troops when their backs were turned."

Whatever the accuracy of Manstein's reporting about such incidents, they hardly explain or justify the policies that the Germans would ruthlessly employ from the very beginning of their campaign. To be sure, the German occupiers initially promised to improve the lives of the peoples they were "liberating." On the first day of the invasion, for instance, German radio broadcasts promised that "one of the first measures of the German administration will be the restoration of religious freedom. . . . We will allow you to organize religious parishes. Everyone will be free to pray to God in his own manner." But Hitler, whose contempt for churches was almost as visceral as Stalin's, quickly made clear that he had no intention of delivering on such promises. He forbade German army units to do anything to help churches and missionaries to enter the newly occupied Soviet territories. "If one did it at all, one should permit all the Christian denominations to enter Russia in order that they club each other to death with their crucifixes," he declared.

Hitler's vision of what awaited the conquered east didn't allow for anything but death and subjugation by terror. He spelled out the essential elements of his approach before Operation Barbarossa began, leaving no doubt about the nature of the occupation he envisaged no matter how Soviet troops and civilians behaved. On March 30, 1941, he convened his generals and—as recorded in summary form by Franz Halder, his chief of staff—delivered a blunt message about the nature of the battle:

"*Clash of two ideologies.* Crushing denunciation of Bolshevism, identified with a social criminality. Communism is an enormous danger for our future. We must forget the concept of comradeship between soldiers. A communist is no comrade before or after the battle. This is a war of extermination. If we do not grasp this, we shall beat the enemy, but thirty years later we shall again have to fight the Communist foe. We do not wage war to preserve the enemy. . . . Extermination of the Bolshevik commissars and of the Communist intelligentsia."

That approach quickly translated into a blueprint for the policies of terror that swept aside all the traditional rules of warfare. The premise was simple: the Russians and other peoples of the Soviet Union were an inferior, primitive race, who weren't worthy of normal human considerations. As Erich Koch, Hitler's brutal governor of the Ukraine, would put it: "The attitude of the Germans . . . must be governed by the fact that we deal with a people which is inferior in every respect." The object of the occupation wasn't "to bring blessings on the Ukraine but to secure for Germany the necessary living space and a source of food."

None of this was empty rhetoric. Hitler's pronouncement on forgetting the concept of comradeship between soldiers led to the infamous Commissar Decree—the order to execute all political officers in Red Army units, even if they attempted to surrender. "Political commissars in the [Red] Army are not recognized to be prisoners of war and are to be liquidated, at the latest in the prisoner of war transit camps," read the order drawn up on May 12, more than a month before the German forces launched their attack. General Jodl added a note that leaves no doubt about the cynical nature of subsequent protestations that such policies were prompted by Soviet behavior. "We must reckon with retaliation against German fliers; therefore it will be best to picture the whole action as retaliation."

The Commissar Decree had the predictable effect of convincing Red Army commissars that they had to fight back at any cost, since they soon realized that defeat amounted to an instant death sentence. When the Germans began encountering Soviet troops who fought back ferociously despite overwhelming odds, the official explanations never made that connection—in fact, the pretence was maintained that no such connection existed. "The main reason why the Russian never surrenders is that, dim-witted half-Asiatic that he is, he fully believes the notion, drummed into him by the commissars, that he will be shot if captured," a directive issued to the German Fourth Army declared.

In order to prepare its forces for the mission ahead, the Wehrmacht distributed propaganda leaflets to them that combined denunciation of the commissars with anti-Semitic themes. Referring to the commissars, one such tract declared: "We would insult the animals if we described these mostly Jewish men as beasts. They are the embodiment of Satanic and insane hatred against the whole of noble humanity."

While the Germans showered the Soviet-controlled areas with propaganda leaflets claiming they were coming to liberate the country and urging Red Army troops to surrender—by the end of 1941 the Luftwaffe had dropped more than 400 million of them—those efforts were undercut by the policies based on Nazi doctrine that were directed at all those who came under their rule in the east. A May 2, 1941, report produced by German economic planners charged with setting the goals for the eastern campaign predicted that by September of that year "the entire German Armed Forces can be fed at the expense of Russia." Far from shying away from the implications of that statement, it went on to point out, "Thereby tens of millions of men will undoubtedly starve to death if we take away all we need from the country."

As *Untermenschen*, or subhumans, the Slavs deserved no consideration, including the staggering numbers of Red Army soldiers who were captured in the early months of the fighting. When German newspapers began publishing photos of the POWs, it was to ridicule their "Asiatic, Mongol physiognomies" and their "degenerate qualities." Little wonder, then, that the German invaders cared little for the POWs' survival and in many cases simply murdered surrendering soldiers. As Field Marshal von Manstein would admit about the early days of the fighting almost in passing, "At this stage we had hardly the time or the men to spare for rounding up prisoners." He pointedly left unsaid what happened to those who weren't rounded up, but their fate isn't hard to imagine. And as word spread of such treatment, the commissars in the Soviet units certainly found it easier to convince their men that captivity would mean death and it made more sense to keep fighting.

Civilians couldn't expect much better treatment. Already on May 6, more than a month before the Germans attacked, the German military command authorized the shooting of all those local inhabitants "who by their behavior constitute a direct threat to our troops" and "collective measures of force" against any location "from which insidious and malicious attacks of any kind whatsoever have taken place." German troops, the orders concluded, "must defend themselves without pity against any threat from the hostile civilian population." And even if German troops committed "punishable acts," they wouldn't be prosecuted if they were motivated by "bitterness against atrocities or subversive work of carriers of the Jewish-Bolshevik system."

In late July 1941, Field Marshal Walther von Brauchitsch, the commander of the army, issued a secret order on Hitler's behalf that bluntly reinforced the message about the nature of the German occupation. "Because of the vast size of the areas occupied in the East, the forces that will be available for establishing security will only be large enough if all resistance is punished not by legal prosecution of the guilty, but by the spreading of such terror by the occupying forces as will remove all desire to resist among the population." As soon as the Germans began encountering partisan activity, the military authorities made good on their pledge to invoke "collective measures," instructing their troops to execute between fifty and a hundred Soviet citizens for every German killed.

Such policies gave German troops carte blanche to murder and destroy at will. And, in that context, any acts of mercy were deemed contrary to official directives. "Feeding inhabitants and prisoners of war who do not work for the German armed forces, from army messes, is as much an act of misplaced humaneness as giving away bread or cigarettes," warned Field Marshal Walther von Reichenau in October 1941. The practical implementation of such policies had immediate consequences for the huge POW population. Hans von Herwarth recalled seeing columns of Soviet POWs "marching arm-in-arm but reeling like drunkards." The next morning a fellow soldier pointed out the corpses of many of the POWs strewn nearby. Suddenly, the truth dawned on him. "They had apparently not been fed for days, and their 'drunkenness' was the result of sheer fatigue," he wrote. A popular German saying summed up the underlying assumption that made this kind of treatment the norm rather than the exception. "The Russian must perish that we may live."

If that left everyone a potential victim, the Germans made special preparations to start the killing of Soviet Jews. In a war where the enemy was defined as "Judeo-Bolshevism," all killings of Jews could be explained as the elimination of the enemy. By the autumn, when partisan activity became more widespread behind German lines, German commanders were calling all resisters Jews, whatever their origin. As they put it, "Where there's a Jew there's a partisan, and where there's a partisan there's a Jew."

But long before the first serious partisan warfare—in fact, before the Germans even launched their invasion—preparations were in the works for massacres of Jews. New mobile SS units called *Einsatzgruppen*, composed of hardened veterans who had carried out killings of intellectuals, clergy, and Jews in occupied Poland, along with special police battalions, followed the advancing German armies into Soviet territory. That summer SS boss Heinrich Himmler made the rounds of those units on the Eastern front to urge them personally to kill Soviet Jews.

The massacres had begun almost as soon as the German troops moved across the border. When Police Battalion 309 entered the city of Bialystok in late June, the unit went on a rampage against Jews, shooting and beating them. When a desperate group of Jewish leaders went to the headquarters of the security division responsible for the area, the general in charge of the division turned his back on them as one of the members of the police battalion urinated on them. Some Jews were lined up and shot, while others were herded into a synagogue, which was set alight. That fire in turn set off fires in nearby houses, where others Jews were hiding.

The tally for the day's macabre events: about two thousand to twenty-two hundred Jews killed.

That wasn't the last of the killings in Bialystok. On July 12, two other police battalions filled the city's stadium with Jewish men. According to their orders: "All male Jews between the ages of 17 and 45 convicted as plunderers are to be shot according to martial law." After collecting the valuables of the victims, the policemen drove them to ditches on the outskirts of the city, formed firing squads, and kept shooting late into the evening, at that point using the headlights of their trucks to light up their targets. In this case, the tally was more than three thousand Jews.

By the end of the summer and early fall, the police battalions were reporting more and more such massacres, which were increasingly composed of any Jews they could capture, including women and children. The terse reports would offer the name of the unit and the number of its victims on any particular day. "August 25: Police Regiment South shot 1,324 Jews," for example, or "August 31: Battalion 320 shot 2,200 Jews in Minkovtsy."

Questioned by American psychiatrist Leon Goldensohn before he was tried at Nuremberg and hanged in 1948, Otto Ohlendorf, the notorious commander of *Einsatzgruppe D*, matter-of-factly described how his unit functioned during those early months of the war. "The Jews were shot in a military manner in a cordon. There were fifteen-men firing squads. One bullet per Jew. In other words, one firing squad of fifteen executed fifteen Jews at a time." The victims were men, women and children. How many perished at the hands of his men during the year he spent in Russia? "Ninety thousand reported. I figure actually only sixty to seventy thousand were shot." Ohlendorf, of course, explained that he was just following orders. "All I had to do was to see to it that it was done as humanely as possible," he added.

By the end of September, after Kiev had fallen, the special squads were in action at the ravine of Babi Yar, where more than thirty-three thousand Jews were murdered. All of this would constitute only the first act of the Holocaust. The industrialized killings in the gas chambers were still in the future. The special killing squads were doing their job, though they weren't as fast and efficient as their leaders wanted them to be. But it certainly wasn't for lack of trying.

* * *

Like so many of their countrymen, Hitler's generals would plead ignorance about the Holocaust, including these early massacres. Field Marshal von Manstein, who also found himself on trial after the war but only spent a few years in prison, admitted to Goldensohn that Ohlendorf's *Einsatzgruppe* was in his district. "But we were told that these SS formations had purely police functions," he insisted. "What they did I never knew."

Manstein also claimed that he knew nothing of the concentration camps until the war ended. While he was among the generals who frequently found themselves at odds with Hitler on military matters, he hadn't been ready to condemn the Führer on moral grounds. "Apparently as time went on Hitler lost all his moral scruples," Manstein told Goldensohn. "However, this is a recognition I have made in retrospect, but which I did not have at the time." It's hard to imagine a more self-incriminating statement, though Manstein clearly didn't see it that way.

The military brass couldn't plead ignorance of the Commissar Decree and other military orders that led to systematic atrocities. In his memoirs, Manstein called that order "utterly unsoldierly." Because it "would have threatened not only the honor of our fighting troops but also their morale," he maintained, he told his superiors that he would not allow his subordinates to carry it out. Heinz Guderian, the famous panzer leader, also claimed that his troops never implemented it—and, just possibly, the stature of these military commanders allowed them to contravene the Commissar Decree.

Manstein made clear that his objection was a practical one. "The order simply incited the commissars to resort to the most brutal methods to make their units fight on to the end," he noted. Even the most obedient generals recognized this probable outcome when the order was first issued. On the eve of the invasion, army commander von Brauchitsch added a line to the instructions on the handling of the commissars that suggested they should be executed "inconspicuously." It wasn't shame that prompted that advice; it was calculation.

Many of the early tensions between Hitler and his generals were triggered by similar disagreements over tactics and goals, certainly not by grand moral principles. Manstein complained later that, from the beginning, the army had tried to stick to its "traditional notions of simplicity and chivalry and its soldierly conception of honor," despite the constant pressure to conform to Nazi doctrine. Given the army's subsequent heinous record, it's certainly an understatement to say that these protestations ring hollow. Even the unsuccessful assassination plot against Hitler by disgruntled officers in 1944 did little to salvage the reputation of a military leadership whose actions put it beyond redemption.

Nonetheless, it would be wrong to overlook the very real disagreements between Hitler and his generals and the role of those disagreements in Operation Barbarossa and the drive to seize Moscow. Hitler and his generals were partners in crime, but, more often than not, they were uncomfortable partners. Hitler had assumed the title Supreme Commander in 1938 and considered himself the supreme military strategist, one who combined a grasp of battlefield conditions acquired during the previous global conflict with a broad understanding of history, economics, and basic psychology that allowed him to outwit his enemies. None of his generals, he felt, came close to matching his mastery of all those fields. The generals, for their part, were alternately awed and alarmed by his behavior, sometimes seeing him as a genius, at other times seeing him as a dangerous fraud, even if they were usually terrified to admit as much even to themselves.

The closest the military brass came to confronting and possibly ousting Hitler during the prewar period came in the summer of 1938, when he began threatening Czechoslovakia. General Ludwig Beck, the army chief of staff at the time, asked Hitler to spell out his plans, seeking reassurance that he wouldn't start a war. While admitting that the crisis over Czechoslovakia could turn into an armed conflict, Hitler claimed that it wouldn't lead to a larger war. But the Führer wasn't about to provide the kind of guarantee that Beck was seeking. "The army is an instrument of politics," he told the general. "I shall assign the army its task when the moment arrives and the army will have to carry out this task without arguing whether it is right or wrong."

In August 1938, Beck was ousted as chief of staff. While he was convinced he had some support among other generals critical of Hitler, he felt bitterly disappointed by General von Brauchitsch, the army commander-in-chief, whom he accused of deserting him. After the war, General Halder, who replaced Beck as chief of staff, and others would claim to have still contemplated a plot against Hitler in September, although their accounts were inconsistent and looked suspiciously self-serving, obvious attempts to distance themselves from their fallen leader. But any resolve they might have had evaporated when British Prime Minister Neville Chamberlain and French Premier Edouard Daladier agreed to come to meet Hitler and then acquiesced in Czechoslovakia's dismemberment by signing the Munich agreement that September. Claiming that he had been preparing a swift putsch and even for Hitler's possible execution, Halder blamed the Western leaders for pulling out the rug from under the plotters. Without the threat of war, Halder argued, "the entire basis for that action had been taken away."

In all probability, Halder and several others embellished their versions of events and of how prepared they were to act. General Beck's role as an early opponent of Hitler's march to war was far more convincing, and he would end up shooting himself after he was captured on the night of July 20, 1944, following the failed assassination attempt against Hitler. But whatever will there was among the generals to resist Hitler in 1938 was, in fact, undercut by his amazing successes: first, the annexation of Austria in March, and then the achievement of his goals in Czechoslovakia without having to go to war. As Field Marshal von Manstein would recall later: "We had watched Germany's precarious course along the razor's edge to date with close attention and were increasingly amazed at Hitler's incredible luck in attaining—hitherto without recourse to arms—all his overt and covert political aims. The man seemed to have an infallible instinct."

Even when his invasion of Poland led to the wider war that they had feared, the generals weren't about to challenge Hitler seriously. He ignored their trepidation about violating Belgium's neutrality and attacking France, and once again the success of his audacious actions made them look as though they were the ones falling short in terms of leadership, although it was their swift victories that made Hitler look so powerful. The Führer didn't hesitate to express his contempt for "the everlasting hesitation of the generals," drumming in the message that he, not they, had the vision and drive to catapult Germany to new heights.

The generals began to perceive slights everywhere. After the defeat of Poland, Hitler came to Warsaw for a victory parade on October 5, 1939. Before flying back to Germany, he made a scheduled stop to visit the commanders and troops. The brass awaited him in a hangar, where they expected to serve him soup from a field kitchen on a table adorned with a white tablecloth and flowers. But when the Führer showed up, he only glanced at these preparations and opted to join the troops outside, where they had their own field kitchen. He tasted the soup, chatted with them briefly, and then headed for his aircraft, ignoring their commanders. Hitler may have been trying to score propaganda points by showing that he felt at home with the ordinary soldiers, but the brass had no doubt it was a deliberate snub.

Hitler also didn't hesitate to promote and demote officers as he saw fit, and even his sudden elevation of a dozen generals to the rank of field marshal prompted speculation that he was trying to devalue the military's highest rank. He left no doubt that he wanted to ensure obedience from his top generals and he was willing to do whatever it took to achieve that aim. In some cases, he simply paid them, providing them with tax-free payments that weren't recorded in the army accounts.

"Although this method of payment was an insult according to the honor code of the German officer, many succumbed because of fear of losing their positions and lure of the money," Fabian von Schlabrendorff, one of the few officers who survived his involvement in the 1944 plot against Hitler, wrote after the war. "In this way Hitler held his higher officers on very effective golden leashes." General Günther von Kluge, for example, received a personal birthday card from Hitler that included a check for 250,000 marks.

In most cases, however, payoffs were hardly necessary. Hitler outmaneuvered his generals again and again, sweeping aside their warnings when he saw fit and overruling them on strategy and tactics at will. Even those generals who tried to stand up to him on occasion were clearly cowed by his track record and the sheer force of his personality. "When considering Hitler in the role of a military leader, one should certainly not dismiss him with such clichés as 'the lance corporal of World War I,'" Field Marshal von Manstein wrote. And notwithstanding his criticism of Hitler for his "excessive self-esteem," his propensity to ignore information that contradicted his theories and his disdainful handling of the top brass, Manstein added, "Hitler possessed an astoundingly retentive memory and an imagination that made him quickly grasp all technical matters and problems of armaments. He was amazingly familiar with the effect of the very latest enemy weapons and could reel off whole columns of figures on both our own and the enemy's war production. Indeed, this was his favorite way of side-tracking any topic that was not to his liking."

The other method Hitler effectively employed was to throw out theories, or just plain smokescreens, meant to trump any purely military arguments. "He had a genius for suddenly confronting his military collaborators with political and economic arguments which they could not immediately refute and of whose value, in any case, the statesman must perforce be considered the better judge," Manstein noted with reluctant admiration. All of which meant that Hitler got the better of his generals time and time again. In most cases, it wasn't even a contest.

And yet Hitler still subjected his generals to withering tirades. "Before I became Chancellor, I believed the general staff was somewhat like a butcher's dog, whom you had to hold tight by the collar to prevent its attacking all other people," he declared on one occasion. "After I became Chancellor, however, I realized that the general staff is anything but a ferocious dog." He then enumerated the decisions the generals had objected to: rearmament, the occupation of the Rhineland, the annexation of Austria, the dismemberment of Czechoslovakia, the invasion of Poland. "The general staff warned me against an offensive in France, and counseled against war with Russia," he concluded. "It is I who at all times had to goad on this 'ferocious dog.'"

It is true that as Hitler decided to abandon plans for an invasion of Britain and to attack the Soviet Union instead, some of the military brass voiced skepticism about such a course. Admiral Erich Raeder, the commander of the navy, argued that the opening of a second front should be postponed "until after victory over England." General von Brauchitsch also expressed reservations. "Purpose is not clear," Halder reported him as saying. "We do not hit the British this way. Our economic potential will not be substantially improved. Risk in the West must not be underestimated." Even Hermann Göring, Hitler's close associate and commander of the air force, would claim in Nuremberg that he had seen the danger of Hitler's plan to attack Russia. "Hitler decided that," he said. "I thought it was stupid because I believed that first we had to defeat England."

Field Marshal von Manstein would later expound on Hitler's misjudgments that led to the ultimate defeat of Germany on the Eastern front. "The first was the mistake committed by Hitler, if by no one else, of underrating the resources of the Soviet Union and the fighting qualities of the Red Army," he wrote. But if Manstein is more credible than someone like Göring, he fatally undermines his case by trying to pin all the blame on Hitler. The German leader was far from alone in underestimating the Soviet Union. On the eve of Operation Barbarossa, much of the top brass—including Brauchitsch, Halder, Jodl—had convinced themselves, or had allowed Hitler to convince them, that the campaign would produce a victory in a matter of weeks, and they were echoing his optimistic predictions.

The skeptics weren't entirely quiet. Shortly before the invasion, Hitler sent military staffers to give briefings on the Soviet economy. They argued that the country wouldn't be capable of producing good armaments to replace its losses quickly. After one such lecture, Admiral Wilhelm Canaris, the head of military intelligence, turned to his colleagues. "Gentlemen, do you really believe all the nonsense you heard today?" he asked. "To the best knowledge of the experts in my department, the entire situation is quite different. So far, no one has succeeded in defeating and conquering Russia!"

But the plain fact was that, by then, even those generals who may have shared those doubts were too intimidated by Hitler to speak up. And most had come to the conclusion that their leader had been proven right before, whatever their reservations, and he'd be proven right again. Before he was hanged in Nuremberg in 1946, another top commander, Field Marshal Wilhelm Keitel, wrote off his willingness to believe the Führer partly to ignorance, partly to blind faith. "I believed in Hitler and knew little of the facts myself," he said. "I'm not a tactician, nor did I know Russian military and economic strength. How could I?"

Whatever the top brass's real feelings about invading the Soviet Union, they quickly began questioning Hitler's military acumen once that invasion was under way. It was one thing to defer to their leader on the major issues of war and peace. It was quite another to sit by quietly while he wavered on how to take advantage of the initial German successes or when he ordered his troops to do battle where they were likely to dissipate rather than concentrate their energy and strength.

While the German propaganda machine was trumpeting the successes of the forces in the early weeks of Operation Barbarossa, the commanders on the ground knew they were often paying a heavier price for them than expected in terms of casualties—and that, in many areas, the German advance wasn't moving as swiftly as they had hoped. The forces of Army Group North were still a long way from reaching Leningrad, and it wouldn't be until late September that they would get close enough to begin the infamous nine-hundred-day siege of the city. Heavy rains were slowing the advance of units in Army Group South, providing a disturbing preview of the much heavier precipitation of late summer and early fall that would bog down entire armies. As the Germans were quickly learning, roads that were marked on their maps would often prove to be no more than mud tracks that would virtually disappear when the weather failed to cooperate.

But there was good news for the Germans about the terrain that led, at least in theory, straight to Moscow. While his Soviet counterparts were scrambling to throw more troops against him, Fedor von Bock, the commander of Army Group Center, was delighted to have made it all the way to Smolensk, and he had no doubt what he wanted to do next. "The enemy is only really beaten at one place on the Eastern Front—opposite Army Group Center," he wrote in his diary on July 13. "If the armored groups now fly apart to the south, east and north, it means forgoing the exploitation of our success. . . . What matters now is to completely smash this foe and make it impossible for him to establish another new front before Moscow. To do so it is necessary to tightly concentrate all armored forces and with them drive quickly to the east until I can report that the enemy is offering no more resistance in front of Moscow!"

But Hitler wasn't ready to make that decision. The German leader, who had accomplished so many of his earlier goals by taking dramatic actions that required supreme self-confidence, wavered for about three weeks before responding to such appeals from his generals. And when he responded, it was to issue orders that directly contradicted the recommendations not only of Bock but also of Halder, Brauchitsch and other top officers. In essence, Hitler suddenly decided that his forces should now concentrate on the drive to Leningrad in the north and the offensive in the south, pushing through the Ukraine all the way to the Caucasus. Directive 34 on July 30 stated specifically, "Army Group Center will go over to the defensive, taking advantage of suitable terrain."

Bock had received the news a couple of days earlier, when Hitler's adjutant Rudolf Schmundt arrived to brief him on his boss's plans. As a clearly angry Bock summarized it in his diary, the gist of the message was: "The main thing is to eliminate the area of Leningrad, then the raw materials region of the Donets Basin [in the Ukraine]. The Führer cares nothing about Moscow itself." A couple of weeks later, Bock vented his frustration again in his diary. "All the directives say that taking Moscow isn't important! I want to smash the enemy army and the bulk of this army is opposite my front!" he wrote. "Turning south is a secondary operation—even if just as big—which will jeopardize the execution of the main operation, namely the destruction of the Russian armed forces before the winter."

The directive from Hitler's headquarters on August 12 at least formally contradicted Bock's assertion. It stated that the objective of German operations was still "to deprive the enemy, before the coming winter, of his government, armament, and traffic around Moscow, and thus prevent the rebuilding of his defeated forces and the orderly working of government control." But if this effectively summarized the thinking of the generals who were convinced that the only way to ensure the success of Operation Barbarossa was to seize Moscow, the directive's most important provision was to mandate a delay in pushing for that objective. "Before the beginning of this attack on Moscow, operations against Leningrad must be concluded," it declared.

As commander of the army, Brauchitsch spelled out his opposing views on August 18, urging the resumption of the drive east toward the Soviet capital. Hitler responded that the army's plan "is not in accordance with my intentions." He then itemized his new priorities. "The most important aim to be achieved before the onset of winter is not to capture Moscow, but to seize the Crimea and the industrial and coal region on the Donets, and to cut off the Russian oil supply from the Caucasus area. In the north, the aim is to cut off Leningrad and to join with the Finns."

In a clash of that kind with his generals, Hitler wasn't going to give any ground once his mind was made up. At about the same time, General von Manstein witnessed a confrontation between Hitler and Halder, the army chief of staff. According to Manstein, Hitler questioned "in the most tactless terms Halder's right to differ with him, declaring that as a front-line infantryman of World War I he was an infinitely better judge of the matter than Halder, who had never been in this position." Manstein was so upset by this "undignified" scene that he left the room, returning only after a calmer Hitler asked him to do so.

Despite his admiration of Hitler's grasp of a broad range of subjects, including military technology, Manstein concluded that the German leader was sorely deficient in precisely the area in which he compared himself favorably to Halder. "What he lacked, broadly speaking, was simply *military ability based on experience*—something for which his 'intuition' was no substitute," Manstein wrote.

But it wasn't just that Hitler lacked the broader military experience of his generals. In those early weeks and months of Operation Barbarossa, he kept changing his mind about the major strategic goals and particularly about the timing for the big German push for Moscow. On September 6, he ordered Army Group Center to focus on "destroying the enemy forces located in the area east of Smolensk by a pincer movement in the general direction of Vyazma"—the next key town and railroad junction on the road to Moscow. And on September 16, Hitler issued the directive that would be the basis for launching Operation Typhoon, which was supposed to be the climactic drive against Moscow, on September 30.

It was the decision the generals had been hoping for, but it came much later than they wanted it, several critical weeks having slipped away in the process. That left them confronting a far more difficult task than they would have faced if Hitler hadn't rejected their pleas to move earlier. It left the field commanders with a growing sense of frustration about their seemingly contradictory orders and, in some cases, growing doubts about the man who was issuing those orders.

During the 1920s, when Germany's army was severely restricted by the Treaty of Versailles, a young Prussian officer by the name of Heinz Guderian single-mindedly dedicated himself to the proposition that the country needed to develop an armored component for its armed forces—panzer brigades or divisions equipped with tanks and other armored vehicles. By the time Hitler took power in 1933, he was able to put on a demonstration for the new leader that included motorcycles, experimental tanks and armored reconnaissance vehicles, all operating together. Hitler was visibly impressed. "That's what I need!" he exclaimed. "That's what I want to have."

Guderian was delighted by the Führer's enthusiasm. Many of his superior officers, who had been brought up in the infantry or cavalry, had been skeptical about the notion that motorized vehicles would play a crucial role in future conflicts. Besides, the Versailles Treaty explicitly forbade Germany to acquire or build armored vehicles or tanks. As Guderian saw it, though, this only proved that "our enemies regarded the tank as a decisive weapon" and Germany had to equip itself with those weapons as soon as possible. To make his case, he had even brought sheet-metal dummies of tanks to take part in army maneuvers, since he couldn't get hold of the real thing yet. "These wretched mock-ups struck the old soldiers from the First World War as so utterly ridiculous that they tended to feel sorry for us and were certainly not inclined to take us seriously," he noted.

With Hitler in charge, all that quickly changed. Germany began rapidly rearming, and new armored units became an essential part of the new armed forces. In the fall of 1935, Guderian was put in charge of the Second Panzer Division, one of three new divisions of the kind. He was no longer a planner but an operational commander of a unit he had done so much to create.

When Germany attacked Poland in September 1939, Guderian's tanks played a crucial role in that first victory. They quickly pushed all the way to Brest, the city with a citadel right on the Soviet border, east of the Bug River. After Soviet troops invaded Poland from the east, Guderian's troops were required to hand over the city to the Russians, since the Bug became the demarcation line of the German-Soviet division of a defeated Poland. Guderian was hardly pleased to give up territory that he had won in a costly battle with the outgunned but defiant Poles. "It seems unlikely that any soldier was present when the agreement about the demarcation line and the cease fire was drawn up," he tersely noted in his memoirs.

While Guderian kept those thoughts largely to himself, he would soon find himself openly at odds with his superiors—all the way up to Hitler—at the very moment of his greatest triumph. During the invasion of France, Guderian's panzers practically raced across the country all the way to the coast, stunning the crumbling French forces. French General Maurice Gamelin issued an order, which was intercepted by the Germans: "The torrent of German tanks must finally be stopped!" But it wasn't the French who finally stopped the onslaught of Guderian and the other tank commanders; it was Hitler. They were suddenly ordered to stop short of Dunkirk, the port to which British and French forces were fleeing to await evacuation. The Luftwaffe was assigned the task of bombing the port, while the tank troops were held back. "We were utterly speechless," Guderian recalled. "We were stopped within sight of Dunkirk!"

A few days earlier, Guderian had threatened to resign when he was told to slow his advance. It had then begun to dawn on him that just when Hitler's support for an aggressive panzer strategy was paying off, the German leader "would now be the one to be frightened by his own temerity," fearing that the German drive was becoming overextended because of the speed of the panzer units. But if that dispute was quickly resolved, allowing Guderian to continue his drive, Dunkirk proved a different matter. Guderian's and the other tank units weren't allowed to attack the port, so the British had enough time to orchestrate the spectacular evacuation of 330,000 British and French forces that could then fight another day. As Guderian saw it, this had been a chance to strike a blow that might have altered the course of the war. "Unfortunately the opportunity was wasted owing to Hitler's nervousness," he complained.

If Guderian was convinced Hitler hadn't been bold enough in the final days of the French campaign, he would soon come to fear the opposite as word spread of an impending invasion of the Soviet Union. He believed that this would be a far more difficult task than defeating Poland or France. But the speed of those earlier successes, he noted, "had so befuddled the minds of our supreme commanders that they had eliminated the word 'impossible' from their vocabulary."

Like some of the other generals, Guderian may have played up his doubts about the Soviet invasion after the war. But he certainly had legitimate grounds for them at the time. With his intimate knowledge of German tank production, he knew that the supply of new vehicles was still far short of what he felt was needed, especially in the case of a lengthy war with the Soviet Union.

An encounter with his Russian counterparts on the eve of that conflict had given Guderian pause. In the spring of 1941, a Soviet military delegation arrived to look at German tank schools and factories. Since Hitler was still pretending to be observing the Nazi-Soviet pact and wanted to keep his invasion plans secret, he had specifically authorized the visit and ordered that the visitors be shown everything so as not to arouse suspicion. When the Germans showed the Russians the Panzer IV, the Russians protested that this couldn't be their newest and heaviest tank as their hosts claimed. In fact, it was the best tank the Germans had at the time, and Guderian and other German experts reluctantly concluded that the Russians must have something better in their own production line. Soon enough, Guderian would be able to confirm that for himself.

As part of Field Marshal von Bock's Army Group Center, Guderian's panzer division was in action from the first day of the invasion, crossing the Bug River and taking most of the Soviet troops by surprise. But two days later, the famed general experienced a close call that almost cost him his life. As he was consulting with several top officers about their next moves, two Soviet tanks suddenly appeared from behind a burning truck that had obscured the Germans' view. Spotting the enemy officers, the Russian tanks opened fire at close range, blinding and deafening them for a moment. Guderian and two other generals immediately hit the ground and survived. A less experienced colonel hesitated and was killed. At a time when the Germans appeared to be heading for a swift victory, this provided a stark reminder that their opponents could still prove to be highly dangerous.

Guderian and his tanks kept pushing due east, taking part in the early victories that culminated in the battles around Smolensk in mid-July. When he flew to his army group's headquarters on July 27, he was expecting instructions to keep going east to prepare for the strike against Moscow. Instead, he was stunned to learn that Hitler had ordered his unit to redeploy to join in the fighting around Gomel, a city located southwest of Smolensk—"that is to say towards Germany," as Guderian angrily noted. In other words, he was being ordered to move away from Moscow.

In many ways, this felt like an even more grievous error than the decision to stop his forces in France before they could hit Dunkirk. Like many of his superiors, he was convinced "that these maneuvers on our part simply gave the Russians time to set up new formations and to use their inexhaustible manpower for the creation of fresh defensive lines in the rear area," thus undermining German ability to achieve a rapid victory. And like Bock, Guderian had the chance to meet Hitler's aide Rudolf Schmundt. He urged Schmundt to convey the message to the Führer that he should reconsider his decision in favor of "a direct push to capture Moscow, the heart of Russia."

In early August, Guderian's forces were involved in fighting to the south of Smolensk, scoring another victory, this time in Roslavl. But their commander was still determined to argue against continuing further south and west to Gomel. His troops were convinced they'd soon be on the move to the Soviet capital, and he watched "with a heavy heart" as they put up signs reading "To Moscow." As Bock wrote in his diary, "Guderian is champing at the bit!"

Toward the end of August, the field marshal agreed to send Guderian along with General Halder to Wolf's Lair, Hitler's military headquarters in East Prussia, for a final attempt to persuade the German leader to change his mind about making the Ukrainian capital of Kiev the next key military target instead of Moscow. But when Guderian arrived, Field Marshal von Brauchitsch, the commander-in-chief of the army, gave him a brusque warning. "I forbid you to mention the question of Moscow to the Führer," he declared. "The operation to the south has been ordered. The problem now is simply how it is to be carried out. Discussion is pointless."

Guderian wasn't one to obey meekly. Finding himself in a room with Hitler that was already crowded with top brass, he waited for an opening to make his case, and he quickly got it. When Hitler inquired whether his troops were ready to make "another great effort," he replied, "If the troops are given a major objective, the importance of which is apparent to every soldier, yes."

"You mean, of course, Moscow?" Hitler said.

Guderian replied "Yes" and asked to be given the opportunity to spell out his reasons. When Hitler agreed, he put forth all the arguments why Moscow should be the target: its role as the country's major communication and transportation hub, which, once captured, would make it difficult for the Soviets to move men and supplies around the country; its role as a major industrial center; and its indisputable role as "the political solar plexus" of the country. A victory in Moscow would lift the spirits of German troops and devastate the Russians psychologically, he added, and would make it considerably easier to achieve victories elsewhere, including in the Ukraine. It would also have a huge psychological impact on the rest of the world. But if that victory wasn't achieved soon and German troops were diverted somewhere else, "it would then be too late to strike the final blow for Moscow this year," since the onset of fall and winter weather would make the task increasingly difficult.

Hitler heard Guderian out without interrupting him. But then he launched into his theory of why the agricultural riches and raw materials of the Ukraine had to be seized first, providing Germany with vital supplies. "My generals know nothing about the economic aspects of war," he complained. As he made clear that the next target would be Kiev and not Moscow, Guderian was stunned to see all the others in the room nodding in agreement. By the end of the session, he felt completely alone, with no support even from those he knew had agreed with his arguments earlier.

So Guderian found himself fighting in the battle for Kiev during the first half of September instead of approaching Moscow. Relying on the kind of pincer movements that they had used at Minsk and Bialystok, the German forces encircled the Soviet forces and then inflicted massive casualties and rounded up hundreds of thousands of prisoners. Aside from the fierce combat, the troops had to deal with the effects of pouring rain. "Only a man who has personally experienced what life on those canals of mud we called roads was like can form any picture of what the troops and their equipment had to put up with and can truly judge the situation at the front and the consequent effect on our operations," Guderian wrote.

The panzer commander admitted that the costly battle for Kiev amounted to a great tactical victory for his side. "But whether great strategic advantages were to be garnered from this tactical success remained questionable," he added. "It all depended on this: would the German Army, before the onset of winter and, indeed, before the autumnal mud set in, still be capable of achieving decisive results?" In other words, would his warning to Hitler prove to be accurate and the remaining window of opportunity too small?

In the wake of the victory in Kiev, Hitler finally issued the orders for Operation Typhoon. As a first step, Guderian's tanks were assigned to advance north toward Moscow by taking Orel and Bryansk. As usual, the panzer leader more than rose to the occasion. When his tanks rolled into Orel on October 3, the local authorities were caught totally by surprise—so much so that the trams were running as if this were any normal day.

Vasily Grossman, the famous war correspondent for the Red Army newspaper *Krasnaya Zvezda,* recalled the pointed exchange he had with his editor after he returned to Moscow from covering the German push from the south. "Why didn't you write anything about the heroic defense of Orel?" the editor demanded. Grossman's reply: "Because there was no defense."

But three days after they seized Orel, the Germans received a nasty surprise of their own. Attacked by Russian T-34 tanks, they sustained major losses. "This was the first occasion on which the vast superiority of the Russian T-34 to our tanks became plainly apparent," Guderian admitted. In order to be effective against them, the driver of a German Panzer IV had to maneuver his tank behind the T-34 and fire an extremely accurate shot at the grating above the engine to put it out of commission. From other angles, the Germans could only damage the tanks but not disable them.

For Guderian, the other unpleasant discovery was that the huge operation and continual combat was exacting a toll not only in terms of higher than expected casualties and exhausted troops but also in terms of strained supply lines. For the first time, the panzer units began encountering occasional fuel shortages. But most troubling, as Guderian saw it, was the looming prospect of a change in the weather and a lack of warm clothing for his troops. He repeatedly requested winter clothing, only to be told that his troops would receive it "in due course" and that he should stop making such "unnecessary" requests. So, too, with their requests for antifreeze for the engines of their vehicles. "We saw as little of this as we did of winter clothing for the troops," he noted bitterly. "This lack of warm clothes was, in the difficult months ahead, to provide the greatest problem and cause the greatest suffering to our soldiers—and it would have been the easiest to avoid of all our difficulties."

Like Stalin, Hitler was ensuring that his officers and men would pay a higher price for both their victories and defeats than whatever the enemy's actions accounted for. Like Stalin, he was responsible for a growing number of self-inflicted wounds. As a result, the German forces finally advancing on Moscow, while still victorious and formidable, weren't quite the juggernaut that they had been during the early weeks of Operation Barbarossa. They had been roughed up on more than one occasion, and the strain of moving so far so fast—including the sudden shifts in their course and targets, as in Guderian's case—was beginning to show. They were about to face their most difficult test to date, with a growing sense of unease about whether they were up to it.

The arrows of the German advance were now unambiguously pointing toward Moscow.

5

"Moscow is in danger"

It was late August 2005, sixty-four years after those early months of the German invasion of the Soviet Union, when I accompanied a trio of searchers on a trip to the dense woods near Vyazma, 140 miles due west of Moscow. To this day, Russians from all walks of life band together in small groups of searchers who take camping trips to the sites of World War II battlefields, combing the areas for the remains of soldiers, their gear, weaponry, and whatever rare evidence they can find to rescue the fallen from anonymity. While the Germans usually buried their dead, the Red Army, especially in the early months of the war, suffered such huge losses and gave up so much territory so quickly that they left most of their dead wherever they had fallen. In the aftermath of the war, Stalin and other Soviet leaders were as uninterested in those remains as they had been in the catastrophic level of casualties that produced them. With a sense of mission that borders on the mystical, the searchers gather what they can and see to it that the remains they find are given at least the approximation of a proper burial, with military honors if at all possible.

On the outskirts of Vyazma, which was the first target of Operation Typhoon when Hitler finally focused on taking Moscow, we stopped at what looked like a small cemetery right near the road. There are a couple of rows of simple rectangular graves, each one with an army helmet placed on it—in many cases a helmet riddled with bullet holes. On modest stone monuments in front of the graves, a few names are listed. Andrei Palatov, my guide and the leader of the *Zvezda,* or Star, group that numbers ten searchers, explained that groups like his had started the cemetery in 1990. Over the fifteen years since, he added, his group alone had brought the remains of about one thousand soldiers for burial there, and they had counted only those remains that were more or less complete. Altogether, thirty thousand remains have been buried in the small cemetery just since 1990, and the search groups are continuing to rebury more soldiers all the time. Each grave represents the last resting place for hundreds—in some cases, thousands—of the fallen.

In most cases, it's impossible to know the names of the soldiers and officers whose remains are found. For all the attention lavished on the military, the Soviet Union hadn't developed the simple but dependable engraved dog tags that the German and other armies had, which allowed easy identification of the dead. Instead, the Soviet army issued its soldiers capsules made of wood or hard rubber with a screw-on cap. The soldier's identification information was written on a small piece of paper that was rolled up and inserted into the capsule. But all sorts of things went wrong. The wooden capsules deteriorated over time, and the handwriting on the slips of paper, whatever the container, tended to fade. But most important, the popular name for the capsule was *smertny medalyon*—death medallion—and soldiers routinely threw them away, fearing that they brought bad luck on the battlefield. That's why only a few names are listed in a cemetery that is the final resting place for thirty thousand soldiers.

A separate grave adorned with fresh flowers lists more names than usual. It contains the bodies of children from the area who died *after* the war, usually when they stumbled upon weaponry or ammunition that then exploded. While neither side had time to lay down mines, there were plenty of grenades, shells, and other dangerous objects, which still occasionally took the lives of those who ventured into the forest.

As hard as it is to imagine that this small cemetery beside the road contains the remains of so many soldiers, it is even more difficult to comprehend the scale of the fighting near Vyazma. During less than two weeks in early October 1941, entire Red Army units were encircled and wiped out by the Germans. Palatov cited the German claims that they had killed four hundred thousand and captured another six hundred thousand—a staggering one million tally. The Germans almost certainly inflated their figures, but not by an exponential amount. There is no doubt that the Soviet losses totaled hundreds of thousands in the Vyazma fighting.

Up to that point, only the battle for Kiev, on the eve of Operation Typhoon, had proven more deadly. In that case, Stalin's refusal to allow his generals to give up the doomed Ukrainian capital allowed the Germans to encircle the Soviet troops and inflict massive losses. General Zhukov and other commanders had argued that a withdrawal would prevent a massacre and would allow those forces to regroup and fight later battles. But Stalin wouldn't hear of it. "How could you even think of giving up Kiev to the enemy?" he barked at Zhukov. Like Hitler, Stalin didn't hesitate to ignore the advice of his generals, overruling them at will.

If the encirclement of the Red Army in Kiev was a clear result of Stalin's refusal to allow his commanders to retreat, the ensuing tragedy near Vyazma was a product of a complete breakdown of communications and command. At the start of Operation Typhoon, the Soviet rulers failed to realize that German forces were quickly moving to encircle and trap as much of the Red Army as possible near Vyazma, making it the next "cauldron," an inferno of death and destruction. The German mission was simple: to trap and destroy the Soviet troops, blocking all means of escape. When the Soviet brass became aware of what was happening, they urged their men to escape by any means, and this time Stalin didn't object. But by then, it was already too late for all but a tiny number of them.

Boris Oreshkin was one of the lucky ones. "In our literature one can hardly find any information about this battle," he noted. "It's quite normal: who wants to talk about defeats?" Manning an observation post atop a hill with three other soldiers, watching wave after wave of German planes flying over on October 2, 3 and 4, with no Soviet planes rising to meet them, Oreshkin felt as though he was in the dead calm of the center of a storm. He could see smoke and explosions on the horizon, indicating the direction of the German attack—right toward Vyazma. But when he and his buddies tried to report what they saw, they could only reach a soldier standing guard at a nearby airfield, who had no interest in their warnings. "I think that we—four ordinary soldiers—were the only people who could see clearly what was going on," he claimed, with hardly any irony.

Soon the Germans began attacking nearby, and their planes dropped bombs on the airfield and anything else they could see. By October 9, Oreshkin was part of the desperate sea of soldiers seeking to find a way out of the German encirclement, under bombardment from the air and pummeled by artillery and machine gun fire on the ground. The Soviet troops were told to break out of the cauldron, but the result was chaos. When a rumor started that some soldiers had succeeded in breaking through the German lines, Oreshkin reported, "People threw away gas masks, helmets and bags. Everybody just had one thought: to have enough time to escape the encirclement." He even threw away his food bag, normally the last item that a panicked soldier abandons, thinking that he would be safe if he could make it only a short distance to the other side of the German lines.

The journey would prove to be sheer torture. Oreshkin and the others spent the night running blindly back and forth in the woods, trying to avoid the bursts of German machine gun fire and cascades of artillery shells. German tanks fired at point-blank range at the Soviet soldiers trying to escape. At one point, Oreshkin heard a sound "as if somebody had taken a sheet of iron and started to shake it," and then there was a blinding light and a hot flame shooting out right next to him. The explosion threw him to the ground. When he opened his eyes, he saw that a friend who had fallen next to him had a gaping wound between his shoulder blades. It was as if a giant stake had been driven through him. "Dress my wound," the soldier pleaded. Oreshkin tried to help him, but it was hopeless, and another round of shells quickly sent him sprawling again.

By the next morning, when he had reached a pond where he

could quench his thirst, Oreshkin felt done for. "I was never more exhausted in my life than I was there. Even death looked like deliverance." Then he saw a junior lieutenant tear up his documents and throw his gun into the pond. He also saw a line of German troops approaching and Soviet soldiers getting up, barely able to raise their hands in surrender. He quickly followed the lieutenant's example and threw his documents and gun into the water as well.

When he joined the group of about twenty surrendering soldiers, Oreshkin was shocked by the disdainful confidence his captors displayed. "We were conveyed to a village by a single soldier," he noted. "He was walking ahead of us and didn't even think that it was necessary to hold the gun in his hands. He was sure that we would do nothing to him and this fact finally broke me down, humiliated me and showed me the whole hopelessness of our situation." Oreshkin would miraculously survive not only to fight again but also, in 1944, to capture German troops who would feel as humiliated and defeated as he felt then. But the overwhelming majority of those who were trapped in Vyazma didn't have a chance of making it.

Now these sixty-four years later on a picture-perfect sunny day, the searchers and I made our way into the shadowed forest about ten miles south of the town of Vyazma, the center of the cauldron where so many had perished. We had hiked only a short distance when Palatov, who was leading our expedition, stopped and climbed down into a ditch where his group had left their most important find on their last outing. He carefully lifted up a plastic bag and pulled out an intact skull, explaining that they would take it to the small cemetery for burial along with any other human remains they'd find during their next trips. The only other skull we'd see during our trip was that of a horse—horses were widely used by both armies—but the evidence of the ferocity of the fighting was everywhere. As Yegor Chegrinets, Palatov's frequent partner on these expeditions, pointed out, "You can't escape the war here. It just grows out of the ground."

I soon saw what he meant. After pitching our tents, we walked deeper into the forest, which was occasionally broken up by wild fields that had once belonged to villages. We waded through the tall grass, stepping gingerly to avoid spraining our ankles in some hidden depression. During the fighting, the villages, too, were obliterated and in many cases were never rebuilt. Although we were only ten miles from the town, it felt as though we were in a different universe, in a forest with dense undergrowth that sprang up even over what once were country roads. Palatov warned me to stay close. The previous year, he said, a pair of hikers had gotten lost in the forest and had set off in the wrong direction. They had a four-day trek before they reached civilization.

Palatov, Chegrinets and Maxim Suslov, the third member of the group, turned on their metal detectors, and soon the quiet of the forest was broken by constant beeps as they zeroed in on metal just below the surface. While cautioning me not to touch anything, they began scooping up bullet casings, shell and bomb fragments, grenades, helmets, bayonets, mess kits, and parts of pistols. The bullet-riddled front of a jeep was lying among some trees, as were other vehicle parts, harnesses, gas masks, and one Soviet boot. Palatov picked up the standard food pouch of a soldier, the kind Oreshkin had thrown away in desperation. There was far more than the searchers could carry, and they left much of what they found in the forest. They took only a few objects for display in the small museum they had set up for that purpose in Moscow.

At a certain point, I was struck by the fact that something was missing in this now deceptively beautiful, wild forest: any form of wildlife, even birds. The searchers explained that while there were deer and wild boar in the forest and certainly some smaller animals, we probably wouldn't see any. The local inhabitants had picked up plenty of battlefield weapons after the war and they shot at anything that moved. The animals stayed well clear of people venturing into the forest—and, my guides added, we'd be smart to do the same in case we saw anyone who wasn't part of our group. That was especially true at night, when drinking and shooting often went together. We didn't run into any outsiders during our outing. Neither did we see any animals during the whole trip.

As we approached a gully, Palatov recounted the story of one of the few Soviet officers who had been experienced and calm enough to lay a trap for the Germans in the heat of the battle. Many of his fellow officers had panicked, just as the soldiers had, but this particular officer had figured out that the Germans were likely to hide in the gully overnight before attacking. As a result, he ordered his men to camouflage themselves in positions surrounding the gully, and when the Germans went down into the gully, as he had anticipated, they opened fire on them. This was one of the few times during the Vyazma battle when the Russians had the upper hand and inflicted heavy losses on the Germans. I followed Palatov into the gully, and his metal detector started going off immediately. He dug just below the surface and found parts of a German belt, spent cartridges, and even a pfennig. It was as if the ground had spoken up to confirm his story.

Just outside our campsite that evening, Palatov found three grenades that had failed to explode. While the TNT had deteriorated over sixty-four years and wasn't particularly dangerous, one grenade still had an intact detonator. Holding them up, he announced: "They're Polish."

Astonished, I asked how that was possible. Palatov explained that it wasn't uncommon to find Polish ammunition and other weaponry. The problem was that it was impossible to know which army it had come from. After Germany and the Soviet Union invaded Poland in 1939, both occupiers seized whatever Polish supplies they could get their hands on and added them to their arsenals. All of which was perfectly logical, but the find had caught me completely by surprise. In one of those bizarre ironies of history, German and Soviet soldiers fighting at Vyazma had killed each other with Polish bullets and grenades. And not only at Vyazma. A report by A. L. Ugryumov, head of the political department of Moscow's Frunzensky district, on the performance of newly formed home guard units composed of Muscovites mobilized to defend the capital, noted that many of the inexperienced soldiers marched into battle in early October equipped only with "Polish trophy rifles."

There are few people left in the region who remember anything from that period. But in 1996 Palatov recorded an interview with Maria Denisova, a woman who has since died. She was fifteen at the time of the Vyazma battle and lived in one of the villages destroyed in the fighting, precisely in the area where we had been hiking. She recalled hiding in terror in the basement of her house along with her mother and a wounded Russian soldier. A German spotted an opening to the basement and tossed in a grenade that killed the soldier and seriously wounded her mother. When Denisova and her mother came out, every house in the village was on fire. The two of them hid in one of the dugouts abandoned by fleeing Soviet soldiers, and her mother died there from her untreated wounds a few days later. Denisova's father had hidden in another dugout with four other men, but the Germans had spotted them and ordered them out. One man's shirt was covered with blood since he had just killed a sheep. The Germans took this as evidence that they were partisans and shot them all.

After the fighting died down, Denisova witnessed a scene of pure horror. "There were so many dead bodies all over the place," she recalled. "We walked on them as if it was a floor covered with bodies. They were next to each other and on top of each other. Some didn't have legs, heads or other parts. We had to walk on them since there was no other place to step. Everything was covered with them: the entire village and the riverbank. It's awful to remember! The river was red with blood as if there was only blood flowing there." She and other survivors had no choice but to pick up the military canteens strewn about and drink from the bloody river, since the village had no well. They also ate the rotting meat of the dead horses that littered the area.

Eventually the villagers buried some of the dead, but they mostly stayed clear of the forest, where the worst fighting had taken place. As late as the following spring, an occasional Red Army survivor would appear among the trees. "They were so ugly with their long beards that almost reached their waists," Denisova recalled. "We were scared of them." But they never harmed the surviving villagers. "I don't know how they survived and what they ate," she added, noting that their clothes were so tattered that it was impossible to tell whether they were ordinary soldiers or officers. Since the area around Vyazma would remain in German hands for two years, it's hard to imagine that many of them lived to see the end of that occupation.

The only individual grave I saw was near the last village before the forest. It was for a Russian general who hid among the villagers as the Germans were completing their job of wiping out the encircled Soviet forces. It's a simple grave with a metal cross. There's no name on the grave, since no one knows who he was. According to the villagers, he helped save some of the local children by instructing them where to hide during the fighting. He changed into civilian clothes, but the Germans heard that he was still in the village and demanded his surrender. They then lined up the villagers and announced that they would start shooting every tenth person unless the village gave him up. At that point, the general stepped forward himself, and he was promptly executed.

In a place where hundreds of thousands perished without a trace, as if they had never existed, the nameless general stands out as one of the few who anyone still remembers. For the rest of the fallen, it's only the ground that remembers and tells their story to those willing to listen.

Foreigners have long been confounded by the way Russians have displayed a seemingly limitless stoic endurance in the face of suffering and despotism. In his classic account of his journey to Russia in 1839, the Marquis de Custine described the country as "an absolute government and a nation of slaves." In Russia, the Frenchman added, "fear replaces, that is to say, paralyzes thought." Push Russians to explain their history and their behavior as they have dealt with the long list of tragedies that make up that history, and, sooner or later, they are likely to start talking about *sudba*—fate. After all, Russians point out, so much of life is not an accident. Just as it is no accident that Vasily Grossman's epic novel about how Russians endured the terror of both Hitler and Stalin during World War II is entitled *Life and Fate*.

But fate can deliver blessings, not only curses. And Ella Zhukova is firmly convinced that Stalin's decision to entrust the defense of Moscow to her father, Marshal Georgy Zhukov, was one of those blessings. "I'm not a religious person, but I believe he had some gift from above," she said, speaking of her father, who was assigned "such a great responsibility" for the Soviet capital at the moment when the Germans looked virtually unstoppable. Maybe fate was at work, too, in elevating a man to this position who was born in 1896 in a village called Strelkovka. The name comes from the word *streltsy*, or archers, because it was one of the places where

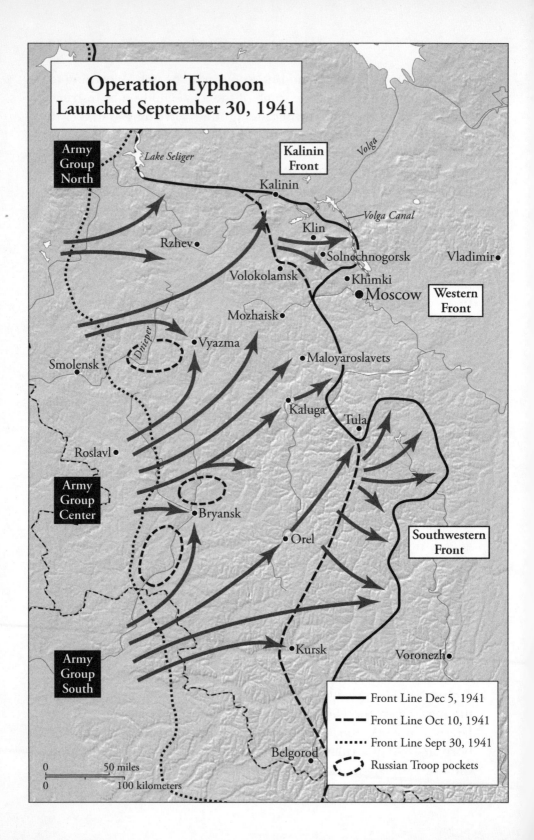

Operation Typhoon
Launched September 30, 1941

Army Group North

Lake Seliger

Kalinin Front

Volga

Kalinin

Volga Canal

Klin

Rzhev

Solnechnogorsk

Vladimir

Volokolamsk

Khimki

Mozhaisk

Moscow

Western Front

Dnieper

Vyazma

Smolensk

Maloyaroslavets

Kaluga

Tula

Roslavl

Army Group Center

Bryansk

Southwestern Front

Orel

Army Group South

Kursk

Voronezh

Belgorod

0	50 miles
0	100 kilometers

— Front Line Dec 5, 1941

--- Front Line Oct 10, 1941

···· Front Line Sept 30, 1941

⬭ Russian Troop pockets

Ivan the Terrible's archers set up camp to defend Moscow from Tartar invaders.

Whatever the case, the man charged with saving Moscow, who would go on to become his country's supreme military leader for the rest of the war, wasn't exactly easy to like. He was famous for his angry tirades laced with obscenities ("You are not a general but a bag of shit!" he would tell subordinates), and he never flinched when it came to sacrificing his men on the field of battle. "If we come to a mine field, our infantry attack exactly as if it were not there," he told General Eisenhower after the war. "The losses we get from personnel mines we consider only equal to those we would have gotten from machine guns and artillery if the Germans had chosen to defend the area with strong bodies of troops instead of mine fields."

In that, along with his unhesitating punishment of anyone who disobeyed orders, he was the perfect general for a leader like Stalin. Like the dictator, he was quick to threaten execution. His message to commanders in the field was all too often brutally simple: carry out the order, no matter how suicidal, or you will be shot for treason. In September 1941, when he was in Leningrad, which was already under siege, he decreed that any soldier who abandoned his post without written permission would meet the same fate.

Marshal Konstantin Rokossovsky, another top commander during the war, who worked closely with Zhukov, offered a decidedly diplomatic but nonetheless revealing description of him after the war. "Zhukov was always a man of strong will and decisiveness, brilliant and gifted, demanding, firm and purposeful," he declared. "All those qualities, unquestionably, are necessary in a great military leader and they were inherent in Zhukov. It is true that sometimes his toughness exceeded what was permissible. For example, in the heat of the fighting around Moscow Zhukov sometimes displayed unjustified sharpness."

Unlike most of his fellow officers, Zhukov wasn't a serious drinker, certainly not by Russian standards, and he didn't smoke. He prized his good looks and wasn't shy about insisting that he had to be portrayed the way he liked. In 1940, he called up the editor of *Krasnaya Zvezda,* the military newspaper, to complain that it was about to print a photo of him that he was convinced did him an injustice. "I look as if I were bald," he said. "You have plenty of artists, don't you? Can't they fix it?" Of course they could—and did.

The son of a shoemaker, Zhukov started as an apprentice furrier in Moscow at the age of eleven and quickly learned some hard lessons. "Grin and bear it when you're beaten," one of his co-workers told him. "A beaten man is worth two who aren't." Conscripted into the tsarist cavalry in 1915, he frequently ran afoul of officers who considered him insolent and unrepentant after his alleged infractions of the rules. But others recognized talent and audacity in the recruit, and he soon proved his courage in battle. In 1919, as part of the new Red Army fighting the Whites, he was wounded by a hand grenade. Hospitalized with multiple fragments in his left side and thigh, he came down with typhus.

But soon he was back in uniform. As a professional military man, he found himself frequently on the move. This wasn't exactly conducive to stable romantic relationships. He married Aleksandra Zuikova in 1922, a union that officially lasted more than forty years and resulted in the birth of two daughters, Era in 1928, and Ella in 1937. In 1929, though, he also fathered a third daughter, Margarita, with another woman. (All three daughters still live in Moscow, but Era and Ella only learned about Margarita's existence in the 1950s and there's no love lost between them.) Zhukov was frequently involved with other women. According to his driver Aleksandr Buchin, he had a long affair during the war with "a young and pretty" nurse by the name of Lidia Zakharova. In 1957, Zhukov fathered a fourth daughter, Maria, with Galina Semyonova, an officer in the army's medical service, who was thirty years younger than he was. In 1965, at the age of sixty-nine, he divorced Aleksandra so that he could marry Galina.

Nonetheless, his daughter Ella, who freely admits that her father had "some lovers," portrays him as "always kind, attentive and loving to his family." He wrote short letters home that indicated he was thinking of his children. In a letter written to Era and Ella in September 1941, he inquired about their health and said, "I think that as soon as I'm done with the Germans, I'll immediately come to you or you'll come over. Please write to me more often. I don't have time at all because we have battles all the time." Even in this letter written to his two young daughters while he was trying to hold off the Germans in Leningrad, he promised to produce a victory. "I'm planning not only to defend the city, but also to pursue them right to Berlin." At a time when the situation looked dire everywhere, this was quite a leap of faith.

Zhukov knew he was lucky to have survived the purges that swept away so many of his fellow officers in 1937. According to his daughter Ella, he always kept a small brown suitcase packed with two changes of underwear and a toilet kit in case the next knock on the door was for him. She remembers that it stood near his bed and that from time to time her mother would put in fresh clothes. While even a child could feel the pervasive atmosphere of fear, she added, "We never spoke openly about it at home."

Zhukov only broke this habit of keeping the suitcase ready in 1957, when Khrushchev, who had always distrusted Zhukov, dismissed him from the post of defense minister and from all his official duties. Zhukov had helped the new Soviet leader arrest Beria and then to outmaneuver his political rivals, but Khrushchev feared that Zhukov might have political ambitions of his own. As the unquestioned military architect of the victory over Germany, Zhukov commanded a high level of prestige and popularity.

Khrushchev's distrust of Zhukov harked back to his relationship with Stalin. Although Khrushchev had also loyally served the discredited tyrant, Zhukov had worked especially closely with him. At the same time, he was prone to speak up more honestly in the presence of Stalin than anyone else. This marked Zhukov as someone who wouldn't be intimidated by power, even of the absolute variety. Marshal Timoshenko would later claim that Zhukov was "the only person who feared no one. He was not afraid of Stalin." Maybe so, but the packed suitcase indicates an acute awareness of the consequences if he fell out of favor.

Not surprisingly, there were distinct limits to what Zhukov could do, particularly in the period of the purges, when he still hadn't risen to the heights he would achieve later. Zhukov would write afterward, in a part of his memoirs that was censored until the 1990s, that the purges constituted "a huge slanderous epidemic" in which "quite often they slandered honest people and even close friends." He also maintained in his memoirs that he tried to protect those officers he could help or at least do them no harm as the interrogators conducted their witch-hunts.

While he was serving in the Belorussian Military District, a member of the military council, Filipp Golikov, interrogated him in Minsk. (Golikov would later play his ignominious role as the military intelligence chief who kept funneling reports to Stalin that downplayed the chance of a German attack in 1941.) Asked about Rokossovsky and other officers who had been arrested, Zhukov defended them as "real patriots." Given another chance to answer the same question, he replied, "Yes, even now I think that they are real patriots and devoted communists."

According to Zhukov's account, Golikov was visibly upset by that response. His face turned red, and he asked if he didn't think it was dangerous "to praise enemies of the people?" But Zhukov held his ground, saying he had no idea why his fellow officers were arrested.

Golikov then shifted gears, bringing up reports that Zhukov was rude to his subordinates and political officers. Zhukov acknowledged he could be sharp-tongued, but he claimed he acted this way only with those who didn't perform well. Finally, the interrogator asked about rumors that Ella, his newest daughter, was baptized—which, if true, would have condemned him on the spot. He denied it, and Ella is convinced to this day that there's no reason to believe that the rumor was anything more than part of the general slander campaign.

Zhukov maintained later that he regarded the purges as a period of mad folly that cost the lives of many good officers. "Of course, I regard them as innocent victims," Andrei Gromyko, the veteran Soviet foreign minister, reported him as saying. Referring to the most prominent victim, the aristocratic commander who had transformed the Red Army into a modern fighting force, he added, "Tukhachevsky was an especially damaging loss for the army and the state." Ella Zhukova also reports that he condemned the purges. But, of course, those condemnations came after Stalin's death. While Zhukov would complain in his memoirs that the purged officers were replaced by "new people who were not so experienced," he was part of a new generation of military leaders whose careers were accelerated to fill that void. In fact, he admits that he was lucky that he wasn't promoted more quickly, since that would have made him a more visible target and made it harder for him to avoid being purged. On another occasion, when he heard that there might be new accusations against him, he admitted, "Actually I was nervous, because at that time it was very easy to be labeled an 'enemy of the people.'"

In the summer of 1939, Zhukov faced the first test of his military leadership skills. Japanese forces had attacked Soviet troops in Mongolia, an action that Zhukov would later characterize as an attempt by Japan to expand its empire and gauge the fighting ability of its Soviet neighbor. Taking command of the Soviet First Army Group, Zhukov demonstrated his willingness to order his troops into the most dangerous situations, knowing full well that they would pay a big price. In one instance, the Japanese attacked in force in an area where Zhukov didn't have access to infantry reserves. So he sent his tanks into battle without infantry support, knowing that this would result in heavy losses, which was exactly what happened. The Soviet brigade lost about half of its tanks and men, but the Japanese suffered high casualties as well, and their assault failed. As Zhukov put it, that fully justified the sacrifice of his men.

But Zhukov also patiently built up his forces to ensure that they would enjoy a healthy advantage in manpower and firepower when he launched his major attack in what was known as the battle of Khalkin Gol on August 20. Despite fierce resistance by the Japanese troops, Zhukov's forces achieved a decisive victory by the end of the month, and two weeks later Japan signed an agreement with the Soviet Union and Mongolia that formally ended hostilities. Both sides had sustained heavy losses, but the Red Army had emerged the clear-cut winner. The Japanese now knew that the Soviet Union was an opponent they couldn't afford to underestimate—which would play a major role in their thinking later, when their alliance with Germany would raise the question whether they should support Hitler by attacking the Soviet Union from the east.

For his role in orchestrating this victory, Zhukov received the title Hero of the Soviet Union and, more important, attracted the attention of Stalin. The following May, he was appointed commander of the Kiev military region. During Zhukov's first face-to-face conversation with Stalin, the Soviet dictator wanted to discuss the successful campaign against the Japanese. Puffing his pipe, he questioned him about the performance of his troops and their officers. Stalin listened attentively and urged him to apply the lessons he'd learned to his new job in the Kiev district and work them into his training courses. When Zhukov returned that night to his room at the Hotel Moskva, he had a hard time falling asleep. He was impressed by Stalin's seriousness and attention to detail, along with his calm demeanor. "If he is always like this, I can't understand why there are so many rumors that he is a monster," he mused, indicating a very different mind-set from the one he would ascribe to himself later. "At the time, I could not believe the bad things."

Even in the fuller version of his memoirs that was released in the 1990s, Zhukov wrote defensively about Stalin's failure to prepare the Soviet Union for the German attack and about the subsequent early successes of the enemy. Stalin had been trying to avoid a war with Germany by all possible means, he pointed out. "Stalin wasn't a coward, but he clearly understood that it was too late to make the important preparations for such a great war against an enemy who was so strong," he added. "He understood that we were late . . . with the rearmament of our troops with new weapons and the reorganization of the armed forces."

Zhukov largely preferred to avoid the question why such preparations hadn't been made earlier and to avoid mentioning Stalin's direct responsibility for these failures. But he was less reticent about pointing out that Stalin had kept most of the key intelligence reports about Germany's intentions to himself, preventing Zhukov and other top military leaders from seeing them. "I wasn't informed by Stalin about information which was in our intelligence reports that he received personally," Zhukov noted. While those reports were shared with other members of the Politburo, they were "kept secret from the military commanders of the country." When Zhukov tried to find out why this was the case, he was told that those were Stalin's orders. On another occasion in early 1941, both Zhukov and Marshal Timoshenko asked the Soviet leader directly why this was happening. "You will be informed only about the things you really need to know," Stalin replied tersely.

On September 11, when it appeared that the Germans were

close to succeeding in their drive on Leningrad, the Soviet leader dispatched Zhukov to take over from Marshal Voroshilov, who was clearly not up to the task of defending the city. "The situation is almost hopeless there," a gloomy Stalin told Zhukov. The new arrival quickly began issuing orders, dismissing or reassigning those generals he felt weren't doing their job, and insisting that the troops stop retreating and launch new attacks, no matter what the odds, or face the firing squad if they disobeyed. By the end of the month, the German advance had been arrested, and it settled into what would become the nine-hundred-day blockade of the city to starve its inhabitants.

Their ordeal would prove to be horrific: With food supplies rapidly dwindling, 632,253 civilians would die during the siege, according to official Soviet figures. But Zhukov's actions—and a bit of good fortune—had prevented the Germans from achieving victory. What Stalin and his generals didn't realize at first was that in the second half of September, Hitler was already redeploying many of his troops to prepare for Operation Typhoon, the attack on Moscow. This eased the pressure on Leningrad.

In the early days of October, as the Germans trapped the Red Army units in the Vyazma cauldron, other troops in the area were desperately fleeing similar encirclements. Vasily Grossman, the *Krasnaya Zvezda* correspondent and novelist, witnessed those events and recorded in his notebooks the impressions that never could be published in his newspaper. "I thought I'd seen retreat, but I've never seen anything like what I am seeing now, and could never imagine anything of the kind," he wrote. "Exodus! Biblical exodus! Vehicles are moving in eight lanes, there's the violent roaring of dozens of trucks trying simultaneously to tear their wheels out of the mud. . . . There are also crowds of pedestrians with sacks, bundles, suitcases. . . . There are moments when I feel with complete vividness as if we have been transported back in time to the era of biblical catastrophes."

The Soviet leaders kept getting more bad news. A Soviet pilot reported that a column of German tanks was only about a hundred miles southwest of the Kremlin, moving steadily along the highway, and there appeared to be no Soviet defenses that could stop them before they would reach Moscow. Alarmed, the Soviet brass sent out a second plane, which confirmed the sighting. Secret police chief Beria was furious, dispatching one of his subordinates to warn Moscow air commander Nikolai Sbytov that he and his pilots could face arrest for "cowardice and panic-mongering." But a third plane confirmed all the bad news, and Stalin realized just how desperate the situation now looked for the Soviet capital. As Zhukov noted, "The grave possibility of an enemy breakthrough hung over Moscow."

On the evening of October 6th, Stalin called Zhukov in Leningrad, ordering him to fly back to Moscow at once. The next day, the Soviet leader, who was suffering from a bad bout of the flu, received him in his Kremlin apartment. "Look, we're in really serious trouble on the Western front, yet I can't seem to get a detailed report about what's going on," Stalin complained. Zhukov's assignment, he told him, was to head immediately to the headquarters of the rapidly disintegrating Western front and to report what was happening. Of course, his real assignment was nothing less than to stop the Germans from marching into Moscow and declaring victory.

Exhausted physically and emotionally, Zhukov got into a car and set out for the headquarters right away, a difficult drive that lasted late into the night. He ordered the driver to stop on at least one occasion and got out to jog a couple of hundred yards to stay awake. He hardly needed to be told that his fate, along with the fate of the country, depended on his ability to stay alert and figure out what could be done to avert the disaster in the making.

The flip side to the deepening pessimism of Stalin was the buoyant mood of Hitler about Operation Typhoon. In September, SS officer Otto Günsche, who would later become the personal adjutant to the German leader, visited Hitler's Wolf's Lair headquarters. When he asked some of the officers stationed there whether this was where the Führer was planning to spend the winter, they laughed as if he had floated an absurd idea. "Spend the winter? What are you thinking of?" one of them replied. "We are fighting a *Blitzkrieg* against Russia." Then referring to Hitler's beloved retreat in the Austrian Alps, he added: "Christmas we will certainly be celebrating on the Obersalzberg as usual."

Hitler called Günsche to his conference room so that he could hear his impressions from the Eastern front. Judging by the cheerful way the Führer greeted him—he was whistling softly to himself—he was expecting good news. While conceding that the Russians were fighting hard, Günsche didn't disappoint him. He said that morale among the SS troops was high and they were happy to be fighting.

Hitler offered a prediction. "We will break them soon, it is only a question of time." Then, describing how his panzer forces, with more than two thousand tanks, were preparing for the assault, he added, "Moscow will be attacked and will fall, then we will have won the war." Once the Soviet forces were defeated and German troops reached the Urals, he added, they would stop there and the Luftwaffe would be charged with bombing any troops that might try to regroup further east. As for the Russians in the areas that he wouldn't bother to occupy, they could starve. Right before dismissing Günsche with a fascist salute, he vowed, "As the reformer of Europe, I shall make sure that a new order is imposed on this land according to my laws!"

Even when the weather began to change in early October, bringing the first snow and rain that would soon do their part to slow the German advance, Hitler continued his ruminations about what awaited Russia once it would be firmly under German rule. At a dinner on October 17, he talked about huge construction projects and the need to lay roads everywhere. According to one of those present who wrote down the highlights of the conversation, Hitler spelled out his vision of the future.

"Where the big rivers are crossed, German cities must arise, as centers of the Wehrmacht, police, administration and Party authorities. Along these roads will lie the German farmsteads, and soon the monotonous steppe, with its Asiatic appearance, will look very different indeed. In ten years four million Germans will have settled there, and in twenty years at least ten million."

The settlers would come from as far away as America, he continued, not just from Germany. His implicit assumption: it would be a German-controlled world once the Soviet Union was defeated. As for the Ukrainians, Russians, and other peoples of that defeated land, "no education or welfare is to be laid on for the native population." In other words, their fate would be total enslavement, and their country's production would only benefit its conquerors.

Hitler's commanders were preoccupied with the more immediate goal: ensuring that their troops would maintain their progress as they prepared to strike Moscow from the south, west and north. A day after Guderian's tanks entered Orel unopposed on October 3, Army Chief of Staff Halder wrote in his diary that all was going according to plan. "Guderian has reached Orel and is now pushing into completely empty space," he noted. "[General] Hoepner has broken through the enemy positions and reached Mozhaisk"—a town about sixty miles due west of Moscow that was at the center of the main Soviet defense line. Northwest of Moscow, German troops were pushing toward Rzhev, a town that was seen as a key staging point for the units that were supposed to carry out the northern portion of the pincer movement aimed at Moscow.

But Guderian wasn't convinced he had completely open space to the north from Orel toward Moscow. And aside from the discovery that the Soviet T-34 tank was proving to be better designed for combat than his panzers, Guderian was troubled by the signs that the Soviet defenders were doing a better job of organizing their counterattacks, even when they were outgunned, than they had before. While Red Army infantry would attack frontally, their tanks would strike at the German flanks. "They were learning," Guderian conceded. And he was worried about the impact on his troops' morale. "The bitterness of the fighting was gradually telling on both our officers and men. . . . It was indeed startling to see how deeply our best officers had been affected by the latest battles."

Even more alarming was that those early days of October produced the first signs of a change in the weather. The first snow fell during the night of October 6 to 7, and, while it was only an early warning of the looming Russian winter, Guderian's officers pleaded for warm boots, shirts, and socks, all of which were in perilously short supply. Despite the admonitions against pestering the high command with repeated requests, Guderian kept doing so—and kept getting nowhere.

The early snows didn't stick, but along with the rains that soon followed, they helped turn the Russian roads into "appalling mud swamps," as Guderian put it. On October 12, he complained, "Our troops were stuck in the mud and immobilized." They still managed to help complete the encirclement of another cauldron, this one in Bryansk, south of the larger action in Vyazma. But just as the German command issued an order for the encirclement of Moscow, Guderian's troops, who were supposed to take care of the southern portion of that task, found themselves increasingly bogged down by both the continued resistance and the weather. In fact, that particular order to encircle Moscow didn't even reach them.

While many of the German generals in the field were convinced they could still produce the victory that Hitler was demanding, they weren't nearly as optimistic as the Führer about the inevitability of it and certainly not sanguine about the price their men would have to pay to achieve it. They had enough of a taste of Soviet resistance and Russian weather to recognize that they were in for a real fight.

As far as Zhukov knew, the Germans had every reason to believe that they had the upper hand and that they could make it all the way to Moscow. "The enemy thought that the Soviet forces were weakened, demoralized and incapable of defending their capital," he wrote later. On October 6, the night he drove out to the Western front headquarters following his meeting with Stalin, Zhukov debriefed the generals there and realized that the situation was grim indeed. The commanders had lost contact with the armies surrounded near Vyazma, and, as Zhukov put it, "there was no longer a continuous front in the west, and the gaps could not be closed because the command had run out of reserves." With the benefit of hindsight, he claimed he knew that, with good planning and leadership, Soviet forces could still manage to hold off the Germans, but his description of the actual situation suggests he was far from certain.

Zhukov phoned Stalin at 2:30 A.M. from the Western front headquarters to give him the report he had been waiting for. As usual, the Soviet leader was up at that late hour. "The principal danger now is that the road to Moscow is almost entirely unprotected," the

weary commander explained. "The fortifications along the Mozhaisk line are too weak to halt a breakthrough of German armor.
We must concentrate forces on the Mozhaisk defense line as soon
as possible from where we can." The line Zhukov was referring to
ran from north to south for about 135 miles, at a distance of about
sixty miles from the capital that his remaining troops were supposed to defend at all costs.

To win time to set up those defenses, about four thousand
cadets from two Podolsk military academies, one for infantry, and
the other for artillery, were ordered to fill one of the most glaring
gaps in the line where German troops were advancing near
Maloyaroslavets. According to postwar Soviet lore, the heroic efforts of the cadets stunned the Germans at first and delayed their
onslaught for several crucial days. One survivor, cadet S. Leonov, is
quoted as rejoicing at their early successes. "We see Germans. They
are running away. We can't believe our eyes. But it's not a dream:
the enemies are running away from us—cadets."

Even if true, that was only a fleeting episode. Boris Vidensky,
the survivor who went on to become a military historian, recalled
the immediate terror of German bombardment, which killed many
of his fellow cadets, and German leaflets fluttering down from
planes with the appeal, "Red young men, surrender to us!" While
the cadets already were wearing the kind of warm underwear, coats
and hats that the Germans lacked, they were completely outgunned. Vidensky pointed out that, as an artillery cadet specializing in cannons, he didn't even know how to fire a machine gun at
first. And while the Germans represented the death threat the
cadets were facing in front of them, there was another threat from
the opposite direction. "This was the first time I saw NKVD blocking units," Vidensky noted, referring to the troops assigned to
shoot any soldiers who tried to retreat. "They were behind us." But
whatever his thoughts were then, he expressed approval of such
terror tactics when looking back more than sixty years later. "The
idea was to resist the Germans at any price," he says. "Such toughness brought us victory."

The official accounts indicate that about 80 percent of the
cadets perished in those few days of fighting. Scattered units elsewhere, including other groups of cadets, also participated in the

improvised defense of a line full of holes. As in the case of the hundreds of thousands of troops who died or were taken prisoner in the Vyazma cauldron, Zhukov would claim that such sacrifices were "not in vain." They bought time for those who were desperately shoring up the defenses all around Moscow, digging trenches, constructing pillboxes and anti-tank barriers, and preparing for the worst. They also bought time for the generals to reorganize their units, shore up the defense lines, and call upon any troops still available.

But Stalin's first instinct, as always, was to punish those whom he blamed for not fending off the German onslaught and for allowing so many troops to get caught at Vyazma. After hearing Zhukov's initial reports, he gave him the command of all the forces defending Moscow and fired several of the top officers who had been in charge during earlier defeats. Although Zhukov had little sympathy for the other senior officers who were dismissed, he defended General Ivan Konev, arguing that he needed him as his deputy commander. Stalin reluctantly agreed but made sure that the new team knew where it stood. "If Moscow falls, both your heads'll roll," he told Zhukov. As always, there was no possibility of assigning any of the blame to Stalin, no matter what happened.

Zhukov calculated he had only about ninety thousand men left to stop the approaching Germans from taking the capital. "These forces were far from adequate to man a continuous defense line," he noted. As a result, the troops were sent to defend key towns and positions. Their officers, from Zhukov on down, watching for where the Germans would strike next, knew they had to do everything possible to deploy them effectively. "Everyone worked day and night," Zhukov wrote later. "People literally collapsed from fatigue and lack of sleep. But everyone did all he could at his post— sometimes even the impossible." The key motivation, he concluded, was "a feeling of personal responsibility for the fate of Moscow." But the Germans kept punching holes in the Soviet defense lines, and Zhukov realized that the most he could hope for was to delay the German advance long enough for the defenses closer to the city to be strengthened.

While anti-tank barriers were hastily erected at the approaches to the capital and German air raids sent Muscovites scurrying for

cover in the city's subway stations, even the official Soviet pro-
nouncements, which always tried to avoid admitting bad news,
sounded increasingly gloomy. The Soviet media didn't report Hitler's speech on October 3 announcing that the "final" drive on
Moscow had begun, but Deputy Minister of Foreign Affairs Solomon Lozovsky indirectly conceded that this might be true when he
told foreign journalists that the capture of any particular city
wouldn't alter the outcome of the war. "If the Germans want to see
a few hundred thousand more of their people killed, they'll succeed in that—if in nothing else," he said on October 7. That same
evening, a report on the news mentioned for the first time "heavy
fighting in the direction of Vyazma."

The next day the army daily *Krasnaya Zvezda* declared that "the
very existence of the Soviet state is in danger" and demanded that
all soldiers "stand firm and fight to the last drop of blood." This
was part of a process that Zhukov would call explaining "the gravity
of the situation, the immediacy of the threat to Moscow, to the
Soviet people." New instructions called on all Muscovites to help
build one defense line outside the city, one right on the boundary
of the city, and then defense lines along the inner and outer boule-
vard rings within the city itself, thus preparing for street fighting.
On October 13, Moscow Party chief Aleksandr Shcherbakov told a
meeting of activists, "Let us not shut our eyes. Moscow is in
danger."

And still the Germans kept coming closer and closer. On October 14, they captured Rzhev. While the town lies 130 miles northwest of Moscow, it was the gateway for the German troops seeking
to sweep in from the north, and its fall meant that they now appeared well positioned to do so. Rzhev would also soon become a
scene of mass killing on a scale comparable to Vyazma, another in-
fernal cauldron that would consume huge numbers of troops. But
for the moment, the twin setbacks in Vyazma and Rzhev signaled
that the endgame for Moscow had really started, and many Muscovites were coming to the realization that it might not last long or
end well.

Ordinary Soviet citizens only had to read or hear the official an-
nouncements to come to that conclusion. They no longer had to
read between the lines, as they normally did, to figure out what was

happening. An official communiqué on the morning of October 16 declared: "During the night of October 14–15 the position on the Western front became worse. The German-Fascist troops hurled against our troops large quantities of tanks and motorized infantry, and in one sector broke through our defenses."

The Germans were closing in, their pincers extended, and by the Soviet government's own admission, they were breaking through. The Moscow Communist Party organization was calling for "iron discipline, a merciless struggle against even the slightest manifestations of panic, against cowards, deserters and rumor-mongers." But that wasn't about to stop the rumors from flying that German troops were already on the capital's outskirts or word leaking out that the government and foreign embassies were already evacuating key personnel. On October 13, Stalin had issued orders for the evacuation of top Party, government, and military officials to Kuibyshev, the Volga River city that had been picked to serve as the temporary capital if Moscow fell.

Nor could it stop the mounting sense of alarm among ordinary Muscovites, who were nervously contemplating the possibility that they'd be left alone to face the German conquerors and occupiers. Suddenly, many of them grabbed their belongings and decided to flee as well, but they had to find their way out of the endangered city on their own.

Moscow was on the verge of panic, not in a metaphorical sense, but in the literal meaning of that term.

6

"The brotherhood of man"

It wasn't only Muscovites or Hitler and Stalin who were anxiously monitoring the German drive on the Soviet capital. It's no exaggeration to say that the world was watching. Certainly Winston Churchill was watching with the hope that the Soviet side would tie down Hitler's forces long enough to ease the pressure on his country, which had held out alone for so long against a military machine that had triumphed everywhere else it had attacked in Europe. Certainly Franklin D. Roosevelt was watching, since he knew, even if he hadn't confided as much to his countrymen, that sooner or later the United States inevitably would be drawn into this global conflict. Certainly Japan's military rulers were watching, carefully monitoring the progress of the German forces and pondering whether they should remain on the sidelines or attack the Soviet Union from the east if that country was about to collapse anyway.

After the initial successes of Operation Barbarossa, most foreign officials and observers were pessimistic about Russia's chances, and they recognized that if their pessimism proved justified, the wider implications would be truly frightening. In the August 4, 1941, issue of *Life* magazine, Hanson W. Baldwin, the country's most authoritative military writer, published "Blueprint for Victory." Despite its upbeat headline, the article amounted to a desperate plea for the United States to enter the war precisely because the Soviet Union's prospects looked so bleak.

"The future depends in large measure upon the Russian campaign," he wrote. "A two to four months' victory in Russia (by 'victory' I mean annihilation of the bulk of the Red Army) will put Germany in a far stronger strategical position than before." By controlling the resources of the Ukraine and other parts of the Soviet Union, he argued, Germany would be "immune to blockade" and would have "completed the conquest of Europe." "Hitler's 'New Order' will be free to grow to its political and economic fruition," he added.

Baldwin did acknowledge that another outcome was theoretically possible. "On the other hand, if the German drive into Russia bogs down into Napoleonic futility, Hitler himself may face eventual defeat," he wrote. But he wasn't betting on that. At best, he believed, Hitler would win in Russia only after a long campaign that would sap German strength and give Britain more time to build up its forces. "But on the basis of all past experience—on our limited knowledge of the Red Army, on the operations of the first month— the world can anticipate in Russia another quick and decisive Germany victory," he somberly concluded. The result would be unequivocal for Britain. "If Russia and its resources fall easily within the Nazi orbit, victory is clearly beyond Britain's grasp," he wrote. "The best she can hope for is a negotiated peace."

Granted, Baldwin was making this case in order to urge his country to join the war effort to stop Hitler, insisting that nothing short of such action would provide hope for success. But his pessimism about Russia's chances was genuine and widely shared at the time. On the eve of the German invasion of the Soviet Union, which the Western powers knew was coming but Stalin refused to see, the conventional wisdom was that this was a disaster in the making.

On June 16, 1941, Sir Stafford Cripps, the British ambassador to Moscow, informed the War Cabinet in London that the consensus among diplomats in the Soviet capital was that Russia could not hold out against the German onslaught for more than three or four weeks. After Cripps's briefing, John Dill, the chief of the Imperial General Staff, told Foreign Secretary Anthony Eden that the Soviet side might be able to resist a little longer but it would be unwise to count on more than six or seven weeks of fighting. Ivan Maisky, the Soviet ambassador to London, was aware of his hosts' pessimism. British defense officials, he wrote, were convinced that the Germans would "go through Russia as a knife through butter," allowing Hitler to become "master of Russia."

Still, Churchill and his ministers were eager to see the Germans concentrate their firepower on the Soviet Union and so force Stalin to join the anti-Nazi alliance after nearly two years of ostensible friendship with Germany. The morning of June 22, Churchill's butler appeared in Eden's bedroom and presented him with a large cigar on a silver platter. "The Prime Minister's compliments and the German armies have invaded Russia," he announced. As Eden noted later, "We savored the relief, but not for me at that hour the cigar." Instead, he and Churchill immediately began discussing how to react, leading to the first of a long series of overtures to the new and, as immediately became apparent, difficult ally.

As the fighting came closer and closer to Moscow, British, American, Japanese and other diplomats in the Soviet capital sent home increasingly gloomy reports about the chances that the German assault could be stopped. But not everyone agreed on the prognosis, and long-simmering tensions between colleagues within some of the missions burst into the open. Moscow was a pressure cooker assignment in the period leading up to the war, with embassies prone to fierce internal battles based on differing assessments of Stalin's regime. The looming prospect of the German conquest of the city only exacerbated them. With the fate of Moscow hanging in the balance, the diplomats, along with top officials in London and Washington, found themselves debating not only what would happen but also how the West should respond to Soviet appeals for help.

While focusing on the pressing question of what Western policy should be, those debates contained explicit or implicit assumptions about the nature of the Soviet system and the personality of Stalin that could be traced back to the very first encounters between Western envoys and the Kremlin leadership. And the ongoing debate about those assumptions and their policy implications would carry on right through the war and beyond. They would all begin to come into focus at Moscow's moment of greatest peril.

Unlike his Republican predecessors, Roosevelt was anxious to reach out to the Kremlin, ending the long period when the United States and much of the West still treated the Soviet leaders as representatives of an illegitimate, dangerous, and quite possibly transient regime. On November 16, 1933, the president signed an agreement with Foreign Minister Maxim Litvinov establishing diplomatic relations between their two countries. He then appointed William Bullitt the first American ambassador to the Soviet Union. Bullitt would also become the first, and not the last, envoy that Roosevelt dispatched to Moscow who would quickly gain a perspective on the Soviet regime that would put him at odds with his boss in Washington.

Born into a wealthy Philadelphia family in 1891 and educated at Yale, Bullitt was eager to serve the president he so greatly admired and he was delighted to be tapped for such an important post. He had visited Moscow with his mother in 1914, just as World War I broke out. Right after the Bolshevik Revolution of 1917, he joined the State Department and quickly became a fervent advocate of recognition of the Soviet regime, which he viewed as a promising experiment in a new form of government. Sent to Russia on a fact-finding mission in November 1919, he expanded his brief to help negotiate an armistice in the civil war directly with Lenin. The Bolshevik leader, he reported, was "a very striking man—straightforward and direct, but also genial and with a large humor and serenity." By any measure, Bullitt appeared to be just the kind of envoy that Roosevelt wanted: someone who shared his positive assumptions about the Soviet Union and belief that a new era of cooperation and progress would be possible.

Less than a month after the Roosevelt-Litvinov agreement was signed, Bullitt arrived for a preliminary short stay in Moscow with the plan that he would then return to the United States to make his final preparations before actually moving and setting up the embassy there. He took along as his aide and interpreter George Kennan, a young foreign service officer who had been working hard on his Russian language skills. Kennan would later describe Bullitt as "charming, brilliant, well-educated, imaginative, a man of the world capable of holding his own intellectually with anyone." But he also noted that this "fine ambassador" was extremely impatient. "He came to Russia with high hopes, and he wanted to see them realized at once."

Those high hopes were on full display during his initial visit to Moscow in December 1933. At a lengthy dinner with "perhaps fifty toasts," as Bullitt recalled, the envoy found himself feted by Stalin and the top Kremlin brass, all there to impress upon him the importance that they attached to the new relationship with Washington. After Stalin promised him a good site for the new embassy, Bullitt recounted, "I held out my hand to shake hands with Stalin and, to my amazement, Stalin took my head in his two hands and gave me a large kiss! I swallowed my astonishment, and, when he turned up his face for a return kiss, I delivered it."

But awed as he was, Bullitt didn't fail to register other, less flattering impressions of the Soviet leader. He had expected "a very big man with a face of iron and a booming voice" but found himself facing someone who was "rather short, the top of his head coming to about my eye level, and of ordinary physique, wiry rather than powerful." And Bullitt was struck by the contrast between Stalin and his predecessor. "With Lenin one felt at once that one was in the presence of a great man; with Stalin I felt I was talking to a wiry Gypsy with roots and emotions beyond my experience," he noted.

Still, the new envoy was in an upbeat mood when, after concluding his rounds in Washington, he returned to Moscow in March 1934. He was convinced that the welcome he had received in December would translate into a friendly relationship between the two countries and, in particular, between the Soviet authorities and the staff of his fledgling embassy. Instead, Soviet officials seemed to go out of their way to disabuse him of that notion. They turned down his requests for a reasonable ruble exchange rate so that the embassy wouldn't have to follow the example of other missions of buying rubles abroad and bringing them in by diplomatic pouch.

They also restricted his use of a small plane he had brought with him to a nine-mile range, making it virtually useless. And on larger issues, such as Russia's debt to the United States left over from tsarist times, he couldn't make any progress, although the idea was to take care of this matter to facilitate the extension of credits to the Soviet regime.

The young and eager embassy staff found itself fighting daily battles just to function, both in initial temporary quarters at the shabby Savoy Hotel and at the new ambassador's residence known as Spaso House, a former fur merchant's mansion badly in need of repairs. Besides Kennan, they included another future ambassador to Moscow, Charles "Chip" Bohlen, and Charles Thayer, a West Point graduate who would go on to write books about Russia. While Bullitt and his team tried to expand their contacts with Russians, they were often frustrated in those efforts and bluntly rebuffed by those who were part of—and, in many cases, soon to be victims of—the hellish regime.

Karl Radek, a revolutionary who would lose his life in the purges, told Bohlen: "You Westerners will never understand Bolshevism. You consider Bolshevism as a hot bath whose temperature can be raised and lowered to suit the bather. This is not true. You are either a hundred per cent in the bath and a hundred per cent for it, or you are a hundred per cent outside and a hundred per cent against it."

Such attitudes, combined with the daily struggle to provide for the most basic needs of the embassy, made the Americans feel isolated and embattled. "We regarded ourselves as a lonely and exposed bastion of American governmental life, surrounded by a veritable ocean of official Soviet ill-will; and we took pride in our accomplishments precisely because of all this adversity," Kennan recalled.

Bullitt soon realized that the embassy also had to worry about maintaining security in a state obsessed with spying on everyone, including the diplomats in its midst. He was followed at all times by four plainclothesmen; whenever he was at his residence, they sat outside. Soviet officials blandly insisted that they were there for his protection and refused to get rid of them. As a result of Bullitt's efforts, six Marines were sent to Moscow to guard the embassy, beginning a practice that would later spread to American embassies all over the world. But that action produced problems of its own. As Bohlen recounted, he witnessed "a highly painted Russian woman" entering the Savoy and declaring to the clerk that she wanted to go up to the room of Sergeant O'Dean, one of the Marines. When the clerk asked why, she replied: "I am his Russian teacher." Bohlen reported that security was improved when the embassy moved to its new site on Mokhovaya Street, but it certainly wasn't the last time that Russian women would be used to compromise Marines on duty in Moscow.

Bullitt was soon completely disillusioned with the regime that he had once seen as inspirational. He wrote Roosevelt that "the honeymoon atmosphere has evaporated," and he became so frustrated by his dealings with the Kremlin that he informed Secretary of State Cordell Hull that "perhaps it would be best to bring all commercial and financial relations to a standstill" until the Soviet side adopted a more positive attitude. With Roosevelt, he argued that while maintaining as friendly personal ties with Soviet officials as possible, the Americans should "let them know clearly that if they are unwilling to move forward and take the carrot they will receive the club on the behind." In other words, Washington shouldn't accommodate Stalin's regime at any price.

It wasn't only the bilateral issues that produced Bullitt's new thinking. Like Kennan, Bohlen, and others, he found the purges and the heightened atmosphere of paranoia and xenophobia increasingly alarming and depressing. In March 1936, he wrote in a letter to a friend that he was stunned by the scope of the arrests, and he noted that those victims he knew personally "were without question loyal to the Soviet regime." A month later he warned Secretary Hull that it was Soviet policy to make friends with democrats "in order the better eventually to lead those democrats to the firing squad."

But Roosevelt wasn't pleased with Bullitt's new perspective and his recommendations for a tougher policy. He didn't want to believe that Stalin's regime had gone as far down the path of arbitrary terror as the evidence indicated, since he clung to the notion that the Soviet Union would eventually develop more democratic institutions and abandon its more aggressive notions of spreading communism elsewhere. The president was much closer to the views of the one embassy staffer who consistently accepted Soviet propaganda at face value. Colonel Philip Faymonville, the chief military attaché, reported that the purge victims were guilty as charged and believed that there had been only "individual instances" of violence against peasants during Stalin's brutal forced collectivization campaign. As Bohlen saw it, Faymonville's "definite pro-Russian bias" made him the "weak link in the staff."

In fact, Faymonville actively undermined his own ambassador, making it clear to Soviet officials that he disagreed with his policies. Those officials, in turn, complained openly about Bullitt, while praising the military attaché. Yevgeny Rubinin, a senior Foreign Ministry official, noted that government agencies took a "most friendly attitude toward Faymonville." Back in Washington, Roosevelt decided that he wanted someone to run the embassy who would receive the same kind of praise. By late 1936, he had found his man: Joseph Davies, who would quickly embrace Faymonville as an ally and radically change the tenor of the mission's reporting from Moscow.

A presidential friend, golf partner and—thanks to his second wife, General Foods heiress Marjorie Merriweather Post—major campaign contributor, Davies had no Russian expertise. This suited Stalin's team just fine. Foreign Minister Litvinov was cheered by the report from the Soviet ambassador in Washington that "Davies understands nothing about our affairs but that he is full of the most sincere desire to work with us in complete co-operation and to carry out strictly Roosevelt's instructions."

To Kennan and others at the embassy, all of this was distressing news. "Had the President wished to slap us down and to mock us for our efforts in the development of Soviet-American relations, he could not have done better with this appointment," Kennan stated. Along with several of his colleagues, Kennan briefly considered resigning in protest, but they backed off, feeling that the new man had to be given a chance to prove himself. Nonetheless, Davies recognized from the start that he faced internal opposition. While praising Kennan's performance in a report to the State Department, he engineered his transfer to Washington by arguing that he had been in Moscow "too long for his own good."

From the vantage point of the Kremlin, Davies was a dream ambassador—someone who was blind to what was happening right in front of him and willing, even eager, to accept the most transparently absurd rationalizations of the regime for its actions. His observations about the Soviet leaders were nothing short of fawning. "Stalin is a very strong, able man who is practical, with a lot of common sense and wisdom," he wrote in his diary on March 11, 1937. "Molotov is an exceptional man with great mental capacity and wisdom." In a letter to his daughter on June 9, 1938, as he was preparing to leave Moscow, he continued in that vein. "He [Stalin] has a sly humor. He has a very great mentality. It is sharp, shrewd, and above all things else, wise, at least so it would appear to me. If you can picture a personality that is exactly opposite to what the most rabid anti-Stalinist anywhere could conceive, then you might picture this man."

Davies attended many of the most infamous purge trials, sending reports to Washington that varied only slightly from the Soviet propaganda accounts of those events. Reporting to Secretary Hull about the trial of Bukharin and other top Bolshevik leaders, he wrote, "It is my opinion so far as the political defendants are concerned sufficient crimes under Soviet law, among those charged in the indictment, were established by the proof and beyond a reasonable doubt to justify the verdict of guilty of treason and the adjudication of the punishment provided by the Soviet criminal statutes." In other words, Stalin's regime was perfectly justified in executing them.

In an earlier message to Hull about the execution of Marshal Tukhachevsky and other Red Army generals, Davies asserted that most of Moscow's diplomatic corps was convinced "that the accused must have been guilty of an offense which in the Soviet Union would merit the death penalty." And he concluded: "The Stalin regime, politically and internally, is probably stronger than heretofore. All potential opposition has been killed off."

In fact, many other diplomats were far less credulous about the Soviet rationalizations of the wave of executions and were startled by Davies' behavior. A German embassy staffer recalled that even his country's ambassador, Count von der Schulenburg, felt "indignation and bewilderment" when he heard about Davies' attendance at the show trials. Charles Bohlen, who had returned to the American embassy after a stint in Washington, was appalled by Davies' reports and tried to fathom his motives. "He ardently desired to make a success of a pro-Soviet line and was probably reflecting the views of some of Roosevelt's advisers to enhance his political standing at home," he wrote. And while Davies was claiming that Stalin was strengthening his country, Bohlen came to the opposite conclusion. "I could not understand why Stalin chose, at a time when the Soviet Union was imperiled by both Germany and Japan, to wreck the structure of officialdom that he had erected and to destroy the leadership of the Red Army."

As Bohlen bitterly noted, Davies never asked him his opinion of the trials, preferring instead to confer with Colonel Faymonville, the military attaché who would invariably confirm the Soviet version of events, and with those American correspondents who were of a similar inclination. His clear favorite among them was Walter Duranty, the Pulitzer Prize–winning *New York Times* reporter who denied the existence of the Ukrainian famine during the forced collectivization campaign and routinely served as an unabashed apologist for Stalin. "I shall always feel under a special obligation to Walter Duranty who told the truth as he saw it and has the eyes of genius," Davies wrote in his diary.

When he published his book *Mission to Moscow* shortly after the Germans launched their attack against the Soviet Union, Davies felt more than ever impelled to offer a benign explanation of all Soviet behavior. "In my opinion, the Russian people, the Soviet government, and the Soviet leaders are moved, basically, by altruistic concepts," he wrote. "It is their purpose to promote the brotherhood of man and to improve the lot of the common people. They wish to create a society in which men may live as equals, governed by ethical ideals. They are devoted to peace." Since he believed almost everything his Soviet hosts had told him, he also accepted their assurances that the country was ready to defend itself. "It is my judgment that both the Soviet government and its army are a great deal stronger than is generally recognized in certain European quarters," he wrote to Roosevelt on January 18, 1939, from his new posting as the ambassador in Brussels.

As for the impact of the army purges, he wrote after the Germans invaded: "There were no Fifth Columnists in Russia in 1941—they had shot them. The purge had cleansed the country and rid it of treason."

On September 7, 1939, just a few days after Germany had invaded Poland to start World War II, a new military attaché arrived to take up his post at the American embassy in Moscow. His name was Ivan Yeaton. This army major arrived with a set of assumptions about the Soviet Union opposite to the ones Davies and Faymonville had subscribed to. His initial experiences only reinforced his conviction that Stalin's Russia was a sinister, violent netherworld. Yeaton had barely unpacked, he recalled in his unpublished memoir, when the Red Army attacked Poland from the east and the Polish military attaché showed up at his door. "We are ordered to evacuate the embassy within hours and allowed to take only one suitcase," the Pole explained. "I have been warned that as soon as I leave the embassy for good I will be arrested and eventually shot. Therefore, I must escape. It will cost a lot of money; so I will appreciate it if you will buy any or all of my household equipment at your own price."

Yeaton offered him the cash he had available by buying his wine cellar at a dollar a bottle and never saw his Polish counterpart again, although he later heard that the NKVD was searching for him in Kiev. Recalling the fate of thousands of Polish officers who were shot the following year in the Katyn forest, the American pointed out, "He had nothing to lose by making a desperate attempt to escape." And Yeaton was quick to register what was happening to others whose countries were falling under Soviet rule. "The wife of the Latvian ambassador, a delightful, gracious and charming hostess, who had had servants all her life, was seen with a group of women prisoners waiting to be crowded into an empty box car attached to a train heading east," he wrote.

Properly suspicious, Yeaton immediately fired his young Russian driver, who was "a little too cocksure of himself." Two weeks later, Yeaton encountered him on the street in the uniform of a NKVD captain, commanding the four "guards" who were assigned to follow him day and night. "He laughed in my face," Yeaton noted.

There was nothing the new attaché could do about that, but he was determined to follow a very different routine from Faymonville's, whose quarters he had inherited. He scorned his predecessor's "dependence on Soviet hand-outs" and sought out military attachés from other embassies who were similarly critical. "The one thing that opened other doors for me was the unanimous dislike and fear of communism on the part of all missions in Moscow," he asserted. That kind of observation gave the impression that he was reporting from a different capital than the one Davies and Faymonville had inhabited.

Yeaton also waged a campaign to tighten security at the embassy. He noted that many consulate clerks gave cocktail parties that were replete with young Russian women "generously provided" by the NKVD. "These 'party girls' were well-trained linguists and informers known in intelligence circles as 'pigeons,'" he pointed out. "Having attended a few of these parties, I was amazed at the freedom with which these lads discussed embassy affairs before the pigeons." He made one other observation: "It also became obvious, at least to me, that there were homosexuals in the group. From the security point of view, this was a dangerous situation." Without informing his colleagues, he urged the F.B.I. to send "an expert on homosexuality" to Moscow. An agent arrived for a visit, and, as Yeaton recorded with satisfaction, "a week or so later we had a small group of bachelors ordered home."

Such actions didn't exactly make Yeaton a popular figure at the embassy, even among those diplomats who shared his bleak view of their surroundings. But the new ambassador, Laurence Steinhardt, was quickly coming to appreciate those members of his staff who displayed none of the kind of willful blindness that Davies and Faymonville had exhibited.

A lawyer firmly established in New York's wealthy Jewish community who had already served as ambassador to Sweden, Steinhardt was a liberal Democrat with—from Roosevelt's perspective—excellent family connections. His uncle Samuel Untermeyer was a major campaign contributor who was openly sympathetic to the Soviet Union. When he appointed Steinhardt to the Moscow post, the president clearly believed he'd be more in the Davies than the Bullitt tradition. But, as Yeaton observed, Steinhardt soon proved "ready to stand up to Soviet obstruction tactics when necessary." As soon as the new envoy began displaying those tendencies, Soviet officials derided him in typically virulent terms. Konstantin Umansky, the Soviet ambassador in Washington, reported that Steinhardt was "a wealthy bourgeoisie Jew who was permeated with the foul smell of Zionism."

Steinhardt quickly became irritated by the routine harassment of diplomats in Moscow—the constant surveillance and climate of suspicion and the Soviet practice of making daily life as difficult and full of restrictions and bureaucratic regulations as possible. Like Bullitt, he began pushing for an American policy of reciprocity, proposing that the State Department should treat Soviet diplomats in Washington the same way and in general taking the approach that American behavior should respond in kind to Soviet actions. Although he had rejected such recommendations before, Roosevelt appeared to change his mind after the series of Soviet actions following the Molotov-Ribbentrop pact—the invasion of Poland and the takeover of the Baltic states and then the attack on Finland. "I think we should match every Soviet annoyance by a similar annoyance here against them," he told Hull and Under Secretary of State Sumner Welles in December 1940.

Despite the restrictions, Yeaton moved around as much as he could, carefully observing what was happening. He would take long walks, and in the early months of 1940 noted that as more Soviet men were called up for military service, "more and more women and boys replaced able-bodied men workers." One day an experimental fighter plane, with its designer aboard, disintegrated as it flew almost right over him. The police quickly cordoned off the wreckage, and the Foreign Office replied to Yeaton's inquiries by claiming no such accident had happened. But a few days later the Soviet press reported that the designer had died, making it sound like it was from natural causes.

On June 18, 1941, Yeaton spotted a German diplomat loading his two prize boxer dogs on a plane to Germany. This prompted him to cable Washington that Hitler would strike "within days." When the attack came, Yeaton's driver was called up, so he was allowed to drive on his own. And he quickly discovered that his bodyguards had disappeared as well. This was a result of the desperate need for manpower, not any Soviet shift in policy, but Yeaton decided to exploit the situation as much as he could. He soon collected more than a half dozen militia citations for violating the wartime rules, including driving at night and trying to slip out of the city, making for the fighting to the west. By comparing his impressions with those of other foreigners in the capital and the accounts of refugees fleeing the fighting, he put together highly pessimistic assessments of the Soviet Union's chances of holding off the Germans. "If my reports appeared to follow the German propaganda line more closely than the Soviet releases, I was unaware of it, and I could find no shred of evidence on which to base an optimistic report," he recalled later.

But it was more than Yeaton's pessimism about the military situation that would get him in trouble. After all, his view that the Red Army couldn't withstand the German assault wasn't uncommon. It was the combination of that pessimism with his instinctive aversion to Stalin's regime that pushed him to oppose the policies that would quickly be championed by Churchill and Roosevelt in response to the German attack on the Soviet Union. In those summer months of 1941, those policies became a matter of both public and very personal disputes.

On the night before the German invasion, Churchill hosted a dinner at his country retreat, Chequers, for Foreign Secretary Eden, Cabinet Secretary Edward Bridges, U.S. Ambassador John Winant, and their wives. The British leader declared that the invasion of the Soviet Union was now certain and that Hitler was hoping that he could count on garnering support from right-wingers in both Britain and the United States for that action. The German dictator would be proven wrong, Churchill assured his guests, and Britain would do everything possible to help Russia in this conflict. Winant quickly added that this certainly would be true for his country also.

After dinner, Churchill and his personal secretary, John Colville, took a walk on the croquet lawn and picked up on the same theme. Colville asked him whether, as a staunch anti-communist, he wasn't troubled by the notion of helping the Kremlin. "Not at all," Churchill replied. "I have only one purpose, the destruction of

Hitler, and my life is much simplified thereby. If Hitler invaded Hell, I would make at least a favorable reference to the Devil in the House of Commons."

Woken at four the next morning with the news about the German attack, Churchill prepared a radio address that he broadcast on the BBC that evening. It would prove to be one of his most memorable orations, pledging his nation to a fight for total victory against Hitler. "We shall fight him by land, we shall fight him by sea, we shall fight him in the air, until, with God's help, we have rid the earth of his shadow and liberated its people from his yoke," he said. Declaring that "any man or state who fights on against Nazism will have our aid," he added, "It follows, therefore, that we shall give whatever help we can to Russia and the Russian people. We shall appeal to all our friends and allies in every part of the world to take the same course and pursue it, as we shall faithfully and steadfastly to the end."

Churchill hadn't forgotten the Kremlin's earlier behavior or talked himself into believing that Stalin suddenly would be an ideal partner. Writing about Hitler's invasion of Russia, he noted, "Thus the ravings of hatred against Britain and the United States which the Soviet propaganda machine cast upon the midnight air were overwhelmed at dawn by the German cannonade. The wicked are not always clever, nor are dictators always right." But even the canny British prime minister probably didn't realize just how much time, energy, and frustration would go into nurturing the relationship with the dictator who was now his ally.

Right from the start, Stalin and his entourage frequently ignored their new Western allies or were downright dismissive of them. Churchill was stunned that his emotional radio speech of June 22 in support of the embattled Soviet Union at first met with no reaction from the Kremlin. Finding that silence "oppressive," Churchill wrote to Stalin on July 7 again promising as much help as possible to Russia. It wasn't until July 18, nearly four weeks after Churchill's speech, that Stalin wrote the prime minister to thank him for those assurances of support. But that first letter also contained a demand that the Kremlin would consistently push from then on: the establishment of a second front against Hitler in the West—in other words, sending British troops to the Continent to fight the Germans there.

Churchill responded with barely concealed impatience that his country was in no position to launch an attack on the Continent at that time. "You must remember that we have been fighting alone for more than a year, and that, though our resources are growing and will grow fast from now on, we are at the utmost strain both at home and in the Middle East," he explained. A steady stream of demands and complaints from the Soviet side would follow, and, as Churchill put it, "I received many rebuffs and rarely a kind word." He added, "The Soviet government had the impression that they were conferring a great favor on us by fighting in their own country for their own lives."

Though Churchill found himself struggling to keep his irritation in check, he faced little internal opposition to his policy of providing aid to the Russians. Across the Atlantic, Roosevelt had also offered "all the aid we possibly can to Russia," but there were public and private dissenting voices. Former president Herbert Hoover warned that "we find ourselves promising aid to Stalin and his militant conspiracy against the whole democratic ideals of the world" and that if the United States entered the war and helped make a Soviet victory possible, this would facilitate Stalin's expansionist ambitions. Senator Harry Truman came up with what sounded like a more coolly calculated approach. "If we see that Germany is winning we ought to help Russia, and if Russia is winning we ought to help Germany, and that way let them kill as many as possible, although I don't want to see Hitler victorious under any circumstances," he declared on the day the Germans attacked the Soviet Union.

Even George Kennan, serving at that time in the American embassy in Berlin, wrote to Loy Henderson, a former Moscow colleague now back in the State Department, to warn that "we should do nothing at home to make it appear that we are following the course Churchill seems to have entered upon in extending moral support to the Russian cause." He argued that Russia had "no claim on Western sympathies," since it clearly wasn't fighting for the same ideals as the West. "Such a view would not preclude the extension of material aid wherever called for by our own self-interest," he concluded. "It would, however, preclude anything which might identify us politically or ideologically with the Russian war effort."

Other government and military officials had a purely practical concern. Did it make sense to send military and other aid to the Soviet Union if, as many were predicting, it wouldn't be able to hold out anyway? If the pessimists proved right, the Germans would seize those supplies as soon as they completed their conquest.

But Roosevelt and his closest aides had no intention of accepting such advice. In fact, they would soon outdo Churchill and his team in lavishing praise on Russia for its war effort and adopt a see-no-evil approach that precluded any real consideration of extracting concessions from Stalin in return for aid. In theory and practice, it quickly became apparent that Roosevelt viewed Russia as an ally worthy of unconditional support. Steinhardt's notion of reciprocity in relations, which the president had briefly endorsed, was unmistakably trumped by the new policy.

The point man for that policy was Harry Hopkins, one of the president's closest advisers, whose pro-Soviet tilt had already attracted the notice of Moscow. In mid-July, Hopkins was dispatched to London for consultations with Churchill about how to deliver on the promise of aid to Russia, and the prime minister introduced him to Soviet ambassador Maisky. The Russian envoy was elated by Hopkins' "obvious sympathy for the Soviet Union" and came away convinced that he was "much more sympathetic" to Soviet needs than Churchill was. In his memoirs, Maisky wrote, "Harry Hopkins has remained as one of the most advanced people among the leading personalities in the bourgeois world during the second world war."

Hopkins was closely attuned to the thinking of former ambassador Joseph Davies, who was still acting as Roosevelt's adviser on Russia and dining regularly with Soviet ambassador Umansky in Washington. Not surprisingly, Davies was a fervent advocate of aid to Russia and, reflecting the Kremlin's official line, he sought to accent the positive even during the first weeks of Operation Barbarossa, when the Red Army was suffering major losses. In a "My dear Harry" letter to Hopkins on July 18, Davies declared, "The resistance of the Russian army has been more effective than was generally expected." At the same time, he argued that the Russians would continue to resist even if the Germans occupied much of their territory. All of which meant that no matter how bad the military situation looked, Western aid to Russia wouldn't be in vain.

It was no accident that Davies' favorite former military attaché re-emerged onto the scene at the same time. After Colonel Faymonville had returned from Moscow, the War Department had effectively banished him because of his reputation as an apologist for Stalin's regime. But on July 13, he was assigned to Washington's Division of Aid Reports, which oversaw Lend-Lease, the military aid program that, up to that point, was channeling supplies to Britain. While the formal head of this operation was General James Burns, this was Hopkins' bailiwick. Faymonville was assigned to helping get the Russian aid program going, and he did so with his usual enthusiasm.

When a Soviet military mission arrived on July 26, he served as their escort around Washington as they pressed their hosts for quick action. Faymonville was so eager to accommodate them that he even showed them classified documents. This led to charges that he had violated military regulations. But Hopkins'—and by extension Roosevelt's—backing ensured that no action was taken against him. In fact, he would soon be given broader responsibilities for the Russian program.

At about the same time, Hopkins left London for Moscow. When the RAF flew him as far as Archangel, he got a first taste of official Soviet hospitality: a four-hour "monumental" meal, with multiple courses featuring cold fish and caviar, and the inevitable vodka toasts. "Vodka has authority," Hopkins reported later. "It is nothing for the amateur to trifle with." Then, after only two hours' sleep, it was off to Moscow, where he was met by Ambassador Steinhardt.

In their first conversations, Hopkins wanted to know whether Steinhardt considered the reports of Major Yeaton, the current military attaché, to be accurate. In other words, was the war going as badly for the Russians as Yeaton maintained? Steinhardt replied that it would be a mistake to underestimate the Russians, since their history indicated that they would defend their homeland. But the ambassador pointed out that it was extremely hard to know where things really stood, since the Kremlin's obsession with secrecy and fear of foreigners meant that all diplomats assigned to Moscow could only piece together fragmentary information and impressions of what was happening.

During Hopkins's three-day visit to Moscow, Stalin offered a personal welcome in several hours of face-to-face talks that left his visitor clearly awed and confident that he had been made privy to inside information. After conveying his messages of support from Roosevelt and Churchill, Hopkins found himself treated to an overview of the military situation and a detailed discussion of what kinds of supplies the Kremlin was looking for. Despite the setbacks his army had suffered, Stalin insisted that the Germans had under-estimated his forces. "Stalin said that his soldiers did not consider the battle lost merely because the Germans at one point and an-other broke through with their mechanized forces," Hopkins later reported. The Soviet leader noted that the German troops were overextended and "even the German tanks run out of petrol."

Most significantly, Stalin's specific requests for supplies such as anti-aircraft guns, machine guns, aluminum for the construction of planes, high-octane airplane fuel, and more than one million rifles indicated he envisaged a long-term war. "Give us anti-aircraft guns and the aluminum and we can fight for three or four years," he told Hopkins. He also claimed that resistance fighters behind German lines were already making life difficult for the invaders. Moreover, Hopkins could see for himself that Moscow was a city well prepared for air raids. It was blacked out completely at night, and when German bombers appeared in the skies, they were met by a hail of anti-aircraft fire.

Stalin argued that the United States would eventually find it necessary to join in the fight against Hitler, and he told his visitor to convey the message to Roosevelt that he would welcome Ameri-can troops under their own command on the Russian front. As a surprised Hopkins noted in his report, "I told him that I doubted that our Government, in event of war, would want an American army in Russia but that I would give his message to the President." The Soviet authorities' consistent refusal to allow Yeaton and other military attachés to visit the front, let alone participate in any action there, suggested that Stalin was simply throwing out this offer for dramatic effect.

Hopkins was impressed as much by Stalin's delivery and appear-ance as by his message. "He talked as he knew his troops were shooting—straight and hard," he recalled later. He described the Soviet leader as "an austere, rugged, determined figure in boots that shone like mirrors, stout baggy trousers, and snug-fitting blouse. He wore no ornament, military or civilian. He's built close to the ground, like a football coach's dream of a tackle.... His hands are huge, as hard as his mind."

Little wonder, then, that Hopkins had no patience for Major Yeaton, the military attaché who had been sending reports predicting a Soviet defeat, when they ran into each other over breakfast at the embassy. The visitor promptly told Yeaton that he was convinced that the Soviet Union would prevail in the conflict, and that the United States would provide it with "all possible" military and economic aid. This assistance, he added, would never be used as a bargaining chip.

Yeaton was dismayed. Alluding to Hopkins's poor health, he wrote later, "His enthusiasm to get us involved in this war and his readiness to negotiate with Stalin on an 'I trust you' basis gave me reasons to question whether or not his illness had affected his mind." Facing Hopkins, Yeaton launched into his counterarguments, explaining his far more pessimistic view of the military situation and the nature of Stalin's regime. "When I impugned the integrity and methods of Stalin, he [Hopkins] could stand it no longer and shut me up with an intense, 'I don't care to discuss the subject further,'" Yeaton reported.

The next morning, Yeaton tried to patch things up. He apologized to Hopkins for upsetting him and requested his help. If the United States and the Soviet Union were to be allies, he explained, it was important for him to be allowed to move about freely to assess the military situation. In other words, the Kremlin should be told to stop restricting the movements of Western military attachés. As Yeaton reported it, Hopkins responded with "a cold, emphatic 'no.'" There could be no more convincing evidence that Hopkins meant it when he told Yeaton that American assistance would never be used as leverage with the Russians, even on such procedural matters. Aid would be truly unconditional.

It wasn't just the Americans who were split in their predictions about whether the Soviet Union could withstand the German invaders. In dispatches that were intercepted by the NKVD, two of Japan's military attachés stationed in Moscow were delivering diametrically opposite assessments to their superiors in Tokyo. Back in April, Colonel Michitake Yamaoka, the senior attaché, was predicting a summer invasion, and he was convinced that the Germans would be victorious by the end of the year. A Japanese newspaper correspondent who was in close contact with Yamaoka wrote in his diary on July 19, "The fate of Moscow will be resolved within the week." On August 11, he predicted, "Moscow should fall in early September."

But Captain Takeda Yamaguchi, the naval attaché, reported on August 11 that the Germans' initial goal of achieving victory within two months was unrealistic. "If the war is conducted according to such plans, it will undoubtedly be lost and we should probably expect an extremely dangerous situation in the future," he wrote to the Ministry of the Navy. The result, he predicted, would be a protracted war. Reporting on the German drive from the south against Moscow in September, he added that the Red Army had been "pretty successful" in inflicting losses on the enemy, particularly on General Guderian's units.

This was a far from academic debate. Japan and the Soviet Union had signed a five-year neutrality pact in April 1941, but Stalin was worried that Japan might decide to attack from the east, especially if the Germans looked as though they were about to score a swift victory. From inside the German Embassy in Tokyo, Soviet master spy Richard Sorge was reporting persistent German pressure on the Japanese to join the fighting. On July 1, Foreign Minister Ribbentrop had argued in a cable to his Japanese counterpart that "the impending collapse of Russia's main military power and thereby presumably of the Bolshevik regime itself offers the Japanese the unique opportunity" to seize Vladivostok and then keep going. "The goal of these operations," Ribbentrop added, "should be to have the Japanese Army in its march to the west meet the German troops advancing to the east halfway even before the cold season sets in."

That was a case of rhetorical overkill, since not even Germany's top generals envisaged such a meeting of the two armies, which would have required both to advance thousands of miles before the winter. But the idea was to entice Tokyo to strike. And as long as Japan's intentions remained uncertain, Stalin felt he couldn't afford to redeploy large numbers of troops from the Soviet Far East to help their beleaguered comrades trying to stop the German drive toward Moscow. Thus, Japan was looming larger and larger in the Soviet leader's strategic thinking.

During his Moscow visit, Hopkins had discussed this situation with Molotov. The American reported that, while not expecting an immediate blow, the Soviet foreign minister "felt the Japanese would not hesitate to strike if a propitious time occurred." Molotov told Hopkins that given this uncertainty about Japan's intentions, he hoped that Roosevelt might warn the Japanese that any such action would prompt the United States to join in the defense of Russia. Hopkins cautiously responded that the U.S. government was monitoring the situation "with great care" but didn't want to be "provocative" in its relations with Japan.

In other ways, however, Roosevelt and his advisers sought to demonstrate that they were responding quickly and positively to Soviet appeals for help. On August 2, Roosevelt wrote a no-nonsense note to Wayne Coy, who had been given oversight of the Soviet aid program while Hopkins was away. The president pointed out that he had complained in the last cabinet meeting that six weeks after the German invasion, the U.S. had done "practically nothing" in terms of actually delivering the supplies the Russians had requested. "Frankly, if I were a Russian I would feel that I had been given the runaround in the United States," he complained. He ordered Coy to "with my full authority, use a heavy hand—act as a burr under the saddle to get things moving." And he concluded with a blunt order: "Step on it!"

At their famous summit at sea from August 9 to 12, Roosevelt and Churchill reviewed the situation in Europe and the Far East and prepared their joint statement of principles known as the Atlantic Charter. Among them were the promises that there would be no territorial changes "that do not accord with the freely expressed wishes of the people concerned" and everyone should be free "to choose the form of government under which they will live."

In theory, those principles should immediately have raised concerns about the Soviet Union's long-term goals, since Stalin was already pushing for acceptance of his country's territorial and political gains that had been made possible by the now defunct Molotov-Ribbentrop pact. But that was hardly the priority at the time. Proceeding from Hopkins's report about his Moscow visit, Roosevelt and Churchill discussed how best to respond to Stalin's requests. They sent him a joint statement on August 14. "We are at the moment cooperating to provide you with the very maximum of supplies that you most urgently need," they assured him. "Already many shiploads have left our shores and more will leave in the immediate future." But they cautioned against grandiose expectations, since the war was taking place on many fronts and they had to allocate their resources carefully. They then proposed sending a high-level British-American delegation to Moscow to work out a detailed joint plan of action to ensure an effective aid program for Russia.

Fearing that Hopkins wasn't up to another trip to Moscow, Roosevelt designated Averell Harriman, chairman of the Union Pacific Railroad, for the mission. Churchill appointed Lord Beaverbrook, the press baron and minister of supply, to represent the British side. While both men would prove to be eager to demonstrate what they could do to help the Soviet war effort, their leaders were already displaying some differences in attitude. Churchill told Beaverbrook, "Your function will be not only to aid the forming of plans to aid Russia, but to make sure we are not bled white in the process."

On the other side of the Atlantic, Roosevelt was more preoccupied with finding ways to present his Russia policy in the best possible light. On September 11, he met Ambassador Umansky and suggested that the Russians could help their cause by publicizing their putative commitment to freedom of religion, since this "might have a very fine educational effect before the next lend-lease bill comes up in Congress." At the same time, Roosevelt wanted to reassure the Russians that the Americans would be coming to Moscow as friends. One key signal was the decision to include Colonel Faymonville, the former military attaché, in Harriman's delegation.

While every bit as committed to providing Stalin with vital military supplies, Churchill was more calculating in his handling of the Soviet leader and not about to allow him or his envoy to browbeat him into decisions that he might regret. On August 29, he wrote

Stalin that in response to ambassador Maisky's pleas for fighter air-craft, forty Hurricanes would reach Murmansk by September 6 and two hundred Tomahawks were also in the works. He offered to send another two hundred Hurricanes, for a total of 440 fighters, "if your pilots could use them effectively." But he warned against unrealistically high expectations since "fighter aircraft are the foundation of our home defense" and were needed in North Africa as well. Politely but firmly, the prime minister was making the point that he had to attend to his country's needs first.

On September 4, Maisky showed up to deliver Stalin's reply, the Soviet leader's "first personal message since July," as Churchill bit-terly noted. Admitting that the position of Soviet forces had "con-siderably deteriorated" in the previous three weeks, Stalin made clear that he considered Churchill's offer insufficient to help slow the German drive deep into his territory. To tip the balance, he de-clared, Britain needed "to establish in the present year a second front somewhere in the Balkans or France, capable of drawing away from the Eastern front thirty or forty divisions," supply the Soviet Union with thirty thousand tons of aluminum by early Octo-ber and provide "a *monthly* minimum of aid" consisting of four hundred planes and five hundred tanks.

Not content to allow Stalin's letter speak for itself, Maisky com-plained that Russia had been under attack for eleven weeks, strug-gling on its own to repel the huge concentration of German forces arrayed against them. Churchill was sympathetic to Russia's plight, but his temper flared when Maisky asked, almost threateningly, how Britain could expect to win the war if it allowed Russia to be defeated. "Remember that only four months ago we in this Island did not know whether you were not coming in against us on the German side," the prime minister replied. "Indeed, we thought it quite likely that you would. Even then we felt quite sure that we would win in the end. We never thought our survival was depen-dent on your action either way. Whatever happens, and whatever you do, you of all people have no right to make reproaches to us."

Maisky backed off. "More calm, please, my dear Mr. Churchill," he pleaded. As the Soviet ambassador recalled, "I began to fear that at the height of his irritation he might say a good deal that was unnecessary."

Stalin didn't help matters by sending a telegram on September 15 with another suggestion. "It seems to me that Great Britain could without risk land in Archangel twenty-six to thirty divisions, or transport them across Iran to the southern regions of the U.S.S.R. In this way there could be established military collaboration between the Soviet and British troops on the territory of the U.S.S.R." Churchill was stunned that Stalin could believe, even for an instant, that Britain was in the position to contemplate such an action. "It is almost incredible that the head of the Russian Government with all the advice of their military experts could have committed himself to such absurdities," the prime minister wrote in his memoirs. "It seemed hopeless to argue with a man thinking in terms of utter unreality."

Later, Maisky showed that he understood the need for the occasional gesture to help keep such tensions in check. When a new edition of *War and Peace* was published, for example, Maisky's wife presented a copy to Mrs. Churchill with the inscription: "1812–1942: We destroyed our enemy then, we shall destroy our enemy also today."

But in the summer of 1941, any sense of confidence that the enemy would be destroyed was hard to find, particularly among Moscow's foreign community. For the Americans, the tenuousness of the situation was brought home by a thousand-pound bomb that exploded only about fifty yards from Spaso House, blowing out almost all the windows of Ambassador Steinhardt's residence. Moscow felt far from safe.

On September 28, the Anglo-American delegation led by Beaverbrook and Harriman arrived in Moscow. Quentin Reynolds, who had tried but failed to get a visa to Russia as a war correspondent, managed to arrange to go in as the mission's press officer. *Collier's Weekly,* his regular employer, had agreed to lend him for the duration. Given the grim news that the Germans were fast approaching Moscow, he wanted to get there any way he could. On the flight over in an army bomber, he sat in the frigid cabin next to Colonel Faymonville. "He was one of the few Americans I had met who doubted the Germans could conquer Russia," he recalled.

While other members of their delegation convened in subcommittees with their Soviet counterparts, Beaverbrook and Harriman met for three consecutive evenings with Stalin, each time for about three hours. At their first meeting, the Soviet leader reviewed the overall military situation, dwelling particularly on the three-to-one or even four-to-one ratio of German to Soviet tanks. Then he went on to provide a wish list of supplies—tanks, anti-tank guns, planes, anti-aircraft guns, even barbed wire. Addressing Beaverbrook, he again raised the possibility of British troops joining Soviet forces in the Ukraine. Like his prime minister, the British envoy offered no encouragement. Harriman tried to raise the issue of religious freedom, noting that it was of concern to the American public, but Stalin hardly bothered to respond. Nonetheless, Harriman and Beaverbrook were pleased with that first session, reporting that it was "extremely friendly."

But the next evening was a different story. "Stalin was very restless, walking around and smoking continuously, and appeared to both of us to be under an intense strain," Beaverbrook recounted. While the two visitors later concluded he must have been preoccupied with the reports indicating that the Germans were about to seize Moscow, they were taken aback by his brusque, seemingly deliberately rude behavior. He picked up the phone and made three calls in their presence, dialing himself. When Beaverbrook handed him a letter from Churchill, Stalin barely glanced at it and left it on the table, ostentatiously ignoring it.

On the issue of supplies, the Soviet leader was more combative than appreciative. "Why is it that the United States can only give me 1,000 tons of armor plate steel for tanks—a country with a production of over 50,000,000 tons?" he demanded of Harriman. When the American tried to explain that it took time to increase capacity for this kind of steel, Stalin shot back, "One only has to add alloys." The one time he appeared grateful was when Harriman offered him 5,000 American jeeps, and he immediately asked if more would be available.

The next day the Germans were proclaiming the talks a failure. Chief propagandist Joseph Goebbels gloated that no agreement was possible between the visitors and the "Bolshevists." But when the downcast duo of Beaverbrook and Harriman arrived at the

Kremlin for their final meeting, Stalin promptly signaled a change in tone. "It is up to the three of us to prove Goebbels a liar," he declared.

Beaverbrook responded by going down the list of supplies requested by the Soviet side, pointing out which ones Britain and the United States could provide quickly and adding some suggestions of their own. While he also indicated which supplies would be harder to get, Stalin was visibly pleased. Maxim Litvinov, the former foreign minister who was serving as the interpreter in the talks, jumped up and exulted: "Now we shall win the war."

The visitors were delighted. "The meeting broke up in the most friendly fashion possible," Harriman reported. "Stalin made no effort to conceal his enthusiasm. It was my impression that he was completely satisfied that Great Britain and America meant business." Beaverbrook observed the Soviet leader carefully, even noting that his doodling habits included "drawing numberless pictures of wolves on paper and filling in the background with red pencil" while Litvinov translated his remarks. Speaking for both himself and Harriman, the British visitor offered his conclusions about Stalin. "We have got to like him; a kindly man, with a habit, when agitated, of walking about the floor with his hands behind his back," he declared. "He smoked a great deal and practically never shows any impatience at all." It was as if they were so relieved to find a more cordial Stalin at their final meeting that they had banished any memory of the boorish Stalin they had seen earlier.

But others in the delegation were more observant and less prone to see only what they wanted to see. General Hastings Ismay, who headed the British military contingent, noted that Stalin "moved stealthily like a wild animal in search of prey, and his eyes were shrewd and full of cunning. He never looked one in the face. But he had great dignity and his personality was dominating. As he entered the room, every Russian face froze into silence, and the hunted look in the eyes of the generals showed all too plainly the constant fear in which they lived. It was nauseating to see brave men reduced to such abject servility."

Reynolds, the American correspondent who was serving as the press officer for the mission, was stunned for a completely different reason when he saw Stalin coming to greet Beaverbrook and Harri-

man. From the Soviet leader's pictures, Reynolds had expected someone "huge, forbidding, surly." Instead, "the rather bowlegged little
man who walked toward us, his face a broad grin when he caught
sight of Beaverbrook and Harriman, was a shattering contradiction
of the public image," he recalled. "I gather that he wore elevator
shoes." Reynolds quoted a British correspondent as saying, "He looks
like the kindly Italian gardener you have in twice a week."

At the farewell banquet in the Kremlin, the Brits and Americans
were treated to a veritable feast, as Reynolds carefully noted, "a
twenty-three course orgy," featuring caviar in huge bowls, mush-
rooms sautéed in sour cream, sturgeon in champagne sauce, and
pilaf of quail. All this was accompanied by endless vodka toasts,
with glasses instantly refilled from carafes of different varieties of
the liquor. "Feasting thus, I found it a little difficult to remember
that the Germans were now less than a hundred miles from
Moscow—or to recall the lines of the hungry of this classless society
doubtless even now waiting at the doors of food stores," Reynolds
wrote. Stalin may not have awed him, but the surreal scene made
him wonder if this was a modern-day instance of the emperor fiddling while Rome burned.

The American newsman stayed behind in Moscow after the rest
of the delegation left, fulfilling his wish to see what would happen
next in the Soviet capital. He wasn't the only person who didn't
catch the flight back. Hopkins had quietly arranged for Faymonville to stay behind so that he could handle the Lend-Lease program in Russia. This amounted to an end run around Ambassador
Steinhardt and other embassy staffers, who viewed the military officer as in the pocket of the Russians. They protested this action to
no avail. Roosevelt, Hopkins, and Harriman all wanted someone in
that post who would please the Kremlin, and they now had their
man in place.

No one was more incensed by that maneuver than Yeaton, who
charged that Faymonville "was irrefutably a captive of the NKVD."
Yeaton was equally scathing in his denunciation of "Harriman's ob-
sequious attitude towards Stalin." But his main concern was judging how quickly the Germans would succeed in taking Moscow,
which he increasingly was convinced was inevitable. While militia
units and whatever workers could still be found dug trenches and

set up tank traps on the outskirts of the city, Yeaton concluded, "It was an even question which would arrive first—the Germans or the first snow storms of the season."

On October 14, Yeaton decided to spend the night at the embassy dacha, eleven miles from the city on the Smolensk highway. "My morale was low and I needed country air," he recalled. He awakened the next morning to artillery fire, and when he looked out the window, he saw Red Army soldiers setting up machine guns in the front yard. He was convinced that this was the end. "I knew I would never see the place again," he wrote.

By the time he returned to Spaso House on October 15, that view was virtually unanimous among the assembled Americans. Ambassador Steinhardt had already sent his wife to safety in Sweden, and the purpose of the gathering was to discuss evacuation procedures for everyone else. According to Charles Thayer, one of the original Russia hands at the embassy, Yeaton predicted that the capital would only hold out for another thirty-six hours. Even Faymonville, as Thayer recalled, "now had completely lost his nerve and gave them only five hours more before the Germans would arrive." During this discussion, Molotov summoned Steinhardt to the Kremlin and issued him instructions to evacuate all Americans to Kuibyshev, the Volga city about six hundred miles away that was supposed to serve as the new base for the government once the capital fell.

Molotov told Steinhardt and Cripps, the British ambassador, who had also been summoned, "The fight for Moscow will continue and the fight to defeat Hitler will become more furious." But when both ambassadors asked to stay in the capital as long as he and Stalin were there, Molotov refused, telling them that he and Stalin would join them in Kuibyshev in a day or two. The message seemed clear: the fight for Moscow would continue from outside Moscow.

Steinhardt returned to Spaso House and told his staffers the news that they all had to assemble at the Kazansky Station for an evening train. He delivered the same message to the American correspondents, telling them that, along with their censors, they would be leaving, too. "You have no discretion in the matter," he declared.

After hours of milling about the station, the assembled foreigners—diplomats and journalists from all the countries represented in the Soviet capital—boarded a train consisting of thirty-three coaches and one locomotive "that seemed to tire frequently," as Reynolds put it. The diplomats traveled in the "soft" cars, and the journalists in the "hard" cars, but the five-day, snail-paced ride wasn't comfortable for anybody. The drinking water supply gave out on the first day, and only some of the cars were heated. But the good news for Moscow was that it began to snow on October 16. "It turned into a five-day blizzard and was the best defense Moscow had," Yeaton noted.

When the exhausted foreigners got their first glimpse of their new home—a dreary Volga city that nonetheless startled them with its twinkling evening lights, since it was far enough east not to require the blackouts that had been the norm in Moscow—they saw little reason to believe that anything would stop the Germans from seizing the capital. After all, Molotov had all but conceded that it was about to fall. As represented by those diplomats and journalists, the world was still watching but finding it increasingly difficult to cling to the slim hope that any other outcome was still possible.

7

Panic in Moscow

If there's one overarching theme in the official accounts of the Great Patriotic War, it's that the Russian people never wavered in their fight against the German invaders, no matter how desperate their situation or how great the sacrifices demanded of them. They believed, so those versions tell us, in the justice of their cause and the inevitability of victory, however long it would take. In short, heroic patriotism was the order of the day. But no single day shatters that myth more decisively than October 16, 1941.

Just as the foreign diplomats and journalists were pulling out of the Soviet capital, the city erupted in panic. It was a panic that Soviet historians were eager to forget, which goes a long way toward explaining why their accounts of the battle for Moscow are so often abbreviated and full of glaring omissions and distortions. No sleight of hand can reconcile those two versions of events—the highly sanitized ones and the reality of the sudden breakdown of law and order, which included looting, strikes, and other previously unimaginable acts of outright defiance of the regime, which played itself out at a moment when most Muscovites were convinced that their city was about to be taken over by the Germans.

The city wasn't united; it was divided and perilously close to spinning out of control.

"A threat hangs over Moscow and our country," *Izvestia* proclaimed that day. "As always, the Soviet people look danger straight in the eye." Not quite, since there was a rush for the exits from the Soviet capital. While there was an official evacuation of top government and Party officials, key factories and other installations deemed essential to the continuation of the regime, many of the city's inhabitants fled on their own. Here the registration statistics tell the story. On January 1, 1941, Moscow's population was 4,216,000. With refugees from other regions more than making up for those leaving the city, it had increased to 4,236,000 by September. But from then on, the capital's population began dropping dramatically—to 3,148,000 in October and, by January 1942, to only 2,028,000.

On October 16, the rush to leave was close to a stampede. Dmitry Safonov, who was working at an artillery factory near Moscow that was to be evacuated to the Urals, had just returned to the city to collect some belongings and was startled by what he saw. "All of Moscow seemed to be streaming out somewhere," he recalled. Cars and trucks were loaded down with personal belongings, while many of the people rushing about on the street "didn't seem to know where to go or what to do." Some claimed to have already seen Germans inside the city. At the railroad station where he hoped to catch a train, Safonov saw suitcases, bags, clothes, lamps, even a piano, all abandoned by those who were trying or had managed to board anything that was moving out. The train platforms were jammed with people. Compared to his visit less than two weeks before, "I hardly recognized the city," he said.

While ordinary citizens fought to get any place they could on a train, even if that meant abandoning their personal belongings, Party bigwigs and factory managers vociferously argued with train dispatchers that they should be allowed to take as much as they wanted. "They tried to take pianos, tables, sofas and other furniture with them," F. Rostovtsev, the chief of the Leninskaya Station, who was the chief dispatcher for all the trains involved in the evacuation from October 14 to 16, recalled. "They demanded 'Supply more wagons for me, my wife and whoever else.'" He added that the train crews had to ignore those incessant demands and force the evacuees to "curb their appetites."

On the roads heading east, there was usually no one to keep any semblance of order, since the normally ubiquitous police had largely disappeared. Quite a few of the seemingly lucky Muscovites who had cars to take them out of the city were in for a nasty surprise. "Some people stopped automobiles driving on the highway," G. V. Reshetin, an art editor, wrote. "They pulled the drivers and passengers out of the cars, beat them and threw their belongings to the ground." Some of the attackers would pile into the cars themselves, while others appeared to be joining in out of sheer vindictiveness. Reshetin witnessed a crowd yelling "Kill the Jews" before they attacked a car carrying an elderly man and a young woman with bundles of documents. Both were pulled out of the car. The man was hit repeatedly, and his face was bleeding. The young woman tried to defend him, shouting he wasn't Jewish and they were simply transporting the documents—to no avail. Although Reshetin had witnessed minor anti-Semitic incidents before, he was "shocked" by the violence of this episode.

Almost everywhere, it seemed, normal rules no longer applied and normal services could no longer be taken for granted. Movie theaters were suddenly all closed for "renovation," the metro stopped running, and those trams that were still operating often failed to stop since they were so crammed with people. Slava Yeremko, who was fourteen at the time, remembers the strange sight of the state bank next to her apartment building. "There was nobody in the bank—the doors were open and there was money on the floor." Large groups were streaming by, on their way to the Belorussky train station, seemingly oblivious to the bank and the money strewn about.

Yuliy Labas, who was only eight, recalls going out with his mother in search of milk. He was already accustomed to the sight of blimps in the air with dangling nets that were meant to entrap German planes, but now he looked up and saw something new. There was black smoke rising from the chimney of the NKVD headquarters on Lubyanka Square, which was right next to where he lived, and black snow on the ground. "They must have been burning papers," he said.

Not far away from her apartment near the Central Committee building, Ella Braginskaya, who was fifteen, also saw dark ashes and partially burnt papers swirling in the air and people looting the shops in the neighborhood. "Most of the looters were women, not men," she said. Looters attacked shops in other parts of the city as well, although other eyewitnesses don't mention a preponderance of women among them. While shops with food that had been rationed up to that point were the main targets, nothing was off limits anymore, including the apartments of those Muscovites who had already left. Looters also attacked the now empty British Embassy.

Valeria Prokhorova, at the time a twenty-two-year-old graduate of the Institute of Foreign Languages, remembers the looting and another common sight. "People were dumping communist literature and portraits of the party leaders," she said. In fact, Muscovites were ridding their apartments and offices of the obligatory pictures of Stalin and Lenin along with the volumes of Marx and other communist literature. Garbage bins were overflowing with this detritus of Stalin's regime, which no one would have dared to throw away at any other time. Many did so out of fear that the Germans, whom they were expecting any moment, would identify them as communists. But some Muscovites vented their pent-up anger. Prokhorova heard people cursing Stalin. "We suffered from hunger and they kept telling us that we are living in the richest country," she quoted them as saying. "What about now? Where is Stalin? He's abandoned us."

Tamara Bylinina, the young widow of a military officer who had been executed during the purges a few years earlier, was digging trenches with other women on the outskirts of Moscow when word spread that the Germans were closing in. The women rushed back to the city, and Bylinina reached her communal apartment, which she shared with about a dozen other people. The portraits of Stalin and Lenin were gone from the walls, and someone had incinerated a twelve-volume collection of Lenin's speeches and writings. "People were scared that the Germans could execute them for worshipping those idols," she explained.

But that fear was mixed with visible elation and occasionally eagerness to welcome anyone who would rid the Kremlin of its current rulers. "Good, they've sucked enough of our blood," one of her neighbors told her. Having heard that Hitler supposedly had said he wanted to drink tea in Moscow, some of her neighbors had set up samovars on their tables. "It was done to greet the Germans," she said.

Ella Braginskaya, the fifteen-year-old who lived near the Central Committee building, recalls that she was worried that her neighbors might see a German occupation as a good chance to settle scores. Her Jewish mother was highly unpopular, she pointed out, as much because of her "arrogance"—she'd tell her daughter that she was from much too good a family to play with the children of the proletariat—as because of her religion. Ella's best friend was a girl named Valya, the daughter of a communist official. As the Germans drew closer to Moscow, Ella would be greeted by catcalls when she walked through her building's courtyard. "You're living your last days," they'd say. "Soon the Germans will come and kill you and Valya."

Not everyone acted this way. At least one neighbor, a woman who lived on the ground floor, vowed to help Ella and her mother. "The Germans are decent people," she assured the mother. "We'll dig a cellar and you'll hide there and later everything will be all right."

And even as countless Muscovites fled to the east, others were still leaving for the front to try to stop the Germans from taking the city. During the chaos of October 16, Valeria Prokhorova and several friends went to the Belorussky Station to bid farewell to two volunteers going off to fight—Aleksandr Aniks, her favorite teacher from her language institute, and Grisha, the husband of her neighbor. They rushed in the dark through the cold snow mixed with rain, carrying a food parcel that they had managed to pull together from their meager rations. At the station, they found the train and, since it was pitch dark, they ran up and down the track, shouting "Grisha! Aleksandr!"

Miraculously, they located the two men, hugged them, and gave them the food. The neighbor kissed her husband good-bye. When the train began to pull away, the teacher shouted, "Girls, tell everybody that we will defend our country. We will protect you!" This could have been a scene from a propaganda movie—except for one thing. "He never said anything about Stalin," Prokhorova noted. "He left to fight for his country."

When the young women began making their way back home, Prokhorova recalled, the streets were filled with "criminals and drunks" and there were no police in sight. "It felt like doomsday," she said.

Standing between the German troops and Moscow, soldiers such as Albert Tsessarsky knew they weren't well equipped to prevent doomsday from happening. A medical student who had volunteered for service after the Germans attacked, Tsessarsky was assigned to a thirty-three-man unit whose main weapon was a broken machine gun that they couldn't make operable. At the beginning of October, the unit was deployed west of Moscow near Mozhaisk, a town at the center of the defense line about sixty miles from the capital. By that time, they had a functioning machine gun, which they set up to face the Germans, who were arrayed on the opposite side of the Moscow River. Their assignment was to dig dugouts where they would hide if the Germans broke through the thin Soviet defenses. At that point, Tsessarsky and his unit would find themselves behind enemy lines, where they were supposed to continue operating, gathering intelligence, and harassing the Germans whenever possible.

As the medical orderly for the unit, Tsessarsky was sent with a driver to Moscow for supplies, arriving on October 16. On his trip to the capital, he was shocked to see that there were no Soviet troops in sight. "The Minsk highway was open," he noted. If the Germans crossed the river, he realized, "all of them would march to Moscow."

Once he was in the capital, Tsessarsky drove right to the center of town, swinging by the Bolshoi Theater, and never saw a policeman. He did see the swirling ashes and bits and pieces of burned documents that everyone else remembers from that day. When he reported to the warehouse for military medical supplies, the manager looked at his list of requested medications and sent him away with next to nothing, claiming that Tsessarsky didn't have the proper authorizations. He did say, however, that Tsessarsky could come back later and try again.

Tsessarsky then set out to find his wife, Tatyana, who was still a

medical student and living in a dormitory next to the medical institute. Tatyana had left Moscow on October 15 to visit her family
home in Dmitrov, almost forty miles away, returning to a very unfa-
miliar Moscow the next afternoon. Since the metro had stopped
running for the first and only time since it was built, she had to
trudge back to her dormitory on foot, only to discover that it was
largely empty. Most of the students and staff had fled, and both
their rooms and the offices of the institute were strewn with the belongings and papers they had left behind, attesting to the haste of
their departure. "They had run away and left everything," she said.

"For me, October 16 was a day like no other—the worst I ever
experienced," she recalled. "Nothing like this had ever happened
to me before or after. The people who know about the war and the
military say that if the Germans had known what was happening
that day, they could have easily taken the city."

Tatyana was relieved to see her husband back at least briefly
from the front, but that wasn't enough to calm her fears about
what would happen next. They both saw a big swastika painted on
the fence running near the dormitory. "Not everyone felt patriotic," Tatyana noted. "There were a lot of people who felt aggrieved. Most forgot those feelings once the fighting started, but
not everyone." Presumably one of those people was responsible for
decorating the fence with the swastika.

After spending the night with his wife in the nearly empty dormitory, Tsessarsky took the warehouse manager at his word and returned to try again to get the supplies he had been sent for. He
discovered that everyone except for a solitary clerk had abandoned
the warehouse. "Take what you want," the clerk told him. As Tsessarsky recalled with evident satisfaction, "We filled the truck with
medicine and I went back to my unit."

Tsessarsky succeeded in his mission only because of the breakdown of virtually all authority in the capital. Even on October 17,
the morning after the panic, the authorities were strangely silent.
While radio broadcasts appealed for calm, the only good news was
that the Germans hadn't arrived during the night.

As far as most Muscovites were concerned, however, this hardly
meant the Germans wouldn't make it at all. Long after the war,
Mikhail Maklyarsky, a top NKVD official who was a key member of

the team charged with preparing underground activity in a German-occupied Moscow, made an admission to his son Boris that ran contrary to the official accounts, which maintained that the capital's inhabitants never wavered in their belief in victory. "He told me that ninety-eight out of a hundred Muscovites thought that Hitler would conquer Moscow sooner or later," Boris said. Along with his mother and other wives and children of the NKVD top brass, Boris, who was only eight at the time, had been evacuated to Kuibyshev back in July. When it came to their own families, the Kremlin's enforcers had decided very early that Moscow wasn't safe.

On October 18, the head of the NKVD's directorate for Moscow and the Moscow region, Mikhail Zhuravlev, filed a lengthy report on "the people's reaction to the fact that the enemy is approaching the capital." In particular, it focused on the "anarchistic behavior" of factory workers during the two previous days. A few examples:

"Some workers of factory No. 219 . . . attacked cars with evacuees from Moscow who were traveling on the Highway of the Enthusiasts. . . . They began seizing the evacuees' belongings. Six cars were thrown into a ravine by this group."

At another factory, a personnel director by the name of Rugan loaded his car with food and tried to leave the factory grounds. "On the way he was stopped and beaten by the workers of the factory. The soldiers on guard at the factory were drunk."

Workers at a shoe factory weren't paid on time "due to the shortage of banknotes" in the local branch of the state bank. "The protesting workers demolished the gates and entered the factory. Cases of stealing footwear from the factory were detected."

Buzanov, the director of the Red Front factory, tried to pacify his workers by distributing sweets. "During the distribution of cookies and candies, there was a fight between some of the drunk workers."

Near a synthetic leather factory, "a group of workers stopped a car with the evacuated members of the same factory's workers' families. Some passengers were beaten unmercifully, and their belongings were seized. At the same factory, four cars were disabled."

"The workers didn't get paid in factory No. 58. Some workers shouted 'Beat the communists!' The group of workers forged a key to the chemical warehouse, stole spirits and got drunk."

At Factory No. 8, there was "counter-revolutionary agitation," including an arson attack on a warehouse and ransacking the belongings of a group of workers and their families singled out for evacuation. "The damage from the fire is about 500,000 rubles."

"About 500 students of the trade school of the Stalin factory gathered waiting to get paid. The director of the school, Samoilov, wasn't there since he had fled from Moscow. The students didn't get their money and started destroying the school. They tore up textbooks ... broke cupboards, stole warm clothes and foodstuffs."

The report also noted incidents of theft of cattle from collective farms in the Moscow region, apparently by farmers preparing to flee. One group of collective farm workers even tried to rob an NKVD office. And most alarming, at 2 P.M. on October 17 in the villages of Nikulino and Toropovo "white flags were hung on some of the houses of the collective farmers." They weren't preparing to surrender to any of the Soviet authorities. They were expecting the Germans.

Zhuravlev's report indicated that the breakdown of authority wasn't complete. In a few cases, the NKVD "with the help of party activists and factory guards" arrested the perpetrators. In other cases, he noted that officers were sent to investigate the incidents. Special NKVD patrols were deployed around the city to try to restore order. But the overwhelming impression the report leaves is that the NKVD and the other "organs," as the machinery of Soviet repression was called, were suddenly fighting a losing battle with a population that no longer was intimidated by them.

During the initial panic of October 16, even the NKVD units were sometimes undecided about how to react. Aleksandr Zevelev, a history student who had volunteered for service on the day the Germans invaded and was assigned to the NKVD, found himself on patrol on Gorky Street, the main thoroughfare in the center of town. "There was marauding," he recalled. "Food shops were abandoned open and people were looting, so we had to stop them. They were stealing sugar, bread and flour." He also saw looters taking food from a restaurant near the Mayakovsky metro station. Although he and the other young men in his unit were armed with rifles, they didn't fire. They only shouted at the looters to stop and then reported these incidents to higher-ups, who would supposedly send others to make arrests. It was as if the dreaded enforcers no longer knew what to enforce.

But others within the NKVD were ignoring the confusion on the streets and acting as if nothing had changed. One scene epitomized the surrealistic feeling of that remarkable day. At midnight, thousands of political prisoners were marched to the square in front of the Kursky railroad station. Among them were several prominent scientists and academicians, including geneticist Nikolai Vavilov. Andrei Sukhno, a colleague and fellow prisoner, later described their ordeal. "Guards with dogs encircled the square and ordered us to stand on all fours. The day before it had been snowing, it was the first snow of the year, and it had melted. People stood [on all fours] in the cold slush of water and mud. They tried to creep away from the big puddles but they stood close to each other and the guards reacted violently. . . . So we were standing on all fours for six hours."

The prisoners were then herded onto a train bound for Saratov. Twenty-five prisoners were jammed into each compartment designed for five passengers, and the 450-mile journey took a grueling two weeks. While Sukhno would live to tell his story, Vavilov died of starvation two years later in Saratov's prison. Ironically, his brother Sergei Vavilov, who was also a scientist, rose to such prominence that in 1945 Stalin summoned him to the Kremlin to appoint him head of the U.S.S.R.'s Academy of Sciences. During that encounter, Sergei inquired about the fate of his brother. In his presence, Stalin picked up the phone and called Beria. "Lavrenty, what about Nikolai Vavilov?" he asked the NKVD chief. "Dead?" Then with no hint of irony, the Soviet leader mournfully added, "Oh, we've lost such a man."

While most of the Kremlin leadership remained oddly silent during the chaos of October 16, Anastas Mikoyan personally intervened in the strike at the Stalin Motor Vehicle Plant. After the fac-

tory director had called him, appealing for help, the Politburo member drove up and found about five to six thousand workers demonstrating in front of the locked factory gates. The workers immediately recognized Mikoyan and bombarded him with questions. Why hadn't they been paid in two weeks? Why were they locked out of their own factory? Why had the government fled Moscow, along with party and Komsomol officials from the factory? Why was no one explaining anything to them?

Mikoyan heard them out and then did his best to defuse the situation. "Comrades, why are you so outraged? There is a war on and anything can happen," he declared. "Who told you the government left Moscow? These rumors are provocations: the government hasn't fled. Those who have to be in Moscow are in Moscow. Stalin is in Moscow, Molotov as well—all the people who have to be here." He admitted that some government departments had been evacuated as a result of the fact that "the front approached the city." But he assured the workers that the government was proceeding according to well-prepared plans and that they shouldn't worry about their livelihoods since they had already received some extra payments. "Now you have to stay calm, obey the instructions that are defined by the war situation. We need composure and discipline to deal with the enemy."

Mikoyan's personal intervention calmed things down and the workers gradually dispersed. But he had neatly ducked some of their questions, and his answers were often disingenuous. He failed to mention that Stalin had already ordered many top officials to leave Moscow and that at that point most of his aides were assuming that the Soviet leader was planning to join them very soon. He also didn't tell the workers that the reason that they were locked out was that explosives had already been planted on the factory grounds to blow it up. On October 15, Stalin had issued a directive "to blow up factories, storage facilities and institutions that cannot be evacuated as well as electrical equipment of the metro (excluding water pipe and sewage systems)." The automobile factory was one of those designated facilities.

But some workers had got wind of reports that the NKVD was planting explosives in their factories. This had prompted, as the NKVD's Moscow region counterintelligence chief Sergei Fedoseyev recalled much later, "a serious incident" at Factory No. 6, a defense plant that had also been designated an object that should be blown up rather than allowed to fall into the hands of the Germans. The factory machinery was packed in special containers to be sent east of Moscow, where it was supposed to be reassembled so that production could be resumed. But as the factory managers were dispatching the containers, they panicked and decided to load their families in the cars with them. "The factory workers could see all of this and they were furious about it, which made them demonstrate," Fedoseyev recounted. "They demanded that the evacuation be aborted and that the factory would not be closed. They were afraid of losing their jobs."

At that point, one of the workers shouted that the factory could blow up at any moment, and tensions escalated dramatically. Terrified, the workers assigned five people to search the factory. They insisted that a high security official, I. M. Serov, accompany them. Although Serov knew that the explosives were already planted there, he pretended not to be aware of anything as he went with the workers on their rounds. Since the devices were well hidden, they didn't find them.

That didn't end the drama. Serov quickly informed his superiors about the incident. Although the factory managers had precipitated the confrontation by their sudden decision to send off their families, the government ordered the NKVD to arrest the ringleaders of the demonstration. Agents rounded up about fifteen people. "They were all shot a few days later and then rehabilitated only in 1953," Fedoseyev laconically noted. That, of course, was the year that Stalin died, which allowed for the posthumous rehabilitation of at least some of his millions of victims.

The handling of those protesting workers—at first with caution and even a seeming willingness to address their concerns, then with more typical violent retribution—reflected the initial uncertainty of the Kremlin leadership followed by a sudden new determination. To be precise, it reflected Stalin's actions at a time when, once again, he initially kept everyone guessing about what he intended to do.

* * *

Why did Stalin largely disappear from view and much of his government remain silent during those few days in mid-October when it looked as though Moscow was about to fall and lawbreakers roamed the streets? What was he doing and what was going through his mind?

On October 14, as the mood in Moscow was growing increasingly volatile, Stalin met with Georgi Dimitrov, who as head of the communist international, the Comintern, maintained contacts with communist movements throughout the world. No stranger to the leader's inner sanctum, Dimitrov was struck by the degree to which everyone assumed that evacuation was inevitable. "Since Moscow itself is becoming the front, preparations must be made for the worst possible scenario," he wrote in his diary. Molotov issued him clear instructions. "Evacuation is necessary. I advise you to leave before the day is out." According to Dimitrov, Stalin's message to the two of them was simple: "Moscow cannot be defended like Leningrad."

Switching the subject, the dictator launched into a list of complaints about Ernst Thälmann, the leader of the German communists who was then a prisoner in the Buchenwald concentration camp. Thälmann, he charged, wasn't a committed communist, and his writings showed he had been tainted by fascist ideology, although Hitler had him arrested as soon as he came to power. Which was why the Nazis wouldn't kill him, Stalin concluded. (In fact, Thälmann was executed at Buchenwald two years later.) Once again, the dictator was demonstrating his obsession with spotting any sign of potential heresy among his followers, even at a time when his world was threatening to collapse around him.

As Molotov and Dimitrov prepared to leave, Stalin added, "Have to evacuate before the day is out!" According to Dimitrov, he said this as casually as if he were saying "Time for lunch!" While Stalin didn't specifically say when he might follow them, Dimitrov was convinced it would be very soon.

Dimitrov and Molotov took the same train to Kuibyshev. En route on October 17, they met over tea with several other top officials on the train, their minds focused on the fate of the capital that they were leaving behind. "Everyone is in good spirits, although quite concerned. Everyone is contemplating the imminent capture of Moscow by the Germans," Dimitrov recorded in his diary. In an appeal to Communists around the world, he tried to accentuate the positive—the plans to reestablish Soviet industries in the east and to continue the fight against Hitler—but his main message was a plea "not to give way to despondency in view of the fascist gang's temporary successes."

Long after the war, Molotov would deny that the mood had been that bleak or that Stalin had ever considered abandoning the capital, even when he was sending many of his closest aides to Kuibyshev. "That's nonsense. He had no doubts," Molotov maintained. "He wasn't going to leave Moscow. I went for two or three days to Kuibyshev and left Voznesensky in charge there. Stalin told me, 'See how they are settling in there and come back right away.'"

But Molotov was a Stalin loyalist to the end, and he wasn't about to admit how much his boss had wavered during those crucial days in mid-October or how grim the situation looked. Dmitri Volkogonov, the former Red Army general and Stalin biographer, argued that the Soviet leader was so profoundly shaken by the threat to Moscow that "he was tormented by alarming presentiments."

Everything was prepared for Stalin's evacuation: a special train, fully equipped and waiting at the station, and—just in case he needed to make an even hastier exit—his personal Douglas DC-3 and three other planes were also standing by, ready to go. On the evening of October 15, Stalin decided to drive out to his dacha, only to be told it was already mined in preparation for the Germans and that he shouldn't go there. Irritated, Stalin ordered his aides to "clear the mines" and announced that he was going to stick to his plan to spend the night there. That decision was probably more a matter of Stalin, as always, asserting his power to overrule anything he wanted than an indication that he had made up his mind about whether or not to leave Moscow.

The next day, Stalin was driving back to the Kremlin when, according to one of his bodyguards, he was greeted by the sight of "people carrying bags with flour, bundles of sausages, hams, boxes of macaroni and noodles"—in other words, everything they had looted from the stores. Ordering his driver to stop, Stalin got out and was immediately surrounded by a crowd. Some people applauded, and someone asked him, "Comrade Stalin, when will we stop the enemy?"

"There is time for everything," Stalin replied.

The fact that he reportedly didn't rebuke anyone for looting only showed how much the disorders on the streets must have taken him by surprise.

Arriving at the Kremlin, he told his entourage that not only the foreign embassies but also the government should be evacuated to Kuibyshev. Some ministries would be scattered in several cities, but Kuibyshev would be the capital in exile. And Stalin declared that the Politburo members should leave as well. As for his own plans, he announced, "I'll go tomorrow in the morning." It was very much the same message that Molotov had given the foreign diplomats: the leader would follow shortly.

Mikoyan wasn't happy with this plan. "Why do we have to leave today if you're going tomorrow?" he asked. "We can leave tomorrow as well." He pointed out that Moscow Party leader Shcherbakov and the NKVD's Beria could only leave the city once they had made the final preparations for the underground resistance that would be left behind. He added, "I'm staying and I will go with you tomorrow."

Stalin didn't object and turned his attention to the preparations for a German takeover of the city, pinning down which factories and other installations were to be blown up and getting military briefings on how the army would continue to try to stop the attackers, retreating to defense lines closer and closer in until they were right at Moscow's ring road.

But Mikoyan did make the trip to Kuibyshev after all. Stalin insisted Molotov should go there and see that the new setup was functioning properly. "Let Mikoyan go with me," the foreign minister implored him. Though Mikoyan tried to object at first, he realized he didn't have any choice. Stalin approved of the idea and told him, "Why don't you go with him?" It wasn't so much a question as a command. Like Molotov, he would spend a few days in Kuibyshev before returning to Moscow.

During all of this, Stalin kept his own counsel. He read a new biography of Field Marshal Mikhail Kutuzov, who had led the Russian army to victory over Napoleon in 1812, and underlined the observation "until the last minute no one knew what Kutuzov intended to do."

The sense of danger was almost palpable. Mikoyan reported that German troops on motorcycles had been sighted about fifteen to eighteen miles from his family dacha, which was about nine miles southwest of Moscow. That meant the troops were only about twenty-five miles from the city's outskirts. Other reports put German scouts even closer, though it was hard to sort out what was real and what was only rumor.

From the air, the Germans made their presence known on an almost daily basis with new bombing raids. Stalin was often forced to take refuge in the Kirovskaya metro station, where he could work and sleep in a specially prepared compartment of a train that was hidden from the rest of the station and other trains by plywood paneling. But at least on one occasion, Stalin witnessed a bombing raid from above ground. Returning to his dacha in the early morning hours, he got out of his car to the din of anti-aircraft fire aimed at a large group of German bombers, which were lit up by searchlight beams trained on them by Moscow's defenders. He refused to move even when a shell fragment fell to the ground nearby. His security chief picked it up and handed it to Stalin. It was still warm.

Whether Stalin felt courage or fear at that moment, he was far from certain about his next moves on October 16, when Moscow looked as though it might collapse from within and without. Air Force Marshal Golovanov saw him sitting in his office that day, asking himself again and again, "What shall we do? What shall we do?"

With many Muscovites convinced Stalin had already fled, this was far more than a personal issue. His decision to stay or go would be seen as a signal of desperation or resolve. Which was probably why he agonized for what seemed like a never-ending couple of days.

In his book about his father, Sergo Beria claimed that the NKVD chief insisted that the Soviet leader should stay put. According to his account, the older Beria told Stalin, "If you go, Moscow will be lost. To ensure your security we can turn Red Square into an airstrip. The army and the people must know that you are in

Moscow." When Moscow party chief Shcherbakov and some other top officials urged the opposite course, Stalin reportedly turned on them. "Your attitude can be explained in two ways," he said. "Either you are good-for-nothings and traitors or else you are idiots. I prefer to regard you as idiots."

The younger Beria's account isn't necessarily reliable, since he was eager to put his father in the best possible light. In retrospect, all the top Soviet officials wanted to be seen as in agreement about the need for Stalin to remain in Moscow. But at the time, they had no assurance that Moscow could hold out, and the last thing any of them wanted was to be associated with a course of action that might have led to Stalin's capture or death.

Ultimately, of course, the decision was only Stalin's to make, but he was still in no hurry to make it. On October 18, he went to the station where his special train was waiting. Some accounts claim it was at the Kalanchevskaya station, while others say it was the Kursky station. As he was approaching his hundredth birthday in 2005, Pavel Saprykin insisted it was at the Kursky station, since he was working there at the time and had helped prepare the special train. He also saw Stalin on that pivotal day. As Saprykin recalled, the Soviet leader walked up to the train, paced the platform beside it, but didn't board it. Instead, he left the station.

Vowing not to leave Moscow, Stalin suddenly took charge again, reverting to the tactic he had relied on his entire career—brute force. Declaring martial law on October 19, he ordered NKVD troops into the street. They were told to shoot almost anyone who looked suspicious. Emergency tribunals were empowered to deal with looters and all other violators of law and order—which also meant prompt death sentences. Surviving members of the NKVD patrols, such as Yevgeny Anufriyev, are cautious in describing what they actually did, but they don't hold back from discussing their instructions. "We had an amazing order to shoot spies and deserters on the spot," he said. "We were ordered to do this, but we didn't know how to figure out who was a spy. So the order had no practical significance." Perhaps in his case, it didn't. But reluctantly he hinted that there were plenty of cases in which it did. "Well, a lot of stupid things were done then. What more can I say?" he added.

There's no reliable tally of how many Muscovites perished in the subsequent clampdown, but the message came through loud and clear: Stalin was back in charge, and few people needed much of a reminder about what that meant. The looting abruptly ended, and those Muscovites who had remained in the city began to sense a new determination to stop the Germans from taking it.

Even Muscovites like Valeria Prokhorova, who distrusted the regime that had swept up many of her relatives in the purges, welcomed that change. "We started to feel that we were being defended, we felt that the regime was defending our land," she said. "Nobody cared for Stalin, but people were fighting for our country."

The panic had threatened more than the internal order of the capital. It had threatened to undermine the entire effort to defend Moscow from the Germans. It demoralized its population, the military, and even its leaders. Long after those events, many Russians would still find it extremely difficult to discuss them, precisely because they were nearly responsible for an implosion that would have had disastrous consequences—and because they are so much at odds with the popular image, nurtured by the regime's propagandists, of a brave, always united people resisting the German aggressors.

In his memoirs, Marshal Zhukov dutifully maintained that most Muscovites had behaved well during mid-October. "But, as the saying goes, there are black sheep in every family, and, in this case, too, cowards, panicmongers, and self-seekers started fleeing the capital in all directions, spreading panicky rumors about an inevitable surrender," he wrote. The proclamation of a state of siege, or martial law, was necessary for "mobilizing the troops and civilians of Moscow to repel the enemy and . . . preventing a repetition of the panic stirred up by provocative elements on October 16." While couched in Soviet rhetoric, his statement amounts to an admission that far more than a few black sheep were involved and much more was at stake than the official accounts suggest.

Perhaps the most honest examination of the painful, conflicting emotions triggered by what happened on October 16 appears in Konstantin Simonov's classic Soviet war novel *The Living and the Dead*. Long after the war, his main character "found it intolerable to remember Moscow as it had been on that day, even as it is intolerable to see a loved one's face distorted with terror." While Simonov praised the heroism of those who continued to fight the Germans, he recognized that it appeared that the war had taken a disastrous turn "and there were other people that day ready in their despair to believe that the Germans were going to enter tomorrow." Clearly upset by the memory of the frantic mass exodus from the city, he added the major caveat: "To be fair, only a few thousand of those tens of thousands could rightly be condemned afterwards by history." In other words, their panic, while hardly laudable, was completely understandable.

In a letter to his wife or girlfriend, Heinrich Lansen, one of the German soldiers advancing on Moscow, wrote on October 8, "The coming victory over the Red Army should be and will be ours. The mighty Führer promised to end the most difficult campaign in history victoriously before the beginning of the severe cold weather. . . . My darling, your wish for the victorious end of the war will be fulfilled soon. Moscow, the stronghold of world-wide Bolshevism, will fall in a few days and the rest of the Red Army will be annihilated together with the enemy capital. . . . You can expect a quick end to the war and a joyful meeting. . . . Maybe when you read these lines, the war in the East will be over."

Lansen's letter never made it back to Germany, winding up in the hands of the NKVD instead almost certainly after its author had perished. But when he penned those words, Moscow looked extremely vulnerable and his predictions, while inspired by Nazi propaganda, far from outlandish. To prevent them from proving to be accurate, the Soviet political and military leaders had to mobilize everyone they could to shore up the capital's wobbly defenses. It wasn't enough to quell the panic. The authorities needed Moscow's inhabitants to pitch in, making this a huge joint military-civilian effort.

With most men already in uniform, teams of women, along with some teenage boys too young to serve, constructed huge networks of trenches, tank traps, and barriers made of felled trees strewn with barbed wire that, taken together, stretched thousands of miles on the approaches of the city. Working night and day, they also dug thousands of artillery emplacements. And in the capital itself, they prepared street barricades in case the Germans breached all the other obstacles. Irina Bogolyubskaya, a teenager at the time, recalled that soldiers arrived at her apartment in October and her family was convinced they were about to be evicted. Instead, they placed a machine gun in one of the windows overlooking the street. "They were preparing for street fighting," she concluded.

"Muscovites made their city into an unassailable fortress," one of the official accounts claimed. "Every building became a bastion, every street a fortified area. Moscow bristled with barricades, metal tank traps and barbed wire." Zhukov reported that more than half a million inhabitants of the Moscow region, mostly women, participated in this gargantuan effort and that their example dramatically boosted the morale of the troops, "augmenting their strength and their will to fight."

In Soviet accounts of this period, this kind of claim was milked for its full propaganda value, quickly skipping over the panic, flight, and chaos to present a picture of a city that was far more united than it really was. Nonetheless, many Muscovites were determined and dedicated, doing everything possible to contribute to the defense of their city, no matter how shaken they were by the exodus of many of their neighbors, by the brief but unnerving near collapse of all authority, and by the hardships they endured during a prolonged period of acute food shortages, with bread in particularly short supply.

The other hardship—and danger—were German air raids. From the time of the first raid on July 22, Moscow lived with regular bombings. According to an NKVD report submitted to Beria, Shcherbakov and other top Moscow party officials on November 24, 1941, there were ninety German raids on the city during the first five months of the war. "Enemy planes dropped 1,521 demolition bombs and 56,620 incendiary bombs on the city," it added. As a result of those attacks, 1,327 were killed, 1,931 seriously injured, and 3,122 lightly injured. While young people, especially young women, raced around the roofs of buildings to toss off the small incendiary bombs before they could do much damage, those devices set off 1,539 fires. Taken together, the two types of bombs destroyed 402 apartment buildings and damaged another 852. Twenty-two industrial plants were also destroyed, and another 102 industrial facilities were partly destroyed. Later tallies, which included subsequent bombing raids, upped all those figures: 2,196 dead out of a total of 7,708 casualties, 577 apartment buildings destroyed and 5,007 damaged, seventy-one industrial plants destroyed and eighty-eight damaged.

But such reports may have understated the damage. In his memoirs, Moscow air commander Nikolai Sbytov recalled the toll from just one day's attack, on October 10. He reported that seventy German planes were involved, ten of which were downed. "The bombs hit the Bolshoi Theater, the Kursky station, and the Central Telegraph," he wrote. "Fifty apartment buildings were destroyed, 150 Muscovites were killed, 278 were lightly wounded and 248 were seriously wounded." Pointing out that this was just one raid out of a total of 122 during the entire period of the air raids on Moscow that stretched all the way to the spring of 1943, Sbytov maintained that this demonstrated a much higher casualty toll than generally reported. "Simple arithmetic will show that Moscow became a cemetery not only for German aviation, but also a grave for thousands and thousands of the civilian population."

All Muscovites lived in fear of those raids, ducking into metro stations that served as bomb shelters whenever the air raid sirens sounded. But the warnings sometimes came too late. Irina Bogolyubskaya, the young woman who had watched soldiers install a machine gun in the window of her apartment, happened to enter the Central Telegraph building to send a telegram on the day of the raid that Sbytov described. She was planning to then join a line of people in front of a food store on the other side of the street. Suddenly, an explosion shattered the windows of the Central Telegraph building. "A plane had dropped a bomb between the store and the Central Telegraph," she recalled. "It was horrible." When she ran out of the building, she saw that almost all the people who had been lined up in front of the food store on the opposite side of the street were dead and many others were severely wounded.

The bombers also targeted the civilians who were dispatched to the city's outskirts to prepare the defense lines. Olga Sapozhnikova and other workers at the Trekhgorka Cotton Mill were ordered to dig trenches several miles outside the city center. "Those were dreadful days," she told British correspondent Alexander Werth.

Referring to the Germans by the popular derogatory term, she added, "On the very first day we were machine-gunned by a Fritz who swooped right down. Eleven of the girls were killed and four wounded."

Vera Stepanova, who was sixteen at the time and lived in the city center, recalls that the first time she was caught in a bombing raid, she froze in fear, completely unable to run. An enemy plane came in so low that "I had the feeling that I could see the German pilot's eyes," she said.

The Kremlin wasn't spared by the bombers either. Mikoyan reported that he knew of six times when German bombs fell on the territory of this leadership enclave during the fighting. One crashed into the Kremlin palace but failed to explode, and another one narrowly missed one of the Kremlin churches and also didn't explode. But on a different occasion, a bomb blew out the windows of a reception hall of a building, and in one case, Mikoyan and his NKVD security guard were thrown to the ground by the force of an explosion near the Spassky Gate, which killed two people. When a bomb hit the Arsenal building, about thirty soldiers were killed. On October 28, Malenkov was summoned to the Kremlin by Stalin, only to learn that the Central Committee building he had just left had sustained a direct hit. "I saved your life," Stalin pointed out.

Still, the Germans didn't accomplish all that much with their air raids, which never reached anything approaching the scale or ferocity of the London Blitz and weren't nearly as effective. According to the figures of the Moscow Defense Museum, only about 3 percent of the city's buildings were damaged during the raids, a far cry from the extensive destruction in the British capital. And even if the civilian deaths in Moscow were understated, they were far less than the more than twenty thousand deaths in London.

The Germans were in no position to mount the kind of massive air assault on Moscow that they had conducted against the British capital. And pilots they could commit to the battle quickly discovered how difficult it was to penetrate the intense anti-aircraft fire they encountered on the approaches to Moscow and in the city itself. Lieutenant Richard Wernicke, who flew one of the notorious Ju-87 Stuka dive bombers, recalled how surprised he was, along with the other German fliers, by the hail of anti-aircraft fire they faced as they dove down over their targets. "It was terrible: the air was full of lead, and they were firing very accurately. We hadn't seen anything like this before," he said, alluding to the fact that German planes had encountered little resistance in the early months of the war.

This was no accident. The Soviet leadership had concentrated about 40 percent of all its anti-aircraft batteries in or around the capital. There were anti-aircraft batteries on the roof of the Moskva Hotel, right next to Red Square, and at Stalin's dacha on the outskirts of town. The city also installed giant searchlights, which were operated by women, who alternated four-hour shifts all day and all night seven days a week. "They wore men's clothes and their hair was cut close to the skin because they were afraid of different diseases, typhus and lice," recalled Tatyana Petrova, whose mother served in a searchlight unit. "It was very important to catch the German planes in crisscrossing searchlights quickly to determine their altitude and direction and speed." That information was then relayed to the anti-aircraft batteries so that they could zero in on them. As a final obstacle, there were the blimps deployed over the city with dangling nets that ensnared a few low flying planes. The Soviet side claimed to have downed 1,392 German planes over Moscow.

German pilots discovered all sorts of dangers even before they reached the capital. Guns would pop up from concealed artillery emplacements, and newly built Soviet fighters, such as the Yak-7, appeared in the sky. "They were very dangerous," Wernicke recalled. "They even dived right behind us." After their initial knockout blow to the Soviet air force, the Germans hadn't had much to worry about from that quarter. During the battle for Moscow, that began to change.

Like the soldiers on the ground, the German fliers also began to learn about the ferocity of the Russian climate. They, too, hadn't been supplied with winter clothing. On the ground, this meant they were always cold, and, flying at sixteen thousand feet, they were literally freezing in temperatures that reached minus 49 degrees Fahrenheit. "You couldn't stand the cold," Wernicke said, still shuddering at the memory of how this further diminished the chance of survival. During November and December 1941, almost half of his squadron's hundred planes, which flew from an airfield in Kalinin north of Moscow, didn't return from their missions.

But the real danger to Moscow was on the ground, not in the air. It would be the ground troops on both sides who would determine the outcome of the battle, and the Kremlin tried to add fresh troops any way it could. In the midst of the panic in the city on October 16, the Moscow region reported that it had collected 11,500 volunteers for Communist brigades, as the home guard units were dubbed then. Since they consisted of workers who hadn't been called up earlier or in some cases had been rejected because of health reasons, that number had shrunk to about ten thousand by the end of the month.

From the start, these newly minted fighters were at a serious disadvantage. They received whatever leftover weapons could be found, usually obsolete guns of Polish, French, or other foreign make, some dating back to World War I. Many of them were defective or lacked appropriate ammunition. These were problems that had been evident from the beginning of the German invasion, when the first volunteers were hastily assembled. Abram Gordon, who had just graduated from the State Pedagogical Institute, had volunteered right away. He found himself in a unit equipped with Polish rifles without any cartridges at all. Outfitted in whatever uniforms could be patched together, they hardly looked like genuine soldiers. Gordon recalled rescuing a fellow volunteer by the name of Petrovsky, who had been surrounded by a crowd yelling that he was a German spy, which prompted the police to race to the scene. "Our buddy was wearing a black uniform, carrying a strange Polish rifle and, with his beard and mustache, was taken for a German paratrooper," he said.

Even when they received more modern Soviet guns, the volunteers had the chance to try them only a couple of times before they found themselves in action. "It definitely wasn't enough practice because many of us were handling guns for the first time in our lives," Gordon pointed out. But soon they'd be thrown into battle against German tanks, sometimes armed only with grenades and Molotov cocktails. In many cases, these encounters amounted to suicide missions.

And death could come from any quarter. Boris Kagan, a young

engineer who volunteered on October 15, found himself in a battle about twenty-five miles from Moscow. As his unit came to a village, he saw Soviet soldiers fleeing the Germans. "Suddenly a tall [Soviet] officer ran out of a house with his gun and started shooting the soldiers who were running," he said. Four of the soldiers were killed.

During the fighting in the second half of October, Zhukov's military command issued an appeal to the troops for courage "in this grave hour of danger for our state." The message was one of patriotism: "The homeland calls on us to stand as an indestructible wall and to bar the Fascist hordes from our beloved Moscow. What we require now, as never before, are vigilance, iron discipline, organization, determined action, unbending will for victory and a readiness for self-sacrifice."

For the Soviet leadership, this, as always, translated into a willingness to sacrifice anyone they saw fit, as the shooting of the retreating soldiers demonstrated. The Kremlin saw no reason to dial back on its policy of terror, whether or not it had anything to do with the current fighting. On the contrary, the machinery of repression kept on working, often with redoubled intensity. Only a few days after Zhukov's appeal, Stalin's executioners were at work again, this time dispensing with those who had just barely survived the military purge trials of the 1930s. Among the victims: the widows of Marshal Tukhachevsky and several other top officers who were tried and shot in 1938, and the famed fighter pilots of the Spanish Civil War, Pavel Rychagov and Yakov Smushkevich. Nothing, not even the desperate efforts to save Moscow, could stop the internal bloodletting.

With the arrival of the first special evacuation trains in mid-October, Kuibyshev began to adjust to its role as the alternate Soviet capital, a designation it would keep until the summer of 1943, when it was no longer deemed necessary. Led by top Soviet officials and foreign diplomats, accompanied by entire theaters and orchestras from Moscow, the new arrivals would triple the size of the city's population, from three hundred thousand to nine hundred thousand. Many local inhabitants were given twenty-four hours to vacate their apartments so that they could be taken over by government offices and foreign embassies, and no provision was made for where they were supposed to go. The message was simple: as locals, they should fend for themselves, moving in with relatives or anyone else who would take them.

Not surprisingly, one of the top priorities of the officials dispatched to Kuibyshev was to prepare safe accommodations for Stalin, on the assumption that he'd have to relocate there. While offices and living quarters were quickly readied in a five-story building in the center of the city, the officials weren't about to stint on providing full protection for their leader in case the Germans kept pushing past Moscow. They drew up plans for the construction of a massive bunker sunk deep into the ground, whose existence was kept secret not only during the war but even until the end of the Soviet Union nearly five decades later.

Construction of the bunker didn't begin until February 1942, when 597 highly experienced construction workers from the Moscow subway system came on special assignment for the project. Working sixteen to eighteen hours a day, they dug out 918,000 cubic feet of soil so that they could build the bunker 121 feet deep, making it the deepest bunker in the world—the equivalent of a twelve-story building below the surface. By comparison, Hitler's bunker in his Wolf's Lair headquarters in East Prussia was forty-five feet deep. Completed in November 1942, the bunker's main hall, which was to serve as Stalin's working area, was the size of the Aeroport subway station in Moscow, and built of similar materials. Today, the bunker serves as a museum and an emergency shelter, capable of holding six hundred people.

But after he imposed martial law in Moscow, which put an abrupt end to most of the looting and other disorders, Stalin decided he wasn't going to join the evacuation after all—at least, not yet. As the building of the bunker attested, he wasn't ruling out that possibility completely. But his instinct was to hang on in Moscow as long as he could, recognizing that his presence there would have a huge psychological impact. Whether they feared or loathed Stalin, many Muscovites and the Soviet troops trying to defend them were watching his movements. It was no accident that the panic had started when rumors spread that he was leaving or had already left Moscow and that people took heart when they learned he was still in the capital.

As November 7 approached—the anniversary of the Bolshevik Revolution, which was normally the occasion of a lavish display of Soviet military might—Stalin startled Molotov and Beria by asking, "How are we going to have the military parade? Maybe two or three hours earlier?"

Neither of those two cronies nor the Moscow military commander, General Pavel Artemyev, had contemplated the possibility of holding a parade at a time when the Germans were pushing closer and closer to Moscow and their planes were conducting regular raids on the city. Artemyev said flat out that a parade was impossible.

But Stalin had made up his mind. "The anti-aircraft defenses around Moscow must be reinforced," he declared. "The main military leaders are at the front. [General] Budenny will take the parade and General Artemyev will be in command. If there's an air raid during the parade and there are dead and wounded, they must be quickly removed and the parade allowed to go on. A newsreel should be made of it and distributed throughout the country in large numbers. The newspapers should give the parade wide coverage." He added that he'd use the occasion to give a speech. "What do you think?" he asked.

Molotov raised the obvious objection. "But what about the risk? There would be a risk, though I admit the political response here and abroad would be enormous."

"So it's decided!" Stalin concluded. "Make the appropriate arrangements."

It was almost as if the Soviet leader knew something—or had reason to hope for something—that would prove that this risk was worth taking.

8

Saboteurs, Jugglers, and Spies

During the summer of 2005, in the midst of the building boom in Moscow, the city's inhabitants were provided with a vivid reminder of the legacy of the battle for the capital sixty-four years earlier. As construction workers began knocking down the Moskva Hotel, the Stalin-era landmark close to Red Square, they discovered more than a ton of explosives in the building's foundations. Luckily, the TNT had deteriorated over time and there were no detonators, which suggested that either the hotel had served as a storage site for the explosives or the authorities had never completed the preparations to blow up the building. But whatever happened, there was no doubt that the hotel had figured in the Soviet leadership's plans for a German-occupied Moscow. The idea was to welcome the Germans with as many explosions of key buildings and installations as possible.

The battle for Moscow was full of secret plans and conspiratorial activity, most of it organized by the NKVD, an organization that always thrived in the shadows. By early October, the NKVD bosses were working on the assumption that the Germans would soon be occupying Moscow and the only resistance left would be whatever underground cells they could put together. At one of three hidden printing plants that they hoped to keep operating under the noses of the new masters of the capital, the first of what promised to be a series of pamphlets was prepared in galley form. It read:

> *Comrades! We left Moscow due to the continuous attacks of the Germans. But it's not the right time for us to weep. We know that Russians at times have had to leave Moscow and then liberate it from the enemy. Death to the German occupants!*
> *—Underground Party Committee*

And the NKVD bosses worked frantically to make death happen in a German-occupied Moscow. Along with planting explosives all over the city, they trained the agents who would be left behind and set up radio stations and sites for dead drops to maintain a clandestine communications network. The object was clear: to kill top Germans at every opportunity and to deprive them of vital facilities, sabotaging their efforts to maintain control over their conquered territories.

Not surprisingly, it was the assassination part of the program that appealed the most to the men who were in charge at the Lubyanka, the headquarters for those who had been conducting a systematic war of terror against their own people in Stalin's name. The prospect that they could target Hitler's cronies was enough to pump adrenaline into their system and get them thinking, as we would put it today, outside the box. They were suddenly free to concoct the kind of murder plots that hadn't been necessary when they were targeting "internal" enemies who had no chance of fighting back. These schemes would require an unprecedented combination of imagination and courage, for the planners knew that their foreign enemies were every bit as ruthless as they were.

Mikhail Maklyarsky, one of the senior NKVD officials charged with the preparations, came up with the most audacious scheme. He recruited four performers who would plan the show of their lives in an occupied Moscow. Among them was nineteen-year-old Nikolai Khokhlov, who knew how to entertain crowds by whistling tunes. "The Moscow situation does not look good, Nikolai," Maklyarsky told the teenager. "Apparently we will have to give up the city. For a short duration, of course. But anyhow, if the Germans enter Moscow, they must feel as though they have entered a hornet's nest."

The hornets, in this case, were to be Khokhlov and the other members of the vaudeville group: Sergei Panilov, who was an experienced writer of skits; Tasya Ignatova, a singer; and a young woman whom everyone simply called Nina the juggler.

The group's assignment was to get into the good graces of the German occupiers by offering to entertain them. "Germans like art, especially if it is not too serious," Maklyarsky explained to Khokhlov. The group would try to wangle an invitation to perform in front of the German brass when they held their victory celebration, possibly in the House of Columns near the Kremlin. "Perhaps even Hitler would honor it with his presence," Maklyarsky continued. "Imagine a big stage show for the Nazi command! German generals, state officers, all kinds of ministers . . . and then, suddenly—an explosion . . . one, two grenades." Whomever those explosions would kill, the message that the Russians were continuing to resist, despite the loss of their capital, would be loud and clear.

The four performers underwent their training in a Moscow apartment, where Khokhlov remembers having the "first big romance" of his life with Ignatova, the singer. Their NKVD handlers delivered large stashes of weapons, explosives, money, ration cards, and food. They also received lessons on how to use their new arsenal, which included yellow bars that looked like soap but were really TNT and a variety of fuses, detonators, bombs, and booby traps. While they were supposed to await instructions from their superiors who were about to abandon Moscow, they all knew that their main task was to give Nina the juggler center stage at the Germans' victory celebration. During the performance, she would be watching for the German VIPs. Then, at the climactic moment, she would toss the pins, prepacked with grenades or other explosives, at her targets, killing as many of them as possible.

As the government was preparing to abandon Moscow on October 15, Maklyarsky summoned the two young men in the group, Khokhlov and Panilov. They walked down a corridor of the Lubyanka full of clerks frantically destroying documents. When they arrived at Maklyarsky's office, he was on the phone issuing an order. "All right. Now listen. Arrest her immediately and execute her at dawn." He turned to the two young men, offering a brusque explanation that the Germans had broken a young NKVD agent who had been sent on a mission. Then he combined that implicit threat with a softer message. "What can I say to you kids? Nothing good. We are leaving Moscow, German tanks are already on the outskirts of the city. Hold on—and remember what you are defending. Don't get excited. Wait for communications and instructions."

In his old age, Pavel Sudoplatov, Maklyarsky's immediate superior, still relished the thought of the star of the show "elegantly juggling the pins and then throwing them at the Germans." Boris Maklyarsky, the son of the mastermind of this scheme, recalls that after the Germans were forced to retreat from the outskirts of Moscow, Sudoplatov went to the apartment where the quartet had been holding its rehearsals to tell them that the show was cancelled. With no German audience, it had lost its purpose, and the performers were informed they were off the hook. To his surprise, the group was visibly disappointed, although Khokhlov would later claim they were also relieved that the pressure was off. Still, they had been looking forward to pulling off the most challenging and dangerous performance of their lives.

That near miss didn't end Khokhlov's career as a risk taker. According to the younger Maklyarsky, Khokhlov, despite his unprepossessing appearance, would prove to be "remarkably brave and cold-blooded." He became a fluent German speaker and was dropped behind enemy lines, successfully passing as a German officer in order to organize the assassination of Wilhelm Kube, Hitler's commissioner general in Belorussia, otherwise known as the "butcher" of the province. After the war, Khokhlov repeatedly tried to break free of the secret services, but his bosses refused to release him. Instead, they trained him for work abroad that would include sabotage and "the physical liquidation of our enemies." As he would put it, he was ordered "to become a murderer—a murderer in the interests of the Soviet State."

But Khokhlov was increasingly disillusioned with the Soviet system. Later in the war, he learned the true story of his father, whom he didn't know that well since his parents had divorced when he was very young. His father served as a commissar in an army battalion during the battle for Moscow, and he made the mistake of confiding in one of his soldiers that Stalin was to blame for the disorder and collapse on the front when the Germans attacked. He added that it was hard to figure out who was the lesser evil, Hitler or Stalin. Convinced that he was being tested, the soldier immediately reported the remarks. The result was that Khokhlov's father was transferred to a penal battalion, the kind of unit that was sent into battle first with the expectation that almost everyone would perish. Which is what happened to Khokhlov's father very quickly.

Khokhlov's stepfather—"an excellent lawyer who probably did not know how to hold a rifle," as Khokhlov put it—volunteered to defend Moscow and died in action almost immediately, too. "The army needed cannon fodder," Khokhlov noted bitterly. "Zhukov achieved all his victories by slaughtering millions. The slaughter was unprecedented."

In 1954, when the Cold War was already in full swing, Khokhlov's Lubyanka superiors dispatched him on an assignment to organize the murder of a prominent Russian émigré in West Germany. Instead, he warned his intended target of his mission, cooperated with U.S. intelligence agents in intercepting other members of his team, and defected to the West. He later wrote his memoirs, *In the Name of Conscience: The Testament of a Soviet Secret Agent,* and ended up teaching psychology at California State University in San Bernardino until his retirement in 1992. That was also the year that President Boris Yeltsin pardoned him, and he was able to return to Moscow for the first time, even dropping in on the Lubyanka, the famed headquarters of his former employers.

As of this writing, Khokhlov is still living the quiet life of a professor emeritus in sunny Southern California. Looking back at the scheme Maklyarsky had cooked up for his group of performers, he didn't hesitate in his response to the question whether they could have succeeded in their plot if the Germans had occupied Moscow. "No, never," Khokhlov said. "The Germans would have immediately located us and all of us would have been hanged." He pointed out that members of the artistic community all traded gossip and everyone quickly found out what everyone else was doing, which meant informers could have easily learned all there was to know. The fact that they had been spending the funds they had been allocated also would have made them easily identifiable. "It really was a charade that never would have worked," he added.

At the time, though, he and the others believed they could pull it off. "The most important trait of a Soviet citizen was naïveté," Khokhlov continued. "We lived in a fog created not only by the weather but by Soviet propaganda. At that time people did not talk about danger."

Aside from Khokhlov's very special group, the NKVD deployed an assortment of operatives to be left behind for undercover work in the city. A handwritten, top-secret memo to Beria from Naum Eitingon, one of the top NKVD officials in charge of those activities, on October 14 offered a partial list along with assignments. The first "diversionary, terror group," identified only by the initials Z.R., consisted of three subgroups, each with two fighters and one munitions specialist. "There are dead drops with explosives and weapons," the memo reported. "Apart from that, explosives are kept outside Moscow in the Agriculture National Commissariat test site. The group commander has two radios—one of them is in reserve in case the first one malfunctions. Radio operators for both radios have been selected and trained. All the group members have cover stories and secret apartments. The group members liaise with the group commanders individually via special agents."

These were the groups that were supposed to carry out Stalin's directive, issued a day later on October 15, to blow up factories and other installations that could not be evacuated. Other groups of agents mentioned in the Eitingon memo carried names such as Fishermen, the Old Men, the Faithful Ones, the Wild Ones and the Little Family.

The report also included brief descriptions of some of the individual agents, identified by their code names, and their more specialized assignments. Agent Markov, the commander of the Wild Ones, for instance, was an ex-burglar. His group's mission was "acts of terror against German army officers." Agent Grip Vice, a member of the Little Family, is described as "an engineer, a sportsman, of noble origin." The report noted that his mother was sentenced to eight years in the Gulag because she had affairs with

German embassy staffers in Moscow, but Grip Vice "is a faithful agent." His assignment was "to join fascist sport and youth organizations in order to get some managing position to conduct some big act of terror." Agent Poet, commander of ex–Red Army officers with combat experience, "will conduct diversions in the railway transport system."

Aside from explosives, the groups had various tools at their disposal. A female member of the Old Men by the name of Gerasimova "is assigned to publish anti-fascist leaflets and she was allotted a typewriter for that." Agent Iron Ore, an engineer and former officer in the tsarist army, was also supposed to publish leaflets and "conduct intelligence operations." "He has been allotted a typewriter and a photo camera," the report pointed out. Agent Kako, a restaurant owner, was expected "to conduct intelligence and terror operations" using his restaurant "for secret meetings and weapons storage." To make his job easier, the report added, "Kako was allotted alcohol." Other sites used as covers for the operatives included a sculptor's workshop, the office of a notary, a medical clinic, and a theater.

As always, the NKVD was particularly eager to identify Soviet citizens who weren't loyal to the cause. Agent Builder, described as a railway engineer and highly successful businessman of noble origin, "has lots of connections among White émigrés, former generals in the tsarist army and dukes." His assignment was to gather members of the intelligentsia "who do not believe we will win the war" and to prepare them "to greet the Germans." He would then start a construction company and move in high social circles under the occupation regime. "He will have intelligence and more active tasks," the report noted tersely. It did not specify whether those "more active tasks" included the assassination of the collaborators or whether that would be left to other agents.

Another report discussed how the operatives should be alerted to evacuate the NKVD offices and set fire to buildings at the moment that the Germans were on the verge of taking the city. One option, it said, was to have ten buglers sound a signal. But the report added that some people might not understand what the signal meant and that there was a risk that German agents would learn of the plan. The other option, which was clearly preferred, was to equip the targeted buildings with radios to make sure the signal would be received and everyone would know this was the moment for the arson attacks on the buildings and their speedy evacuation.

As the German offensive came closer and closer, the NKVD was increasingly preoccupied with planting the explosives and mines necessary to achieve their objectives. In his recollections dated April 4, 1994, Sergei Fedoseyev, head of the Moscow region's NKVD counterintelligence section, explained that factories that could still be used to produce armaments were a priority target. Despite the enormous effort to move key industries to the east, that job was far from completed. Fedoseyev also mentioned the need for twenty tons of explosives to blow up twelve city bridges.

From an intelligence briefing, Fedoseyev and other NKVD officials heard that Otto Skorzeny, the SS officer who was already developing a reputation for ruthless efficiency and later in the war would snatch Benito Mussolini from captivity, was in charge of a "technical section" of the approaching German forces. His mission: to seize and secure Communist Party buildings in the city, the NKVD's Lubyanka, the Central Telegraph and other high priority facilities before they could be destroyed. With this in mind, the NKVD dispatched specialists to double check that everything was arranged to thwart those plans.

Igor and Natalya Shchors are among the last surviving members of the NKVD teams that were prepared for undercover work in an occupied Moscow. They are also a true NKVD couple, since they began their assignments in 1941 as strangers instructed to play the roles of husband and wife, and gradually the role-playing became reality. In 1944, they formally tied the knot and a year later started a family. After all this time, they still feel a little awkward discussing how an NKVD mission blossomed into a full-fledged romance. "In the beginning it was difficult," Natalya recalled, sitting in their cramped apartment on the Garden Ring Road in central Moscow. Her blue eyes sparkled as she looked over at Igor, sitting stiffly in his armchair by the window. "But from that time on, we've been together."

One of six children, Igor was born in 1913 and grew up in the Ukraine, where Stalin unleashed his terror campaign of forced collectivization, which resulted in an artificially induced famine that claimed millions of lives. Igor remembers it well. Although his family would get ration coupons for bread, the shops often had no bread at all for days at a time. "People would storm the shops to get bread, and we would eat it right away so that nobody could grab it from us," he says. "There were even cases of cannibalism."

Still, he managed to be a top student at school, particularly in math, and he was chosen to study at Leningrad's Mountain Engineering Institute, where, as he vividly recalls, "I would get more bread." As a mountain engineer, he learned all about explosives, and he took a two-year artillery course that allowed him to graduate with the rank of an officer. In March 1940, he was called to serve in the NKVD and told to report to the Lubyanka in Moscow. From there he was assigned to a special NKVD school in a wooded area outside the city. The wooden house that served as a school was ringed by barbed wire, and the students weren't allowed to leave the premises without informing their superiors exactly where they would be and who they would be visiting.

The school was primarily geared to teaching the future agents foreign languages, but it also was designed to make them familiar with the customs and behavior of the countries where they might be sent so that they could blend in as much as possible. And of course, they learned basic spycraft. By the end of the course, they were supposed to be ready to operate as illegal agents in a foreign country.

Igor arrived in late August 1940, and he recalls the early drills on outdoor surveillance, safecracking and the skills they'd need to elude capture. (For their final exam, they had to give the slip to instructors who tailed them.) The students used false last names and weren't allowed to question each other about their background. Igor was given the last name Shlegov, but he was allowed to keep using his real first name.

He was assigned to a group of twelve students learning French. There were also similar groups studying English, German, and Italian—forty-eight trainees in all, male and female. He remembers one of his instructors as "a talented criminal who was released and made a tutor." At a time when food shortages were still common, Igor learned how to eat oysters and fois gras. "We were supposed to know how to eat such food in case we went to some fancy event in France," he says. They also learned how to sip wine and other drinks that required a different approach from the normal bottoms-up vodka-drinking in Russia. To be prepared for the other end of the social spectrum, one of the instructors specialized in teaching his charges rude colloquial French. The students were told that once they reached France, they would open a beauty salon, a pub, or a hotel, using it as cover for their spying operations.

Igor formally completed the course on June 21, 1941, graduating with the rank of lieutenant in the NKVD. The next day, when he and a fellow graduate went to the market to buy some food and wine for a small celebration, a shop assistant rushed out to tell them about Molotov's announcement of the beginning of the war. Returning to the school, they received instructions to stay put until they received a new posting. A week later, Igor was assigned to OMSBON, the NKVD's special forces.

As part of that unit, he underwent more military training, but he was impatient to get into action and pleaded for a new assignment. After Stalin's speech on July 3 that called on people to join the resistance, Igor sent a telegram directly to Pavel Sudoplatov, the NKVD boss in charge of "special tasks," who responded by inviting him to the Lubyanka. Sudoplatov advised the eager, freshly minted lieutenant to be patient, assuring him that he'd find a way to use him soon. "The war will last a long time," Sudoplatov added.

Igor then found himself in a small group of men who were instructed to prepare for journeys that might take them directly into the fighting. Two of the men were sent to Smolensk, but one of them stepped on a mine and died immediately, while the other lost a leg. Igor was also supposed to head west, but the rapid advance of the German forces prompted his bosses to change his orders. He was brought back to Moscow, where his path would cross with Natalya's.

Born in 1919 in the village of Pavelkovo, about 150 miles south of Moscow, Natalya was no stranger to hardship either. She was the twelfth child in her family, and when she was only two, her mother died. Raised by her eldest sister, she loved sports and from 1937 to 1941 studied at the Joseph Stalin Institute of Physical Fitness in Moscow. She practiced all kinds of sports, from gymnastics to ice hockey, and took courses in sports medicine, physiology, anatomy, massage, and math and physics. In 1940, she took part in the annual sports parade in Red Square. She fondly recalls standing on a motorcycle and carrying flowers as her contingent paraded past Stalin and the rest of the Soviet leadership. Was she nervous? "I was never afraid of anything," she claims. Later, when the Germans starting dropping small incendiary bombs on the city, Natalya was among the young people who monitored the roofs and tossed away unexploded bombs so that they wouldn't set fire to the buildings.

When she completed her studies in the summer of 1941, Natalya was eager to join the army, but the director of her institute told her that she had been summoned to the Komsomol office downtown. There she and four other young women found themselves in a meeting with an NKVD officer, who asked them pointedly, "Aren't you afraid of going to the war?" All of them, including a soon-to-be-legendary teenager by the name of Zoya Kosmodemyanskaya, responded that this was exactly what they wanted. On the spot, they filled out their applications to join the NKVD.

A day later, Maklyarsky, the man who directed the entertainers preparing their assassination plot, assigned Natalya to an OMSBON unit. She was to work as a nurse in Stroitel, a town in the Moscow region. She had already learned first aid while doing part-time work in a medical institute ("I wasn't afraid of blood," she notes). As part of her OMSBON training, she was also taught to shoot and make explosives.

In early October, a hospital supervisor told the nurses that a senior NKVD officer was arriving to conduct interviews with them. The officer turned out to be Maklyarsky, who greeted her with a smile and called her Natalie instead of Natalya, which is the more common form of her name. "Natalie, we would like you to carry out a special order of Stalin," he told her, adding that she should come to Moscow.

The very next day, Natalya and two other women found themselves in room 1212 of the prestigious Hotel Moskva, the brooding, massive building next to the Kremlin where explosives were discovered in 2005. They were issued new uniforms, but Natalya's boots were four sizes too large for her. Struggling along in them, she was escorted by Maklyarsky to the Lubyanka office of Bogdan Kobulov, Beria's right-hand man. Kobulov sat behind a huge desk, with several officers seated around it.

"What can you do?" Kobulov asked her. "Can you drive?"

Natalya responded that she could but she had a driver's license only for a motorcycle. "I also play hockey and do sports," she added.

Kobulov had his mind on other things. "What if we make you a fictitious wife?" he asked. In preparation for undercover assignments, the NKVD sometimes put male and female agents in fake marriages, which allowed them to work together without arousing suspicion. The brass assumed that a married young couple would attract less attention than a single man or woman.

Natalya still smiles at the memory. "I felt my heart sink for a moment and I turned red. But I said, 'If I need to do this for my country, I'll do it.'" Her lack of enthusiasm was understandable since she had a boyfriend named Dmitry, who had already proposed to her. He had been called up in 1939, and they had kept writing letters to each other. But she felt she had no choice but to agree to pretend to be the wife of a man she hadn't yet even met.

She was sent back to room 1212 at the Hotel Moskva, where the NKVD supplied her with "beautiful dresses, shoes and bedding," she recalls. Then the phone rang, and she was instructed to report to room 525. There she was introduced to Igor and told that a driver would take them to the apartment assigned to him in the Rublevo section on the outskirts of Moscow. It was hardly a romantic beginning to their life together. Since even the NKVD driver wasn't supposed to know that they weren't truly a married couple, Igor put his arm around Natalya in the car, but she stiffened, leaving no doubt how uncomfortable she felt.

That discomfort hardly eased when they arrived at the apartment. Igor's official job was working at the local railroad station, but he was also part of a rescue brigade charged with putting out fires in his neighborhood. The wooden houses there would burn easily as a result of air raids or, if the Germans came close enough, shelling. And then there were other duties, preparation for sabotage activities. All of which meant Igor was rarely in the apartment, often sleeping on the job wherever it was. After bringing Natalya to her new quarters, he quickly left her in the apartment alone. The awkwardness of their situation may have given him added incentive to do so.

Once he had left, Natalya surveyed the apartment's one small room. It contained a bed, a table, and a chair and, she recalls, cigarette butts all over the floor. She swept the floor, straightened the bed, and when night fell, tried to sleep. But she was too nervous to settle down, and at five in the morning she went for a walk in the nearby woods to clear her head. Just then, Igor returned and panicked when he saw that she wasn't there. He immediately contacted Maklyarsky and Sudoplatov, who reprimanded her for not keeping Igor informed of her whereabouts.

Natalya's official job was to monitor the chemical content of the area's water supplies. But her more important assignment was to assist Igor in his preparations for resistance once the Germans took over the city. He was supposed to keep working at the Rublevo railway station, using that job as cover for serving as liaison between different resistance groups and keeping the government, presumably evacuated at that point to Kuibyshev, informed about what was happening in the occupied capital.

The Soviet authorities had already placed explosives or mines in major buildings such as the Bolshoi Theater, where top Germans were likely to appear, and on roads and in other public facilities. Igor knew all about those mines, since they were wrapped in special antimagnetic containers that had been developed in the Leningrad Mountain Engineering Institute, where he had studied. These containers made it almost impossible to detect the mines' presence. But when it came to the Rublevo railway station, where he worked, Igor had a special certificate from Molotov, Stalin's right-hand man, forbidding Soviet troops to burn or blow up the station as they retreated. The idea was to keep it functioning as a resistance center.

Igor's other special privilege: at a time when almost all cars were commandeered for the front lines, he was assigned an M-1 car, a prestigious vehicle normally assigned to government officials, to make his rounds and allow him to send radio messages from different locations. The front seat cushion was an early James-Bond-like creation. It looked perfectly normal on the outside, but the inside was filled with a five-kilowatt battery that powered his radio gear.

The NKVD gave Igor and Natalya forged documents and a new last name: Shevchenko. At times, Igor went out alone; at others, Natalya joined him and helped him with his myriad tasks. Like the good math student that he was, Igor remembers that he buried 4,400 liters of fuel poured into 110 milk containers, which could be dug up and used for making explosives. He also buried sacks of dynamite, guns, and grenades for use by the underground. When she accompanied him, Natalya helped him camouflage the hiding places by covering them with leaves and grass. Since he was an engineer, Igor also monitored the water and sewage systems, keeping tabs on how he could smuggle resistance fighters through them.

That last responsibility led to a sudden summons to Stalin's dacha. As a result of a stray German bomb, the water supply to the dacha had sprung a leak. "You must fix the pipe immediately!" the dictator's chief bodyguard commanded him. Igor kept his cool and ordered the other bodyguards to start digging to find the leak. Within three hours, he had completed the repair job and was awarded the Order of the Red Star for doing so. He was one of the lucky ones whose close encounter with the tyrant ended happily.

Dmitry, Natalya's boyfriend in the army, kept writing to her every day. And Natalya was still bothered enough by her fictitious marriage that she went to Maklyarsky and asked him if she couldn't be assigned to a partisan unit. The NKVD boss wouldn't hear of it.

In the meantime, Igor insisted that Natalya address him by his first name instead of the more formal Igor Aleksandrovich to keep up the pretence that they were married. He tried to act the caring husband, and he tried to coax her to relax. As Igor pointed out, working in the underground meant acting their parts with conviction, since their lives depended on it. Over time, both of them became more accustomed to their roles, and then they no longer felt like roles. In 1943, with Moscow no longer threatened, Natalya was sent to an NKVD radio liaison school for four months. Since the students were not allowed to leave the premises during the course, Igor visited her every night. They were married for real in

1944. By the time her old boyfriend Dmitry returned from the war in 1945, she and Igor had a five-month-old son.

When I visited the couple in May 2004, Natalya—short, stooped but still spry—tallied the rest of the family history: four children, one of whom died, three grandchildren, and three great-grandchildren. The elderly couple live with a daughter, son-in-law, and grandson in their two-room apartment in a Stalin-era building with high ceilings, lugubrious double windows that let in very little light, and shabby Soviet furniture. The bookshelves contain a jumble of wartime memoirs, especially of NKVD agents, and their grandson's toys—miniature cars, Star Wars games, and the latest Harry Potter book in a flashy Russian edition. They had been petitioning everyone to get a separate apartment for her daughter's family, with no success. Ailing and tired, Igor didn't seem particularly interested in fighting anymore for that cause. But always ready to spring into action, Natalya held out a ray of hope. "We've written to Putin," she said. She was waiting for a reply.

For every story that had a happy ending, where the protagonists survived, there were countless others with tragic endings during the battle for Moscow. But the Soviet leaders made sure that carefully selected cases were put to good use, transforming the victims into mythic figures whose courage would inspire others to follow suit, no matter what the price. Zoya Kosmodemyanskaya, the eighteen-year-old who had volunteered for underground work along with Natalya Shchors, was at the top of that list.

Natalya's memory from that single encounter with Zoya was of a teenager who was "tall, pretty, with short, cropped brown hair like a boy's." What else could she say about her? "You could see she was a good girl."

She was also a brave one, who paid the ultimate price for her courage. Dispatched in late November 1941 on an arson mission to the German-occupied village of Petrishchevo about fifty-five miles from Moscow, she was captured, tortured, and executed. That much of her story is clear, but there are differing accounts of the rest of it, and there is a key omission in all the official versions that followed.

For all the obvious pitfalls of relying on NKVD interrogation records, which were often the product of methods that were every bit
as brutal as the Gestapo's, the official report on the interrogation
of Vasily Klubkov, one of two Red Army soldiers who were sent on
the mission with Zoya, appears to be accurate in the main outline
of her story. Dated March 11 to 12, 1942, the top secret document
offers a transcript of the interrogation of Klubkov that started at 10
P.M. and continued until 5 A.M. Klubkov was captured by the Germans, and the NKVD prepared the transcript as evidence that he
was the one who betrayed Zoya and then went on to work for the
Germans. According to some rumors, the villagers may have betrayed Zoya, but no mention of that possibility ever appears in the
report or in other official versions of the events.

Like Zoya, Klubkov was eighteen, a postal worker with seven
years of schooling. He had joined the Red Army only a month
before this first disastrous mission. A three-person team, which
consisted of Zoya, Klubkov, and a soldier named Boris Krainov, was
equipped with bottles filled with fuel—better known as Molotov
cocktails—guns and food before they were sent on their way. The
threesome walked for four days to get to the village, approaching it
through the woods in the middle of the night. Once they reached
their destination, they decided to split up to set fire to buildings in
different parts of the village.

Klubkov told his NKVD interrogators that as he approached the
house that he was supposed to set on fire, he could see that Zoya
and Boris had already set their targeted buildings alight. He
claimed that he tossed his Molotov cocktail but "for some reason it
didn't burn." At that moment, he spotted German guards and ran
for the woods about three hundred meters away. "As soon as I got
to the woods, two German soldiers jumped me and took my gun,
two bags with five bottled explosives and a bag of food from me."
He noted that the food bag also contained a liter of vodka.

The Germans brought their captive to their village headquarters, where an officer took charge of him. The senior man immediately pointed a gun at Klubkov and demanded he tell who else had
accompanied him on his mission. According to the transcript,
Klubkov confessed that he promptly complied. "I was a coward," he
said. "I was scared I would be shot."

The officer gave an order to the German soldiers, who quickly left the house. At that point, Klubkov also told the officer that he was part of a four-hundred-man reconnaissance unit based in Kuntsevo, a village on the southwestern outskirts of Moscow, and that this unit was sending out small sabotage teams, usually of five to ten people, behind enemy lines.

A few minutes later, the soldiers brought in Zoya. Klubkov said he didn't know whether they had also captured Boris. As Klubkov looked on, the Germans began their interrogation of the new prisoner. Asked how she had conducted her arson attack, Zoya denied that she had set fire to anything. "The officer started beating Zoya up and demanded she answer the questions," Klubkov reported. "However, she refused to say anything."

When the Germans asked if this was really Zoya and what he knew about her, Klubkov confirmed her identity and the fact that she had set fires in the southern part of the village. Zoya stubbornly remained silent, and, increasingly frustrated, several officers stripped her naked and beat her with rubber truncheons for two to three hours, trying to force her to break her silence. "Kill me but I won't tell you anything," Zoya reportedly declared. Klubkov added: "After that, they took her out of the room and I didn't see her anymore."

The details of what happened next to Zoya are open to dispute. Her story was subsequently portrayed in a play and a film and depicted in propaganda art, which hardly qualify as unimpeachable historical sources. According to some accounts, the Germans led her through the village with a placard around her neck before torturing her some more, cutting off her left breast, and then hanging her. When Soviet troops finally arrived in the village, they found her frozen, mutilated body still hanging from the gallows.

In the screen version, Zoya's story takes on even more symbolic meaning. The film claims she was born on January 21, 1924, the day that Lenin died. It shows footage of Lenin lying in state, juxtaposing this with shots of baby Zoya, who will keep his spirit alive. She grows up in a loving home, with her parents teaching her all the communist virtues. When the war breaks out, she quickly volunteers for dangerous partisan missions. The film depicts her capture and torture and how she is led to the gallows walking barefoot in the snow. In the execution scene, the villagers are clearly awed as they watch the beautiful young woman bravely face death, shouting out at the last moment: "Stalin will come!" There's nothing subtle about the message: Stalin will be their savior.

But the filmmakers didn't hesitate to rearrange the facts when it suited their purposes, starting with Zoya's date of birth. The public record is clear. Zoya was born on September 13, 1923, a few months earlier than in the film and certainly not on the same day as Lenin's death. Nina Tumarkin, whose book *The Living and the Dead: The Rise and Fall of the Cult of World War II in Russia* examines the mythmaking process at work in the Soviet Union, discovered that Zoya's family situation was also a far cry from the way it was depicted on the screen.

Zoya, Tumarkin writes, "had had a tragic home life that propelled her toward suicide." Her father, who is portrayed in the film as going off to the front when the war starts, was already dead by that time—shot, along with her grandfather, during Stalin's terror campaign in the 1930s. Influenced by an uncle who was a committed communist and by her mother's desire to clear the family name, she volunteered for the Komsomol's local partisan group, even though this was a path to nearly certain death at that time in that particular region. "The forest was sparse and the terrain was flat," Tumarkin notes. "There was no cover for partisans and no opportunity for them to accomplish anything except to turn themselves into exemplars of heroism by getting killed."

After Zoya perished, her mother lobbied intensively to make her into a national hero. "She told me, 'I will die as a hero, or come back as a hero,'" the mother declared. In 1944, she also urged her still underage son, Zoya's younger brother, to volunteer for service. He, too, was killed, another victim of his mother's zeal.

As for Vasily Klubkov, the fellow teenager who was captured by the Germans, the NKVD transcript of his interrogation several months later tells the rest of his story. Once Zoya was led away, the German officer told him, "You are going to work for German intelligence now. Anyway, you have already betrayed your motherland. We will train you a bit and send you to the Soviet home front."

"I accepted the officer's offer to work for German intelligence," he told his NKVD interrogators. He then went on to describe other

Soviet POWs he met when he was sent off for special training in Krasny Bor, a town near Smolensk. There German officers explained how he and the others were supposed to return to Red Army units, claiming that they had escaped captivity. Klubkov's specific mission was to get himself back into his old unit, where he could find out what groups were about to be dispatched behind German lines, and relay that information to his German masters.

When he "escaped," he did manage to return to his unit, but he was quickly arrested and the interrogations began. From the transcript of his interrogation during the night of March 11 to 12, it's clear that he was already broken, willing to confess to anything his interrogators insisted upon. Stalin's working assumption was that any Soviet soldier who allowed himself to be captured was by definition a traitor and that anyone who escaped German captivity was doubly suspect. His interrogators certainly knew that they were expected to share the same set of principles. Which meant getting Klubkov to produce the kind of confession that would only confirm their accuracy.

Klubkov may have been telling the truth, since it's easy to imagine a terrified teenager on his first mission agreeing to his German captors' demands. But there's no way of knowing for sure how he really behaved, since he surely was just as terrified when he was interrogated by the NKVD. Or how much of what he said about Zoya was accurate, since the NKVD may already have been preparing the transcript with the idea of her elevation to mythic status. Only Klubkov's fate is certain. In the Central Archives of the current Russian secret service, now known as the FSB, the top secret report of his subsequent trial on April 3, 1942, accompanies the transcript of Klubkov's earlier interrogation. It's a very short document, which contains Klubkov's confirmation that he betrayed Zoya and his motherland "due to my own cowardice."

The court's verdict: "Execution by shooting, without confiscation of property due to its absence."

As the Germans advanced closer and closer to Moscow, Stalin found himself looking to another type of agent with a secret mission, one who was working under cover in Tokyo for the GRU, the military intelligence arm of the Red Army. This was Richard Sorge, the master spy who had infuriated the Soviet leader before June 22, 1941, by bombarding Moscow with warnings that Hitler was about to strike. In the late summer and early autumn of 1941, the Kremlin desperately needed to know whether Japan's forces were preparing to attack the weakened Soviet Union from the east, as its German ally was urging it to do. So long as that looked probable or even possible, Stalin had to keep a large contingent of his troops deployed in Siberia rather than calling them back to help in the defense of Moscow. All of which meant that nothing would be more valuable than accurate intelligence from Tokyo. No one had a better track record there than Sorge, no matter how much Stalin despised him.

Born of a Russian mother and a German father, Sorge didn't just flirt with danger, he courted it. Officially working as a correspondent for the *Frankfurter Zeitung* in Tokyo, he garnered inside information from the German embassy and senior Japanese officials, which he'd promptly pass on to Moscow. He skillfully maintained his dual identity, even when, as often was the case, he drank heavily. He carried on affairs with a wide array of Japanese and other women, including the wife of the German ambassador, Eugen Ott. His exploits fascinated even the postwar occupiers of Japan, whom he didn't live to see. According to a U.S. military intelligence report, he was "intimate with some thirty women in Tokyo during his years of service, including the wife of his good friend, the German ambassador, the wife of his foreign assistant, and the mistress of this same assistant."

But he took his greatest risks by openly disputing German predictions that they'd quickly seize Moscow and win the war. In effect, he portrayed himself as a patriotic German who was confident enough to air all his misgivings. "This war is criminal! We have no chance of winning!" he told Ambassador Ott shortly after the Germans invaded. "The Japanese laugh when we put out the line that we'll be in Moscow by the end of August!" In his contacts with Japanese officials, he also argued that German calculations were wildly wrong, doing his best to undermine the efforts of Ott and other Germans to convince the Japanese that they should join their country in crushing the Soviet Union. There was certainly some method to Sorge's apparent madness. Ott, for one, was convinced that Sorge's outbursts proved that he wasn't hiding anything from him. Besides, the German ambassador genuinely liked Sorge and, as more of an opportunist than a diehard Nazi, he wasn't about to report his heretical views.

Apart from his role as a Soviet agent, Sorge also hid the fact that he was far more seriously worried that the Japanese would attack the Soviet Union than he let on. Since Ott routinely confided in him, Sorge knew that the German ambassador was trying to sort out the mixed signals he was receiving from his hosts. At times they suggested that Japan would act like a good German ally and jump into the conflict with the Soviet Union and at other times Japan's rulers appeared extremely hesitant. The Japanese remembered that General Zhukov had defeated their forces in Mongolia in 1939, which made at least some of them skeptical about German claims that Germany would achieve an easy victory against the same commander. But those memories made the politicians pause more than the military leaders, who were primed for action. "Now the opportunity to destroy the U.S.S.R. has arrived," proclaimed General Sadao Araki.

In July, the Japanese started a new mobilization, sending more troops north to Manchuria. Ott wanted to believe that this meant that Tokyo was preparing to attack Russia. As for Sorge, he later conceded that this "gave us cause for anxiety." But the Japanese were also intent on pursuing their imperial ambitions to the south, deploying troops to expand their Greater East Asia Co-Prosperity Sphere, despite mounting tensions with the United States and Britain. On July 28, their forces took over French bases in Indochina. The question was whether Tokyo was ready to move in both directions.

Pressed by his superiors in Moscow, Sorge still couldn't provide a clear answer. On July 30, he reported, "Japan will be able to begin war from the second half of August, but will only do so should the Red Army actually be defeated by the Germans, resulting in a weakening of defense capabilities in the Far East." He added that a key Japanese informant "is convinced that if the Red Army stops the Germans in front of Moscow, Japan will not make a move." In other words, the battle for Moscow would be the single most crucial factor in Japan's decision.

This left the Kremlin in a Catch-22 situation. If it pulled a significant number of troops out of the Far East and sent them to defend Moscow, this would provide desperately needed reinforcements that might determine the outcome of that battle. At the same time, it would prove to be a grievous miscalculation if it served as an invitation to the Japanese to attack from the east, possibly delivering the coup de grace to the beleaguered Soviet regime. But that conundrum would evaporate if Sorge could provide the reassurance that the Kremlin so urgently needed that the Japanese weren't going to attack.

Sorge had no doubts about the importance of his mission, and he pushed his Japanese collaborators and unwitting sources hard to pick up any intelligence they could. He endlessly discussed the conflicting signals with Hotsumi Ozaki, a left-wing Japanese journalist he had befriended and then enlisted as an accomplice in espionage. In early August, Ozaki had picked up reports that the Japanese would attack the Soviet Union on August 15. Sorge told him that Ott had heard the same reports and believed them. But Ozaki noted that the Japanese were well aware of the fact that the German offensive was encountering more resistance than expected in some places, which argued for caution. And if the Japanese were to attack, they knew they had to do so very soon or risk fighting a winter war in Siberia.

On August 11, Sorge wrote another ambivalent note to Moscow reflecting those considerations. He pointed out that the Japanese were carefully monitoring the German-Soviet fighting and the losses the Germans were incurring even as they continued their advance. He also noted the growing tensions with the United States, which were increasing the pressure for a decision on what Tokyo's priorities should be. With winter approaching, he added, "In the coming two to three weeks, Japan's decision will be made." But if the tone of his report suggested that Japan was unlikely to attack, he hedged his bets in a way that was hardly reassuring. "It is possible that the General Staff will take the decision to intervene without prior consultation," he wrote.

A couple of weeks later, Sorge and Ozaki were picking up far more encouraging signals. The German naval attaché, Paul Wenneker, told Sorge that the Japanese navy wanted to push south and rule out an attack on the Soviet Union, at least for the current year. And while reporting on Japanese troop strength in Manchuria, Sorge proudly added some vital information he had learned. "Many soldiers have been issued with shorts . . . and from this it can be assumed that large numbers will be shipped to the south." Specifically, he mentioned that the Japanese were discussing plans to occupy Thailand and Borneo. In another message, he relayed news that Ozaki had learned from top government officials about their attitude toward an attack on the Soviet Union. "They decided not to launch the war within this year, repeat, not to launch the war this year." It was a line that radiated triumph and relief.

Would Stalin believe him? The Soviet dictator was as suspicious as ever of a spy who blended so fully into the German community in Tokyo and was well known for his freewheeling lifestyle. Ever since Sorge had angered Stalin with his accurate reports predicting the German attack on the Soviet Union, his own bosses in military intelligence had speculated that he might be an agent for the other side. During the purges, some officers who were convicted of trumped-up charges of spying for Germany or Japan had mentioned Sorge, which was enough to establish guilt by association.

But this time, Sorge was reporting something that the Kremlin hoped was true. And by the middle of September, Ott and other German diplomats were conceding that there was no chance that the Japanese would respond positively to their pleas for intervention. Instead, Tokyo was determined to expand its reach in Southeast Asia, and it saw the United States as the main obstacle to its ambitions. Back in Moscow, General Aleksei Panfilov, a tank commander who was serving as the temporary chief of military intelligence, offered a rare endorsement of Sorge. "Considering his great possibilities as a source and the reliability of a significant amount of his previous reporting, this report inspires confidence," he wrote.

As Sorge would admit later, it was only in September that the Kremlin began to have "complete trust in my reports" that the invasion wasn't about to happen. As a result, Stalin finally felt free to make the decision to send a large part of the forces in the Soviet Far East to defend Moscow. Starting in October, the Siberians, as they were called, were transported to the Soviet heartland. A total of about four hundred thousand troops were redeployed in this period of late 1941 and early 1942, making the one-to-two-week journey in hastily organized special trains. Approximately 250,000 were dispatched to defend Moscow, and the rest were sent to Leningrad and other embattled regions. The arrival of these fresh troops, most of whom were outfitted with proper winter clothing, would dramatically change the situation for Moscow's defenders and shock the Germans, who had fought their way to within striking distance of the city.

In mid-October, Sorge wrote what proved to be his last dispatch to Moscow. Once again, he demonstrated the reliability of his Japanese sources by predicting that "war with the United States will begin in the very near future." But the report was never sent. The Japanese finally caught on and arrested him along with Ozaki and other members of his espionage ring on October 18. During relentless interrogation sessions, he admitted his role, and he was sentenced to death. But his captors were in no hurry to execute him. In fact, they kept him alive in prison until late 1944.

By then, the war was going badly for Japan and it had little interest in further antagonizing the Soviet Union, which it feared might join the war in the Pacific. Japanese officials had suggested several times that they'd be willing to exchange Sorge for a Japanese prisoner held by the Soviet side. Each time they were rebuffed. The standard response, in one case reported as coming directly from Stalin, was, "Richard Sorge? I do not know a person of that name."

The Soviet leader wasn't about to save someone who knew so much about the warnings he had received and ignored when Hitler was preparing to invade his country. And he wasn't moved at all by the fact that Sorge's intelligence coup a few months later, confirming that the Japanese were not going to attack the Soviet Union in 1941, was a critical factor in the battle for Moscow. On November 7, 1944, which happened to be the twenty-seventh anniversary of the Bolshevik Revolution, Sorge was hanged.

9

"O Mein Gott! O Mein Gott!"

The fighting in October hadn't produced any decisive break-throughs for either side. German units were about forty miles out-side Moscow and in some places even closer. Although the invaders were tired, battered, and overextended, they still threatened to make good on Hitler's vow to seize and then annihilate the Soviet capital. The panic in the city had subsided, but Stalin and his en-tourage were far from convinced that the worst was over. Even with fresh troops arriving from Siberia, there was no assurance that Moscow could stave off disaster.

It was at this moment that Stalin insisted on carrying out his most dramatic gesture of defiance: a full-blown celebration of No-vember 7, the twenty-fourth anniversary of the Bolshevik Revolu-tion. He was convinced that precisely because Moscow's fate was still uncertain, such a stage-managed event could provide the city's defenders with a much-needed boost of confidence. That is, if something didn't go wrong, producing exactly the opposite result.

The first part of the ceremonies sent somewhat of a mixed mes-sage. On November 6, the Soviet leaders assembled in the Maya-kovsky metro station for an address by Stalin to delegates of the Moscow City Soviet and other civilian and military officials. Sitting on chairs brought from the Bolshoi Theater for the occasion, the assembled dignitaries applauded as Stalin, along with Molotov, Mikoyan, and other Kremlin leaders, arrived on a subway train they had taken from a nearby station. Broadcast on radio and loud-speakers, the proceedings began with a burst of patriotic music and were followed by the leader's address to the nation. All of which was designed for maximum inspirational effect.

This may have worked for those listening on the radio but not necessarily for the officials gathered below ground in the metro station. British correspondent Alexander Werth pointed out that everyone knew that the venue had been chosen because of the danger posed by German bombers to anything aboveground. "As many who attended the meeting later told me, the underground setting of the meeting was uncanny, depressing, and humiliating," he wrote. Stalin's speech, he added, "was a strange mixture of black gloom and complete self-confidence."

That it was. Talking about the danger facing the country since the Germans first launched their attack, he declared: "Today, as a result of four months of war, I must emphasize that this danger—far from diminishing—has on the contrary increased. The enemy has captured the greater part of the Ukraine, Belorussia, Moldavia, and Estonia, and a number of other regions, has penetrated the Donbass, is looming like a black cloud over Leningrad, and is menacing our glorious capital, Moscow." He also warned that the enemy "is straining all his strength to capture Leningrad and Moscow before the winter sets in, for he knows that the winter holds nothing good in store for him."

But if that part of his speech painted a bleak picture, he also claimed that heroic Soviet troops had "compelled the enemy to shed streams of blood" and that the *Blitzkrieg* had already failed. He then reeled off statistics that were supposed to prove how badly the Germans had been beaten, although only moments before he had effectively conceded that it was his armies that had suffered a devastating series of defeats. "In four months of the war we lost 350,000 killed, 378,000 missing, and have 1,020,000 wounded men," he asserted. "In the same period, the enemy lost over 4,500,000 killed, wounded and prisoners."

As Western historians have pointed out, the Red Army routinely lost more men than the Wehrmacht even later in the war when they were scoring victory after victory and driving the Germans out. For the entire period of the conflict, on average the Red Army lost three times more men than the Germans did. Stalin's numbers, purportedly reflecting the losses during the string of German early victories, were nothing more than fantasy. "It is extremely doubtful that anyone in Russia could have believed those figures," Werth wrote. But as the British correspondent noted, they were meant to buttress Stalin's broader assertion that the *Blitzkrieg* had fallen short, failing to produce the swift collapse of Germany's intended victim that it had achieved in Poland and Western Europe.

To explain "the temporary military setbacks" of the Red Army, Stalin offered a variety of excuses. Although he trumpeted the fact that Britain and the United States were now allied with the Soviet Union, the first excuse he gave was "the absence of a second front in Europe," which allowed the Germans to focus on the Eastern front. "The situation now is such that our country is waging the war of liberation alone without anyone's military aid," he said. Of course, he never mentioned that the Germans were able to invade Poland thanks to their alliance with Russia or how long Britain had fought alone before Operation Barbarossa.

Similarly, he blamed the setbacks on "the shortage of tanks and partly also of aircraft," presenting the problem solely as one of production capabilities, never acknowledging the huge losses that were a direct result of his refusal to believe that the Germans would attack when they did. He vowed that Soviet industry would achieve a "several-fold" increase in the production of tanks and other weaponry, and, in fact, this would prove to be an accurate forecast of what would happen later in the war, wiping out the initial German superiority in firepower.

But the balance sheet of evasions and promises was less important than his invocation of a patriotic duty to resist the invaders who "have already sunk to the level of wild beasts." Portraying the conflict as another in a long line of defenses of Mother Russia, he reminded his listeners of the great figures of Russian history, everyone from Pushkin and Tolstoy to the legendary military commanders Aleksandr Suvorov and Mikhail Kutuzov. Not coincidentally,

Kutuzov was the general who defeated Napoleon's armies. "Napoleon's fate must not be forgotten," he intoned. He mentioned Lenin as well, but the focus was on the national—not the ideological—struggle for survival.

And finally there was his vow of far more than victory. "The German invaders want a war of extermination against the peoples of the U.S.S.R. Well, if the Germans want a war of extermination, they shall have it." It would be an eye for an eye or, more accurately, vengeance at any price.

The traditional military parade in Red Square, the riskiest part of the ceremonies, was scheduled for eight o'clock the following morning, though only those directly involved, who were all sworn to secrecy, knew the timing and details. Most of the commanders of the military units slated to take part received word about those plans at 2 A.M., just a few hours before they had to muster their troops. As the troops, tanks and artillery assembled in the early-morning cold, fears of a German air raid receded. While Soviet planes still patrolled the gray skies, a heavy snowfall had started by the time of the parade, making air strikes highly unlikely. From the Kremlin gate, Marshal Budenny emerged on a white horse with saber drawn and joined Stalin and the other Kremlin leaders on the Lenin Mausoleum to review the troops.

During the night, sand had been scattered on Red Square and the nearby streets, but it disappeared in the morning winds and snowfall. This made the job of the artillery and tank brigades particularly difficult, since they had to deal with slippery surfaces and snowdrifts. With Stalin and the rest of the brass looking on, some of the troops had to push recalcitrant artillery pieces. Two heavy tanks stopped in the square and turned in the wrong direction, triggering a moment of alarm, followed by visible relief when it became clear that this was due to a miscommunication. But most of the soldiers marched through Red Square without incident—and immediately marched out of the city to rejoin the fighting at the nearby front.

With strong winds whipping up the snow that morning, Stalin's voice didn't carry well. Most of those who were marching in Red Square that day registered only his presence, not his message. "We marched past the mausoleum and we saw him," Aleksandr Zevelev, a member the NKVD special forces known as OMSBON, recalled. "He was waving his arm."

But it was precisely Stalin's presence that mattered. On the eve of the parade, Leonid Shevelev, a new recruit, couldn't understand why his instructors were wasting time on marching drills. "For us it was incredible: the enemy was near Moscow and we were practicing our marching!" he said. But early in the morning on November 7, they found out the reason, and their participation gave them a huge morale boost. "We had heard that Stalin had left the capital," Shevelev said, referring to the rumors that had circulated earlier. "It was very important for us to see that our leader chose to stay with us in Moscow. This made us march with the kind of determination as if we were nailing down the coffins of the advancing Nazis."

Another young OMSBON volunteer present that day, Yevgeny Teleguyev, pointed out that the importance of the parade was that it took place at all. When his unit arrived at the front straight from Red Square, the soldiers they were coming to assist had already heard reports of what had happened. "Is it true that there was a parade in Moscow?" they asked. Teleguyev and the others replied, "There was and we even participated in it." As Teleguyev recalled, the soldiers were awed by their testimony.

But Stalin wanted much more than just to prove that he was there. Since the sound technicians had been unable to get a clear recording of his speech at the parade and the cameramen had problems getting decent shots of him, he agreed to deliver his speech again the next day to get a good recording and sound track. The speech that most Soviet citizens heard broadcast on November 8 and the newsreel footage of Stalin that they saw of him reviewing the troops came from this staged session in the Kremlin. The Soviet leader wasn't about to let the bad weather mar his effort to get his message out.

As he did in his speech at the Mayakovsky metro station, the Soviet leader admitted that a lot of territory had been "temporarily lost" and that "the enemy is before the gates of Leningrad and Moscow." But he once again boasted that the Soviet troops were inflicting heavy losses on the invaders and insisted that the Germans "are straining their last forces." "The enemy is not as strong as some terror-stricken would-be intellectuals picture him," he added—a statement that underscored his loathing of intellectuals and set up his prediction that the war would end in disaster not just for Germany's armed forces but also for its masters. "Another few months, another half year, one year perhaps—and Hitlerite Germany must collapse under the weight of its own crimes," he declared.

Whether or not Stalin believed his own words, he knew he had to rally his countrymen. One way was to signal his determination to call up as many troops as needed for the effort to repulse the invaders. "Our reserves in manpower are inexhaustible," he pointed out. The other was to repeat and expand his litany of Russian heroes, this time starting with the thirteenth- and fourteenth-century warriors Alexander Nevsky and Dmitri Donskoi and finishing again with Marshal Kutuzov, the architect of the victory against Napoleon. "Let the manly images of our great ancestors . . . inspire you in this war!" he declared. It was an unabashed appeal to the kind of patriotism that made no distinction between the old and new regimes. It was also a de facto admission that the country was in such danger that he couldn't depend on loyalty to the Communist Party to carry the day.

For all his prophecies of victory and boasting about wildly inflated German losses, Stalin was desperately eager for reassurance that he wouldn't be proved wrong. On or around November 19, he phoned General Zhukov and asked, "Are you sure we are going to be able to hold Moscow? I am asking with an aching heart. Tell me honestly, as a member of the Party."

"There is no question that we will be able to hold Moscow," Zhukov told him. But he took advantage of the occasion to ask for the assignment of two new armies to the defense of the capital and two hundred tanks.

"I am glad you are so sure," Stalin replied. He promised Zhukov two reserve armies by the end of November but claimed he couldn't do anything about his request for tanks. "We have no tanks for the time being," he said.

While Zhukov had to respond with the reassurance that Stalin was seeking, he wasn't nearly as confident as he sounded. Elena Rzhevskaya, who has written extensively about her own wartime experiences, met Zhukov when he was working on his memoirs in

1964. The famed military leader was largely ostracized at the time, a victim of political infighting in the Kremlin, and he talked openly about the crucial turning points of the war with her. "Marshal Zhukov considered November 1941 the most critical and most ominous month for Moscow, when its fate was decided in battle," she recalled.

For all the bravado they had displayed on the anniversary of the Bolshevik Revolution, Stalin and his generals knew that the fight for control of the Soviet capital—and the country—could still go either way.

Hitler continued to exude confidence that his forces would emerge victorious soon, and those charged with keeping up the morale of the troops did their best to spur them on. A proclamation addressed to German soldiers in October declared:

> *Soldiers! Moscow is before you. In the course of two years of war all of the continent's capitals have bowed before you, you have marched along the streets of the best cities. Moscow remains. Force her to bow, show her the strength of your weapons, walk through her squares. Moscow means the end of the war!*
>
> *—Wehrmacht High Command*

But many of the officers and men who were doing the actual fighting were beginning to be plagued by doubts. Although their string of early victories seemed to confirm that the Red Army wouldn't be able to resist their onslaught, there were also early indications that the enemy they had been taught to scorn would be difficult to crush, no matter how terrifying his losses.

General Ewald von Kleist, who commanded the First Panzer Army, was astounded by the refusal of some Red Army units to surrender under any circumstances. "The Russians are so primitive that they won't give up even when they are surrounded by a dozen machine guns," he recalled after the war when he was held in Nuremberg. "I would say it is a difference between German bravery and Russian bravery in the sense that the former is logical and the latter brutal."

A German soldier who was sent to the Eastern front in August 1941 described his shock in discovering that the Red Army was employing the same kind of human wave tactics that were used in World War I. The Soviet assaults "were carried out by masses of men who made no real attempt at concealment but trusted in sheer weight of numbers to overwhelm us," he wrote. In one such attack, "The lines of men stretched to the right and left of our regimental front overlapping it completely and the whole mass of Russian troops came tramping solidly and relentlessly forward."

Describing the vision before him as "an unbelievable sight, a machine gunner's dream target," he added, "It was rumored that the commissars worked out the number of machine guns which we had, multiplied that number by the number of rounds per minute that we could fire, calculated how many minutes it would take a body of soldiers to cross the area and added to the final total a couple of thousand men. Thus some men would get through our line . . ."

The German was convinced that the attack he was seeing had been calculated precisely that way. "At 600 meters we opened fire and whole sections of the first wave just vanished, leaving here and there an odd survivor still walking stolidly forward," he recalled. "It was uncanny, unbelievable, inhuman. No soldier of ours would have continued to advance alone." As German machine guns overheated from the continual firing, the Soviet side kept sending in more waves of troops. "The Ivans," as he called them, kept up their attacks for three days, and he never saw a stretcher-bearer during the entire time.

"The number, duration and fury of those attacks had exhausted and numbed us completely. Not to hide the truth, they had frightened us," the German admitted. He noted that this depressed many of the men in his unit, who now realized that they were in for a much more difficult struggle than they had anticipated. "That we would win, we had no doubt, but what we were now engaged in would be a long, bitter and hard fought war," he concluded.

Many German units were involved in less dramatic engagements and didn't experience these human wave tactics. But they, too, were finding the fighting in Russia unlike any other they had faced so far. Lieutenant Kurt Gruman of the 185th Infantry Regiment, the Eighty-seventh Infantry Division, pondered the contrasts as he wrote in his diary on November 17, 1941, when he was participating in the drive toward Moscow. Looking back at the time he spent in France, he fondly recalled "the beauties of the Versailles countryside," "cozy evenings in the club room, sitting in deep chairs with a glass of absinthe or a bottle labeled 'Martel,' 'Hennessey' or 'Montmousseau,'" and the "intoxicating shimmer" of Paris.

When Gruman took part in the invasion of the Soviet Union on June 22, his life changed immediately. The first battles went relatively smoothly, but soon he was thrust into the fighting at Smolensk, where each victory came at a higher price. "I will always remember the ferocious battles and the heavy losses which both sides suffered," he wrote. His spirits were subsequently lifted by the successes of "the great October offensive." "The great encirclement in which we participated will enter history under the name 'The Battle of Bryansk and Vyazma,'" he wrote. "Nothing could stop us; we quickly surmounted the mined fields and blown-up bridges."

While recalling the difficulties of "a season of a veritable quagmire" of mud that forced him to learn how to ride a horse, Gruman boasted how "we crossed Borodino field, where Napoleon had fought," and then forded the Moscow River. Despite a first clash with Siberian divisions, his faith in victory appeared unshaken. "The charge to Moscow had begun," he noted with evident satisfaction.

Gruman was clearly a loyal officer, but his diary entries dwelled more and more on the hardships that the Germans faced. On November 16, he recorded that his unit "finally received a few pairs of winter boots" from the regimental command, leaving little doubt that he was angry that most of the men still didn't have them. While he observed that it was a beautiful sunny day and that the snowy landscape "casts a spell," he indicated that the cold of "this wonderful winter weather" could be endured during the day "but at night it tortures us." The following morning, he wrote that the thermometer showed minus 9 [16 degrees Fahrenheit], and "the morning is beautiful, almost like a fairy tale."

But Gruman knew that those early signs of winter and the certainty that temperatures would plummet much lower didn't augur well. He was worried not only about the men but also about the horses in his unit. "The poor horses were exhausted. The lack of forage and the cold took their toll—all horses stood in the open," he wrote.

The health of these transport animals was no minor matter. Despite its reputation as a highly modern, mechanized army, the German invasion force relied to a huge extent on horses. There were still some traditional cavalry units, but the horses were primarily used to haul artillery and supplies. When vehicles became stuck in Russia's treacherous mud, as they constantly did, horses would pull them out. As General Günther Blumentritt, chief of staff of Army Group Center's Fourth Army, reported, "The infantry now slithers in the mud, while many teams of horses are needed to drag each gun forward. All wheeled vehicles sink up to their axles in the slime. Even tractors can only move with great difficulty. A large proportion of our artillery was soon stuck fast."

It's estimated that the Germans used about 750,000 horses during the early stages of Operation Barbarossa and a total of two and half million of those animals during the entire war against the Soviet Union. On average, about one thousand horses perished during every day of the fighting.

While shelling and bullets killed most of the horses, many collapsed from heart failure brought on by overexertion, particularly during the mud season. Others succumbed to disease and the cold. The Russians had horses that could withstand low temperatures far better than the horses rounded up by the Germans in their occupied territories. Those horses, it turned out, died faster in the cold than humans did.

As his unit was ordered to advance, Gruman recorded more complaints. "The maps were so inaccurate that it was virtually impossible to use them. . . . Obstructions and congestion along the way. I would not have minded bludgeoning a few drivers and train commanders." The sky was "a fiery red" from the shelling, and the soldiers hit the ground as "missiles are exploding among the trees." One of the greatest fears of the men was the famed Soviet Katyushas, or "Stalin's organs," as the new rocket-propelled artillery fired from trucks was called. While his men hadn't experienced this weapon yet, he pointed out that others had told him "the effect of exploding rockets on morale is far greater than their destructive force."

Morale in Gruman's unit was increasingly shaky even without the Katyushas. The lieutenant noted on November 24, "Each day the combat strength of the troops weakened." Two weeks earlier, the company had seventy men, but now it was down to forty. He reported that some of the best officers had died trying to set an example of bravery for their men and "the new replacement commanders did not know their business well" and "had no conscience," using every opportunity to stay in the rear as others died.

Above all, though, Gruman warned of the dangers of exhaustion. "Our men, who had been fighting since the beginning of August, were tired," he wrote. "The burden of morale was extreme. The cry of 'Medic!' ran through the fighting like stray fire, and the cry of 'Machine guns forward!' was not heard. Such sad episodes formerly were not known in our regiment." Recalling the brave soldiers he saw in earlier engagements, he added, "Such a warrior is not created from a tired, louse-infected, and numerically small company."

In an entry dated November 25 to 29, he wrote that "we were unable to break the enemy resistance" and that they had buried more of their men. While he pointed out that other units were still advancing on the Soviet capital, he no longer believed he and his men would be among those who would achieve "the glory of reaching Moscow first." Instead, he looked to *Schneller Heinz*, the famed panzer commander Heinz Guderian, who was advancing from the south. "Our hopes for penetrating Moscow from the southwest lie with Guderian's tank units," he concluded.

Guderian, who had once been firmly convinced that he'd fulfill those hopes, was now plagued by doubts about the ability of his tanks to succeed in that task. Shortly after he seized Orel on October 3, his tanks came up against more Soviet T-34s and suffered heavy losses. "Up to this time we had enjoyed tank superiority, but from now on the situation was reversed," he recalled. "The prospect of rapid, decisive victories was fading in consequence." To the Soviet side, such a judgment appeared premature, since they still didn't have anywhere near the number of tanks they needed. Nonetheless, there was no question that the T-34s, even in limited numbers, were making their presence felt in a big way.

The other major factor was the weather. The mud of October was proving to be a daunting opponent in its own right. "The Russians are impeding us far less than the wet and the mud!" Field Marshal Fedor von Bock, commander of Army Group Center, complained in his war diary on October 21. Monitoring Guderian's progress as he pointed his forces toward Tula, the arms-producing city guarding the southern approach to Moscow, Bock wrote on October 30, "Guderian's weak spearhead reached the southern outskirts of Tula, which is being defended by the enemy. Everything else is still lagging far behind on the muddy roads."

A day later, Bock added that "our losses have become quite considerable," and reported that Hitler had been demanding an explanation for the lack of progress. "He probably refused to believe the written reports, which is not surprising, for anyone who hasn't seen this filth doesn't think it possible," he noted dolefully.

Guderian was as exasperated by the commands that were coming from Hitler as by the conditions he faced. When his tank troops began their drive from Orel to Tula on the one road linking the two towns, they discovered that the Russians had blown up bridges and set extensive minefields along both sides of the road. Along with the weather and Soviet counterattacks, this hampered the resupply efforts further. As a result, fuel shortages began to limit the speed of the advance. When he received Hitler's order on October 28 for "fast moving units" to seize key bridges, he was furious. Noting that the maximum speed his tanks were reaching on the Orel-Tula road was twelve miles per hour, he wrote, "There were no 'fast-moving units' any more. Hitler was living in a world of fantasy."

On the night of November 3 to 4, a frost hardened the mud roads, making it easier for Guderian's troops to advance. But whatever relief he felt was offset by his forebodings about what the dropping temperatures would mean for his troops, which rekindled his anger with Hitler's earlier decisions that had delayed the push on Moscow until this late date. "It is miserable for the troops and a great pity for our cause that the enemy should thus gain time while our plans are postponed until the winter is more and more advanced," he wrote in a letter on November 6. "It all makes me very sad. With the best will in the world there is nothing more you can do about the elements. The unique chance to strike a single great blow is fading more and more, and I do not know if it will ever recur. How things will turn out, God alone knows."

As temperatures dropped to 5 degrees Fahrenheit on November 12 and then minus 8 degrees the next day, Guderian was summoned to a meeting of the commanders of the armies of Army Group Center that only incensed him more. In the "Orders for the Autumn Offensive, 1941," which the top brass unveiled at that session, the plan of action for the Second Panzer Army bordered on the surreal. Its assignment was to seize Gorky, which Guderian noted was about four hundred miles from Orel and 250 miles *east* of Moscow. The idea was to cut off communication lines to the Soviet capital from the rear. "This was not the month of May and we were not fighting in France!" Guderian noted. With his immediate superior backing him up, he then wrote out a report why "the Panzer Army was no longer capable of carrying out the orders that had been issued it."

Returning to his units in the field, Guderian was even more discouraged. On November 14, he visited the 167th Infantry Division. "The supply situation was bad," he recalled. "Snow shirts, boot grease, underclothes and above all woolen trousers were not available. A high proportion of the men were still wearing denim trousers, and the temperature was 8 below zero!" A few hours later he reached the 112th Infantry Division, where the situation was similar. If some of the troops were managing to deal with the cold, it was only thanks to what they had seized from the enemy. "Our troops had got hold of Russian overcoats and fur caps and only the national emblem showed that they were Germans," he wrote. The supplies of winter clothes provided by their own army were so meager that they constituted "a mere drop in the ocean," he added.

A few days later, the same weary troops of the 112th Infantry Division were in for a terrifying surprise. Siberian troops, fresh off trains from the Far East and fully equipped with winter gear, launched an all-out attack that sent the Germans reeling. Guderian tried his best to explain what happened to his men but didn't attempt to disguise the dimensions of the disaster. "Before judging their performance it should be borne in mind that each regiment had already lost some 500 men from frostbite, that as a result of the cold the machine-guns were no longer able to fire and that our 37 mm. anti-tank gun had proved ineffective against the T-34," he wrote. "The result of all this was a panic. . . . This was the first time that such a thing had occurred during the Russian campaign, and it was a warning that the combat ability of our infantry was at an end and that they should no longer be expected to perform difficult tasks."

While Guderian may have come to that realization a bit later than he indicated in his memoirs, he was increasingly alarmed by the contrast between his "insufficiently clothed, half-starved men" and "the well-fed, warmly clad and fresh Siberians, fully equipped for winter fighting." Writing about those battles in November as he tried and failed to reach Tula, he added, "Only a man who knew all that can truly judge the events which now occurred."

Guderian and other generals in the field were also beginning to recognize that it wasn't just the new Siberian troops who were fighting with greater determination than they had encountered before. There was a growing conviction among many of the Soviet fighters that this was a national struggle, something that wasn't always apparent in the early days of the invasion.

In Orel about that time, Guderian met an old tsarist general, who told him, "If only you had come twenty years ago we should have welcomed you with open arms. But now it's too late." Referring to the devastation of the Russian civil war after the Bolshevik Revolution, the tsarist general added, "We were just beginning to get back on our feet and now you arrive and throw us back twenty years so that we will have to start from the beginning all over again. Now we are fighting for Russia and in that cause we are all united."

Those sentiments were no accident. They were partly the result of the brutal policies of the Germans in the territories they had already occupied, which shattered any illusions of the local populace and surrendering Soviet troops that their new masters would show them any mercy. But they were also the direct result of the change

in tone emanating from the Kremlin. As Waffen SS General Max
Simon would report later, "A *national* concept had not at this time
(summer and autumn 1941) penetrated the minds of the Russian
front-line troops; it was not proclaimed by Stalin till late autumn."
By then, even someone like the former tsarist general Guderian
had encountered was receptive to national appeals coming from
the communists he had once fought.

Stalin's decision to use the defiant Revolution Day ceremonies
in Moscow to proclaim those new national—as opposed to ideological—goals would quickly begin to produce results.

Vasily Grossman, the *Krasnaya Zvezda* war correspondent and novelist, reflected on the differences between the soldiers of the opposing armies as they fought each other and struggled with the
elements, first the rain and mud, then the freezing temperatures.
"Germans are not so well-prepared for the physical hardship, when
a 'naked' man is facing nature," he wrote in his notebook. "A Russian man is brought up to hardship, and his victories are hard
earned. Germans, on the other hand, are prepared for easy victories that would be based on technological superiority, and they give
in to the hardship caused by nature. General Mud and General
Cold are helping the Russian side. (But it is true that only those
who are strong can make nature work for them, while the weak are
at the mercy of nature.)"

Whatever degree of truth in Grossman's generalizations, the
Red Army soldier was no superman, either physically or psychologically. Many of the troops fighting to defend Moscow felt as worn
down as their opponents. They, too, struggled with the elements
and keeping themselves fed and warm. Their superiors nervously
monitored their mood, watching for signs of trouble.

The Moscow region military censorship office boasted in an internal memo that it had checked 2,505,867 letters written between
November 15 and December 1, which accounted for all the correspondence for that period. While it claimed that most of the letters
showed that morale was good, it reported the confiscation of 3,698
letters and deletion of passages from 26,276 others. Since most soldiers certainly knew that their letters could and would be checked,

the fact that a portion of the correspondence demonstrated "low morale, which was connected with questions of provisions and warm clothes" and others contained "anti-Soviet propaganda" indicated that the authorities had serious reason for concern.

"The food is really poor. Soon I won't be able to move because of hunger," a soldier named Ptashnikov wrote. Semyon Leskov was more descriptive. "You know how cold it is and we are sitting in the trenches wearing cold boots," he wrote. "We're sitting here shivering, and the Germans keep pounding us day and night. They want to get to Moscow by any means, but we're standing here by the river and we won't let them break through. Sometimes we have enough food, but usually we don't because we keep changing our position to fight."

The complaints about the cold and the food were widely echoed. "You want me to describe my service. . . . You know that it's very cold in winter and that we don't have enough bread. We haven't had a bath for two months already and everybody has a lot of lice," wrote N. I. Folimonov to his wife or mother. Another soldier complained, "They give us enough food just to keep us alive. And our life is really very difficult—only prisoners live like this, and soldiers should not have to endure such conditions. . . . We have only cabbage and potatoes to eat." V. Sorokin reported that his unit received only "five spoons of soup" in the morning, which was supposed to keep them going until the evening.

But the most alarming letters were the ones that linked the dismal conditions with predictions of defeat. "Wherever we go, the Germans encircle us and pursue us like hunting dogs chase rabbits. Believe neither the newspapers nor the radio—they tell lies! We saw everything and I saw how the Germans chase our soldiers and we don't know where to run. We don't have enough weapons to fight and vehicles to drive. We lack fuel so our troops leave tanks and vehicles and run," wrote E. S. Suslin. Another letter, signed by the name Dronov, went from complaining about the meager rations to predicting flatly, "The Germans will take Moscow within a few days—don't believe the newspapers." All those letters were confiscated.

Even as some of the troops in the field grew discouraged, others responded to the call for volunteers to defend the capital. The Moscow authorities had managed to expand the Communist brigades, or home guard units, which were composed of a combination of volunteers and draftees. By late November, their ranks had swelled to about 48,000, almost a fivefold increase from October, when the first groups were organized. Civilian units were quickly transformed into regular military formations. Some were set up as anti-tank units, while others were prepared for street fighting if the Germans managed to enter the city. Others were quickly deployed in positions guarding the approaches to the capital.

They were thinly deployed—and they knew it. Even with fresh recruits joining their ranks, the forward units hardly constituted an impressive force to stop the Germans. Albert Tsessarsky, the medical orderly who had gone to Moscow for supplies on October 16, was back with his thirty-three-man home guard unit near Mozhaisk, about sixty miles west of Moscow. With about four to five hundred enemy troops facing them on the other side of the Moscow River, they knew they had no chance of stopping the Germans with only a single machine gun once they decided to attack.

But the home guard troops came up with a clever plan to make the Germans nervous about doing so. Starting in early November, they patrolled the riverbank with ten men at a time—that is, with about one-third of their total strength. Normally, that size patrol would be deployed only by a much larger unit—which was precisely the point. The idea was to lead the Germans to believe that they had far more men than they really did. Although they were dressed in winter coats and *valenki*, Russian felt boots, each ten-man unit went out for only two hours at a time. "That was the longest we could stand the cold," Tsessarsky said.

Across the river, the Germans, who lacked winter gear, huddled in their encampments and didn't seem eager to move. Even when the river froze in early November, the Germans didn't try to cross, something that both relieved and perplexed Tsessarsky and the other Russians, who knew that they couldn't stop them if they did.

But some of the local inhabitants who had been trapped on the German side tried to make a break for it across the ice one night. The Germans suddenly came to life, turning on a searchlight and shooting at the fleeing civilians. "There were terrible scenes," Tsessarsky recalled. "I remember a mother was crossing the river with a child on a sled. When she reached us, she wanted us to take the baby, but he had been killed. The next morning, we saw many dead bodies on the ice. The ice was red from blood."

Tsessarsky treated the wounded as best he could. "My first real medical practice was there," he noted. Some of the villagers brought their dead with them. Since it was impossible to bury them in the frozen ground, Tsessarsky and the other soldiers wrote down the names of the dead and attached them to the clothing, offering the vague hope that the bodies might be given a proper burial in the spring. "Even now I don't know what happened to the bodies," Tsessarsky added, still troubled by that memory as he recounted that period of his life sixty-five years later.

That night on the river was a grim reminder of what the Germans were capable of and what would await anyone who was caught in their sights.

Stalin and Zhukov knew that they couldn't count on such home guard units to hold off or fool the Germans for long and that it was the Siberian divisions that offered the best hope of preventing Hitler from achieving his goal of seizing Moscow. While the troops that were hastily redeployed from the Soviet Far East were known as Siberians, not all of them hailed from that region. Some of the men had fought in earlier battles and were among the survivors of units that had been virtually wiped out. Reassigned to the Far East, they were blended into newly organized units undergoing training there. They soon found themselves returning to the battlefronts on the approaches to Moscow once Stalin felt confident he wouldn't be attacked from the east by Japan.

Boris Godov had been in an airborne brigade near Kiev at the start of the war and had sustained a stomach wound while escaping from the German encirclement of the Ukrainian capital. After recovering in a hospital in the Moscow region, he was assigned to the 413th Siberian Division, which was dispatched in late October to defend Tula, the arms-producing city south of Moscow, from the Germans troops led, among others, by General Guderian. "Tula was on the way to Moscow, and who knows if Moscow would have survived if we hadn't beaten the Germans there," he said proudly.

But Godov and his fellow troops in the Siberian division quickly discovered that they weren't prepared for the intensity of the fighting they'd face and, in some cases, weren't properly equipped for it. True, they had good winter clothing: *valenki* (boots), cotton-wool jackets, overcoats, and white camouflage coverings. The field kitchen was also better than in most other units, providing warm soup and kasha morning and evening and even a hundred grams of vodka when the weather turned cold. The bad news, however, was that German planes started bombing the Siberians as soon as they arrived, and they didn't always have the weapons they needed to fight off ground assaults.

In one case, an artillery unit discovered that it had been provided with shells that were too small for their guns, which left it at the mercy of German tanks. "The entire artillery regiment perished since they couldn't do anything," Godov recalled. Many soldiers died trying to blow up German tanks with hand grenades, since that was the only usable weapon they had. Of the 15,400 men in Godov's division, only about five hundred survived. But Guderian was frustrated in his efforts to reach Tula and thus in what he hoped would be his final push from the south to Moscow.

On other parts of the front, the invaders had already penetrated the greater Moscow region, which consisted of eighty-seven districts. In November and December, German troops completely controlled seventeen of them, and occupied parts of another ten. Those living on the outskirts of the capital were never sure whether the next soldiers to show up would be friend or foe.

Natalya Kravchenko, the daughter of a Moscow artist who had died a year earlier, was staying at the family dacha, or country house, in the village of Nikolina Gora, about thirty miles west of Moscow, during that uncertain period. There were seventeen checkpoints manned by Red Army troops on the heavily shelled road leading from the village to the capital, but they were suddenly abandoned, and the sounds of battle—the gunfire and shelling that the villagers had been hearing—disappeared just as abruptly. "It was a very difficult moment," Kravchenko recalled. "The silences were one of the most frightening things during the war."

Kravchenko, her sister, and her grandmother were in their house when the silence was broken by a strange noise. "We didn't understand where the sound was coming from and we went to find out," she said. Right outside their house, all along the village road, there were Siberian troops, fast asleep and snoring. "It's difficult to imagine the speed at which the Siberian troops were moving forward," she added. "They used to sleep only two to three hours a day." This was one of those sleep breaks, and the exhausted soldiers were making full use of it.

When the soldiers woke up, they asked for water, which the Kravchenko women poured into their helmets. They marched off, and the fighting quickly resumed nearby. Kravchenko's dacha was transformed into a first aid station for the wounded. The family's curtains, blankets, and sheets were all used for makeshift operating stations; the wounded were treated on the large drawing tables in her father's study. The intensity of the fighting soon convinced the Kravchenkos that they should return to Moscow, since it was beginning to look safer than the outskirts, where there was no escape from the bloodshed.

The Siberians didn't have that option. Vladimir Edelman was one of the men who had just arrived from the east. Like Godov, he wasn't really a Siberian. A Ukrainian Jew, he had also fought in the losing battle for Kiev in September. Unlike many of his relatives, who were among the victims of the massacre of Jews at Babi Yar, he escaped from his native city and ended up in an infantry unit in the Omsk region composed mostly of Siberian military cadets and recent graduates of military colleges.

As a lieutenant with combat experience, Edelman was put in charge of a twenty-five-man unit. When his superior officers came to check his soldiers' shooting skills, they were angered by what they initially saw. Instead of positioning themselves on the ground and aiming according to standard regulations, the Siberians sprawled and took aim from any position they felt comfortable in. The officers berated Edelman for failing to teach them the proper stances and procedures. But when they saw the targets the Siberians had been shooting at, they quickly overlooked all that. "They were excellent shots because they were hunters," Edelman said. On a scale of one to ten, most of the men had scored nines or tens.

While still in Siberia, Edelman and the other men had been issued long underwear, sweaters, fur vests, cotton-wool pants, gloves or mittens, winter coats, and fur hats. They kept their handguns under their coats and also wrapped up radios so that they wouldn't freeze. Edelman admitted that the Germans had better radios, machine guns, and mortars at that point in the war and the Russians would try to seize their equipment whenever they could. But once he and his twenty-five men were deployed northwest of Moscow, Edelman quickly came to realize that the big advantage his men had was their winter gear. The temperature would drop to as low as minus 40 degrees Fahrenheit at times during November and December, and the Germans suffered the most from those temperatures.

It wasn't only the German soldiers who froze. Some of the lubricants in their tanks and other vehicles would also freeze. The German troops on the approaches to Moscow hadn't been supplied with antifreeze or even chains to tow stranded vehicles. In some cases, German planes dropped ropes to the troops so that they could be used for towing. As temperatures plummeted, the same overoptimistic expectations of an early victory that accounted for the failure of German planners to provide winter uniforms was responsible for the increasingly serious transport problems.

There was no question that the real Siberians could handle the cold better than most Russians and certainly better than the Germans. "We were remarkably enthusiastic and we showed them that we could fight well," Edelman said. "But the severe Russian winter helped us a lot." During November and most of December, he pointed out, he and his men weren't able to wash themselves. Finally they reached a village where there was a crude *banya,* or bathhouse; cold water was available only at a well outside. "The Siberians would have their steam bath and then jump into the snow," Edelman recalled with amazement. Unable to do that, he rubbed soap all over his body in the steam bath and then ran to the well, splashed cold water on himself, and ran back to the steam bath. The Siberians helped to rinse and dry him so that he'd warm up again.

One sight remains vividly etched in Edelman's memory: a group of captured Germans standing at a crossroads where he was directing traffic in the biting cold. They were wearing summer uniforms with light coats and no hats. The only sounds that emanated from them were sighs and moans and the words *"O Mein Gott! O Mein Gott!"* Every so often, one of them would drop to the ground, dead.

Another time, as he led his men across a snow-covered field near Volokolamsk, Edelman realized that they were literally walking on bodies that were just beneath the white surface, packed together so tightly after a recent battle that it was impossible to avoid them. "The fields around Moscow were filled with hundreds of thousands of corpses," he noted. "It's hard to describe what was happening there." Many perished as a result of the mines planted first by the Russians to slow the German invaders and later by the Germans to slow the Red Army's push to drive them back.

When Edelman and his men forced the enemy to retreat, they sometimes found frozen German bodies stacked like logs. The surviving Germans had evidently hoped that they would be able to bury those who had fallen when the ground thawed in the spring.

For all the talk about the enthusiasm of his men, Edelman reluctantly admitted that they were subject to brutal discipline. "I saw the shooting of deserters," he said. "I saw this in my battalion." He didn't shy away from discussing the memories that many veterans prefer to suppress, putting them in the context of the normal terrors of combat. "The first time you have to get out of a trench and run straight into enemy guns, your heart is pounding so hard and you're drenched in cold sweat. You run and the men on your left and right fall, and you know that at any moment the same can happen to you." As an officer, he added, "You have to charge and believe your soldiers will follow you."

And what if someone didn't want to get out of the trench to follow him? Edelman looked away, then replied, "When you see someone is staying behind, you punch him in the face. There are different rules in war. Why should I attack and you don't? There's no time for sentiment."

The Siberians helped recapture several towns and villages northwest of Moscow, but they paid a heavy price for their victories. Of the twenty-five men under Edelman's command when they joined the battle for Moscow in late October, only three were still with him by January 1942. "The rest were either killed, wounded or frozen," he said. "My hands and feet also froze but I still kept fighting." Edelman was wounded five times during the war and decorated after the battle for Moscow for his bravery. His mother, who had escaped from Kiev, was notified twice that he was dead.

Despite his evident patriotism and courage, Edelman was eager to set the record straight on one point. "It's a myth that people yelled 'For the motherland! For Stalin!'" he said. "I never heard anyone yelling that. There are a lot of myths and you can only find out the truth bit by bit."

The truth about the Siberians, as is so often the case about others who participated in the defense of Moscow, has literally remained just below the surface of the fields and villages where so many fought and died. Semyon Timokhin grew up in Toropovo, a tiny village in the Kemerovo region of Siberia. He was only seven when the battle for the capital was reaching its climax and his father was one of the conscripts dispatched to the Moscow region. As his train was approaching its destination, German bombers struck, and he was badly wounded. "His arm was torn to shreds and that was the end of the war for him," Semyon recalled.

Semyon heard plenty of vivid accounts of the Siberians' ordeals. His uncle, Vladimir Timokhin, was also sent to fight near Moscow that autumn and recounted one particularly gruesome night. Around 3 A.M., a huge explosion shook his barracks and one part of the building simply disappeared. Jumping up from his cot, Vladimir looked out and saw that the ground was white, though it hadn't been covered with snow the day before. In fact, there was still no snow. The soldiers had been issued white pajamas the day before, and it was their torn pajamas and bodies that were strewn across the dark ground.

Growing up after the war, Semyon pursued a military career, eventually rising to the rank of general in the army, specializing in aviation. After he retired from his last assignment as head of the Moscow area aviation headquarters in 1989, he was allotted a plot of land not far from Snegeri, a village just northwest of Moscow, where the Siberians had participated in brutal tank and infantry battles. "I began to cultivate and fence it, and found bones all over the place," he said. It turned out that the local inhabitants had tried to bury those who had died in late 1941 and early 1942, once their bodies began to thaw in the spring. "All this territory with more than two hundred plots of land turned out to be a huge common grave," Semyon explained.

A plot of land this close to Moscow was a prize possession, but given all that he already knew about the price the Siberians had paid there, he couldn't continue to treat it as just another place to grow cabbage, tomatoes, parsley, apples and pears as he had planned to do. "I could not stay there," he said. The ghosts of his fellow Siberians drove him away.

2

Stalin and Hitler were kindred spirits, almost perfectly matched in terms of their cynicism and staggering brutality. Stalin was even willing to toast the Führer's health when he thought they had reached a bargain. But Hitler was determined to conquer and enslave Russia, treating it as *Lebensraum* for the German people. Speaking in Berlin's Sportpalast on October 3, 1941, he called the drive to Moscow "the greatest battle in the history of the world."

3

STALINE   HITLER

On August 23, 1939, Soviet Foreign Minister Vyacheslav Molotov (seated) and his German counterpart Joachim von Ribbentrop (left) signed the infamous Nazi-Soviet nonaggression pact, while Stalin looked on. A French cartoon mocked the "love waltz" of the two tyrants.

Stalin believed he had outsmarted Hitler by getting him to accept the Soviet grab of eastern Poland and the Baltic states. He also thought that the nonaggression pact would at the very least delay a war between their two countries for a few years. But the German dictator stunned him by launching the invasion of the Soviet Union on June 22, 1941. At first, German troops met minimal resistance.

Because Stalin had refused to believe all the warnings that the Germans were about to attack, the invaders were able to roll eastward at a rapid pace. *Left:* a German scouting tank passes a signpost indicating that Moscow is only 100 kilometers (62 miles) away. *Below:* Russian civilians flee the invading army.

7

8

Caught by surprise and often without weapons, hundreds of thousands of Soviet troops surrendered to the Germans during the early months of the war. *Right:* the new POWs are marched off to makeshift prison camps. *Below:* weeping Russian women watch their men on a similar march into captivity. Most of these Soviet prisoners would quickly perish.

9

10

When it looked as though Moscow's defenses would no longer hold, Stalin recalled General Georgy Zhukov from Leningrad and put him in charge of saving the capital. Like his master, Zhukov was willing to do anything to ensure obedience to his orders, including executing anyone who tried to retreat. He also never flinched at sacrificing his men on the battlefield, which produced staggering casualty rates.

General Heinz Guderian's panzer units pushed east all the way to Smolensk in less than a month. Guderian urged Hitler to allow him to keep going directly to Moscow, but the German dictator insisted that his troops take Kiev first. As Guderian predicted, this proved to be a huge mistake. It delayed the drive to Moscow until the weather began to change and Stalin could call in reinforcements from Siberia.

13

Prime Minister Winston Churchill and Foreign Secretary Anthony Eden. The British leaders were determined to help the Soviet war effort. But Churchill was infuriated by Stalin's incessant calls for Britain to establish a second front on the European continent and his equally unrealistic demands for huge numbers of planes, tanks and other supplies.

President Roosevelt's aide Harry Hopkins with Stalin during his visit to Moscow in August 1941. A Russian official was elated by Hopkins's "obvious sympathy for the Soviet Union."

FDR with Harry Hopkins in the White House study. Although the United States was not yet in the war, Roosevelt insisted on providing as much aid as possible for Russia. Even as Moscow's fate hung in the balance, Stalin used his talks with Western leaders to begin pushing his plans for Soviet domination of postwar Eastern Europe.

16

On Hitler's orders, the Germans unleashed a reign of terror wherever they advanced. This ensured that even those who initially welcomed the invaders as liberators quickly turned against them. The atrocities, such as the hanging of these alleged Soviet partisans, only helped Stalin rally his people.

17

To stop the German tanks, Russian civilians dug a huge network of trenches, traps and wooden barriers on Moscow's outskirts. At the same time, Soviet officials were presiding over the evacuation of factories and government offices to the east. By the end of 1941, half of the city's population had fled or been evacuated.

ОТСТОИМ МОСКВУ!

A Soviet propaganda poster with an urgent message: "We'll Defend Moscow!" But even as they exhorted their people to fight to save the capital, Kremlin officials were far from confident they could hold off the Germans. They prepared teams of secret agents, trained for sabotage and assassination operations, to stay behind in a German-occupied Moscow.

After the delay caused by
Hitler's insistence on first taking
Kiev, German troops marching
to Moscow found themselves
caught in the autumn rains.
As General Guderian pointed
out, Russian roads turned
into "canals of mud" that
dramatically slowed
their advance.

19

After the panic of mid-October that featured looting, strikes and massive flight from Moscow, Stalin astonished his entourage by insisting on holding a military parade on Red Square on November 7, 1941, the anniversary of the Bolshevik Revolution. Heavy snow minimized the danger of German air raids, and Stalin was able to demonstrate that he was still in control of the city.

Severe winter weather arrived early as German troops attempted to take Moscow. Because Hitler had been convinced that they would triumph before the weather changed, most of them lacked winter uniforms. Soviet forces began capturing more and more ill-clad, freezing German soldiers.

23

Soviet troops, especially those rushed in from Siberia to defend Moscow, were far better equipped to handle the frigid temperatures. Many of them had proper winter boots, cotton-wool jackets, overcoats and white camouflage coverings. This would prove an increasingly critical factor in the fighting.

A Soviet T-34 tank passes a German corpse on the snowy terrain. As one German officer put it, the failure of his side to make the final push for Moscow shattered the myth of the invincibility of Hitler's forces. "The German army never completely recovered from this defeat," he wrote.

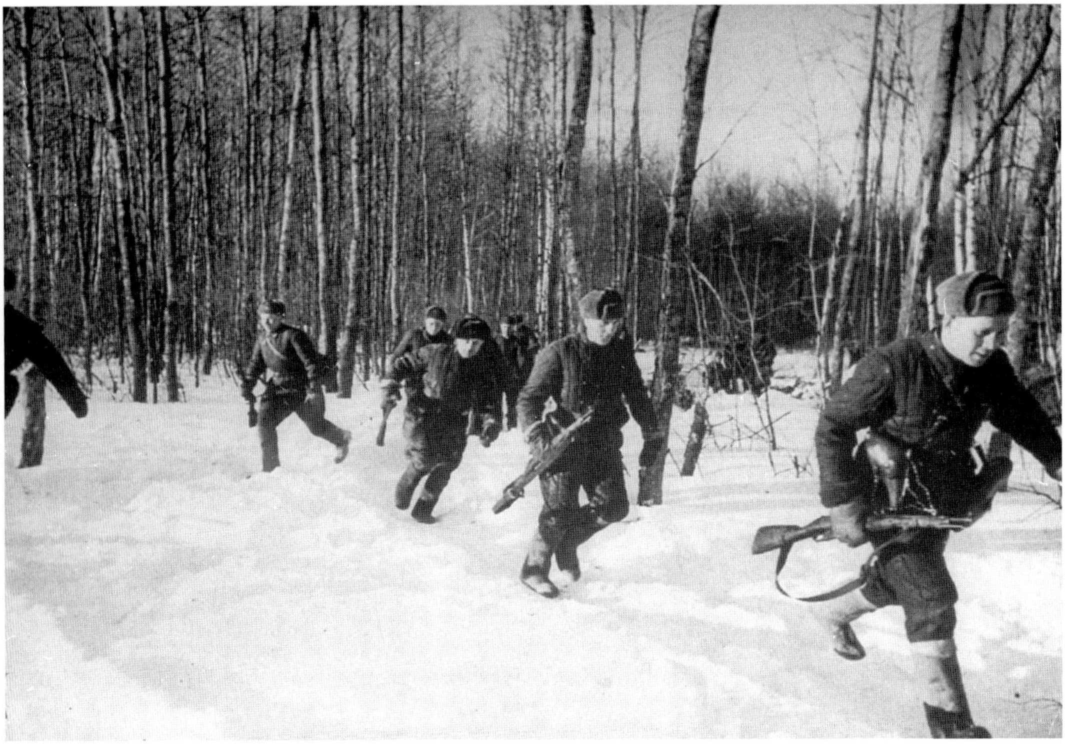

23

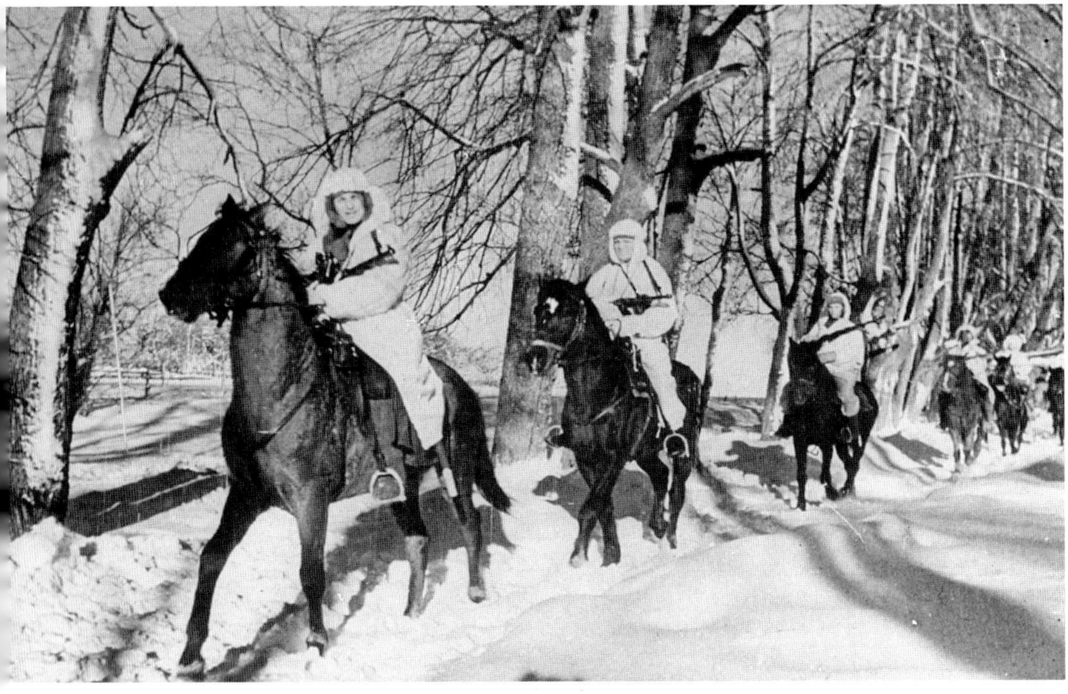

10

"Don't be sentimental"

By late November, Stalin and his generals were beginning to realize that they had survived the worst part of the drive on Moscow.
They knew that the Germans were overextended, running low on
supplies and constantly freezing. They knew, too, that Hitler didn't
have large numbers of fresh reserves to call up at that point, no
saviors like the Siberians to throw into the battle. And they knew
that their men who had rushed to the defense of the capital had,
for the most part, fought as hard as they could. "Our soldiers were
fully conscious of their personal responsibility for the fate of
Moscow, for the fate of their homeland, and were determined to
die rather than let the enemy through to Moscow," Marshal Zhukov
wrote later. Despite the propagandistic tone of that assessment, it
was generally accurate.

But none of that meant that Stalin was ready to ease up on his
generals or his men. Zhukov got a personal taste of that when the
Soviet leader called him about a report that Dedovsk—a town
northwest of Moscow, only twenty miles from the Kremlin—had
been abandoned by his troops and taken over by the Germans.

"Do you know that they've occupied Dedovsk?" Stalin asked.

"No, Comrade Stalin, I didn't know that," Zhukov replied.

"A commander should know what's going on at the front!" the dictator snapped. He then ordered Zhukov to go immediately to the area and "personally organize a counterattack and retake Dedovsk."

When Zhukov demurred, saying that he shouldn't leave the headquarters at such a tense time, Stalin wasn't about to listen. "Never mind, we'll get along somehow," he brusquely informed him, adding that Zhukov's chief of staff could take over while he went off on his mission.

Zhukov quickly found out the real story. General Konstantin Rokossovsky, whose Sixteenth Army was responsible for that region, explained that Dedovsk hadn't fallen to the Germans. In fact, his troops were fighting along the Volokolamsk highway further north to prevent a breakthrough toward Dedovsk and Nakhabino. In the course of that fighting, the Germans had taken a small village called Dedovo. The names were close enough for someone to have mixed them up. "It was plain that the report Stalin had received was all a mistake," Zhukov recalled.

But when he called headquarters to explain the misunderstanding, Stalin flew into a rage and demanded that Zhukov retake the village. It didn't matter that the village had no tactical or strategic significance and that Stalin had been thinking of another place when he had issued the original order. He wasn't about to let Zhukov off the hook.

Somewhat sheepishly, Zhukov proceeded into the field and told Rokossovsky and another general that they had to mount an operation to take back the village from the Germans. In reality, this meant diverting troops to seize a few houses. With far more important battles raging all around them, they at first objected, pointing out that this would be a needless diversion, which would entail sending a rifle company across a deep gully away from the main fighting. Rather than argue a hopeless case, Zhukov informed them that this was an order from Stalin. That ended all discussion.

When Zhukov reported the successful completion of this senseless mission on December 1, he was told that Stalin had called three times. "Where is Zhukov?" he had demanded, apparently having completely forgotten that he'd sent him away. "Why has he gone away?"

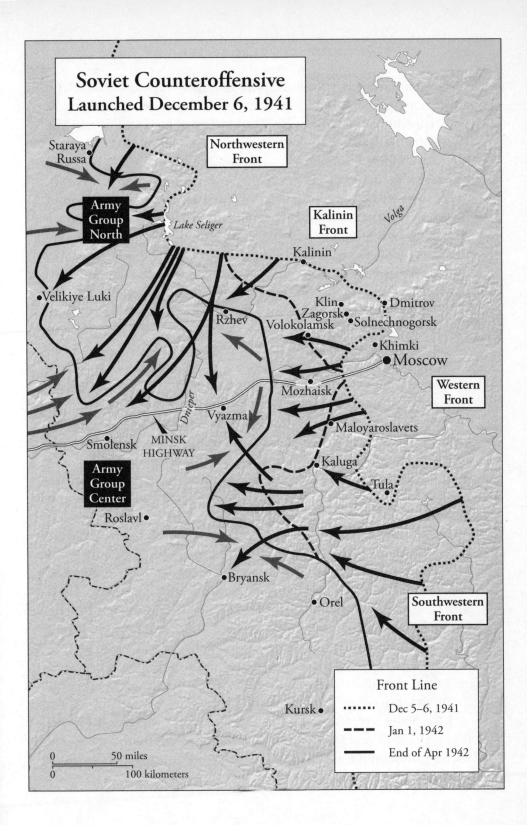

Soviet Counteroffensive
Launched December 6, 1941

Staraya Russa

Northwestern Front

Kalinin Front

Volga

Army Group North

Lake Seliger

Kalinin

Velikiye Luki

Klin
Zagorsk
Volokolamsk
Solnechnogorsk
Dmitrov

Rzhev

Khimki

Moscow

Dnieper

Mozhaisk

Western Front

Vyazma

Smolensk

MINSK HIGHWAY

Maloyaroslavets

Army Group Center

Kaluga

Tula

Roslavl

Bryansk

Orel

Southwestern Front

Kursk

Front Line

.... Dec 5–6, 1941

– – – Jan 1, 1942

——— End of Apr 1942

0   50 miles
0   100 kilometers

On the same day, German troops had launched a new attack on another part of the front that had been fairly quiet until then. Finally back at his headquarters, Zhukov called Stalin to discuss the latest attack. It was only when they were just about done that the Soviet leader mentioned his previous assignment. "Well, and what about Dedovsk?" he asked.

Zhukov knew better than to repeat that the town had never been in danger and that the Soviet leader had confused it with a tiny village. He simply reported that his troops had driven the Germans out of Dedovo. It wouldn't have hurt anyone but himself to underscore the fact that Stalin had been provided with erroneous information and then compounded the error by refusing to acknowledge it. In his dealings with Stalin, Zhukov was more outspoken than almost anyone else ever dared to be, but he, too, was under no illusions about the risks of provoking his ire.

In that respect, Stalin and Hitler ran their military campaigns in similar fashion. Both dictators regularly cowed their generals, overruling them whenever they saw fit. But by late November and early December, the two leaders were in a novel position vis-à-vis each other. The German army's rapid march across Russia had all but stalled just short of Moscow, and the Red Army was finally poised to strike back in some areas. It would not simply keep retreating. This would test Stalin's and Hitler's military leadership skills in new ways.

While Stalin ordered Zhukov to launch the first counteroffensive starting December 6, Hitler belatedly responded to appeals of his generals to acknowledge how overextended and exhausted their troops were by ordering an end, for the duration of the winter, of their drive to seize Moscow and other key objectives. Hitler's Directive 39 issued on December 8 declared, "The severe winter weather which has come surprisingly early in the East, and the consequent difficulties in bringing up supplies, compel us to abandon immediately all major offensive operations and to go over to the defensive."

Like Stalin's refusal to admit the truth about the confusion between Dedovsk and Dedovo, Hitler's directive was deliberately misleading in blaming all his army's misfortunes on the harsh winter weather. His own mistakes—particularly his failure to make any plans for a winter campaign—were at least as big a culprit. And while the German leader was ostensibly allowing his troops to assume defensive positions, the reality was far more complicated and distressing on the ground. He still wasn't listening to his generals. Stalin's refusal to listen at key moments would also prove very costly, but Hitler's unshaken faith in his own military genius would have far more serious consequences in this new phase of the battle for Moscow.

There was another way that the two dictators were alike. Both men demanded that their armies fight this war with no regard to even the most rudimentary concepts of humanity. Brutal treatment wasn't just tolerated; it was encouraged, even demanded. On the German side, Nazi propaganda drummed home the message to the troops on a daily basis that their enemies were *Untermenschen*, or subhumans. On the Soviet side, racist doctrine wasn't officially part of communist ideology but quickly developed its own momentum.

Ilya Ehrenburg, who like Konstantin Simonov was a famous war correspondent for the Red Army newspaper *Krasnaya Zvezda*, penned his most quoted lines about the Germans in August 1942. "Now we know. The Germans are not human," he wrote. "Now the word 'German' has become the most terrible swear word. Let us not speak. Let us not be indignant. Let us kill. If you do not kill the German he will kill you. . . . If you have killed one German, kill another. There is nothing jollier than German corpses."

While that article appeared after the battle for Moscow was over, similar sentiments pervaded the war coverage of Ehrenburg and others during the fighting around the capital. And no wonder. It was Stalin who had set the tone for all the propagandists during his speech in the Mayakovsky metro station on November 6, when he had vowed, "Well, if the Germans want a war of extermination, they shall have it."

From the beginning of the war, the Soviet leader had also left no doubt that he wasn't concerned about how many of his own people died in the process. Back in September, Stalin heard reports that German forces attacking Leningrad had pushed old people and children in front of them as human shields. The Soviet leader responded by denouncing "the German swine" for such tactics, while issuing unambiguous instructions to his generals not to worry about civilian casualties. "My advice is, don't be sentimental, smash the enemy and his willing or unwilling accomplices in the teeth," he declared. "Hit the Germans and their delegates, whoever they might be, with everything you've got, cut the enemy down, never mind if they are willing or unwilling enemies."

Abram Gordon, who had volunteered for service right after graduating from the State Pedagogical Institute in Moscow, quickly learned what this determinedly unsentimental approach to war meant in practical terms. He was part of a unit assigned to blocking the German advance toward the capital along the Warsaw Highway in early October. The two thousand men were outgunned and outnumbered. During one day's pitched battle, they desperately tried to stop German tanks with grenades and Molotov cocktails until they ran out of even those meager weapons. Not more than 300 to 350 of the Soviet fighters were still alive and able to move by the end of the day. Their only hope was to retreat into the forest under the cover of darkness, leaving behind both the dead and the severely wounded. "One can only imagine what happened to them the next day when the Germans occupied that territory," Gordon said.

In the final stages of the battle, Gordon and his fellow soldiers had come across ten Germans who had lost their way and quickly surrendered. "We had to decide what to do with them," Gordon recalled, still visibly uncomfortable with the memory. "The fact is that we had to retreat into the forest as soon as possible. We could not take them with us and we could not release them."

Most Soviet veterans prefer not even to mention such incidents, and Gordon clearly wanted to stop there. But pressed to spell out what he was implying, he added, "We had to shoot them." And he admitted that he was one of the men assigned to the firing squad. "I was ordered to kill them. For quite a long time this memory tormented me, but now I clearly understand that these measures were necessary. We were soldiers in a war where you had to kill or be killed."

The tables were soon turned when the Germans captured him.

Taken to a large farmyard, he found himself behind a barbed wire fence with thousands of other Soviet POWs. Their German captors lined them up and started marching them west, presumably to one of the full-blown POW camps that they had set up farther back from the front lines.

At that moment, Gordon had the first in a series of close calls. Looking straight at him, a German guard shouted out the question, "Are you Jewish?" As Gordon is the first to point out, his dark features leave little doubt about the answer. Too numb with fear to respond, he suddenly heard someone next to him shout back, "No, he's from the Caucasus." Gordon is convinced those words saved his life.

The prisoners were forced to march more than thirty miles before they were allowed to rest near the road. There he met Lieutenant Nikolai Smirnov, who was already thinking about how to escape. When the officer suggested to Gordon that they try to hide in one of several large haystacks nearby, the soldier didn't need much convincing. He figured that his chance of survival in captivity was close to zero.

For about two hours, the two men crawled painfully slowly to the haystacks, since they wanted to make sure that the guards wouldn't spot them. They made it and burrowed deep into one of the haystacks, spending another three or four hours there. During that time, some of the other POWs noticed their absence and, figuring out what they had done, decided to follow their lead. But as they reached the haystacks, the guards saw them. Soon the air was filled with screams as the Germans thrust their bayonets into the places where they had just begun to hide, and shot others. Since Smirnov and Gordon were at the bottom of the haystack, they survived unscathed.

When it was completely dark and the Germans resumed the march of the POWs, Smirnov and Gordon finally emerged from the haystack and began their trek back to Soviet-controlled territory. With the help of villagers who provided them with food and directions, they eventually found their own troops. But their ordeal wasn't over.

Along with several other men who had escaped captivity or simply become detached from their units, they were sent back to

Moscow to be grilled by military interrogators. Smirnov and Gordon decided they would tell their story straight, including everything, even their brief period in German hands. They figured that they could hardly be considered POWs—traitors in the eyes of Stalin's regime—since they had escaped so quickly.

But the military counterintelligence service viewed a quick return as equally suspect. This could mean they were spying for the Germans. Summoned to the dormitory where he had lived as a student, Gordon discovered that it had been transformed into an interrogation center. When it was his turn to face questioning, he was ordered into room 13, the very room that he had lived in earlier. It felt like an eerie coincidence.

There was no time for nostalgia, however. The officer who questioned him was openly skeptical of his story and left little doubt that he viewed him as a possible spy. "I'm a Jew," Gordon declared in frustration, making the point that he couldn't have talked the Germans into sparing him even if he had wanted to spy for them. That finally convinced his interrogator to release him and reassign him to military duty. "This was the only time in my life where my origins helped me," Gordon wryly noted.

Smirnov wasn't so lucky. His interrogator dispatched him to a prison camp in Mordovia, a region southeast of Moscow where many Gulag victims perished. As an officer, he was doubly suspect and, officially, he was sent there so that he could be vetted further. As Gordon would learn later when he tried to find out what happened to the brave lieutenant who had engineered his escape, Smirnov died in the prison camp about four months later. The cause of death was listed as tuberculosis.

Elena Rzhevskaya, the future writer, who had learned German and often served as a Red Army interpreter during interrogations of German POWs, recalled her astonishment when she discovered that the enemy operated under different rules. Questioning a German lieutenant who was part of a group of sixteen men who had given themselves up when they were surrounded by Soviet forces, she asked him whether their action was considered treason. "No, it's not," the lieutenant replied, adding that his men fought better knowing that they could surrender if they had to. Looking back at that encounter decades later, Rzhevskaya still sounded surprised. "Unlike Soviet soldiers, German soldiers weren't punished [by their own side] for being captured," she said. "Those who survived were even promoted."

But most Germans were already in bad shape when they were captured and many wouldn't survive their subsequent ordeals. Like many other Soviet soldiers, Rzhevskaya encountered captured Germans who looked almost comic in their desperation to protect themselves from the frigid winter weather, wearing any clothes they could seize from the local population, which consisted mostly of women, since the men had gone off to fight.

Rzhevskaya recalled one POW in particular, right after he was seized. "The German was frozen and had icicles all over his face and on his clothes. He was bundled up in a woman's thick linen shawl and his military hat was perched on top of the shawl. The shawl was big enough to cover his whole body. He was also wearing straw boots—the kind Germans forced locals to make for them." His bizarre appearance offered him a modicum of protection at first, causing the Russians to smile instead of venting their anger at him. He realized this and lifted his hands to show they were covered with wool socks instead of mittens, adding to the comic effect.

But, as Rzhevskaya noted, the mood changed when the prisoner was led into a hut for his interrogation. "Since it was hot in the hut, the icicles started to melt from his face and he felt he was losing his funny-looking camouflage," she said. "He looked confused and started touching his face as if he were trying to catch his melting armor."

The sightings of "winter Fritz," those Germans who were reduced to taking any kind of clothing from the locals to try to keep warm, became a staple of many recollections of Soviet veterans. Albert Tsessarsky, the medical orderly who was sent with his home guard platoon to block the German advance on Moscow near Mozhaisk, recalled what he saw when his unit joined in the counteroffensive on December 6. After crossing the frozen Moscow River, the Soviet soldiers came across the German corpses left behind by their retreating comrades. One dead German had a bra wrapped around his head, evidently to try to protect his ears from freezing. The others were wrapped in anything else they had found to fight the cold, and they were wearing only light leather boots. "I must say at that moment I felt such joy, such satisfaction that they got what they deserved," Tsessarsky said. Later, he added, those emotions would pass and he only recalled the "awful" sight of these men who had gone "blindly to their deaths."

In the early stages of the fighting, the Germans who were captured had exuded defiance. Zoya Zarubina, another young woman who acted as a translator during interrogations of POWs, recalled her initial "feeling of shock to see the enemy sitting across the table—the arrogance they had." But later, she'd see them increasingly as "sick, frightened, a phantom of the army that had invaded." Some were still firmly convinced that Hitler would prevail, but many of them were simply terrified by everything that was happening to them, worn down by months of combat and an unforgiving climate.

For their Red Army counterparts, there was always the added dimension of terror imposed by a regime that wouldn't accept the possibility of surrender. Yevgeny Anufriyev, who had been studying architecture until the outbreak of the war, was assigned to an NKVD platoon of eighty men that was supposed to attack Germans trying to hold on to their positions during the Soviet counteroffensive. Outfitted in white camouflage overcoats and operating on skis, they moved quickly—but soon learned that they weren't as prepared for combat as they thought. "Men shouldn't fight on skis in a village," he pointed out. "There are gardens and gates, and your feet can get tied up in your skis." During one of their early attacks, their machine guns proved almost useless. "Men had to pay with their own blood for the mistakes of the top brass," he said. "We weren't warned that lubrication in guns could freeze in the winter. Our machine guns didn't work properly because they froze."

The ensuing battle cost the lives of many of the men in the platoon. But even as they tried to extricate themselves from a barrage of enemy fire, no one considered giving up. "We weren't allowed to surrender," Anufriyev declared. By then, most soldiers knew all too well what the consequences would be from their own side, even if they survived German captivity. Huddled in a shed and discovering he had only three bullets left, Anufriyev took his handgun and pointed it at his head, ready to pull the trigger. At that moment, another soldier, who was carrying their badly wounded platoon leader, shouted to him, "Help me!" Somehow the two of them managed to carry their leader and dodge bullets long enough to find more soldiers and escape from the village. The appeal for help saved both the officer and Anufriyev.

The heroism of the ski patrols was later celebrated in articles in the Soviet press, which reported that despite their extraordinarily high death rates, none of the men surrendered. Anufriyev attested to the accuracy of those accounts. "We were ready to kill ourselves rather than be captured," he said. But it was a mixture of courage and fear that produced such fierce determination. Stalin was always willing to pull the trigger if his own men balked.

Hitler was no less intent on making his men stand and fight, triggering an open confrontation with his most famous tank commander, Heinz Guderian, and other top generals who dared to question his decisions. Faced with the Soviet counteroffensive that was launched on December 6, the German dictator began exhibiting the erratic behavior and refusal to acknowledge the realities on the ground that would ultimately lead to his undoing. With the benefit of hindsight, the battle for Moscow provided the first clear demonstration of his failures as a military leader.

While Hitler reluctantly issued the order to halt offensive operations on December 8, he consistently refused to accept the advice of those commanding the troops near Moscow about how they could best defend themselves and preserve their strength during the harsh winter. If the Germans were going to have a chance to resume their drive to seize the Soviet capital in the spring, they had to minimize their losses. But like Stalin, Hitler viewed any consideration of the human toll of his policies as a sign of weakness, despite the mounting signs that the Soviet leader could sacrifice far more men than his German counterpart.

Guderian had set up his forward headquarters at Yasnaya Polyana, the Tolstoy estate south of Moscow. Describing his visit there on December 2, he would later claim that "no stick of furniture was burned, no book or manuscript touched." That didn't jibe with what Soviet troops found when they took back the estate two weeks

later or with what local inhabitants subsequently recounted. Before
the Germans fled, they had warmed themselves by building fires
right in the house—according to some reports, using manuscripts
from Tolstoy's library as fuel. And right next to the famed writer's
grave, they had buried about seventy of their dead, leaving the
garden and park in disarray. A large wooden marker declared that
they had fallen "for Greater Germany."

Maria Shchegoleva, the sister of the Tolstoy Museum's curator,
told the French journalist Eve Curie, who visited the estate in January, that the Germans had tried to burn down the main buildings
as they left. After setting fires in Tolstoy's house, the schoolhouse,
and the remaining buildings, they told the Russians that they
shouldn't attempt to enter them since they were all mined. "We
paid no attention to this, and as soon as the Nazis had left we
started fighting the fires with two extinguishers that the Germans
had not found and that could still be used—and with water painfully brought up from the well, which was covered with ice and two
feet of snow," Shchegoleva said. Thanks to those efforts, the
damage wasn't all that devastating. By the end of May 1942, the
Russians were able to reopen the museum honoring Tolstoy's life
and work.

But Eve Curie noted bitterly that she learned of something
more chilling that happened during the German occupation: the
bodies of two Russians had remained hanging for four days in the
main square of the village. "There could not be a graver offense to
the memory of Leo Tolstoy," she wrote.

It's conceivable that most of the desecration took place after
Guderian's visit to Yasnaya Polyana, but in any case, honoring Tolstoy's memory was hardly the German general's primary concern.
He knew his troops were literally freezing—on December 4, for example, he recorded that the temperature was minus 32 degrees
Fahrenheit—and frostbite was taking an increasingly heavy toll.
"The enemy, the size of the country and the foulness of the weather
were all underestimated, and we are suffering for that now," he
wrote to his wife.

Even before Hitler issued his order to suspend offensive operations, Guderian had concluded that Moscow couldn't be taken that
winter. Although other panzer units attacking from the northwest

had come within twenty miles of the Kremlin, he noted, they "were forced to abandon their attacks because they lacked the necessary strength to seize the great prize that now lay so near." Guderian was convinced that the only way to preserve German strength was for his troops to withdraw to positions further back from the front lines, where possible to areas that the troops had dug in and fortified before the ground had frozen. "But this was exactly what Hitler refused to allow," he complained.

Guderian's immediate superiors were sympathetic to his appeals, since they recognized their weaknesses even before Zhukov launched his counteroffensive. "The fighting of the past 14 days has shown that the notion that the enemy in front of the army group has 'collapsed' was a fantasy," Field Marshal Fedor von Bock, the commander of Army Group Center, wrote in his diary on December 1. "Halting at the gates of Moscow, where the road and rail net of almost all of Eastern Russia converge, is tantamount to heavy defensive fighting against a numerically far superior foe. The forces of the army group are not equal to this, even for a limited time."

Field Marshal von Brauchitsch, the commander-in-chief of the army, authorized Guderian to start some limited withdrawals, which Guderian quickly acted upon. But Hitler was intent on delivering the message that these were the exceptions rather than the rule. He reached Guderian by phone on the night of December 16. Although the connection was patchy, he got his main points across: the general was supposed to hold his current positions and no further withdrawals would be tolerated. As army chief of staff General Franz Halder noted in his war diary, Hitler reiterated those instructions to his command team at midnight along with a contemptuous dismissal of those who were arguing for a broader pullback. "General withdrawal is out of the question," Halder recorded. "Enemy has made substantial penetration only in a few places. The idea to prepare rear positions is just driveling nonsense."

Field Marshal Erich von Manstein drew a direct parallel between the German leader's behavior when he began suffering his first setbacks and that of his Soviet counterpart at the beginning of the conflict. "Hitler's reaction when the first crisis occurred in front of Moscow was to adopt Stalin's precept of hanging on doggedly to every single position," he wrote after the war. "It was a policy that had brought the Soviet leaders so close to the abyss in 1941."

By the time Guderian was summoned to Hitler's headquarters on December 20, the German leader had dismissed Brauchitsch, the commander-in-chief of the army who had agreed to some of Guderian's redeployment plans, and assumed direct command of the army himself. If there were any doubts left that Hitler believed in his superior abilities and held his generals in contempt, that decision completely dispelled them. "This little matter of operational command is something anyone can do," he told Halder. "The task of the commander-in-chief of the army is to train the army in National Socialist ways. I know of no general who could do that as I want it done, so I have decided to take over the command of the army myself."

Hitler also had gotten rid of Bock, the commander of Army Group Center, who had argued in vain against his orders to hold on to the forward positions on the approaches to Moscow. Guderian knew that those moves didn't augur well for his face-to-face meeting with Hitler, although he still hoped that the German leader retained some of his previous positive feelings about him.

Guderian was quickly disabused of that notion when he entered the dimly lit room where Hitler and his entourage awaited him. "As Hitler came forward to greet me, I saw to my surprise, for the first time, a hard unfriendly expression in his eyes," he wrote later. The panzer general who had once entranced the Führer with his bold plans and brilliant performance was now entering hostile territory.

Asked for a summary of his army's movements, Guderian signaled his intention to continue the withdrawal to safer positions that Brauchitsch had authorized.

"No, I forbid that!" Hitler shouted.

Guderian explained that the only way to prevent needless losses of his men was to continue with the redeployment he had already started. But Hitler had already made up his mind and insisted that his troops "must dig into the ground where they are and hold every square yard of land!"

grim reports he began to hear from his fellow fliers who took part in raids south of the capital. They spoke of the "unforgettable sight" of hundreds of German tanks burning on the ground. It was particularly striking because the fliers could see that their own crews had set these tanks alight after they had run out of fuel or the engines had conked out. Since the soldiers had to retreat, they were forced to resort to such measures to prevent the tanks from falling into Soviet hands.

On the ground, Kurt Gruman, the infantry lieutenant who kept a diary as his regiment tried to fight its way to Moscow, noted that this was true for anything the Germans had brought with them. "Everything that we cannot take with us and that must not fall into Bolshevik hands must be destroyed," he wrote on December 15. The next day, he complained, "Morale and discipline during this withdrawal have been subject to heavy blows. How much valuable property has been lost in vain! They did not even bother destroying it all. I fear those munitions will come down on our head."

Supply lines weren't simply overextended; they had broken down completely in many cases. Pointing out that the severe weather was preventing planes from taking off, Gruman reflected the widespread feeling of hopelessness. "Now we cannot rely on any more deliveries," he wrote on December 21. "What will this do to us? There is a feeling among the men as if they had been put on duty but then someone forgot to send replacements. Have we not been abandoned?" He added plaintively, "One could howl with frustration."

As always, the merciless cold added to that sense of desperation. Gruman tried to keep warm by wearing two overcoats and a blanket but still found the cold "all-penetrating." An improvised field hospital was full of men with second- and third-degree frostbite. "Swollen legs are covered with blisters, so that they are no longer even legs, but rather some kind of formless mass," Gruman recorded in his diary. "In some cases gangrene had already set in. Those who managed to make it through the deluge of shrapnel have become invalids here." In some units, far more soldiers were crippled by frostbite than by battlefield wounds during this period.

While Gruman still tried to talk himself into believing that Germany would ultimately win—"There is no doubt that in the summer the Bolsheviks will once again feel our might," he wrote—his diary radiated growing despair. It included more and more references to Russians penetrating their positions as they retreated further. In January, his entries grew shorter, and the final entry was on February 17. On that day or shortly thereafter, he, too, probably perished. There's no way of knowing whether he died in battle or simply from the cold.

As some of the badly wounded and frostbitten soldiers were sent back to Germany for treatment, it became harder and harder for Hitler's regime to maintain the fiction that the war was proceeding according to plan. "The anxiety of the German people about the Eastern front is increasing," Hitler's chief propagandist, Joseph Goebbels, confided in his diary on January 22, 1942. "Deaths owing to freezing are an especially important factor in this connection." Goebbels complained especially bitterly about the "devastating effect" of the mail that soldiers were sending to their loved ones. "Words cannot describe what soldiers are writing back home from the front," he wrote. Apparently, the German authorities were far less effective in weeding out complaining letters than their Soviet counterparts were.

Even in his diary, Goebbels couldn't admit the truth of those letters. He blamed the negative tone of many of the letters from the front on soldiers who wanted to feel important by dramatizing their situations. "The passion for showing off here plays a considerable role," he wrote. "When the soldier writes and exaggerates he doesn't stop to think that he may be causing his family and his relatives a lot of worry." While Goebbels stated he was recommending stronger indoctrination of the soldiers, he didn't hold out much hope that this would produce the desired effect. "It is a question of human weakness against which one is powerless," he concluded.

Like his boss, Goebbels was already blaming the officers and men for falling short, never accepting responsibility for the decisions that had left them in those extreme winter conditions without even the proper clothing. If morale was plummeting, it was the soldiers who were to blame. If they couldn't put up with the hardships without complaining, they hadn't been properly indoctrinated.

This conveniently overlooked two key facts. The first was Hitler's belief that his troops could achieve victory before the harsh winter weather set in. This proved to be a fatal miscalculation, in large part because of his tactical mistakes. And the second was the German leader's decision on transport priorities.

Throughout the early months of the invasion, Hitler faced the choice of sending winter clothing, food or ammunition to the front. He had to decide which of those three needs to fill first, since German rail capability was severely limited. The Soviet rail system operated on wide-gauge tracks, which weren't used elsewhere in Europe, and only a portion of German-controlled trains were equipped for them. On top of that, German locomotives broke down frequently as temperatures dropped. While sending some food supplies and ordering his troops to seize whatever provisions they could from the territory they controlled, Hitler decided to make ammunition the top priority for transport. As for warm clothing, even when it was prepared for shipment, there was usually no space made available for it on the trains rolling east. That had been the case with the winter clothes Guderian had located at the train station in Warsaw, for instance.

In a radio broadcast on December 21, 1941, Goebbels appealed to the German people to donate winter clothing for the soldiers at the front, asking that they provide anything they could that would help keep the soldiers warm. Guderian was convinced that this was a direct result of his complaints about the lack of winter clothing in his meeting with Hitler the day before. But given the transport problems, this clothing drive was too little, too late for many of the soldiers trying to survive the first winter of the war. Most of the warm clothing didn't make it in time for that deadly cold period.

In a diary entry on March 6, 1942, Goebbels tallied the German losses on the entire Eastern front, not just in the fighting near Moscow, since the beginning of Operation Barbarossa. He put the number of dead around two hundred thousand and the total for those killed, wounded, or missing at nearly one million. He also made special note of the impact of winter conditions. "Until February 20, 112,627 cases of freezing or frostbite were reported, including 14,357 third-degree and 62,000 second-degree cases. . . . The number of those who suffered from freezing is considerably higher than we had at first imagined." Once again, he worried about the impact on morale. "Even as it is, the final figure is only a small fraction of what is being spread around among the people in the form of rumors," he wrote.

As always, the implication was that those sacrifices weren't being borne with the kind of dignity and stoic acceptance that the Nazi leadership demanded and expected.

Zhukov was pleased to see his army pushing the enemy back from the outskirts of Moscow, but he knew that the Germans still had considerable firepower left. He also knew the limitations of his own troops, who were continuing to die in far greater numbers than the Germans, while those who survived were often battered and exhausted. So when he was summoned to the *Stavka,* or Supreme High Command, for a meeting on January 5 with Stalin, other political leaders and the top military brass to discuss the next phase of the counteroffensive, he was understandably wary. He was acutely aware of the limitations of the forces at his disposal that would have to carry out any new orders.

At the start of the meeting, Marshal Boris Shaposhnikov, the crusty former tsarist officer who had survived the purges and risen to the position of chief of the General Staff, provided an overview of the military situation. Much to Zhukov's dismay, he also outlined plans for a massive new offensive that would be aimed not just at pushing the Germans farther back from Moscow but also at breaking the blockade of Leningrad and defeating German forces in the Ukraine and the Caucasus. In other words, the Red Army was supposed to attack on all fronts.

Shaposhnikov certainly didn't dream up those plans on his own—he knew who would endorse them. "The Germans seem bewildered by their setback at Moscow and are poorly prepared for the winter," Stalin declared. "Now is the time to go over to a general offensive."

Zhukov warned that this would be a dangerous strategy. While urging a continuation of the offensive on the Western front to keep driving the Germans further from Moscow, he pleaded for more reinforcements and equipment, especially tanks, for the divisions under his command. "As for offensives near Leningrad and in the southwest, forces there face formidable enemy defenses," he pointed out. "Without powerful artillery support, our forces would be unable to break through, they would be worn down and suffer heavy and completely unjustified losses." Coming from a commander who never flinched at sacrificing his men when it served to achieve his goals, the message was clear: a general offensive would inevitably fail and would prove counterproductive.

Nikolai Voznesensky, who was in charge of wartime economic planning, sided with Zhukov, pointing out that he couldn't provide the necessary military equipment to support such an ambitious military undertaking. But Malenkov and Beria quickly dismissed his objections, claiming that he was always exaggerating the difficulties. (In 1950, during another round of purges, Voznesensky was tried and shot.)

As Zhukov had figured out by then, Stalin's mind was completely made up, and nothing he or Vosnesensky said would make any difference. "I've talked with [Marshal] Timoshenko, and he favors the attack," the dictator added. "We must quickly smash the Germans so that they cannot attack when the spring comes." Then there was the final flourish. "So this, it seems, ends the discussion," Stalin said.

As they walked out of the meeting, Shaposhnikov turned to Zhukov. "It was foolish to argue," he told him. "The Chief had already decided."

Zhukov asked why Stalin had bothered to ask for his opinion. Shaposhnikov sighed. "I just don't know, old fellow, I just don't know."

Like Hitler, Stalin wasn't about to listen to his generals when they tried to tell him anything he didn't want to hear, even when this obstinacy resulted in precisely the "completely unjustified losses" that Zhukov had warned against. As always, the human price of his decisions was the least of Stalin's concerns. On February 7, for instance, the Germans intercepted the orders radioed to Soviet commanders in the field. The gist of the message: the commanders had to do everything to spare their ammunition but not their men.

Looking back at those battles with their huge body counts,

Mikhail Geykhman, a lieutenant in one of the Siberian artillery divisions that participated in the offensive west of Moscow that winter, waxed philosophical. "We hadn't been prepared to fight a war with fewer losses," he said. While claiming that morale was high because they were finally moving forward and the soldiers were increasingly convinced that they could drive back the enemy, he pointed out that even Siberian units like his weren't nearly as well equipped as the Germans believed—and as popular lore later had it. "We didn't have enough supplies of anything," he said.

During that first winter of the war, many of the men in his unit still wore short boots with leg wrappings and a cloth cap shaped like a helmet called a *budyonovka,* which also required inserting extra lining and wrappings to keep head and ears warm. It was only toward the end of the winter that most of the troops received the full-length *valenki,* or felt boots, and *ushanki,* fur caps with thick ear flaps, that were soon standard issue. As Goebbels had done on the German side, the Soviet authorities appealed to civilians to donate anything warm, including underwear, for the troops at the front.

When it came to weaponry, the problems were even more serious. Some of the cannons in Geykhman's division dated back to the civil war and were mounted on wooden wheels and pulled by horses. Most officers considered their handguns inferior to the ones their German counterparts carried. When they could, they seized any handguns they found on dead Germans. They were also short of machine guns and anti-tank weapons. The most frightening moments for Geykhman and his unit were in early February, when they had to face German tanks near Mozhaisk, the town sixty miles due west of Moscow, with whatever firepower they had. "They were coming straight at us," he recalled. "We understood that we were facing a very strong enemy who knew how to fight."

The other shortage was of experienced officers. Geykhman, who had volunteered after graduating from high school at seventeen, a year earlier than most students, had been made a lieutenant after a three-week training course, still short of his eighteenth birthday. As proud as he is of his role in saving Moscow, he noted that many of the best officers had perished in the purges before the war, and everyone was still paying the price. "Our officers weren't ready for this war," he said. "We only really learned how to fight in 1943."

Finally, it wasn't just the Germans who had to grab any opportunity to scrounge for food. Strict food rationing had been imposed in major cities such as Moscow and Leningrad right after the Germans invaded, and it spread throughout the country as the fighting intensified. With bizarre precision, the planners determined that ordinary workers should get 1,387 calories per day, while those who did heavier work received 1,913 calories. Their dependents were allocated a meager 750 calories, and there were no provisions for anyone who didn't work.

The troops were usually supplied with at least minimal rations, but the soldiers had to look to supplement them in any way they could. Yevgeny Teleguyev, the young volunteer in the NKVD's special forces known as OMSBON, recalled his platoon's search for food when they traveled on skis, often behind enemy lines. On one occasion when their rations had run out, they found a horse in the forest and killed it. Then they had to figure out how to skin and cook it. "We were city guys and didn't know how to do that kind of stuff," he said. Since they didn't have an axe to chop off the hooves, they boiled the horse's legs with its hooves and horseshoes intact.

Other soldiers stripped horses that had been dead for quite a while, which could be a dangerous way to quell their hunger. One officer of a unit fighting near Rzhev reported that his men were falling ill after eating the rotting remains of a horse. But with some soldiers dying of starvation, it was hard to restrain anyone. If the soldiers were lucky, they found potato pits, holes in the ground or in the basement of huts where peasants stored their potatoes for the winter. Like the Germans, they grabbed whatever they saw.

The fighting soon was reduced to a struggle for survival on every level. Vera Katayeva, a nurse assigned to troops fighting along the Mozhaisk Highway, recalled that after the Red Army retook the town of Mozhaisk in January, the fighting beyond it settled into a blood-soaked standoff in a narrow corridor that became known as Death Valley. "Soviet and German soldiers spent three months there—January, February and March—killing each other," she said. "The ground was covered with dead bodies and dead horses."

By late January, the Germans were not just following Hitler's orders and holding their ground in several places. They were also beginning to launch some modest counterattacks of their own. On January 26, Goebbels noted in his diary an "extraordinarily favorable" report from an unnamed commanding general on the northern front, who claimed that Soviet forces there were "being bled white." As Goebbels wrote, "He believes the Soviet Union will collapse in the spring, provided we are in a position to deliver a few decisive blows. Even though I am not able as yet to share this optimism I nevertheless believe he has something . . . possibly it is actually true that the Bolsheviks are now using up their last resources and will break down under a severe blow. But let us not cling too much to such hopes," Goebbels added. "Our preparations for the coming spring and summer must be made just as though the Bolsheviks still had very great reserves. That will make us immune to surprises and we won't have moral setbacks like those of last summer and autumn."

Those setbacks, particularly the failure to seize Moscow as planned before the end of 1941, had clearly shaken his confidence. Optimistic predictions, while still welcomed, were no longer automatically believed.

Stalin's general offensive in early 1942 didn't achieve any of its grandiose goals. New attempts to break the siege of Leningrad and to regain control of key areas of the Ukraine were costly failures, and the costliest failure of them all was the attempt to encircle and destroy the troops of Army Group Center that were still threatening Moscow from the west. As with every previous stage of the battle for Moscow, everything seemed to conspire to produce maximum suffering and maximum losses, in most cases instigated by the decisions flowing from the top.

One of those decisions was nothing less than a scorched earth policy. On November 17, 1941, Stalin dictated Order 0428, which declared, "All inhabited locations up to a distance of 40–60 kilometers [25 to 37 miles] in the rear of German troops and up to 20–30 kilometers [12 to 19 miles] on either side of the roads are to be destroyed and burnt to ashes." The destruction was to be carried out in a variety of ways—by aerial bombing, artillery fire, and ski patrols and partisan guerrillas armed with petrol bombs. On top of that, the order stipulated: "Each regiment is to have a team of volunteers of 20–30 men to blow up and burn down inhabited locations." Those who excelled in this destruction, it added, would receive special awards.

All of which was a recipe for countless tragedies for civilians hoping to survive the fighting raging around them, since the implementation of that order meant the destruction of their meager homes in the middle of the winter. "Whether the decision was made in light of military necessity or insane cruelty remains an open question," Stalin's biographer Dmitri Volkogonov wrote, "but in either case it was a typically Stalinist, callous act."

Those policies provided yet another reason for many local inhabitants to distrust all the warring parties, including the partisans who were beginning to operate behind enemy lines. They soon learned that the partisans might be targeting their homes for destruction, and even when that wasn't the case, their presence would expose them to brutal retaliation from the German occupiers. In a top secret report submitted on November 8, 1941, N. P. Krasavchenko, a Komsomol secretary who had found himself behind enemy lines after the German victory at Vyazma, 130 miles west of Moscow, reported on local "anti-Soviet" attitudes after he managed to escape. He encountered one partisan who said he was forced to operate alone because he couldn't trust anyone. "Most people don't like me because they are afraid of German vengeance and they threaten to turn me in," he told Krasavchenko.

In his own encounters with villagers, the Komsomol secretary came across similar attitudes. "Thank God there are no partisans here," he reported them as telling him. "But if there were some, we'd give them up to the Germans." The villagers explained that if they failed to do so, the Germans would burn down their houses and execute them. Those German atrocities, of course, would begin to generate their own backlash, shattering any remaining illusions that the local populace could count on quietly surviving the occupation, no matter how obedient they were. As Soviet troops began to take back towns and villages near Moscow, an all too common sight was partisans or ordinary citizens still hanging from makeshift gallows. For anyone caught in the vicinity of this titanic struggle, there was no easy escape.

That was doubly true for the warriors, especially those who were ordered to carry out their leaders' most dangerous orders. On the Soviet side, this meant Stalin and Zhukov's plan to encircle and destroy Army Group Center, the main body of German troops west of Moscow. The idea was to encircle the German forces near Vyazma, in the same general area where Soviet troops had been encircled and virtually wiped out in October. As Stalin envisaged it, this would deal a huge blow to the German war machine. But by pushing the exhausted Soviet forces deeper and deeper into enemy territory, it also increased the risk that they would be stretched too far without the means to protect their own flanks. In that case, the Germans would have the chance of once again closing in on them instead of the other way around.

To avoid such an outcome, Stalin and his generals needed to work closely together, making sure that troop strength was buttressed at key points. But already, in the first part of the offensive, the Soviet leader demonstrated that he felt free to ignore the urgent pleas of his military commanders, even in the case of Zhukov, who normally held more sway with him than anyone else.

After his troops scored victories near Volokolamsk, northwest of Moscow, Zhukov received an order on January 19 to pull out a major part of those forces, the First Shock Army, so that they could rejoin the reserves. He phoned Stalin to argue that he needed that unit to keep the drive going in that crucial area. "Don't argue," Stalin snapped. "Send it along." When Zhukov continued to protest the weakening of his forces, the dictator replied: "You have plenty of troops—just count them." When that, too, failed to silence Zhukov, Stalin hung up on him.

When it came to the push against Vyazma, Zhukov would later admit that both he and Stalin made crucial mistakes. "We overestimated the capabilities of our forces and underestimated the enemy's, and the nut proved to be harder to crack than we had expected," he wrote later. But, as with the fundamental decision of launching a general offensive in the first place, he shifted most of the blame to Stalin. He pointed out that the Germans had withdrawn to the prepared defensive positions that Hitler's generals had wanted to retreat to earlier and that they had begun to reinforce those positions with reserve troops brought in from France.

This allowed them both to dig in to resist attacks and to mount counterattacks of their own.

Zhukov also warned Stalin that his artillery units were woefully short of ammunition, forcing the infantry to mount attacks without anything approaching adequate artillery support. Stalin remained unmoved, and he continued to order more and more attacks, many of which ended with disproportionately high body counts on the Soviet side. "If you don't achieve results today, you will tomorrow," Stalin blithely told Zhukov. "If you attack, you may at least tie down the enemy, and the results will be felt on other parts of the front."

That was little consolation for the commanders and the men dispatched to fight those battles without the planning and support that would give them a chance to achieve victory. Under the command of General Mikhail Yefremov, the Thirty-third Army had pushed its way to within striking distance of Vyazma. It was supposed to be joined by troops moving from the Kalinin region in the north. Together they were supposed to deal a decisive blow to the enemy's Army Group Center not just in Vyazma but also up to Rzhev, the city further to the north that remained a likely jump-off point for a new push against Moscow.

The mission of the Soviet forces was to encircle and destroy the Germans, but more often than not, they found themselves encircled instead. General Yefremov and his Thirty-third Army, along with General Pavel Belov's First Cavalry Corps, were cut off behind enemy lines near Vyazma. During February and March, other Soviet forces trying to dislodge the Germans holding Rzhev shared their fate. The fighting was at such close quarters that it was hard for the Soviet command to organize parachute drops of food and ammunition, since the enemy often seized the supplies. "Hey Russians! Ivan!" the Germans taunted them over megaphones when they did so. "*Danke schön.* We're eating your pork and peas. It's delicious." For troops who were often near starvation, nothing could be more demoralizing.

Forced to recognize that many of the troops under the command of Yefremov and Belov were hopelessly stranded behind enemy lines, Stalin and Zhukov agreed to allow the two generals to try to fight their way back east to avoid complete encirclement. Belov eventually succeeded in making his way back with some of his forces, but the remaining troops of Yefremov's Thirty-third Army were virtually wiped out during their last desperate attempt to break through in April. The popular commander was among those who perished. According to most accounts, Yefremov was wounded and then shot himself to avoid capture.

The Soviet counteroffensive pushed the Germans back about forty-five to sixty-five miles along the central front, but it fell far short of its objectives. "Events demonstrated the error of Stalin's decision calling for a general offensive in January," Zhukov concluded. Although he had argued against that decision and he claimed that he opposed some of the tactical calls Stalin made at the time, Zhukov was also tarred by the huge losses during that offensive. Since the Germans were every bit as battered and exhausted, neither side felt triumphant.

In fact, Moscow felt safer and was safer, since subsequent events would demonstrate that the Germans wouldn't be able to mount another serious drive to seize the Soviet capital. But the Germans were still occupying such towns as Vyazma and Rzhev, which had been launch points for the first drive on Moscow. For Stalin, who had been particularly intent on liberating Rzhev, this was a major source of frustration. This also meant that even after the battle for Moscow was effectively over in late April, at the start of the spring thaw, which ruled out any further major actions by either exhausted army for several weeks, the Moscow-related fighting would continue. Rzhev, already the scene of some of the most intense fighting, would still be a major killing field for almost another entire year. Even if the threat to Moscow had largely receded, no one was celebrating.

11

"The worst of all worlds"

In December 1941, as Soviet troops began their counterattacks aimed at pushing the Germans back from the approaches to Moscow, Anthony Eden embarked on the long roundabout journey to the Soviet capital that wartime conditions necessitated. Weakened by the flu, the British foreign secretary spent four days on a destroyer bound for Murmansk largely confined to his bed. Since the Arctic port city was fogged in when they arrived on December 12, the British delegation couldn't be flown the next leg of the trip. Instead, they faced the prospect of a two- or three-day train ride to Moscow. But when they were still waiting on the ship, the Soviet side arranged a surprise for Eden.

The foreign secretary had undertaken the journey because relations between Stalin and his Western allies remained tense, despite the professions of friendship on both sides. Since Lord Beaverbrook and Averell Harriman's visit to Moscow in September, the Soviet leader had continued to press his demands for speedier delivery of the promised Lend-Lease supplies and any sort of military action that would take some of the pressure off his weary troops, no matter how often Churchill and others reminded him that Britain was hardly prepared to start fighting on the Continent, much less entertain his far-fetched suggestions that it should dispatch troops to Russia.

There was also another issue that Stalin was pushing: an agreement about postwar boundaries. Much to the dismay of both Churchill and Roosevelt, Stalin was intent on defining the new geopolitical contours of the Continent after Hitler's eventual defeat. His armies had barely held their own on the outskirts of Moscow, but their leader was already looking ahead to a new European order that would satisfy his territorial ambitions.

Eden had volunteered for his mission in order to try to dampen those expectations and to keep relations between these uneasy allies on an even keel. Neither he nor Churchill knew what kind of reception to expect, since Stalin had demonstrated his testiness on more than one occasion already, though he often adopted a softer tone immediately following a nastier exchange. Ivan Maisky, the Soviet ambassador to London, who regularly conveyed his leader's complaints, accompanied Eden on his journey and provided the first signal of Stalin's frame of mind.

After they docked in Murmansk, Eden stayed on board while Maisky went into town to make the arrangements for a heavily guarded train. Returning to the destroyer, the Soviet ambassador asked for a private word with Eden, and they went into the foreign secretary's cabin. Maisky placed a black bag on the table and delivered a message from Stalin. The Soviet leader, he said, didn't want Eden and his delegation to feel "embarrassed" during the visit by the dispute between Britain and Russia over the ruble exchange rate. Like the Americans, the British had repeatedly protested an exchange rate that inflated all their expenses in Russia. Without conceding any ground on that issue, Maisky explained that Stalin was putting enough rubles at Eden's disposal for him and his delegation to have no problems during their visit. Then, as an astonished Eden looked on, the ambassador pulled out "package after package" of bills that he put in rows on the table.

"I was agape at so much wealth," the foreign secretary recalled. But he had the presence of mind to ask Maisky to thank Stalin for his generosity and to assure him that his delegation could cover its expenses and that they wouldn't need the money on the table.

Maisky was visibly upset by Eden's polite refusal, but when the foreign secretary refused to change his mind, he gathered up the packages of rubles, placed them back in the black bag, and locked it.

This was typical Stalin. He wanted to appear conciliatory and soften up his British visitor before their talks but with an ostensibly generous gesture that put Eden in an awkward position, since he had no choice but to reject it. The Soviet leader probably had no idea why his guest couldn't accept the money, since, in his world, he rewarded or punished anyone as he saw fit—and no other rules applied.

The next morning, December 13, Maisky went back on board to tell Eden the news that *Pravda* was trumpeting: the Soviet victory in the battle for Moscow. Although the foreign secretary knew the fighting was far from over, he was elated. "That's marvelous!" he told Maisky. "For the first time the Germans have suffered a reverse!"

On their train journey, which began the late afternoon of the same day, Eden was impressed by the ability of the Russians to deal with the unrelenting cold that reached minus 15 degrees Fahrenheit at night. The special train was equipped with anti-aircraft guns mounted on open wagons between the passenger carriages, which were manned by crews in two-hour shifts. "The cold which these men had to endure when moving at a fair pace through these Arctic temperatures must have been cruel," Eden observed.

During one of the occasional stops along the way when they got off to pace alongside the tracks, he asked Maisky, "How can your people stand such cold?" When the ambassador assured him that the crews were appropriately dressed and used to the icy temperatures, Eden added, "Well, the Germans are not used to such frosts."

When the train pulled into Moscow on the evening of December 15, icicles hung from the carriages and the station was plunged into darkness. Suddenly, it was bathed in light for fourteen minutes as Molotov greeted his British counterpart. The Soviet foreign minister eagerly reported that Soviet troops had just driven German troops out of Klin, fifty miles north of Moscow. Then the lights went out, and people moved like shadows through the steam and smoke of the train and the continuing blackout of the capital, which had been established to avoid providing visible targets for German bombers. The capital didn't feel as triumphant as the official proclamation had made it sound a couple of days earlier.

If Eden had any doubts about the impact of the improved military picture on Stalin's frame of mind, they promptly evaporated when the two men sat down for their first meeting the next evening. Right from the start, the Soviet leader focused on his territorial ambitions, along with his other ideas for the postwar period, no matter how premature such a discussion inevitably felt. He wasn't going to let Eden off the hook by merely discussing the current situation. The first real success of his army, stopping the Germans just short of Moscow and then beginning to push them back, only strengthened his resolve to press his British guest for the commitments he wanted. Stalin could try to appear magnanimous by offering wads of rubles, but his generosity didn't extend to his country's neighbors, whose prewar status and borders were not to his liking.

Even during the earliest days of the German invasion, when the Red Army was in retreat everywhere and a catastrophic defeat seemed in the making, the Soviet leadership had signaled its determination to stake out its future claims. In July 1941, at the urging of Churchill's government, Maisky had conducted negotiations in London with the leader of the Polish government in exile, General Wladyslaw Sikorski, aimed at getting these hostile neighbors to reestablish diplomatic relations and cooperate in the struggle against Germany. The talks provided the first clues to how the Soviet side intended to achieve its territorial goals.

The Poles, of course, were the aggrieved party, since Stalin had joined forces with Hitler in dismembering their country as envisaged by the Molotov-Ribbentrop pact. After invading Poland from the east in September 1939, the Soviet Union annexed a large swathe of territory that had been eastern Poland, and deported about two million Poles from those areas to Soviet labor camps, prisons or exile in remote regions. Among them was the equivalent of several divisions of Polish soldiers that Soviet forces had captured during the invasion. Several thousand of their officers had disappeared without a trace, including more than four thousand whose bodies were later discovered in a mass grave in the Katyn forest near Smolensk in 1943. The victims had their hands tied behind their backs, and had been shot in the head.

Sikorski's government wanted two clear commitments from Moscow: a declaration that the Nazi-Soviet partition of Poland was null and void, which would mean that the country would be restored to its pre-1939 borders at the end of the war, and the freeing of all Polish military personnel and civilians who were deported and imprisoned. This would allow the formation of Polish army units in the Soviet Union who would join the fight against the Germans.

But at their talks in July 1941, Maisky immediately indicated that the Kremlin's idea of a reestablished Poland was at odds with Polish goals. "I explained that as we saw it the future Polish state should only consist of Poles, and should cover those territories which were inhabited by Poles," he recalled. As the Polish negotiators understood, this formulation meant that the Soviet side intended to hold on to a large part of the territories it had annexed in 1939, since it viewed them as Ukrainian and Belorussian and already had conducted its version of ethnic cleansing there. If these were to be the criteria for the postwar boundaries, the ostensible Soviet willingness to renounce the territorial agreement with the Nazi regime would have little practical significance.

Sikorski felt compelled to conclude an agreement, no matter how troubled he was by the Soviet stance. As Jan Ciechanowski, the Polish ambassador in Washington, pointed out, "The British government was strongly pressing General Sikorski to speed up the conversations with the Soviets, instead of pressing the Soviets to accept the just conditions of Poland." Churchill conceded as much in his memoirs. Although Britain had gone to war over Poland, he was now particularly intent on keeping his new Soviet ally in the fight against the Germans and, at least according to some reports, he still suspected Stalin might cut another deal with Hitler if circumstances changed once again. "The issue of the territorial future of Poland must be postponed until easier times," the prime minister wrote. "We had the invidious responsibility of recommending General Sikorski to rely on Soviet good faith in the future settlements of Russian-Polish relations, and not to insist at this moment on any written guarantees for the future."

The agreement concluded on July 30 did include provisions for the formation of Polish army units on Soviet soil and amnesty for Poles imprisoned there, and it restored diplomatic relations between the two countries. But while the Soviet-German treaties of 1939 were declared invalid, the territorial question remained unresolved. In Washington, Under Secretary of State Sumner Welles stated that he understood that the agreement "was in line with the United States policy of non-recognition of territory taken by conquest." In the House of Commons, Eden reiterated his government's position that it didn't recognize the territorial changes of 1939, but he added that this "does not involve any guarantee of frontiers by His Majesty's Government." For Poles, as Ciechanowski put it, this was "the first swallow on the rising dawn of a new British policy of appeasement."

Less than two weeks before Eden's visit to Moscow, Sikorski had also undertaken the circuitous journey to the Soviet capital, flying from London, via Cairo, Tehran and Kuibyshev. Meeting with Stalin on December 3 and 4, he pushed for information about his missing officers and for the implementation of the proclaimed amnesty for all Polish military prisoners so that they could form the basis of a new fighting force. Sikorski only encountered denials and feigned ignorance when it came to the fate of the missing Polish officers. "They must have escaped somewhere," Stalin declared. But Sikorski managed to win the Soviet leader's agreement to permit the newly freed Poles to cross to Iran, where the British had promised to provide the supplies they needed to outfit themselves as a proper army again. Under the command of General Wladyslaw Anders, those troops would later fight valiantly in North Africa and, most famously, capture the monastery at Monte Cassino during the Italian campaign in 1944.

In return, Stalin tried to maneuver Sikorski into a discussion of the postwar boundary between Poland and the Soviet Union. "I think it would be useful if we discussed it," he said. "After all, the alterations I want to suggest are very slight." The Polish leader insisted that he had no right to discuss even the tiniest change in his country's "inviolable" borders, and Stalin dropped the subject.

Sitting down for his first meeting with Stalin in Moscow on December 16, Eden was hoping that he'd also succeed in skirting this politically charged issue and new suspicions that his government was caving in to Soviet demands. In Washington, Roosevelt had been trying to reassure the Poles that he was sensitive to their concerns and that he was sticking by the commitment he and Churchill had made in the Atlantic Charter, which they had proclaimed during their summit at sea back in August. At that meeting, they had promised there would be no territorial changes "that do not accord with the freely expressed wishes of the people concerned." He urged Churchill not to make any commitments to Stalin about postwar arrangements. For Eden, the less said about all this in Moscow, the better.

Stalin wasn't about to play along. The Soviet leader immediately handed Eden drafts of two treaties, one for the wartime military alliance between their two countries and the other for dealing with postwar arrangements. He then jolted his guest by proposing a secret protocol to the second treaty, which would spell out the future of European borders. "Russian ideas were already starkly definite," Eden grimly noted later. "They changed little during the next three years, for their purpose was to secure the most tangible physical guarantees for Russia's future security." There was a recent precedent for such secret protocols on the redrawing of borders: the Molotov-Ribbentrop pact.

While this time Stalin wasn't plotting to wipe out the Polish state, the similarity didn't end there. Once again, Poland and the Baltic states figured as the primary losers in such an arrangement. For Poland, Stalin insisted that its eastern border should run along the Curzon line, the armistice line suggested by British Foreign Secretary Lord Curzon during the Russo-Polish War of 1919–1920. Polish victories during that war produced a border that ran much farther east, which meant that interwar Poland controlled a large swathe of territory that the Kremlin coveted. As a result of the partition of Poland under the Molotov-Ribbentrop pact, the Soviet Union seized this portion of Poland and set up a boundary very close to the original Curzon line. Now Stalin wanted to make that arrangement permanent.

To compensate for the loss of its territory, Stalin indicated that

Poland should be given a good chunk of eastern Germany. He also called for restoration of a separate Austrian state, depriving Germany of the Rhineland and possibly Bavaria, and creation of a council of the victors who would decide what to do with a defeated Germany. And he wanted to know what Eden thought about the possibility of Germany paying reparations for the damage it was inflicting. As for the Baltic states, they were to be swallowed up once again by the Soviet state, and the Soviet borders with Finland and Romania would revert to what they had been before the Germans attacked. In short, he was proposing many of the terms that would eventually figure in the discussions of the great powers in Tehran in 1943 and Yalta in 1945.

Eden knew how he had to respond and tried to do so as tactfully as possible. His government, he said, was open to considering such issues as how to organize military control over a defeated Germany, and it certainly favored an independent Austria. Given the disastrous impact of reparations after the previous war, it would oppose any effort to demand reparations after this one. As for the key issue of future borders, he explained that his hands were tied. "Even before Russia was attacked, Mr. Roosevelt sent a message to us, asking us not to enter into any secret arrangement as to the postwar reorganization of Europe without first consulting him," he told Stalin.

In fact, John Winant, the American ambassador in London, had been instructed to deliver a precise message to Eden from Secretary of State Cordell Hull shortly before his British counterpart left for Moscow. Dated December 5, the cable stressed that the postwar policies of both countries and the Soviet Union were encapsulated in the Atlantic Charter and it would be "unfortunate" for any of these governments "to enter into commitments regarding specific terms of the postwar settlement." It added, "Above all, there must be no secret accords."

With those warnings in mind, Eden kept emphasizing to Stalin that Russia, Britain and the United States needed to be in agreement on the major issues and that he couldn't commit to anything on his own.

"What about the attachment of the secret protocol?" Stalin asked, refusing to give up.

When Eden reiterated that this would require consultations with his own government and Washington, the Soviet leader claimed to agree, saying that a united front was crucial to their efforts. The discussion then shifted to the military situation. While there were some tricky issues there as well, the foreign secretary felt that he had succeeded in shelving the territorial issue, at least for the time being.

Their next meeting proved that he was wrong. "Stalin began to show his claws," he noted. Seemingly oblivious to Eden's previous explanations, the Soviet leader bluntly asked for British recognition of his country's 1941 borders—in other words, those that it had established under the Molotov-Ribbentrop pact.

It was back to square one, and, in what Eden described as a "frigid" atmosphere, he had once again to explain that he couldn't endorse anything of the sort. He pointed out that Churchill had declared earlier that Britain wouldn't recognize changes in the borders produced by the war—and that this was at a time when Germany was advancing and any recognition of such borders would have hurt Russia.

"If you say that you might as well say tomorrow that you do not recognize the Ukraine as forming a part of the U.S.S.R.," Stalin curtly interjected.

"That is a complete misunderstanding of the position," Eden replied. "It is only changes from the prewar frontiers that we do not recognize."

Stalin wouldn't let the subject go, insisting that the British refusal would leave his country a supplicant. "It makes it look as if I should have to come cap in hand," he said.

This was the petulant Stalin, who turned indignant any time his demands, no matter how far-reaching, weren't immediately accepted. He would push and push, seeing how much he could get away with. It was a preview of the Stalin that the British and American leaders would see again and again as the war progressed. But the Soviet leader knew when to ease up, especially when he sensed that his aggressive tactics could backfire. He also instinctively understood that after a round of bullying, he would score extra points by suddenly appearing to be more reasonable.

Which was exactly how events played out with Eden. The foreign secretary realized that he, too, had to put on a display of pique if he wanted Stalin to ease up. Driving back to his hotel after the acrimonious session, he decided he could speak freely in the car. He figured this was the one place where his conversations were unlikely to be monitored. He told his British colleagues that once they were back in his hotel suite, he would vent his frustration loudly for the benefit of the listening devices there. Pacing back and forth in his sitting room, he did exactly that, decrying Soviet behavior and saying that it would have been better if he hadn't come to Moscow. "My conclusion was that, with the best will in the world, it was impossible to work with these people even as partners against a common foe," he recalled. "The others joined in the chorus."

A few hours later, Eden received the first indication that his Soviet hosts were trying to undo that impression. Earlier he had asked to visit the front, since he was eager to get a more direct feel for the military situation, but his request had been ignored. Now, however, Maisky was on the phone with the news that he would be allowed to travel to just-liberated Klin the next day. Driving with Maisky, he saw burned-out villages, German and Russian tanks that had been destroyed in the fighting, and both German and Russian dead strewn across and alongside the road. "The corpses were already frozen still, often in the most strange and incomprehensible poses: some with arms flung apart, some on all fours, some standing up to their waist in the snow," Maisky recalled.

Eden was moved to pity by the sight of six young German prisoners, "little more than boys," as he put it, who had been captured the previous day and were shivering from both cold and fear. "They were miserably clad in thin overcoats with only a poor cardigan and no gloves," he noted. "God knows what their fate will be, but I can guess: Hitler's victims."

During the ride back to Moscow, Eden reinforced the message that he had tried to convey by speaking to the microphones in his hotel suite. He told Maisky that if, as it appeared, his trip ended in failure because of the Soviet side's insistence on pushing treaty terms that he couldn't accept, only the Germans would be pleased.

Convinced that the two sides wouldn't be able to work out an agreement, Eden went to his final meeting with Stalin on December 20, taking along the draft of a short communiqué. To his surprise, though, the Soviet leader was far more accommodating than he had been earlier. While he still called for recognition of the borders he wanted, he said he now understood that the British side had to consult with the United States first and that any treaties could wait. In the meantime, relations between their two countries would continue to improve, he added. He also offered a communiqué that, as Eden put, "was longer and more forthcoming than mine." The foreign secretary recalled that he felt a sense of relief, which was precisely what Stalin wanted him to feel.

To cap things off, Stalin invited Eden and his party to the Kremlin for dinner. The guest of honor noted that the meal was "almost embarrassingly sumptuous." He recorded that there was borscht, sturgeon, "the unhappy little white suckling pig," a variety of meats, and, of course, wine, champagne, and vodka. Marshal Timoshenko, he added, "appeared to have been imbibing before we had met." Seemingly embarrassed that Eden had noticed, Stalin asked him, "Do your generals ever get drunk?" Eden replied that they rarely got the chance to do so.

According to Maisky, Eden suffered his own awkward moment. At one point, he asked Stalin about a large bottle of a yellowish liquid that was sitting on the table. It was pepper brandy, but Stalin smiled and told him, "This is our Russian whisky." When Eden said he'd like to try it, the Soviet leader poured him a large glass. Taking a big sip, he turned red and choked, "his eyes nearly bursting from their orbits," Maisky recalled. Stalin then announced, "Only a strong people can take such a drink. Hitler is beginning to feel this."

Eden didn't mention this incident in his memoirs. He preferred to stress that his mission had ended "on a friendly note." But the lavish banquet left him with "a feeling of unreality, which was not due to the hunger, even misery, in our midst, or to the German armies, so near that their gunfire was almost within sound." What really bothered him was something deeper. "Within these gilded rooms the atmosphere was unhealthy, because where one man rules all others fear," he observed.

He also realized that while he had managed to avoid making

any of the commitments that Stalin was pushing for, his visit represented only the first act of a drama that would continue. The Soviet leader wasn't about to give up on his territorial ambitions, he pointed out in his cable to Churchill, "and we must expect continued badgering on this issue."

During that winter of 1941 to 1942 when the Germans were stopped and then pushed back from the outskirts of Moscow, Churchill largely put aside his earlier irritation with the frequently arrogant tone of Stalin's demands, as relayed by Maisky, and didn't want to allow any further Soviet badgering to sour the Anglo-Soviet relationship. It was a change that didn't escape the notice of Berlin. "Stalin's bust has been unveiled in the London Stock Exchange. That's where it belongs," Goebbels noted bitterly in his diary on January 28, 1942. "The collaboration between Bolshevism and super-capitalism is thereby publicly symbolized. England has sunk low. She is facing difficult times. She can thank Churchill."

In a later entry, Goebbels mentioned that he knew there was speculation in London that the Soviet Union might still make a separate peace with Nazi Germany. "Such fear, however, is unwarranted," he wrote on March 6. "The Soviet Union will and must be knocked out, no matter how long that may take. The situation is ripe for putting an end to Bolshevism in all Europe, and considering our position, we can't give up that aim."

In fact, Churchill is unlikely to have been seriously worried about a new separate Soviet-German peace agreement at that point. If there ever was such a possibility—and there's no hard evidence to support that notion—it was during the early days of the German invasion, when the Soviet Union appeared on the verge of collapse. But after the Germans fell short in their push to Moscow, Stalin had no incentive to contemplate such a course. Like Hitler, he was committed not just to victory but also to the destruction of the opposing system.

Like Hitler, too, he made overoptimistic predictions. Stalin sent a message to Churchill on March 14 declaring his confidence that "the combined efforts of our troops, occasional setbacks notwithstanding, will culminate in crushing the common enemy, and that the year 1942 will see a decisive turn on the anti-Hitler front." When Maisky handed Churchill the telegram, the prime minister didn't hide his skepticism. "I don't see how 1942 can become a decisive year," he said.

During his talks with Eden in December, Stalin had seemed more realistic. While he made the far-fetched claim that Soviet troops might be able to join Britain and the United States in the fight against Japan in the spring, he then added the huge caveat that it would be better if Japan attacked his country rather than vice versa. "War would be unpopular with our people if the Soviet government were to take the first step," he said.

This was a highly disingenuous statement, implying that Stalin was a democratic leader who acted only when he could count on public opinion to back him. It also overlooked the fact that the Japanese were unlikely to oblige since, as Eden pointed out, they'd prefer "a policy of dealing with their opponents one by one." The foreign secretary understood the import of Stalin's message: just as the Western powers wouldn't accede to the Soviet leader's demands for launching a second front anytime soon, Moscow wouldn't be ready to help with Japan for the foreseeable future.

Churchill and Roosevelt were in full agreement on a different issue: the urgent need to step up the flow of Lend-Lease supplies to the Soviet Union, which would strengthen its forces during the coming battles. Although Roosevelt kept pushing for faster production and delivery schedules, the early results were disappointing, since this was a hugely ambitious project. Eventually, it would provide the Soviet Union with 409,500 vehicles, mostly Studebaker trucks, which would keep its army mobile, and 1,900 locomotives, along with 43 percent of all Soviet tires, 56 percent of the rails for the railway network and about one-third of its explosives. In addition, the United States supplied huge amounts of food, copper, aluminum and high-octane airplane fuel. As insistent as Stalin was in demanding these supplies, he consistently refused to acknowledge the scale of that foreign assistance effort to his own people. He wanted them to believe that any military successes were purely the result of his inspired leadership and the Red Army's prowess.

Roosevelt and Churchill were willing to overlook these slights, since they were united in the view that such aid was vital. But they took a different tack when it came to the territorial claims Stalin had put forward during Eden's visit to Moscow. Despite his predisposition to trust the Soviet leader, Roosevelt initially appeared more resolute in resisting those demands. In reality, however, the rift revealed the weaknesses of both leaders when it came to handling someone as wily as Stalin.

Upon his return to London, Eden had urged Churchill, with the support of several other top officials, to consider a compromise that would entail acceding to Soviet demands on the Baltic states while refusing to give ground on Poland. In March, the prime minister had come around to that position. "The increasing gravity of the war has led me to feel that the principles of the Atlantic Charter ought not to be constructed so as to deny Russia the frontiers she occupied when Germany attacked her," he told Roosevelt, requesting his support for his government's plans to accept those demands. That would mean accepting the creeping Soviet annexation of the Baltic states, which was the result of the Nazi-Soviet pact of August 23, 1939.

Roosevelt refused to back this willful mangling of the charter's principles. Under Secretary of State Welles pointed out that the British willingness to cave in on the Baltic states was "not only indefensible from every moral standpoint, but likewise extraordinarily stupid" since it would only lead to more demands, including the annexation of Polish territory. Eden caustically noted, "Soviet policy is amoral; United States policy is exaggeratedly moral, at least where non-American interests are concerned."

But this was far from the complete story. If Churchill's approach exhibited the cynical calculation that would ultimately doom any efforts to contain Stalin's ambitions at the end of the war, Roosevelt would prove to be both naïve and inconsistent. He genuinely wished to avoid secret protocols and other written commitments on territorial issues that he wanted resolved later, which, not insignificantly, helped him maintain good relations with Polish officials and his good standing with Polish-American voters. At the same time, though, he sent very different signals in private and maintained his faith in Stalin's good intentions.

All of which helped generate the Anglo-American tensions in dealing with Russia that would carry right to the Yalta conference in 1945, when most of the postwar arrangements were finalized. Those tensions were first clearly visible during the final phase of the battle for Moscow, a time when some officials still doubted a Soviet victory. It was then that Roosevelt signaled his intentions to negotiate directly with Stalin, bypassing the British. With British-American talks about Russia "tangled," as Eden put it, Welles informed Lord Halifax, the British ambassador in Washington, that the president would take precisely that course.

British officials were aghast. "Here was the first of several occasions when the President, mistakenly as I believe, moved out of step with us, influenced by his conviction that he could get better results with Stalin direct than could the three countries negotiating together," Eden wrote. "This was an illusion."

On March 18, Roosevelt delivered a blunt message to Churchill. "I know you will not mind my being brutally frank when I tell you that I think I can personally handle Stalin better than either your Foreign Office or my State Department," he declared. "Stalin hates the guts of all your top people. He thinks he likes me better, and I hope he will continue to do so."

Roosevelt had never met Stalin at that point, which made his confidence in his ability to "handle" the Soviet leader all the more astonishing. But along with his conviction that their presumed personal rapport would trigger Stalin's goodwill, Roosevelt displayed his own level of cynicism that alarmed even the putatively more jaundiced British allies.

In his conversations with Maxim Litvinov, who was then the Soviet ambassador in Washington, Roosevelt hinted broadly that while he couldn't yet accept Soviet claims on the Baltic states and Romanian territory, he would do so later. As Litvinov reported to Moscow, the president described himself and Stalin as "realists." Then, with a smile, he indicated "he will deal with these issues at the end of the war."

Presidential aide Harry Hopkins, who had been a systematic advocate of sending such signals to please Stalin, was at Roosevelt's side when he met with Lord Halifax on March 9. The president told the British ambassador that he was planning to tell Stalin that he recognized his country's need for firm security arrangements after the war but that it would be dangerous to put anything in writing yet. He would then add that Stalin had no reason to worry about the future of the Baltic states, since once the Red Army had retaken them, the United States and Britain wouldn't do anything to dislodge it.

When Halifax reported back to him the gist of this plan, Eden was appalled. "I did not like the method of this statement, because I was sure that it would fail to satisfy Stalin and because it seemed to me to give us the worst of all worlds," the foreign secretary recalled. "We would be ungraciously conniving at the inevitable, without getting any return for it."

The immediate beneficiary of these Anglo-American tensions was Stalin, who, according to Eden, "as a negotiator was the toughest proposition of all." There were very few voices in either the British or the American camp calling for a genuinely tough negotiating posture. Someone like Ivan Yeaton, the American military attaché in Moscow who viewed unconditional aid for the Soviet Union as a huge mistake, was on the losing side of the debate, which flickered only briefly. After his clash with Hopkins during the presidential aide's visit in July 1941, he found his warnings about the nature of Stalin's regime largely ignored, and all the more so after he was sent back to the War Department in Washington later in the year. While Churchill initially seemed more eager to please Stalin, Roosevelt's team emphatically stressed that its Lend-Lease aid had no strings attached.

The conventional wisdom holds that the fate of Eastern Europe was determined at the Yalta conference in 1945, consigning it to Soviet control and redrawing the borders according to Stalin's wishes. But that was merely the final step in a long process. The Soviet leader first revealed his plans in considerable detail during the battle for Moscow. As Molotov put it later, "My task as minister of foreign affairs was to expand the borders of our Fatherland. And it seems that Stalin and I coped with this task quite well."

However much they differed on tactics, Churchill and Roosevelt responded in a way that only encouraged the Soviet leader's conviction that he would ultimately prevail. On December 1, 1941, just before Stalin met with Sikorski and then Eden, the Soviet side organized a secret meeting of Polish communists in Saratov. This was the first step in the creation of a puppet government, which would ensure Soviet control of a postwar Poland. Stalin still faced a huge threat from the German invaders, but most Western resistance to his political ambitions had effectively already crumbled, and the little bit that was left would continue to erode as the fighting progressed. The Soviet ruler wasn't just revealing his plans for the postwar world during the battle for Moscow; he was also acting on them.

For the Western correspondents in the Soviet Union, the job of trying to report on the battle for Moscow, or any other aspect of the war, was more often than not an exercise in frustration. Quentin Reynolds, the *Collier's Weekly* correspondent who had reached Moscow by assuming the role of press spokesman for the Beaverbrook-Harriman mission back in September, had stayed on as he had planned to but then quickly began to wonder if the assignment had been worth the effort. Referring to the twice-weekly press conferences of Deputy Minister of Foreign Affairs Solomon Lozovsky, Reynolds noted, "Always graciously inviting us to ask him any questions we wished, he succeeded in answering none. Actually, most of our news about what was going on came from American and British embassies or from the German radio."

When, along with the diplomats, the journalists were evacuated to Kuibyshev in mid-October, their already sour mood took a decided turn for the worse. Larry Lesueur, a CBS radio correspondent who reached Russia too late to get to Moscow and made his way to the alternate capital instead, found the other correspondents there "extremely despondent" about their plight. He had been so eager to report from Russia that he had arrived on a British convoy carrying tanks, boots, and other war aid to the northern port city of Archangel and then endured a seventeen-day, winding, stop-and-go two-thousand-mile train journey to Kuibyshev. Exultant at first that he had finally made it, he was soon infected by his colleagues' bleak mood. "One of the world's decisive battles was thundering six hundred miles away and the only news we could get was what came over the Russian radio," he wrote.

Spending most of their time in Kuibyshev's Grand Hotel, which was off-limits to most Russians, the foreigners had plenty of reasons to feel isolated. Delivery of newspapers from Moscow was erratic, Lesueur reported, and even when they arrived, they were at least three days old. The battle for the Soviet capital also disrupted cable communications, which meant that he would often miss instructions on broadcast times. In those cases, he would go through the entire exercise of tramping across town in the evening to drop off his report at the censorship office, returning to his hotel for a bit of rest and then walking the icy streets to the Kuibyshev radio station to make his broadcast in the middle of the night—only to learn later that his voice hadn't necessarily reached his listeners.

Even when the correspondents managed to get out of Kuibyshev to see something for themselves, they had trouble reporting anything beyond official information. Trying to find an acceptable excuse to travel, Reynolds and Arch Steele of the *Chicago Daily News* asked to visit a munitions factory. To their surprise, their request was approved. Accompanied by an army lieutenant who served as their guide, they drove by a cluster of bleak wooden buildings surrounded by a barbed-wire fence, which left no doubt it was a concentration camp for Soviet citizens who were trapped inside Stalin's network of terror. "A few soldiers with rifles were guarding the camp quite carelessly," Reynolds recalled. "It was obvious that there was no place for any of the prisoners to run and hide." About a mile past the camp, they came across a large group of women prisoners working on the road with picks and shovels. "Dressed in their shapeless gray clothing, they stood just off the road and watched us pass, their faces expressionless," Reynolds wrote.

Knowing that the censors would never permit the two Americans to report this unexpected glimpse of Soviet reality, their guide freely admitted that these women were political prisoners. When Reynolds wrote a glowing report about high morale in the munitions plant and tried to slip in a mention of the prisoners working on the road, the censors gutted it. They cut not just that passage but even most of the laudatory description of the factory visit. Reynolds was so furious that he cabled his editor requesting a transfer for himself and another colleague, Alice-Leon Moats. Since "service cables" weren't censored, he didn't hold anything back. "Moats and I would like to remain to write about the heroic Russian people and the great Red Army but stupid censorship prevents us from doing this," he wrote. "Moats wants to go to India. I want to go to London. What do you think?"

His editor replied twelve hours later, telling them, "You two go wherever you can find stories." Moats did head off to India, while Reynolds ended up going to Cairo to cover the war in North Africa. In any case, both reporters were happy to leave Russia.

When the American correspondents left behind heard the news on the night of December 7 to 8 that the Japanese had attacked Pearl Harbor, they threw their fur coats over their pajamas and gathered in the room of Henry Cassidy, the Associated Press bureau chief. Cassidy decided to pull out a bottle of scotch that he had been saving for Christmas, and the reporters plotted their next moves. "Everyone talked at once and all of us made plans to leave Russia immediately for the Far East," CBS's Lesueur recounted. "Although we knew Russia would keep on fighting even if Moscow were taken, nevertheless her armies would be split up if the Germans captured the Soviet capital." Besides, for the Americans this meant that their war would be taking place elsewhere. As Cassidy put it, "The big story seemed to have gone from Russia to the Pacific."

But cut off as they were, the correspondents didn't know anything yet about the Soviet counteroffensive that Stalin had just launched to push the Germans back from Moscow. When they saw the official communiqué on December 12 proclaiming the success of that effort and victory in the battle for Moscow, they were stunned. "That night I wondered if the Japanese would have dared strike at Pearl Harbor if they had known that their Axis partners on the other side of the world were really doomed to failure only twenty-five miles from Moscow," Lesueur wrote.

The next day Soviet press officials began extending invitations to the correspondents to return to Moscow. The invitees couldn't have been more delighted and promptly put aside, at least for a while, their earlier plans to bail out of Russia. "The Red Army had not only saved Moscow from the Germans," Cassidy exulted. "It had also saved the correspondents from Kuibyshev."

It would prove to be a temporary respite, since the correspondents would be ordered back to Kuibyshev in late December, but an exciting one because they could finally get out and do something. And they would be offered more trips to the front in January, when the Soviet counteroffensive pushed the Germans back further. As always, even when they were allowed to get closer to the action, they only caught a glimpse of what was happening and could easily be misled by patently false Soviet propaganda. Cassidy reported that the battle for Moscow "was won by as smart and successful a trick play as has ever been sprung on an unsuspecting opponent." A Soviet officer had told him how this "trick" worked. "We could have stopped them [the Germans] earlier, but we waited until it would cost us less—and cost them more," he said. In other words, the Soviet side had cleverly lured the Germans closer and closer and then sprung its trap. This was the Kremlin's version of spin, and highly effective, since correspondents like Cassidy were so eager to have something fresh to report.

Nonetheless, the journalists could see enough to begin to get a more accurate picture. Driving on the Klin-Volokolamsk road north of Moscow in late December, Cassidy recognized that the Germans still had a lot of punch left and Soviet claims of victory were somewhat premature. "Out there, I could see, it was not a broken German army that was being pursued to the west. It was a still powerful machine which had stalled and was backing up for a fresh start," he reported. "I could see, too, it was not a feeble Red Army that was tottering after a beaten foe. It was a still-growing force which was just beginning to feel its own offensive power and was actively precipitating the retreat of its enemy."

In Moscow itself, Lesueur and other correspondents were struck by how few buildings had been hit by German bombs and how quickly bomb craters had been filled in. "Compared with London, the Soviet capital was untouched," he wrote. But as soon as they traveled outside the capital, they could see how close the war had come. Driving about twenty-five miles out of the city on the Leningrad Highway, the CBS correspondent saw burned-out villages, knocked-out German and Soviet tanks strewn across a field that resembled a junkyard, and a forest "devastated as by a hurricane" by fierce artillery fire and tank battles. "The blackened wreckage of the villages was appalling," he recounted. He saw a couple of peasant women sifting through the remains of their homes that were "only charred, smoking embers."

And everywhere the reporters saw the dead of both armies. While the Germans had managed to bury some of their fallen comrades, even erecting crosses for them with their names and ages burnt into the wood, many of the dead were like the ones Cassidy came across on one outing. "Here, the bodies, in small groups of twelve to fifty, frozen in strange positions, many with bent arms still uplifted as though to ward off the inevitable, seemed more like wax statues than men," he wrote. "The snow and ice clothed their deaths in merciful cleanliness."

In many cases, the frigid temperatures preserved the evidence of the kind of deaths the soldiers had met. Lesueur drove along a road littered with stiff bodies of Red Army soldiers. They were barefoot and shot through the head. "Prisoners," the Soviet officer escorting him explained. "The Germans shot them when they couldn't keep up with the retreat."

Lesueur also took note of the other kind of casualties. "The war was hard on horses," he wrote. "All along the roadside their frozen bodies lay in snow-covered blasted chunks."

One of the Westerners who was particularly moved by the plight of the Russians was Eve Curie, the daughter of the Nobel Prize–winning scientist Marie Curie. She had come to Russia both as a reporter and as an avid supporter of the Free France movement. Because of the fame of her mother, she sometimes was given more leeway than other correspondents. As she traveled outside Moscow, she told herself, "Russia happens to be the only place in Europe where, today, one can see towns, villages, and people liberated from the Germans." Meeting the inhabitants of those villages and towns and hearing their stories, she felt a personal connection to them, as she put it, "perhaps because I was French and because my mother came from Poland."

Curie was fascinated by what the local inhabitants had to say about the German occupation. One woman told her that the German officers in her village near Istra, just west of the Soviet capital, talked about "taking Moscow and then going back home to Germany." And they'd keep repeating, "Moscow is finished, *kaput;* the Soviet Union is *kaput.*" When they received the order to withdraw, an embarrassed German officer declared, "This is not a retreat. Our tanks and trucks simply need repair. We must go away, but we will soon be back." But as they left, the German troops threw incendiary grenades into houses, leaving the village in flames.

Almost everywhere she stopped, Curie came across stories of German terror. The occupiers drove villagers out of their houses into the forests, shot people at random, including a young mother with five children who refused to give up some firewood she was carrying, and slaughtered cows and stole any other food available. They left bodies of their victims hanging in towns and villages, and there were endless tales of atrocities—Soviet prisoners burned alive and children machine-gunned who had laughed at the occupiers, for instance. "These crimes seemed so dreadful and so pointless that, at times, I hesitated to believe them," she wrote. Nonetheless, she found the accounts of different people in each town or village remarkably consistent.

But Curie—and, independently, CBS's Lesueur—would stumble across a story that would prove even more revealing than the soon to be all too familiar accounts of German atrocities. It was a story the import of which they had no way of recognizing at the time, a story that the Soviet authorities would soon try to excise from all accounts of the battle for Moscow. Which was precisely why their reporting would prove so valuable.

In its triumphant article on December 13, 1941, proclaiming the collapse of the German drive to seize Moscow, *Pravda* prominently mentioned several generals who had distinguished themselves in the fighting around the capital. One of them was Andrei Vlasov, whose troops had taken Solnechnogorsk, northwest of the city. But soon Vlasov's name would disappear from reprints of that article and from all other Soviet accounts of the battle for Moscow. In the official histories, he simply vanished.

The thirteenth child of a peasant family, Vlasov was born in 1900. In 1919 he was called up to fight in the civil war. After joining the Communist Party in 1930, he rose rapidly in the ranks, and in the late 1930s served as a military adviser in China. In 1940, he was awarded the Order of Lenin. When the Germans invaded the following summer, he fought on the Ukrainian front and won plaudits for breaking out of the Kiev encirclement with his troops at the last moment. In November, Stalin put him in command of the Twentieth Army, with the assignment of keeping the Germans from breaking through to Moscow from the north. At a personal meeting with Vlasov in the Kremlin on November 10, the Soviet leader reportedly dismissed his appeal for reserve troops to help him with his mission and only provided him with fifteen tanks. Despite that typical harsh treatment, Stalin considered him one of his best commanders.

On December 16, three days after the *Pravda* article that hailed the exploits of Vlasov, Lesueur, accompanied by a censor and two Red Army officers, drove north of Moscow for a promised interview with the now famous general. As they drew closer to the expected rendezvous point, they encountered signs warning of mines. One of the officers told Lesueur that as they retreated, the Germans were planting thousands of mines, which required minimal concealment since the snow quickly took care of that problem. They pulled up to a small house where they had been told to find Vlasov, which until a few days earlier had been used by his German counterpart and still bore the sign "German Divisional Headquarters." But Vlasov was no longer there, since he had already moved further with his troops.

Finally reaching Vlasov's new temporary headquarters, Lesueur witnessed the arrival of the general and another top officer. "With a smile they approached us, and automatically we walked toward them, followed by a group of obviously admiring Red Army men," he recounted. "The soldiers had no fear of the commanding officers, but seemed drawn to them as an admiring college boy is drawn to a respected professor."

After an exchange of greetings with his troops, Vlasov shook hands with his visitors. Lesueur sounded awed by his appearance, noting that he "looked more like a teacher than a soldier, so tall that his high gray astrakhan hat with the crimson and gold crown made him tower. He wore gold-rimmed spectacles at the tip of his nose." Vlasov told his visitors that his troops were preparing to liberate Volokolamsk that same night and that he had already sent his ski battalion to surround the town. As the general talked about his next moves, "his eyes had a look of bright elation," Lesueur reported.

When Lesueur asked Vlasov where he expected the Germans to dig in and hold their positions that winter, the reply indicated just what it was that Stalin liked about this general. "I am not planning my offensive on the basis that the Germans will hold somewhere," he said. "I intend to drive them as far as I can."

"Do you think they'll try to hold at Smolensk?" Lesueur continued, referring to the city 230 miles to the west of Moscow.

The general looked away. "Smolensk—that's a different story," he said.

Lesueur concluded that Vlasov's message was that he shouldn't get carried away with his expectations about what the Soviet troops could accomplish during their counteroffensive that winter. This was only the beginning of the effort to drive the Germans back.

A month later, when Vlasov's troops were in control of Volokolamsk and had succeeded in beating back several German counterattacks in the region, Curie paid a similar call on the general, since she, too, was anxious to meet "one of the young leaders whose fame was rapidly growing." And she, too, was impressed by the commander who came to greet her. "Vlasov was a strong, tall man of forty, with sharp features and a face tanned by the snow and sun," she wrote. "He wore a plain, olive-green uniform: high leather boots, breeches, and a coat in Russian style, shaped like a peasant's tunic. He had no insignia of any kind, no badges, no stars, no medals."

Over tea and *zakuski*, Russian hors d'oeuvres, an animated Vlasov described his recent battles, how his troops had launched their latest on January 10 and advanced eighteen miles within about a week, beating back three German divisions in the process. With a triumphant laugh, he spilled out the contents of a waterproof bag, which included emblems of German tank and cavalry regiments and several Iron Crosses, dated 1939, probably awarded to soldiers for the Polish campaign. "There was something very stimulating in talking with this energetic man, completely obsessed by his hard job . . . [who] judged everything from a purely military point of view," Curie observed.

Vlasov was also eager to talk about military leadership. He mentioned Peter the Great and expressed his admiration for Napoleon. "What utter nonsense to compare constantly Hitler to

Napoleon," he said. "Napoleon was a real military genius, a great captain of war!" He questioned Curie about Charles de Gaulle and was clearly intrigued by Guderian, the legendary tank commander who had recently been relieved of his duties by Hitler.

Above all, he was focused on hitting the Germans as hard as possible. "It is not so much the number of miles retaken which counts, but the number of casualties inflicted on the enemy," he told Curie. "Our aim is to weaken Hitler. This is why Stalin's orders are not simply to push the Germans back, whenever we can, but to encircle their units and annihilate them. The enemy is now a wounded beast—although still very strong."

Curie concluded that this was a man obsessed by his mission, someone who was totally committed to his cause. Along with his declarations about the need to destroy the enemy, he repeatedly invoked Stalin's commands by prefacing his statements with "Stalin's order is" or "Stalin's plan is." As for himself, he declared, "My blood belongs to my Fatherland."

Six months later, the unthinkable happened. On July 12, 1942, while commanding the Second Shock Army on the Volkhov front south of Leningrad, Vlasov was captured by the Germans. But that was hardly the unthinkable part. After all, many top officers had perished or been captured when their armies were encircled. What was truly startling was that the famed general then proposed to his German captors that he should be allowed to set up a "Russian Liberation Movement" whose mission would be to topple Stalin's regime. In other words, Vlasov decided to switch sides.

Stalin was stunned. When Beria showed him copies of Vlasov's statements announcing his intentions, he asked the secret police chief if they could be German forgeries. Beria told him that there was no doubt that Vlasov was now working for the Germans. "How is it we missed him before the war?" Molotov asked.

Looking for a scapegoat, Stalin summoned Khrushchev to the Kremlin and pointed out "in an ominous tone" that he was responsible for giving Vlasov the command of the Thirty-seventh Army during the battle for Kiev. Khrushchev refused to play the fall guy, reminding Stalin that it was his decision to put Vlasov in charge of the Moscow counteroffensive. That was enough to make the Soviet leader drop the subject. But that fencing failed to address the key issue. "It was difficult to understand how a man who had displayed such devotion, bravery, and skill and who had earned such respect, could betray his country," Khrushchev wrote.

In December 1942, Vlasov issued the "Smolensk Declaration," spelling out his goals and in part explaining his change of allegiance. "Bolshevism is the enemy of the Russian people," the statement proclaimed. "It has brought countless disasters to our country and finally has involved the Russian people in a bloody war waged in others' interests." The "others" were identified as the British and American capitalists, while Germany was portrayed as fighting against Bolshevism, not against the Russian people. According to the statement, Vlasov's group would concentrate its efforts on deposing Stalin and his regime and then conclude "an honorable peace with Germany." It also promised an end to terror, the freeing of all political prisoners, and the dismantling of collective farms.

Despite his rapid rise in the Soviet military, Vlasov probably had harbored doubts all along about the political system he served. According to some accounts, during the civil war one of his brothers fell victim to the Reds, who executed him as a traitor, and his parents were branded "rich peasants" when he gave them a cow. Whatever role such incidents may have played, Vlasov later emphasized that he was still proud of what he did during the battle for Moscow. "I did everything I could to defend the country's capital," he wrote in an open letter. But he was angry at the "indecisive and chaotic leadership corrupted by commissar control" that was responsible for the "heavy defeats" suffered by the Red Army. And looking back at how Stalin had ruled the country even before the war, he expressed sorrow and anger at the loss of millions of lives during forced collectivization and the wave of political arrests and executions.

Like many of the Soviet POWs who later joined his movement, Vlasov may have also calculated that he had better odds for survival if he took up arms again. It was no secret that Soviet POWs were dying in German captivity in huge numbers and that Stalin viewed those who managed to escape as traitors. Ironically, though, Hitler was also extremely suspicious of Vlasov and other Soviet officers who wanted to fight. He wanted a clearly subjugated Russia, not a liberated Russia.

It wouldn't be until very late in the war, when Germany was facing defeat, that Hitler officially sanctioned Vlasov's movement. Vlasov finally got the chance to send his divisions into action in March and April 1945, when German troops were fighting a rearguard action in Prague. But when the SS began a shooting spree there, Vlasov's troops switched sides once again, turning their guns against the Germans to defend the Czechs.

That did nothing to help Vlasov and his doomed followers. Captured by the Red Army, some were immediately shot. Vlasov and other top officers were brought back to the Soviet Union, tortured, and hanged. And, of course, Vlasov's name was expunged from all official accounts of the battle for Moscow. It wouldn't do to admit that one of its heroes had decided that he would rather die fighting Stalin than defending him. From the very beginning, the history of that battle was riddled with deliberate omissions, blatant distortions, and outright lies. Only the eyewitness testimony of Western correspondents such as Curie and Lesueur kept alive the memory of Vlasov's role in the battle for Moscow.

12

The Deadliest Victory

On January 11, 1942, Stalin sent a typically brusque order to the commander of the Kalinin front about Rzhev, the town of 54,000 people that the Germans had occupied since October 14, 1941. Located 130 miles northwest of Moscow, Rzhev was seen by both sides as a crucial jumping-off point for German troops still hoping to seize the capital. "In the course of the 11th, and in no case later than the 12th of January, the town of Rzhev must be captured," Stalin commanded. "Staff recommends for this purpose that all available artillery, mortars and aircraft be used to smash the entire city and that you should not be deterred from destroying it."

Russian historians maintain that the battle for Moscow ended on April 20, 1942, when the Soviet counteroffensive stalled and both exhausted armies were trapped in another muddy season, making it impossible to launch major new assaults. But the battle for Rzhev, which was in reality an extension of the battle for Moscow, would continue for almost another year. Despite Stalin's repeated orders to his commanders to drive the Germans out, the result was one unsuccessful drive after another, with Soviet troops suffering losses that were staggering even by the inflated standards of the time. Surviving veterans talk in hushed tones about the

"Rzhev meatgrinder," a killing machine that wouldn't stop grinding up its hundreds of thousands of victims until the Germans decided to withdraw without a final fight and Soviet troops entered the town on March 3, 1943.

To this day, the inhabitants of Rzhev resent the fact that in most accounts of the period those who were caught up in those epic battles haven't received the recognition they deserve. At the town's modest museum dedicated to the fighting there, researcher Olga Dudkina pointed out that Soviet forces mounted four major operations to liberate Rzhev, all of which failed, in some cases right at the outskirts of the town. Those included some of the largest tank battles of the entire war, along with other clashes of infantry and artillery units. The Germans also suffered tremendous losses, but the fact that they held on to Rzhev for so long infuriated Stalin. "For many years Rzhev was forgotten, probably because they didn't want a reminder of the failures there," Dudkina explained. "In the history of the Great Patriotic War, this was the biggest military failure."

The Soviet troops that were supposed to encircle and destroy the enemy were frequently encircled and destroyed themselves. This was what had happened with General Yefremov's Thirty-third Army and General Belov's First Cavalry Corps near Vyazma in April and would happen again and again with units fighting closer to Rzhev. According to a Wehrmacht report dated July 13, 1942, for example, the Germans surrounded and annihilated a Soviet tank brigade and several rifle and cavalry divisions. The ensuing fighting resulted in the capture of more than thirty thousand Soviet troops who survived the onslaught. The victors also reported that they had destroyed 218 tanks, 591 artillery pieces and 1,300 machine guns, along with an assortment of other weaponry.

With the Germans preparing their offensive in the south that would lead to the beginning of the battle for Stalingrad later that summer of 1942, the Soviet forces found themselves spread out and highly vulnerable. Stalin's insistence on launching the general counteroffensive back in January to keep pushing the Germans farther from Moscow had already started that process. When Soviet commanders had to begin bolstering their forces to meet the German challenge in the south, this meant dispatching some of the troops there who were supposed to participate in the fighting near Vyazma and Rzhev.

Both armies were stretched thin, desperate for supplies of all kinds, and conditions in and around Rzhev became steadily more gruesome as the fighting dragged on. When soldiers from either side heard planes approaching, they'd send out "hunters" to search for any food drops, racing to get to them before the enemy did. Soviet officers from Zhukov on down complained that many of the units had to ration their shells and other ammunition carefully. Otherwise they'd find themselves completely defenseless.

When a squadron of Soviet planes tried to make a drop of desperately needed food to General Ivan Maslennikov's troops, who were surrounded by the Germans, the soldiers watched with dismay as the parachutes fluttered down into German-held territory. "We're starving here and you feed the Germans!" Maslennikov radioed General Pavel Zhigarev, who was in charge of these operations. Informed of that message, Stalin promptly summoned Zhigarev to his office. According to General Aleksandr Vasilevsky, who was present, Stalin was "so furious that I thought he would kill Zhigarev with his own hands in his office." Luckily for Zhigarev, the ruler's anger didn't last long, since he was preoccupied with plenty of other problems, and the air force general emerged unscathed.

In contrast to the chronic shortages of food and ammunition, there was a constant overflow of the wounded that overwhelmed the medical teams working in field hospitals. Faina Sobolevskaya, a nurse assigned to a medical unit for Soviet troops trying to seize Rzhev in the summer of 1942, recalled that her team of two surgeons and seven nurses worked frantically in the tents they set up in the woods; their two operating tables were constantly occupied. "We didn't know how to care for so many wounded," she said. "We were always full."

During the heavy rains in August, there wasn't enough room inside the tents for all the wounded. Since there was no way to wash and change clothes, almost everyone was swarming with lice. (The same was true for the Germans on the other side of the front lines.) Accompanied by the nerve-rattling sound of nearby artillery barrages, the doctors and nurses kept at their jobs around the clock, catching the occasional short nap whenever they could. "We

were young and somehow we managed," Sobolevskaya said. When
one of her fellow nurses was killed, she recalled, her already heavy
workload increased further, and the chances for rest became even
less frequent. What kept her going was the visible gratitude of the
soldiers they saved or mended. "The soldiers loved us," she said
simply.

The scale of the fighting meant that there often wasn't time to
bury the dead on the battlefields or provide aid to the dying. There
were also cases of the dead and the severely wounded not being
sorted out properly. In the winter of 1942, Lieutenant Mirzakhan
Galeyev of the 174th Rifle Division sustained a severe head wound
near Rzhev. When the battle ended, the bodies of the fallen were
placed in a common grave, and Galeyev was put in with them. As
the gravediggers began refilling the hole in the ground, they noticed his body's convulsions. Galeyev was unconscious but very
much alive. Hauled out of the grave and treated in a nearby hospital, he pulled through. He would live to the age of eighty-six, but
the headstone on the common grave where he nearly perished still
bears his name, along with those of his friends who really did die
there.

Inside Rzhev, those inhabitants who hadn't managed to flee
before the Germans arrived faced their own daily terror. The occupiers distributed leaflets warning that anyone who hid or fed Red
Army soldiers would be hanged, and they set up a gallows in the
middle of town to prove they were serious. Since they had arrived
in mid-October, when the weather was already unusually cold, they
seized whatever clothing they could from the locals. Nikolai Yakovlev, who, at sixteen, had been too young to join the Red Army, recalled seeing German soldiers seizing *valenki*, Russian felt boots,
right off people's feet. "They would take your *valenki* and give you
their summer boots—or let you run home barefoot," he said.

The Germans seized whatever food they spotted as well. And
both the soldiers and Rzhev's inhabitants made swift work of any
dead horses they found, chopping them up and eating them, re-
gardless of the risks. Hunger pangs routinely trumped any fear of
catching a disease from rotting horsemeat.

Marching the locals across the bridge that spanned the Volga
from one part of town to another, the Germans shot those who

lagged behind and, according to Yakovlev, lobbed hand grenades into any place where they thought people were hiding. "There were a lot of corpses all over the place," he recounted. They also began selecting the healthy younger inhabitants to serve as forced laborers, herding them onto trains for the trip west, tearing screaming mothers from their children whenever they decided they only wanted one member of the family.

In the autumn of 1942, Zhukov orchestrated Operation Mars, the most ambitious offensive yet to dislodge the German forces in the Rzhev region and finally rid Moscow of the threat they represented. *Stavka,* the Soviet military headquarters, sent out the order for the operation on October 10. "The forces of the right wing of the Western Front and the left wing of the Kalinin front are to encircle the enemy Rzhev Grouping, seize Rzhev, and free the railroad line from Moscow to Velikiye Luki," it declared. In the three weeks of the actual operation that was launched in late November, Zhukov's troops paid a tremendous price as they were ordered to attack entrenched German positions again and again. The Soviet tally was about 100,000 dead or missing and another 235,000 wounded. And, once again, they failed in their mission.

Zhukov and his defenders would later claim that these sacrifices kept German troops tied down that otherwise might have been sent south to rescue Field Marshal Friedrich Paulus's beleaguered Sixth Army at Stalingrad. Carrying out the plan dubbed Operation Uranus, the Red Army succeeded in encircling Paulus's troops in November, setting the stage for the Germans' devastating defeat there. While Zhukov was one of the architects of that victory, military historian David M. Glantz points out that the attempts to portray the failures at Rzhev as a clever diversion are "at best disingenuous and at worst blatant lies." In his book *Zhukov's Greatest Defeat,* he argues that the northern offensive, Operation Mars, represented a huge failure of Stalin's top military commander. It was supposed to deal as big a blow to the Germans as the highly successful Operation Uranus in the south. Instead, while the Germans had to surrender at Stalingrad in January 1943, they continued to occupy Rzhev until March of that year.

Inside occupied Rzhev, the German terror continued right up until the first Soviet troops finally entered the town on March 3,

1943, although the Germans had fled two days earlier. By that time, most of the town's buildings had been leveled—first by German bombers and artillery when the Germans were attacking, then by successive Soviet bombardments when the Soviet forces sought to take it back, and finally by the retreating Germans, who torched whatever they could on their way out. Only 297 of 5,434 buildings were still standing by early March, and only a few hundred inhabitants were left in the city. The others had fled, died, or been deported. Most of the remaining residents had lived in dugouts and other improvised shelters to survive the shellings and minimize contact with the Germans.

When a Soviet intelligence platoon entered the town, they couldn't find any of the local inhabitants at first. Then they discovered 362 of them locked up in a church. The Germans had planted explosives to blow up the church, but the retreating troops had failed to detonate them. Those trapped inside could only assume the worst. With temperatures dipping to minus 4 degrees Fahrenheit, they burned bibles and other church literature to stay warm. They also had no food. But all these terrified people survived.

The teenager Nikolai Yakovlev considered himself relatively lucky. A few months after the Germans took control of Rzhev, they rounded him up with his mother and first put them into the town's makeshift concentration camp for a couple of days. During that time, his mother made soup from a dead cat they found, which nourished them till they were sent to another camp in Vyazma, where they weren't fed at all. Those prisoners who tried to make a run for it were shot. A few days later, the others were loaded on trains again and traveled to Brest, where they were disinfected from lice. The next stop was Königsberg in East Prussia, and from there Yakovlev and his mother were dispatched to a farm, where they worked until the Red Army approached the area near the end of the war.

Yakovlev would soon feel doubly lucky. The Germans herded all the forced laborers into a concentration camp as the fighting drew near, and they were later abandoned. Unlike in other camps, there was no final death march. The Soviet forces arrived and SMERSH, the dreaded military counterintelligence unit whose mission it was to ferret out traitors, began vetting everyone who had fallen into

The Eastern Front
December 5, 1941 to the end of April, 1942

Lake Ladoga

FINLAND

Leningrad Front

Baltic Sea

Leningrad

Volkhov Front

ESTONIA

Army Group North

Novgorod

Staraya Russa

Northwestern Front

Volga

Pskov

Kalinin Front

Kalinin

SOVIET UNION

LATVIA

Western

Velikiye Luki

Rzhev

Klin

Moscow

LITHUANIA

Dvina

Mozhaisk

Vyazma

Western Front

Wilno

Smolensk

Tula

E. PRUSSIA

Army Group Center

Minsk

Roslavl

Southwestern Front

BELORUSSIA

Bryansk

Orel

Warsaw

Brest

Gomel

Kursk

Dnieper

POLAND

Kiev

Kharkov

Don

Southern Front

UKRAINE

Dniester

Dnepropetrovsk

Army Group South

Zaporozhye

HUNGARY

ROMANIA

Odessa

Sea of Azov

Caucasus Front

CRIMEA

Novorossiysk

———— Limit of German advance Dec 5, 1941

Areas reoccupied by Soviet forces from Dec 6, 1941, to end of Apr 1942

Sevastopol

Black Sea

0   100 miles
0   150 kilometers

BULGARIA

their hands. "I wasn't a POW—I was clean," he said, still breathing a sigh of relief that he wasn't in the position of Soviet POWs, who were automatically considered traitors by Stalin's regime. Since he had been too young to serve, he was considered less of a security threat. "The ex-POWs were sorted out and led away," he added.

The leader who was responsible for such policies of internal terror rarely ventured out of Moscow during the war. He had no urge to get closer to the fighting or to make morale-boosting excursions to other cities or towns. On the night of August 4 to 5, 1943, however, Stalin stayed in a small wooden house in Rzhev. No one quite knows why he chose to do so, but local inhabitants like to think that maybe it was his way of honoring the memory of those who perished there—which, to say the least, would have been a highly unusual gesture for a man who never flinched at sending millions to their deaths.

Preserved as a modest library, the house contains a plaque informing visitors that Stalin stopped there and ordered an honor guard to fire a volley of shots in honor of the troops who had liberated more towns from the Germans. After Khrushchev launched his de-Stalinization campaign in 1956, the plaque was removed. Put back in the 1980s, it remains there today, serving as a small reminder of the deeply ambivalent feelings Stalin still inspires among so many of those who survived both his reign of terror and the war.

Like the larger battle for Moscow that it was a part of, Rzhev's ordeal put the horror of the Soviet-German conflict on full display and demonstrated the strengths and weaknesses of both sides. It showed how tenaciously the invading army held on to a strategic piece of real estate long after the Kremlin had declared that the capital had been saved but also showed the self-destructive nature of Hitler's policy of terrorizing the Soviet people. It showed how Stalin pushed Zhukov and others to continue hurling their troops into battles without adequate preparation or equipment and the Soviet leader's refusal to ponder, even for a moment, whether a more carefully calibrated, less callously brutal strategy could have saved lives and scored at least as many victories.

Until he died at the age of ninety-six in late 1986, Vyacheslav Molotov remained completely faithful to the ruler he served so long, always defending his actions, never admitting that he could have been seriously wrong about anything either before or during the war. As he saw it, Stalin couldn't be faulted for anything. After all, he was "a genius" and a strikingly handsome one at that. His eyes were "beautiful," Molotov said, and he couldn't understand how anyone could see any imperfections in his appearance. "He had pockmarks on his face, but you could barely notice them," he told an interviewer long after the war.

The former foreign minister was at his most strident when faced with questions about Stalin's paranoia, which led him to launch wave after wave of terror and to distrust the reports of his best spies about Hitler's intentions. Molotov suggested at one point that Stalin couldn't act upon the warnings since this would have given Hitler an excuse to attack the Soviet Union earlier than he did; then, without acknowledging the contradiction, he declared that Stalin failed to act because his spies couldn't be believed. "Provocateurs everywhere are innumerable. . . . You couldn't trust such reports," he said.

As for the notion that Stalin had been lulled into believing Hitler, Molotov responded with a mixture of contempt and pride. "Such a naïve Stalin. Stalin saw through it all. Stalin trusted Hitler? He didn't trust all his own people! And there were reasons for that. Hitler fooled Stalin? As a result of such deception, Hitler had to poison himself, and Stalin became head of half the world!" In other words, the ultimate outcome of the war proved Stalin had been right all along.

It was also nonsense to suggest, as the tyrant's critics did, that the terror, particularly the sweeping military purges of 1937, weakened the Soviet state and contributed to the disarray of its armed forces once the Germans attacked in 1941, Molotov insisted. In his view, this was a total misreading of history. The victims of the purges were "enemies" beyond a doubt, and if they hadn't been eliminated before the war, the conflict with the Germans would have been even bloodier than it was. "There would have been more victims," he asserted. "We would have prevailed in any case. But it would have required millions more victims. We would have had to beat back the German invasion and fight the internal enemy at the same time."

The specious nature of that logic aside, it's hard to imagine still more victims. Today, Russian historians estimate that approximately 27 million Soviet citizens died during the war, of which at least 8.6 million constituted Soviet military personnel. Even during the later period of the war, when Hitler's forces were retreating, Soviet losses were higher than German losses on the Eastern front; on average, they were at least three times as high. Retired general Vyacheslav Dolgov, who had just graduated from a military school in June 1941 and served as a political officer in the early fighting, looked back at the battle for Moscow and the rest of the war that he miraculously survived and stated a simple truth. "I suppose it's right to trumpet the victories to today's young generation," he said. "However, our victory wasn't only the result of successful battles; it was mainly the product of brutal defeats."

The horrific toll of those victories and defeats was a direct result of Stalin's decisions that weakened rather than strengthened his country: first by decapitating his military in 1937, second by keeping up the steady delivery of Soviet supplies for Hitler's war machine during the period of the Nazi-Soviet pact and by turning a willfully blind eye to the German dictator's preparations for an invasion.

"It would be hard to find a worse beginning to a war than that of June 1941," Stalin's biographer Dmitri Volkogonov, another retired general, noted. "All the leading political and military authorities had thought the U.S.S.R. might survive at most three months. But the Soviet people had proved them wrong. However, the fact of unbelievable resistance and staunchness would be ascribed to the 'wise leadership' of Stalin, the very person most directly responsible for the catastrophe." Stepan Mikoyan, the son of Politburo member Anastas Mikoyan and a fighter pilot during the war, put it more succinctly. "All things considered, I believe—contrary to the opinion of some war veterans who still say that 'we won the war thanks to Stalin'—it would be correct to say that we won the war *despite* Stalin's dictatorship," he wrote.

Similarly, the Soviet Union emerged victorious despite Stalin's continued policy of terror during the conflict. The arbitrary executions of Soviet soldiers for alleged treason, desertion and other crimes, the killing sprees in which the Red Army and NKVD targeted civilians and prisoners as they retreated before the German onslaught and the "blocking units" behind Soviet lines machine-gunning those of their own men who tried to retreat all contributed to an unprecedented number of defections. It wasn't just General Vlasov who switched sides, later organizing his Russian Liberation Movement. There were "Hiwis"—the abbreviation for *Hilfswillige,* Soviet volunteers—from the beginning of the conflict. Many were Soviet POWs who were desperate to find a way of surviving and hoped that by switching sides they'd better their chances. But there were plenty of defectors who genuinely believed they had made the right decision.

They included members of disparate national and other minorities—Ukrainians, Balts, Cossacks, Georgians, and others—whose accumulated grievances against Stalin's regime prompted them to fight for anyone who promised to destroy it. The very policies that Stalin had instituted to subdue his subjects—executions, mass deportations, the Gulag—helped set the stage for this wave of defections. During the course of the war, the defectors numbered in the hundreds of thousands.

But Stalin may have been saved from the consequences of his policies by Hitler's own policy of terror. If some inhabitants of the Ukraine and other Soviet territories initially welcomed the Germans as liberators, the draconian occupation that followed quickly opened their eyes to the nature of the conquerors. In village after village, town after town, from the border to places such as Rzhev on the approaches to Moscow, the litany of atrocities grew longer and longer and the notion of liberation at the hands of the Germans was thoroughly discredited. The number of defectors was at its highest in the early period of the war and declined precipitously as the fighting progressed. In part, this was due to the realization that the pendulum was swinging against the invaders, but it was also the clear result of the nature of the German occupation. Hitler's reign of terror was the greatest gift the German leader could have given to his Soviet counterpart.

Stalin indirectly hinted as much in a speech he delivered on May 24, 1945, right after the war in Europe had ended. "Our government has made many mistakes," he declared. "We had some desperate moments in 1941–42 when our army was in retreat, forced to abandon our native villages and cities . . . abandoning them because there was no other way out. Some other nation might well have said to its rulers: You have not fulfilled our expectations, go away, we shall set up another government, which will conclude peace with Germany and will secure us quiet."

That was a rare admission on Stalin's part, although as always he failed to take any personal responsibility for those "mistakes," blaming them instead on the government, as if it operated independent of his control. More important, though, this statement constituted an implicit recognition that he might have faced far more defections, even a general revolt, if the German invaders had behaved differently. Stalin ruled by fear and, given an alternative that offered a life without fear, there's no telling what his people would have done. But with Hitler giving the orders to the invading army, a life without fear was never an option. His terror began to trump Stalin's terror.

If the early period of the war puts the terror tactics of both sides in stark relief, they don't account for the outcome of the battle for Moscow, which would prove to be the largest and deadliest battle of World War II. They don't explain why Hitler's powerful war machine came up short, why the *Blitzkrieg* strategy that had been so successful in Poland, France and most of the rest of western Europe failed to achieve the same results in the Soviet Union, why the capital managed to hold out.

Top German officials and generals often blamed the Russian weather—first the mud season that trapped and wore down their armies, then the exceptionally cold winter—for their setbacks. "Will this winter never end? Is a new glacial age in the offing?" Goebbels wrote plaintively in his diary on March 20, 1942. "Certainly one is inclined at times to yield to this suspicion when one contemplates the constant, repeated attacks by winter weather." Hitler, he added, never liked winter and he had never imagined that it would "inflict such suffering upon German troops." In his memoirs, Churchill drew the obvious parallel with Napoleon. "Like the supreme military genius who had trod this road a century before him, Hitler now discovered what Russian winter meant," he wrote.

This kind of explanation infuriated Zhukov. He saw it as an effort to convince everyone that "German troops were beaten at Moscow not by the iron steadfastness, courage and heroism of Soviet soldiers, but by mud, cold and deep snow." He added, "The authors of these apologetics seem to forget that Soviet forces had to operate under the same conditions." Of course they did, but they were much better prepared—which by no means absolved Hitler of his responsibility for failing to outfit his soldiers with proper winter gear.

Walter Kerr, a correspondent for the New York *Herald Tribune* who reported from Russia that winter, offered a more judicious verdict. "It was cold, all right," he wrote, describing December 1941, "but the weather could never explain what happened to the German Army in the next two months. Still, it played its part."

Aside from his failure to prepare his troops for a winter war, Hitler's other colossal blunder was to refuse to listen to Guderian and his other generals who wanted to keep driving due east from Smolensk in August, making Moscow their immediate goal. Instead, the German leader chose that moment to divert his invading army south to the Ukraine and its capital, Kiev, delaying the assault on Moscow for nearly two crucial months.

During his talks with Roosevelt's envoy Averell Harriman, Stalin left no doubt about his view of the magnitude of that decision. "Stalin told me that the Germans had made a great mistake," Harriman recalled long after the war. "They tried a three-pronged drive, remember, one at Leningrad, one at Moscow and one in the south. Stalin said that if they had concentrated on the drive toward Moscow they could have taken Moscow; and Moscow was the nerve center and it would have been very difficult to conduct a major operation if Moscow had been lost. He said the Germans had made that kind of mistake in World War One—by not going to Paris. So Stalin said they were going to hold Moscow at all costs."

By all accounts, Hitler kept changing his mind about the importance of seizing Moscow. He'd predict that a quick victory there would produce the collapse of the Soviet Union, but after encountering more resistance than expected, he'd act as if it wasn't at the top of his list of priorities. One clear reflection of this can be found in Goebbels' diary entry on March 20, 1942. In it he flatly declares: "The Führer had no intention whatever of going to Moscow." Yet a few lines later, he states that Hitler's plans for the coming spring and summer consist of "the Caucasus, Leningrad, and Moscow." For a leader who had scored his first victories by a string of audacious actions, his behavior during the battle for Moscow revealed a new vacillating side to his character, which would become increasingly visible as the war dragged on.

The one firm decision Hitler made then—to dismiss several top generals and assume direct command of all military operations in December 1941—meant that he drew the conclusion from the defeat at Moscow that he needed to rely on his generals less, not more. "He wanted to be another Napoleon, who had only tolerated men under him who would obediently carry out his will," Field Marshal Erich von Manstein would write later. "Unfortunately he had neither Napoleon's military training nor his military genius." Hitler also continued to believe that he could outdo Napoleon by winning the war in Russia even after many of his generals were coming to the opposite conclusion.

The battle for Moscow set another pattern in Hitler's behavior as a military leader. When things went wrong, as they did on the outskirts of the Soviet capital, it was always his underlings who were to blame, never him. In this, as in his total disregard for the sacrifices he was demanding of his troops, Hitler and Stalin were very much alike. But it was Hitler's decision to postpone the push on Moscow, over the objections of many of those who served him, that allowed the weather to play the part it did. An earlier drive would have given the German forces the chance to seize the Soviet capital before the arrival of the autumn rains that bogged them down and the icy winter that was often as deadly as enemy fire.

The delay proved costly in another way as well. It provided Stalin with the time he needed to reassure himself that the Japanese weren't about to invade from the east. This allowed him to make the key decision to send in the Siberian troops to defend Moscow. During Eden's visit in December 1941, the Soviet leader told the British foreign secretary, "The bringing in of fresh reinforcements was the cause of the recent successes."

However much Hitler had bailed him out by making enormous mistakes, Stalin emerged from the battle for Moscow convinced that he had engineered this first Soviet victory, and that had an immediate impact on his behavior. Summoned to the Kremlin for a talk with his boss, Khrushchev was stunned by what he saw. "I found myself confronted with a new man. He was much changed from the way he'd been at the very beginning of the war," Khrushchev wrote. "He had pulled himself together, straightened up, and was acting like a real soldier. He had begun to think of himself as a great military strategist, which made it harder than ever to argue with him. He exhibited all the strong-willed determination of a heroic leader."

Khrushchev couldn't resist throwing in a barb that made his own feelings clear. "But I knew what sort of hero he was," he concluded. "I'd seen him when he was paralyzed by his fear of Hitler, like a rabbit in front of a boa constrictor. And my opinion of him hadn't changed in the meantime." Nonetheless, a big victory always makes a leader look better, and there was no doubt that the outcome of the battle for Moscow cheered Stalin's people and his allies.

Churchill's words summed up the reaction at the time. "All the anti-Nazi nations, great and small, rejoiced to see the first failure of a German Blitzkrieg," he wrote. "The threat of invasion to our Island was removed so long as the German armies were engaged in a life-and-death struggle in the East." But he added cautiously, "How long that struggle might last no one could tell."

What would have happened if the battle for Moscow had gone the other way? The standard Soviet line was that the war would have continued and that it would only have been a matter of time before the Germans were driven back—in other words, the outcome of the conflict was never in doubt. But as Stalin had confided to Harriman, Moscow was the nerve center, and a German victory there would have dealt a huge blow to his efforts to mobilize the country to defeat Hitler's forces. For the German invaders, this would also have served as a huge psychological boost, proof that Hitler had been right once again when he invaded the Soviet Union.

R. H. S. Stolfi, who taught Modern European History at the Naval Postgraduate School in Monterey, California, argued in his book *Hitler's Panzers East: World War II Reinterpreted* that Hitler's decision to divert his forces to the Ukraine in August cost the Germans the war. If the German leader had listened to the advice of Guderian and the other generals who wanted to capitalize on the swift victories in June and July, Stolfi maintained, his troops would have taken over the Soviet capital by the end of August.

"The arrival of Army Group Center at and beyond Moscow on roughly 28 August 1941 in the communications center of European Russia would have disintegrated the resulting isolated Leningrad and Ukrainian fronts," Stolfi wrote. And he insisted this would have meant the defeat of the Soviet Union by October 1941, which in turn would have produced a cataclysmic ripple effect. "By the magnitude of the victory and its timing, the Germans would have also won the war in Europe," he concluded.

It's impossible to prove or disprove that thesis. Many historians are more inclined to agree with Soviet assertions that Stalin's regime would have kept fighting no matter how far east it was pushed and that it would eventually have mobilized the resources and the men to push the Germans back. After all, it had successfully evacuated much of its war production to the east, and soon those factories would outpace their German counterparts in churning out the weaponry and supplies that were needed on the battlefields. But even if this had proved true, the war on the Eastern front would have taken much longer than it did. And this would have meant that World War II would have been a much longer, even more harrowing conflict than it actually was.

The reality of the German defeat hit the invaders hard, particularly those troops who had almost made it to the Soviet capital. CBS correspondent Larry Lesueur described his trip on the Leningrad Highway leading out of the city in December 1941. "This was the high water mark of the German advance. We were about twenty-five miles from the city limits of Moscow," he wrote. "The German failure must have been the greatest disappointment for an invading army in history."

With the benefit of hindsight, many of the Germans conceded as much. Richard Wernicke, the Stuka pilot who had participated in dive-bombing raids over Moscow, declared, "After Moscow, we were absolutely without any hope, and we felt that this was a great catastrophe." By that he meant the entire war, not just the one battle.

While it was indisputably a huge defeat for the Germans, a more contentious question is how big a victory Moscow was for the Soviet side. "The battle for Moscow allowed Stalin to fight another day, but it was not the turning point of the war, as is so often asserted," British historian Richard Overy has argued. "Moscow was a first, faltering step, a brief success almost squandered by Stalin's own military ineptitude."

The Red Army losses of almost two million soldiers during the battle for Moscow represented, to a considerable extent, the price of that ineptitude. And, yes, the next big battles—Stalingrad, Kursk—would prove to be more decisive victories, more clear-cut turning points. But Moscow was the first turning point, even if Overy is right about the shakiness of that victory. In retrospect, Hitler's failure to reach Moscow did signal the beginning of his end, but only the very beginning.

And for all his mistakes and all his brutality, Stalin deserved credit for one key decision that helped produce that outcome, no matter how much Hitler contributed to it as well. Magomed-Ganifa Shaidayev, who served as a political officer in a unit that fought on the northern approaches to Moscow, voiced the view of many veterans and civilians who lived through those chaotic days in October 1941 when the capital looked as though it was about to fall. "If Stalin had decided to leave Moscow during the panic, if the leader of the country had left the capital, this could have led to the destruction of the city," he said. "The fact that he stayed in Moscow with his people inspired us and saved the capital."

But Stalin and his successors haven't wanted to dwell on that moment or much else about the battle for Moscow, preferring instead to talk about the subsequent battles, which don't provide so many reminders of what went wrong in the early period of the war. Nor have they wanted to dwell on the staggering scale of Soviet losses. There's no way around the fact that Stalin was responsible for most of the mistakes that produced those huge casualty counts. Moscow was the first Soviet victory in World War II, but just barely. And it was the deadliest by far.

The battle for Moscow demonstrated that the Soviet people were far less united and determined in the early days of the war than official propaganda proclaimed. While that wasn't so surprising when it came to areas such as the Ukraine and the Baltic states, Moscow was another story. Even to explain Stalin's most laudable display of leadership, his decision not to abandon the capital, would require an honest discussion of conditions there at the time—the panic, the looting, the strikes, the brief but complete breakdown of law and order. All that is completely at odds with the standard image of Stalin's Soviet Union and its propaganda line about the unflinching unity and heroism of its people at their moment of greatest peril. So Soviet history books have generally whitewashed what happened, moving on quickly to the later victories, which don't require nearly as much tap-dancing around inconvenient truths.

The irony is that this whitewashing has done a huge disservice to the genuine heroes of a pivotal confrontation and contributed to a popular version of the war in which the battle for Moscow plays only a minor role, with many of the key events shrouded in an artificial mist. Today the battle for Moscow should take its proper place, front and center, in all accounts of the conflict between two monstrous political systems. Moscow's defenders paid a horrific price, but they changed the course of history not just for their own country but also for everyone locked in the struggle against Hitler's Germany. They deserved better from their leaders then, and they deserve better from all those who recall that struggle now.

Notes

INTRODUCTION

PAGE
2   *"This defeat"*: Fabian von Schlabrendorff, *The Secret War Against Hitler*, 131.

2   *the totals:* Moscow battle statistics on troop levels and losses from *Moskovskaya bitva v khronike faktov i sobytii*, 474.

2   *battle for Stalingrad:* Ibid., 468.

2   *battle of Gallipoli:* Most sources put the number at about 500,000 or slightly higher. A BBC report dated February 28, 2002, for example, put Turkish losses at 300,000 and Allied losses at 214,000 ("The Battle for Gallipoli: February 1915–January 1916").

3   *battle of the Somme:* R. R. Palmer and Joel Colton, *A History of the Modern World*, 681.

3   *El Alamein: Moskovskaya bitva v khronike faktov i sobytii*, 468.

4   *"The object of operations":* H. R. Trevor-Roper, ed., *Hitler's War Directives: 1939–1945*, 150.

4   *"To Moscow":* Heinz Guderian, *Panzer Leader*, 195.

4   *"In a few weeks":* Alan Bullock, *Hitler and Stalin: Parallel Lives*, 799.

5   *"It was the lowest point":* Alexander Werth, *Russia at War: 1941–1945*, 221.

6   *"lose nothing, except":* Simon Sebag Montefiore, *Stalin: The Court of the Red Tsar*, 609.

7   *"the greatest battle in"*: Richard Overy, *The Dictators: Hitler's Germany, Stalin's Russia*, 493.

1: "HITLER WILL NOT ATTACK US IN 1941"

PAGE

10   *"Undeserved and severe beatings"*: Bullock, 4. Other biographical details 1–4.

11   *"His contempt for"*: Dmitri Volkogonov, *Stalin: Triumph and Tragedy*, 155.

11   *"Don't waste time"*: Ibid., 156.

11   *"Groaning are"*: Isaac Deutscher, *Stalin*, 40–41.

12   *"spent nearly seven years"*: Ibid., 97.

12   *"This creature softened"*: Montefiore, 29.

13   *marriage to Nadezhda Alliluyeva:* Ibid., 86–87.

13   *a Walther pistol:* In Nadezhda's case, Volkogonov, 154. (But in Montefiore, 101, the pistol is described as a Mauser.) In Geli's case, Ronald Hayman, *Hitler + Geli*, 160.

13   *"Comrade Stalin"*: Lars T. Lih, Oleg V. Naumov, and Oleg V. Khlevniuk, eds., *Stalin's Letters to Molotov 1925–1936*, Appendix, 241–242.

14   *"Hitler responds"*: Otto Strasser, *Hitler and I*, 62.

15   *Stalin only wrote:* Robert Service, *Stalin*, 361.

15   *"As I am watching"*: Valentin M. Berezhkov, *At Stalin's Side*, 117.

15   *"leader of the party"* and rest of Mekhlis quote: Volkogonov, 241.

16   *"Stalin struck me"*: Hans von Herwarth with S. Frederick Starr, *Against Two Evils*, 54.

16   *"Hitler, what a"*: Overy, *The Dictators*, 53.

16   *"After the victory"*: Berezhkov, 57.

16   *Ronald Freisler:* Schlabrendorff, 318.

16   *"Shoot the mad dogs!"*: Deutscher, 373.

16   *"Never forget"*: Adolf Hitler, *Mein Kampf*, 660–661.

17   *He also had read* and *"His promises"*: Volkogonov, 352.

17   *"I know how much"*: Bullock, 676.

17   *"The Soviet Union could not"*: Ronald Seth, *Operation Barbarossa*, 9–10.

17   *"Of course, we are"*: Volkogonov, 385.

17   *"Hitler wants to"*: Jerrold L. Schecter with Vyacheslav V. Luchkov, eds., *Khrushchev Remembers: The Glasnost Tapes*, 46.

18   *the German-Soviet Agreement* and *"laid the solid foundations"*: Werth, 81.

18   *"A short blow at Poland"* to *"a struggle for 'democracy'"*: Ibid., 84.

19   *"shamefully conducted war"* and *"He was confident"*: Anastas Mikoyan, *Tak bylo*, 385.

19   *"Most of our troops"*: Schecter, 55.

19   *Winter War:* Montefiore, 330.

19   *"The Germans could see":* Schecter, 55.

20   *"The Red Army was":* Montefiore, 330.

20   *"He was racing":* Schecter, 54.

20   *"to beat our brains in":* Strobe Talbott, ed., *Khrushchev Remembers,* 166.

20   *"Everything I undertake":* Bullock, 697.

21   *"Britain's hope lies," "With Russia smashed"* and *"Decision":* Charles Burdick and Hans-Adolf Jacobsen, eds., *The Halder War Diary,* 244–245.

21   *"I will not":* Albert Axell, *Marshal Zhukov,* 76.

21   *According to General Henning von Tresckow:* Schlabrendorff, 134–135.

22   *"to beat England":* Alexander Dallin, *German Rule in Russia 1941–1945,* 17.

22   *"Ribbentrop was a":* Leon Goldensohn, *Nuremberg Interviews,* 445.

22   *The origin:* Dallin, 15.

22   *"The German Armed Forces":* Trevor-Roper, 93–94.

22   *"with the intention":* Ibid., 96–97.

22   *"For three years":* Hitler, 196.

23   *"visibly at":* Overy, *The Dictators,* 490.

23   *"Since Russia":* Bullock, 774.

23   *"We have only":* Ibid., 759.

23   *"Russia will collapse":* Axell, 63.

23   *"fourteen days of":* Overy, *The Dictators,* 490.

24   *"Führer, we are":* William L. Shirer, *The Rise and Fall of the Third Reich,* 1070.

24   *"regrettable blunder":* Ibid., 1071.

24   *"The beginning of":* Ibid., 1081.

24   *"This postponement":* Ibid.

25   *"a Slavic-Tartar":* Dallin, 9.

25   *"One day that":* Sergo Beria, *Beria, My Father,* 49.

26   *"He struts":* Ibid., 51.

26   *"I rather liked":* Goldensohn, 186.

26   *"He reminded me":* Ibid., 448.

26   *"England, despite":* Deutscher, 441.

26   *"If that's so":* Montefiore, 340.

27   *"So while":* Schecter, 55.

27   *Dergachev:* David E. Murphy, *What Stalin Knew,* 63.

27   *Ariets* and *Major General Vasily Tupikov:* Ibid., 64–66.

28   *Bucharest quoted:* Ibid., 73–75.

28   *Soviet military attaché in Budapest:* Ibid., 79.

28   *"Rumors and documents":* Donald Rayfield, *Stalin and his Hangmen,* 394.

28 *Prague station* and *Stalin's note:* Murphy, 81.
29 *"the Germans could":* Ibid., 84–87.
29 *"a little shit":* Ibid.
29 *Starshina* and *"sent back":* Ibid., 101.
29 *"Stalin's attitude to"* and *"grind them":* Stepan Mikoyan, *Memoirs of Military Test-Flying and Life with the Kremlin's Elite,* 102.
30 *Steinhardt* and *Churchill:* Murphy, 262.
30 *"They're playing us":* Montefiore, 349.
30 *"until the spring of 1941":* Berezhkov, 150.
30 *"Stalin, concerned":* Ibid., 181.
30 *German planes* and *"In case of violations":* Murphy, 165–166.
30 *lame explanation:* Ibid., 167–170.
31 *"so long as":* Ibid.
31 *"I'm not sure":* Montefiore, 352.
31 *"We must remain"* and *"We will remain":* Deutscher, 453.
31 *When he reassured:* Adam B. Ulam, *Expansion and Coexistence,* 306.
31 *"I honestly believe":* Seth, 36.
31 *Goebbels asserted:* Louis P. Lochner, ed., *The Goebbels Diaries: 1942–1943,* 87.
32 *"Stalin is about":* Ulam, 311.
32 *"To argue that":* Schecter, 49.
33 *"I do not know":* Petro G. Grigorenko, *Memoirs,* 46–47.
33 *Isaac Deutscher:* Deutscher, 439.
33 *"Germany is observing":* Volkogonov, 391.
34 *"to dull the":* Ibid.
34 *"Is the German Army":* Ivo Banac, ed., *The Diary of Georgi Dimitrov,* 159–160.
34 *calling up of five hundred thousand reservists:* Montefiore, 352.
34 *30 percent of* and *"Fulfillment of the plan":* Volkogonov, 375–376.
35 *Havas reported, "one must do," Stalin reacted,* and *"We see nothing":* Murphy, 24–27.
35 *"My people":* Montefiore, 356.
36 *German deserters:* Ibid., 357–358.

2: "LOOK HOW SMART WE ARE NOW"

PAGE
37 *General Georgy Mikushev:* V. Ananko, A. Domank, and N. Romanichev, *Za kazhduiu piad,* 15–34. Romanichev and Boris Nevzorov provided additional details of Mikushev's experiences in interviews for this book.
38 *"to not respond":* Murphy, 214.
40 *Hans von Herwarth:* Hans von Herwarth with S. Frederick Starr, *Against Two Evils,* 197–198.

43 *"Moscow has surrendered":* Werth, 164.

43 *the Germans destroyed:* Volkogonov, 408.

43 *Major General I. I. Kopets:* Constantine Pleshakov, *Stalin's Folly,* 126–127.

43 *450 miles:* Deutscher, 465.

43 *letter home: Biulleten' Assotsiatsii istorikov vtoroy mirovoi voyny,* issue 8, 2003, 21–25.

44 *Yuri Druzhnikov:* Yuri Druzhnikov, who teaches Russian Literature at the University of California at Davis, recounted his family history in an interview. He also included some of these experiences, only slightly altered, in his novel *Passport to Yesterday.*

46 *"It's going to":* Anastas Mikoyan, 378.

46 *"Hitler surely":* Service, 410.

47 *a meeting with Molotov:* M. M. Gorinov and others, eds. *Moskva Voennaia, 1941–1945: Memuary i arkhivnye dokumenty,* 26.

47 *"the German government has declared war":* Service, 411.

47 *"Ribbentrop deceived us":* Georgii Kumanev, *Riadom so Stalinym: Otkrovennyye svidetel'stva,* 24.

47 *3.05 million men:* Bullock, 790.

47 *The Germans divided:* Overy, *Russia's War,* 84–85.

48 *"When the showdown":* Werth, 155.

48 *"Comrade Boldin":* Ibid., 159–160.

48 *"are being killed all over the place":* Ibid.

48 *issuing orders:* Ibid., 165–166.

49 *"Let Molotov speak"* and *"That was certainly a mistake":* Anastas Mikoyan, 388–389.

49 *Stalin helped him:* Montefiore, 368.

49 *"This unheard-of":* Werth, 167–168, Montefiore, 368.

50 *"Lenin left us":* Volkogonov, 410.

50 *"Comrade Stalin is":* Montefiore, 374.

50 *"What have you"* and *"He had the strangest":* Volkogonov, 411.

50 *Stalin assumed:* Montefiore, 376.

50 *"With whom":* Ibid., 376–377.

50 *"Fine":* Volkogonov, 411.

50 *Council of Evacuation:* Overy, *The Dictators,* 500.

50 *"a different Stalin"* and *"Well, they":* Schecter, 65.

50 *Khrushchev* and *Malenkov:* Talbott, 168.

51 *"Tell me":* Ibid.

51 *On July 3, he finally addressed:* Joseph Stalin, *The War of National Liberation,* 9–17. I have corrected a few words of the translation.

53 *Lenin was sent on a long journey:* The story of Lenin's voyage and the treatment of his body is based on interviews with Ilya Zbarsky. A few details are taken from *Lenin's Embalmers* by Ilya Zbarsky and Samuel Hutchinson.

59   *"Since I struggled":* Dallin, 3.
59   *"It is thus"* and *"The sheer geographical":* Burdick, 446–447.
59   *"It is the Führer's":* Ibid., 458.
59   *Over dinner:* Bullock, 764–765.
60   *"Russians, surrender":* Pleshakov, 245.
60   *"The Russians are":* Fedor von Bock, *The War Diary,* 225.
61   *"Some people in":* Berezhkov, 184.
61   *Goebbels:* Fred Taylor, ed., *The Goebbels Diaries: 1939–1941,* 426–433.
61   *home guard:* Overy, *Russia's War,* 80.
61   *On July 4, Goebbels:* Taylor, 446.
62   *"The Führer has":* Bullock, 798.

3: THE PRICE OF TERROR

PAGE
63   *Ilya Vinitsky:* This account is based on interviews with Vinitsky and on personal notes he wrote about his experiences during the war and made available for this book.
68   *censors' internal report:* Moskva Voennaia, 52.
69   *"The local population":* Herwarth, 201.
70   *"It was not":* Beria, 69.
70   *"traitors who":* Pleshakov, 255.
70   *Order 227:* Bullock, 813.
71   *German report dated February 19, 1942:* Ibid.
71   *Order 270:* Volkogonov, 427.
71   *"I am Stalin's son," "The fool"* and *daughter-in-law Yulia:* Montefiore, 379–380.
71   *to exchange Yakov:* Ibid., 445–446.
71   *"There are no":* Steven Merritt Miner, *Stalin's Holy War,* 56.
72   *Nikolai Pisarev:* Based on my interview with Pisarev. I first wrote about him in *Newsweek,* January 16, 1995, "The POW."
72   *"The officers who":* Volkogonov, 416.
72   *"What can one think":* Beria, 70.
73   *shooting of hundreds:* Miner, 57.
73   *"a great number of":* David M. Glantz, *Colossus Reborn,* 567.
73   *prompt execution:* Antony Beevor and Luba Vinogradova, eds., *A Writer at War,* 19.
73   *NKVD report:* Robert Conquest, *The Dragons of Expectations,* 128.
73   *supplying the Gulag:* Pleshakov, 270, reports that between July and December 1941, 1,339,702 people were put on trial, and 67.4 percent of them were sent to the Gulag.
74   *Pavlov* and *"No appeal":* Volkogonov, 421–422, Bullock, 795.
74   *"A great war was":* Stepan Mikoyan, 49.
74   *an estimated 158,000 Soviet soldiers:* Overy, *The Dictators,* 535.

74 *German military tribunals:* Ibid., 517.

75 *"Did you notice":* Pechenkin, 21.

75 *the Great Terror. During 1937 and 1938:* Service, 356.

75 *44,000 names* and *"Stalin, a busy man":* Ibid., 352–353.

76 *"Give the dog":* Ibid., 353.

76 *"Without any noise":* Pechenkin, 15.

77 *"will make even":* Rayfield, 322.

77 *"What are you":* Overy, *The Dictators,* 475.

77 *bloodstains:* Rayfield, 324.

77 *"as if he":* Pechenkin, 96.

77 *"Stalin, do you hear":* Ibid., 95.

78 *"There was"* and *"Spies, spies!":* Ibid., 47–48.

78 *Germans reportedly leaked:* Rayfield, 323, Robert Conquest, *The Great Terror,* 198–199.

78 *"When I saw":* Pechenkin, 84.

78 *General Jonah Yakir:* Rayfield, 324.

79 *"wives of enemies":* Conquest, *The Dragons of Expectation,* 115.

79 *"The purge was":* Pechenkin, 118–119.

79 *"This is worse":* Overy, *Russia's War,* 30.

79 *The purges hit:* Conquest, *The Great Terror,* 450.

80 *"So many were":* Schecter, 52.

80 *"I have repeatedly":* Stepan Mikoyan, 106.

80 *"disastrous":* Herwarth, 115.

80 *"forged the defeats":* Volkogonov, 324.

80 *"Let us imagine":* Deutscher, 377.

81 *"Among all the documents":* Ibid., 379.

81 *to deport* and *"At a time when":* Norman Davies, *Heart of Europe,* 66–67.

82 *"those who were":* Bullock, 718.

82 *March 1940, the Kremlin decreed:* Andrew Nagorski, "At Last, a Victory for Truth," *Newsweek,* October 26, 1992.

82 *the arrests began:* Ronald J. Misiunas and Rein Taagepera, *The Baltic States,* 38–39.

82 *a list of no less than fourteen categories:* Ibid., 40.

83 *the numbers involved:* Ibid., 41.

83 *Ukrainian uprising:* Anne Applebaum, *Gulag,* 416.

84 *"Those who can walk":* Ibid., 418.

84 *"our Himmler":* Rayfield, 392.

84 *such as Orel, where 154:* Ibid., 401.

84 *Butyrka prison:* Ibid., 400.

84 *42,776 prisoners:* Aleksei Toptygin, *Lavrentii Beriia,* 250.

85 *"We used to":* Montefiore, 382.

85 *allowed him to sit:* Rayfield, 401.

85 *"There're too many"* and *surprise:* Montefiore, 331.

85 *"Of course there were excesses"*: Overy, *The Dictators*, 217.
85 *"If trouble started"*: Albert Resis, ed., *Molotov Remembers*, 26.
86 *"My father explained"*: Beria, 33.
86 *"Warfare reverted to"*: Service, 423.

4: HITLER AND HIS GENERALS

PAGE
88 *"Let us kill"*: Overy, *The Dictators*, 516.
88 *"All the Soviet"*: Herwarth, 201.
88 *collective farms* and *"against whom"*: Ibid., 202–203.
88 *Captain Karl Haupt*: Ben Shepherd, *War in the Wild East*, 79–80.
89 *"All its members"* to *"their backs were turned"*: Erich von Manstein, *Lost Victories*, 180–187.
89 *"one of the first"*: Miner, 53.
89 *"If one did it"*: Ibid., 54.
90 "Clash of two": Burdick, 346.
90 *"The attitude of the"*: Miner, 54.
90 *"Political commissars"* and *"We must"*: Dallin, 30–31.
91 *"The main reason"*: Shepherd, 72.
91 *"We would insult"*: Ibid., 74.
91 *400 million:* Dallin, 66.
91 *"the entire German"*: Ibid., 39.
91 *"Asiatic, Mongol"*: Ibid., 69.
92 *"At this stage"*: Manstein, 183.
92 *"who by their behavior"*: Dallin, 31.
92 *"Because of the"*: Seth, 38.
92 *to execute between fifty and a hundred:* Overy, *The Dictators*, 520–521.
92 *"Feeding inhabitants"*: Dallin, 71.
93 *"marching arm-in-arm"*: Herwarth, 208.
93 *"The Russian must"*: Overy, *The Dictators*, 537.
93 *"Where there's a"*: Shepherd, 89.
93 *Einsatzgruppen* and *Himmler*: Christopher R. Browning, *Ordinary Men*, 10–11.
93 *Police Battalion 309 entered the city of Bialystok:* Ibid., 11–12.
94 *Bialystok. On July 12:* Ibid., 13–14.
94 *"August 25"* and *"August 31"*: Ibid., 17.
94 *"The Jews were"* and *"All I had to"*: Goldensohn, 389–390.
94 *Babi Yar:* Browning, 18.
95 *"But we were"* and *"Apparently as time"*: Goldensohn, 356–357.
95 *"utterly unsoldierly"* and *"would have threatened"*: Manstein, 180.
95 *Guderian:* Guderian, 152.
95 *"The order simply incited"*: Manstein, 180.
95 *"inconspicuously"*: Overy, *The Dictators*, 513.

96   *"traditional notions of":* Manstein, 77.
96   *"The army is":* Schlabrendorff, 80.
97   *felt bitterly disappointed:* Ibid., 81.
97   *"the entire basis":* Shirer, 556. Full account of the Halder plot, 547–559.
97   *"We had watched":* Manstein, 23–24.
98   *"the everlasting":* Ibid., 77.
98   *scheduled stop:* Ibid., 61.
98   *devalue the military's:* Ibid., 150.
98   *"Although this method"* and *Kluge:* Schlabrendorff, 146.
99   *"When considering":* Manstein, 274–275.
99   *"excessive self-esteem":* Ibid., 74.
99   *"Hitler possessed":* Ibid., 274–275.
99   *"He had a genius":* Ibid., 74.
99   *"Before I became"* and *"The general staff":* Schlabrendorff, 127.
100   *"until after victory":* Dallin, 15.
100   *"Purpose is not":* Ibid., 16.
100   *"Hitler decided":* Goldensohn, 102.
100   *"The first was":* Manstein, 175.
100   *"Gentlemen, do you":* Schlabrendorff, 125.
101   *"I believed in Hitler":* Goldensohn, 160.
101   *"The enemy is":* Bock, 247.
102   *"Army Group Center":* Trevor-Roper, 146.
102   *"The main thing":* Bock, 265–266.
102   *"All the directives":* Ibid., 289.
102   *"to deprive the":* Trevor-Roper, 150.
103   *"Before the":* Ibid.
103   *"is not in"* and *"The most important":* Ibid., 151.
103   *"in the most tactless":* Manstein, 261–262.
103   *"What he lacked":* Ibid., 275.
103   *"destroying the":* Trevor-Roper, 153.
103   *September 16:* Geoffrey Jukes, *The Defense of Moscow,* 77.
104   *Heinz Guderian:* All quotations and information in the account of Guderian's career and dealings with Hitler are from Heinz Guderian, *Panzer Leader* (his memoirs), except where otherwise noted.
107   *"Guderian is champing":* Bock, 285.
109   *"Why didn't you"* and *"Because there":* Beevor, *A Writer at War,* 56.

5: "MOSCOW IS IN DANGER"

PAGE
113   *"How could you":* Service, 421.
113   *Boris Oreshkin:* Boris Oreshkin, "Viaz'ma," anthology *Podvig,* issue 38, Moscow, *Molodaia Gvardiia,* 1991, 102–114.

117 *report by A. L. Ugryumov: Moskva Prifrontovaia 1941–1942*, 180, 185.

119 *"an absolute government"* and *"fear replaces"*: Phyllis Penn Kohler, ed., *Journey for Our Time*, 128, 146.

119 *Strelkovka*: Georgi K. Zhukov, *Marshal Zhukov's Greatest Battles*, 5 (Harrison Salisbury's introduction).

121 *"You are not"*: Pleshakov, 165.

121 *"If we come"*: Zhukov, *Marshal Zhukov's Greatest Battles*, 8 (Harrison Salisbury's introduction).

121 *he decreed:* Axell, 5.

121 *"Zhukov was always"*: Zhukov, *Marshal Zhukov's Greatest Battles*, 12 (Harrison Salisbury's introduction).

122 *"I look as if"*: Pleshakov, 164–165.

122 *"Grin and bear it"*: Axell, 15.

122 *Conscripted:* Ibid., 21–36.

122 *relationships:* interviews with his daughter Ella, Axell, 213–222, interview with his driver Aleksandr Buchin.

122 *In a letter:* letter courtesy of Ella Zhukova.

123 *"the only person"*: Overy, *Russia's War*, 69.

123 *the purges:* G. K. Zhukov, *Vospominaniia i razmyshleniia*, Vol. I, 228–246.

124 *"Of course, I regard"* and *"Tukhachevsky was"*: Andrei Gromyko, *Memoirs*, 168.

124 *the purged officers:* Zhukov, *Vospominaniia i razmyshleniia*, 221–249.

125 *Japanese forces:* Axell, 55–56.

125 *face-to-face conversation* and *"If he is always"*: Zhukov, *Vospominaniia i razmyshleniia*, 287.

126 *"Stalin wasn't a coward"*: Ibid., 368.

126 *"I wasn't informed"* and *"You will be informed"*: Ibid., 378, 380.

127 *"The situation is"*: Montefiore, 387.

127 *Soviet figures:* Overy, *Russia's War*, 112.

127 *redeploying:* Zhukov, *Marshal Zhukov's Greatest Battles* (Harrison Salisbury's introduction), 22–23.

127 *"I thought I'd"*: Beevor, *A Writer at War*, 48.

127 *A Soviet pilot reported:* Stepan Mikoyan, 68.

128 *Beria was furious:* Montefiore, 391.

128 *"The grave possibility"*: Zhukov, *Marshal Zhukov's Greatest Battles*, 30.

128 *"Look, we're in"*: Ibid., 30–31.

128 *Otto Günsche:* Eberle, *The Hitler Book*, 77.

129 *dinner on October 17:* David Irving, *Hitler's War*, 424–425.

130 *"Guderian has reached"*: Burdick, 546.

130 *Guderian:* Guderian, 232–240.

131 *"The enemy thought"*: Zhukov, *Marshal Zhukov's Greatest Battles*, 26–27.

131 *"there was no"*: Ibid., 32.

131 *"The principal danger":* Ibid., 33.
132 *"We see Germans":* Brochure on Podolsk Cadets provided by the Museum of the Defense of Moscow.
133 *"If Moscow falls":* Montefiore, 393.
133 *"These forces were":* Zhukov, *Marshal Zhukov's Greatest Battles,* 42–43.
134 *"If the Germans," "heavy fighting"* and *"the very existence":* Werth, 231.
134 *"the gravity of":* Zhukov, *Marshal Zhukov's Greatest Battles,* 44.
134 *"Let us not":* Werth, 232.
135 *"During the night":* Ibid., 233.
135 *"iron discipline":* Ibid., 232–233.
135 *October 13, Stalin had issued orders:* David M. Glantz and Jonathan M. House, *When Titans Clashed,* 81.

6: "THE BROTHERHOOD OF MAN"

PAGE
138 *"Blueprint for Victory":* *Life,* August 4, 1941.
138 *Sir Stafford Cripps:* Anthony Eden, *The Reckoning,* 312.
139 *John Dill:* Ibid.
139 *"go through Russia":* Ivan Maisky, *Memoirs of a Soviet Ambassador,* 161.
139 *"The Prime Minister's"* and *"We savored":* Eden, 312.
140 *William Bullitt:* Dennis J. Dunn, *Caught Between Roosevelt & Stalin,* 13–34.
140 *"a very striking man":* Dunn, 34.
141 *"charming, brilliant"* and *"He came to":* George F. Kennan, *Memoirs,* 79.
141 *"perhaps fifty toasts"* and *"I held out":* Dunn, 23, 28.
141 *"a very big man"* and *With Lenin:* Ibid., 18–19.
141 *returned to Moscow:* Ibid., 40–41.
142 *"You Westerners":* Charles E. Bohlen, *Witness to History,* 26.
142 *"We regarded":* Kennan, 81–82.
142 *plainclothesmen:* Bohlen, 32.
142 *Marines:* Ibid., 21.
143 *"the honeymoon"* and *"perhaps it":* Dunn, 41.
143 *"let them know":* Ibid., 42.
143 *"were without question":* Ibid., 47.
143 *"in order the better":* Ibid., 49.
144 *"individual instances":* Ibid., 58.
144 *"definite pro-Russian":* Bohlen, 47.
144 *"most friendly attitude":* Dunn, 58.
144 *"Davies understands":* Ibid., 70.
144 *"Had the President":* Kennan, 83.
144 *transfer* and *"too long for":* Dunn, 71.
145 *"Stalin is a":* Joseph E. Davies, *Mission to Moscow,* 112.
145 *"He [Stalin] has":* Ibid., 357.

145   *"It is my opinion":* Ibid., 272.

145   *"that the accused":* Ibid., 201.

145   *"The Stalin regime":* Ibid., 202–203.

145   *"indignation and bewilderment":* Herwarth, 110.

146   *"He ardently desired":* Bohlen, 55.

146   *"I could not":* Ibid., 57.

146   *"I shall always":* Davies, 352.

146   *"In my opinion":* Ibid., 511.

146   *"It is my judgment":* Ibid., 432.

147   *"There were no":* Ibid., 280.

147   *Ivan Yeaton: Memoirs of Ivan D. Yeaton, USA (Ret.):* 14–45.

149   *"a wealthy bourgeoisie Jew":* Dunn, 107.

149   *"I think we":* Ibid., 103.

150   *dinner at his country retreat, Chequers* and *"Not at all":* Winston S. Churchill, *The Grand Alliance,* 370.

151   *"We shall fight him":* Ibid., 372.

151   *"Thus the ravings":* Ibid., 367–368.

151   *silence "oppressive"* and *Stalin wrote:* Ibid., 380–383.

152   *"You must remember":* Ibid., 385.

152   *"I received many":* Ibid., 388.

152   *"all the aid":* Dunn, 126.

152   *"we find ourselves"* and *"If we see":* Ibid., 127.

152   *"we should do":* Kennan, 133.

153   *"obvious sympathy":* Maisky, 179, 183.

153   *"The resistance of":* Davies, 493.

154   *Faymonville* and *Lend-Lease:* Robert Huhn Jones, *The Roads to Russia,* 41–42.

154   *classified documents:* Dunn, 129.

154   *Hopkins:* Robert E. Sherwood, *Roosevelt and Hopkins,* 325–327.

155   *"Stalin said":* Ibid., 334.

155   *"Give us":* Ibid., 328.

155   *blacked out:* Ibid., 330.

155   *"I told him":* Ibid., 343.

155   *"He talked as"* and *"an austere, rugged":* Ibid., 343–344.

156   *Hopkins* and *Major Yeaton:* Yeaton, 37–38.

157   *Japan's military attachés* and *Japanese newspaper correspondent:* FSB archives courtesy of V. P. Yeroshin and V. Iampol'skii, *Organy gosudarstvennoi bezopasnosti SSSR v Velikoi Otechestvennoi voine.*

157   *Sorge was reporting:* Tsuyoshi Hasegawa, *Racing the Enemy,* 17.

157   *"the impending collapse":* Ulam, 323.

158   *Hopkins* and *Molotov:* Sherwood, 332.

158   *Roosevelt wrote a no-nonsense note to Wayne Coy:* Susan Butler, ed., *My Dear Mr. Stalin,* 39.

158   *"that do not"* and *"to choose":* Ibid., 41.

159   *"We are at"* and *British-American delegation:* Ibid., 41–42.

159   *"Your function"* and *"might have a":* Ibid., 43.

159   *August 29, he wrote:* Churchill, 454.

160   *On September 4, Maisky showed up to deliver Stalin's reply:* Churchill, 456.

160   *"Remember that"* and *"More calm":* Churchill, 457–458.

160   *"I began to":* Maisky, 191.

161   *"It seems to"* and *"It is almost":* Churchill, 462–463.

161   War and Peace: Maisky, 208–209.

161   *bomb that exploded:* Dunn, 151–152.

161   *"He was one":* Quentin Reynolds, *By Quentin Reynolds,* 233.

162   *first meeting:* Sherwood, 387–388.

162   *the next evening:* Ibid., 388–389.

162   *Goebbels gloated:* Jones, 61.

163   *"It is up to":* Ibid.

163   *Beaverbrook responded* and *"Now we shall":* Sherwood, 389.

163   *"The meeting broke up"* and *Beaverbrook observed:* Ibid., 389–391.

163   *"moved stealthily like":* Dunn, 134.

164   *"huge, forbidding":* Reynolds, 238–239.

164   *farewell banquet:* Ibid., 239.

164   *arranged for Faymonville:* Dunn, 132–133.

164   *"was irrefutably":* Yeaton, 40–44.

165   *Steinhardt:* Reynolds, 244.

165   *Charles Thayer, "now had completely"* and *Molotov told Steinhardt and Cripps:* W. Averell Harriman and Elie Abel, *Special Envoy to Churchill and Stalin,* 106–107.

165   *"You have no":* Reynolds, 242.

166   *a train:* Reynolds, 242–245.

166   *"It turned into":* Yeaton, 44.

7: PANIC IN MOSCOW

PAGE

168   *"A threat hangs":* Information Bulletin of the Soviet Embassy in Washington, October 17, 1942 (Hoover Institution archives).

168   *Moscow's population:* Oleg Matveev, *"Bedstviia zatiazhnoi voiny," Nezavisimoe Voennoe Obozrenie,* 20.06.2003, #20 (335).

168   *"They tried to take":* Gorinov, 376.

169   *"Some people stopped":* Ibid., 111.

170   *British Embassy:* Montefiore, 398; Col. Albert Seaton, *The Battle for Moscow,* 118.

174   *Mikhail Zhuravlev filed a lengthy report:* Gorinov, 116–119.

176   *geneticist Nikolai Vavilov:* S. E. Shnol, *Geroi i zlodei rossiiskoi nauki,* 99–100.

176 *Anastas Mikoyan personally intervened in the strike:* Anastas Mikoyan, 420.

177 *"to blow up factories":* Moskovskaia Bitva v postanovleniiakh Gosudarstvennogo Komiteta oborony, 70.

177 *Sergei Fedoseyev:* Gorinov, 92.

179 *"Since Moscow itself"* and *train to Kuibyshev:* Banac, 196–200.

180 *"That's nonsense":* Resis, 42.

180 *"he was tormented":* Volkogonov, 434.

180 *special train* and *planes:* Ibid., 435.

180 *dacha* and *"clear the mines":* Montefiore, 397.

180 *driving back to the Kremlin:* A. T. Rybin, *Riadom so Stalinym,* 23.

181 *at the Kremlin* and *Mikoyan wasn't happy:* Anastas Mikoyan, 418–419.

181 *"Let Mikoyan go":* Ibid., 422.

181 *Kutuzov:* Montefiore, 399.

182 *Kirovskaya metro:* Ibid.

182 *bombing raid:* Volkogonov, 434.

182 *"What shall we":* Stepan Mikoyan, 108.

182 *"If you go":* Beria, 75–76.

183 *"Your attitude":* Ibid.

183 *Kalanchevskaya station:* V. K. Vinogradov, *Lubianka v dni bitvy za Moskvu,* 17.

183 *Pavel Saprykin:* Interview with Pavel Saprykin.

184 *"But, as the saying":* Zhukov, *Marshal Zhukov's Greatest Battles,* 46.

184 *"found it intolerable":* Konstantin Simonov, *The Living and the Dead,* 304.

185 *"The coming victory":* Biulletten' Assotsiatsii istorikov vtoroy mirovoi voiny, 21–25.

186 *"Muscovites made":* Gorinov, 307.

186 *Zhukov reported* and *"augmenting their":* Zhukov, *Marshal Zhukov's Greatest Battles,* 53–55.

186 *NKVD report* and *"Enemy planes":* Gorinov, 427–428.

187 *Later tallies:* Y. Y. Kammerer, V. S. Karaulov, S. E. Lapirov,. Moskve— vozdushnaia trevoga! Mestnaia PVO v gody voiny, 414–415.

187 *Nikolai Sbytov:* Gorinov, 170–171.

187 *"Those were":* Werth, 236–237.

188 *Mikoyan reported:* Anastas Mikoyan, 415.

188 *"I saved your life":* Montefiore, 404.

188 *twenty thousand deaths in London:* Museum of London exhibition "Remembering the Blitz: The Big Story."

189 *Soviet side claimed:* Moscow Defense Museum figures.

190 *volunteers for Communist brigades:* V. K. Ivanov, *Moskovskaia zona oborony,* 22.

191 *"in this grave hour":* Zhukov, *Marshal Zhukov's Greatest Battles,* 49.

191 *Kuibyshev:* Vyacheslav Kharlamov, the director of the Stalin Bunker Museum.
192 *Construction of the bunker:* Ibid.
193 *"How are we":* Volkogonov, 436.
193 *Artemyev:* Montefiore, 404.
193 *"The anti-aircraft defenses":* Volkogonov, 436.

8: SABOTEURS, JUGGLERS, AND SPIES

PAGE
195 *Moskva Hotel:* Kevin O'Flynn, "A Ton of Explosives Unearthed at Moskva," *Moscow Times,* July 11, 2005.
195 *three hidden printing plants:* Gorinov, 91.
196 "Comrades! We left": Ibid.
196 *Nikolai Khokhlov:* Unless otherwise indicated, Nikolai Khokhlov, *In the Name of Conscience,* 3–32, and from interview with Khokhlov.
198 *"elegantly juggling":* Gorinov, 103.
198 *Khokhlov's career* and *his father:* Khokhlov, 138, 85–86, and from interview with Khokhlov.
200 *memo to Beria from Naum Eitingon:* Vinogradov, 82–90.
201 *Another report:* Ibid., 78–79.
202 *Sergei Fedoseyev:* Gorinov, 87–93.
210 *report on the interrogation of Vasily Klubkov:* Vinogradov, 182–190.
211 *screen version, Zoya's story:* Nina Tumarkin, *The Living and the Dead,* 76–78.
212 *Tumarkin writes:* Ibid.
212 *"She told me":* Moskva Prifrontovaia 1941–1942, 572.
212 *Zoya's younger brother:* Tumarkin, 78.
213 *report of his subsequent trial:* Vinogradov, 190–194.
214 *"intimate with":* Robert Whymant, *Stalin's Spy,* 218.
214 *"This war is":* Ibid., 209.
215 *"Now the opportunity":* Ibid., 194.
215 *"gave us":* Ibid., 212.
215 *"Japan will be":* Ibid., 217.
216 *Ozaki:* Ibid., 221.
216 *August 11, Sorge wrote:* Ibid., 222–223.
216 *Wenneker, told Sorge:* Ibid., 232–234.
217 *"Many soldiers"* and *"They decided":* Ibid.
217 *military intelligence:* Murphy, 88.
217 *German diplomats* and *"Considering his":* Ibid., 89.
217 *"complete trust":* Whymant, 239.
218 *four hundred thousand, 250,000* and *the rest:* Provided by Russian military historian Kirill Dryannov.
218 *last dispatch:* Whymant, 258.

218 *"Richard Sorge?":* Murphy, 90. (Whymant, 316, attributes a similar response to Soviet officials, not to Stalin directly.)

9: *"O MEIN GOTT! O MEIN GOTT!"*

PAGE

219 *assembled in the Mayakovsky metro station:* Montefiore, 405, Werth, 240.

220 *"As many who":* Werth, 240.

220 *"Today, as a result":* Stalin, 18–34.

221 *the Red Army lost three times more men:* Catherine Merridale, *Ivan's War,* 188.

221 *"It is extremely":* Werth, 241.

222 *military parade:* Gorinov, 147–152; Overy, *Russia's War,* 113, Montefiore, 405–406.

223 *newsreel footage of Stalin:* Details of reshoot provided by Boris Maklyarsky, son of top NKVD official Mikhail Maklyarsky; also mentioned in Overy, *Russia's War,* 115.

223 *"temporarily lost"* and other quotations from Stalin's speech: Stalin, 35–38.

224 *"Are you sure":* Zhukov, *Marshal Zhukov's Greatest Battles,* 62.

225 *"Marshal Zhukov considered":* Elena Rzhevskaya, "Roads and Days: The Memoirs of a Red Army Translator," *The Journal of Slavic Studies,* Volume 14, March 2001, 59.

225 *A proclamation:* Ibid., 61. The proclamation was found by the Soviet side and translated by Rzhevskaya.

225 *"The Russians are":* Goldensohn, 344.

226 *"were carried out":* James Lucas, *War on the Eastern Front,* 32–33.

226 *Lieutenant Kurt Gruman:* Gruman's diary was found by Soviet troops and translated by Rzhevskaya in *The Journal of Slavic Studies,* 59–69. The diary ends on February 17, 1942, which Rzhevskaya assumes is when he died.

227 *in his diary:* Ibid.

228 *"The infantry now":* Seth, 151.

228 *750,000 horses:* James Lucas, *War on the Eastern Front,* 114–115.

229 *"Up to this time":* Guderian, 237.

230 *"The Russians are":* Bock, 337.

230 *"Guderian's weak":* Ibid., 345.

230 *"our losses"* and *"He probably":* Ibid., 347.

230 *"There were no":* Guderian, 244–255.

233 *"A national concept":* Lucas, 13.

233 *"Germans are not":* Beevor, *A Writer at War,* 223.

233 *military censorship office* and *letters:* Gorinov, 165–170.

235 *home guard units:* Ivanov, 22.

237 *eighty-seven districts:* Shvetsova, *Moskva i Moskvichi, 32.*

237 *Natalya Kravchenko:* Interview with her and her written account, which is to be published by the village of Nikolina Gora in an anthology of such recollections.

239 *antifreeze or even chains* and *dropped ropes:* Seth, 151.

10: "DON'T BE SENTIMENTAL"

PAGE

243 *"Our soldiers":* Zhukov, *Marshal Zhukov's Greatest Battles,* 70.

243 *Dedovsk:* Ibid., 77–79.

244 *Dedovo:* Ibid.

246 *"The severe winter weather":* Trevor-Roper, 166.

247 *"Now we know":* Overy, *Russia's War,* 163–164.

248 *"the German swine"* and *"My advice is":* Volkogonov, 420.

253 *"no stick of":* Guderian, 257.

254 *using manuscripts from Tolstoy's library as fuel:* Overy, *Russia's War,* 124.

254 *buried about seventy* and *fires:* Yasnaya Polyana Museum.

254 *fallen "for Greater Germany":* Eve Curie, *Journey Among Warriors,* 214.

254 *"We paid no attention":* Ibid., 213.

254 *the bodies* and *"There could":* Ibid., 216–217.

254 *"The enemy":* Guderian, 261.

255 *"were forced to"* and *"But this was":* Guderian, 259.

255 *"The fighting of":* Bock, 376.

255 *"General withdrawal":* Burdick, 590.

255 *"Hitler's reaction":* Manstein, 279.

256 *"This little matter":* Seth, 158.

256 *Guderian* and *Hitler:* Guderian, 265–271.

258 *"Everything is":* Beevor, *A Writer at War,* 63.

259 *Kurt Gruman:* Rzhevskaya, 65–68.

259 *crippled by frostbite:* Lucas, 89. Lucas cites medical reports of the Fourth Army indicating more than double the casualties from frostbite than from battle.

260 *Goebbels:* Lochner, 37–38.

261 *on transport priorities* and *Hitler decided:* Lucas, 97.

261 *Goebbels appealed:* Lochner, 33.

261 *Guderian was convinced:* Guderian, 267.

261 *"Until February 20":* Lochner, 112–113.

262 *"The Germans seem bewildered":* Zhukov, *Marshal Zhukov's Greatest Battles,* 81.

263 *"As for offensives":* Ibid., 82.

263 *"I've talked with":* Ibid.

263 *Shaposhnikov turned to Zhukov:* Ibid., 83.

263 *Germans intercepted:* Seaton, 260.

265 *food rationing:* Overy, *The Dictators,* 500.

265 *rotting remains:* I. Z. Ladygin, N. Smirnov, *Na Rzhevskom rubezhe,* 26.
266 *"extraordinarily favorable"* and *"He believes":* Lochner, 49.
266 *Order 0428* and *"All inhabited locations":* Volkogonov, 456.
267 *"Whether the decision":* Volkogonov, 456.
267 *In a top secret report* and *"Most people": Moskva Prifrontovaia 1941–1942,* 187–189.
268 *"Don't argue":* Zhukov, *Marshal Zhukov's Greatest Battles,* 85.
268 *"We overestimated":* Ibid., 88.
269 *"If you don't":* Ibid., 89.
269 *"Hey Russians!":* Ladygin, 26.
270 *"Events demonstrated":* Zhukov, *Marshal Zhukov's Greatest Battles,* 90.

11: "THE WORST OF ALL WORLDS"

PAGE
272 *Eden, Maisky* and *black bag:* Eden, 332.
273 *"That's marvelous":* Maisky, 227.
273 *"The cold which these men":* Eden, 333.
273 *"How can your people":* Maisky, 228.
273 *When the train pulled into Moscow:* Ibid., 228–229.
275 *"I explained that":* Ibid., 173.
275 *"The British government was":* Jan Ciechanowski, *Defeat in Victory,* 36.
275 *he still suspected Stalin might cut another deal with Hitler:* Ciechanowski, 33, 37, Butler, 62.
275 *"The issue of":* Churchill, 391.
276 *"was in line with":* Ciechanowski, 40.
276 *Eden reiterated* and *"does not involve":* Churchill, 392–393.
276 *"the first swallow":* Ciechanowski, 41.
276 *"They must have escaped":* Ibid., 68.
276 *"I think it would be"* and *"inviolable":* Ibid., 78.
277 *"Russian ideas":* Eden, 335.
278 *Eden knew how he had to respond* and *"Even before Russia":* Ibid., 336.
278 *Dated December 5, the cable:* Sherwood, 401–402.
278 *"What about the":* Eden, 337.
279 *"Stalin began to show his claws":* Ibid., 342–345.
280 *listening devices* and *"My conclusion":* Ibid., 345.
280 *"The corpses":* Maisky, 234.
280 *German prisoners:* Eden, 347, Maisky, 235.
280 *He told Maisky:* Eden, 347.
281 *meeting with Stalin on December 20:* Ibid., 348.
281 *to the Kremlin for dinner:* Ibid., 349–351.
281 *pepper brandy:* Maisky, 236.
281 *mission had ended:* Eden, 351–352.
282 *"Stalin's bust":* Lochner, 53.

282   *"Such fear":* Ibid., 113.

282   *Stalin sent a message* and *Churchill:* Maisky, 252–253.

283   *During his talks with Eden in December, Stalin:* Eden, 348–349.

283   *Lend-Lease supplies* and *it would provide:* Overy, *The Dictators,* 502–503.

284   *Upon his return to London, Eden:* Dunn, 160.

284   *"The increasing gravity":* Ibid.

284   *"not only indefensible":* Ibid., 161.

284   *"Soviet policy is":* Eden, 370.

285   *British-American talks about Russia "tangled":* Ibid., 375.

285   *"Here was the first":* Ibid.

285   *"I know you will not mind":* Dunn, 161.

285   *conversations with Maxim Litvinov* and *"he will deal with":* Ibid.

285   *March 9:* Eden, 376.

286   *"I did not like":* Ibid.

286   *"as a negotiator":* Ibid., 595.

286   *"My task as minister":* Resis, 8.

286   *secret meeting of Polish communists in Saratov:* Ciechanowski, 103.

287   *"Always graciously":* Reynolds, 241.

287   *"extremely despondent":* Larry Lesueur, *Twelve Months That Changed the World,* 56.

288   *disrupted cable communications:* Lesueur, 56–58.

288   *"A few soldiers":* Reynolds, 246–247.

288   *"Moats and I":* Ibid., 248.

289   *Pearl Harbor* and *"Everyone talked at once":* Lesueur, 74.

289   *"The big story":* Henry C. Cassidy, *Moscow Dateline,* 158.

289   *"That night I wondered":* Lesueur, 77.

289   *"The Red Army had":* Cassidy, 160.

290   *"was won by"* and *"We could have":* Ibid., 161.

290   *"Out there, I could see":* Ibid., 193–194.

290   *"Compared with London":* Lesueur, 82.

290   Lesueur's description of drive on Leningrad Highway: Ibid., 85–88.

291   *"Here, the bodies":* Cassidy, 195–196.

291   *Lesueur drove:* Lesueur, 122.

291   *"The war was hard":* Ibid., 91–92.

291   *"Russia happens to be":* Curie, 173.

291   *by what the local inhabitants had to say:* Ibid., 172–173.

292   *stories of German terror:* Ibid., 172–177.

292   *The thirteenth child:* Overy, *Russia's War,* 129–130; Catherine Andreyev, *Vlasov and the Russian Liberation Movement,* 19–22; and George Fischer, *Soviet Opposition to Stalin,* 26–32.

293   *Lesueur, accompanied by a censor and two Red Army officers, drove north:* Lesueur, 93–94.

293   *"With a smile":* Ibid., 97.

293 *looked more like:* Ibid., 98.
294 *Lesueur asked Vlasov:* Ibid.
294 *"one of the young leaders":* Curie, 179–184.
295 *"My blood belongs":* Ibid.
295 *Beria* and *"How is it":* Volkogonov, 442.
295 *Stalin summoned Khrushchev:* Schecter, 181–182.
296 *"It was difficult":* Ibid.
296 *"Smolensk Declaration"* and *"Bolshevism is the enemy":* Andreyev, 206–209.
296 *one of his brothers* and *parents:* Overy, *Russia's War,* 130.
296 *"I did everything I could":* Andreyev, 210–215.
297 *action in Prague:* Overy, *Russia's War,* 131.

12: THE DEADLIEST VICTORY

PAGE
299 *"In the course of":* Volkogonov, 456–457.
300 *Wehrmacht report dated July 13, 1942:* O. Kondrat'ev, *Eto bylo na Rzhevsko-Viazemskom platsdarme (kniga tret'ia),* 24.
300 *Germans preparing their offensive:* Ibid., 20.
301 *from Zhukov on down:* Ibid., 16.
301 *Soviet planes tried to make a drop:* Ladygin, 29.
302 *Lieutenant Mirzakhan Galeyev:* Svetlana Kukhtina, "Grandfather Was Reborn Near Rzhev," *Our Victory Day by Day: The Frontline Album,* RIA Novosti Project.
303 Stavka, *the Soviet military headquarters, sent out the order:* Glantz, *Zhukov's Greatest Defeat,* 22. (Glantz's book is the most detailed—and damning—account available of this operation.)
303 *The Soviet tally:* Ibid., 319.
303 *"at best disingenuous":* Ibid., 317.
303 *the German terror continued:* Rzhev Battle Museum researcher Olga Dudkina.
307 *Vyacheslav Molotov:* Resis, 22–23, 164–165, 267–269.
308 *27 million* and *8.6 million:* Merridale, 337.
308 *three times as high:* Ibid., 188.
308 *"It would be hard":* Volkogonov, 446–447.
308 *"All things considered":* Stepan Mikoyan, 106.
309 *"Our government has made":* Ulam, 314.
310 *"Will this winter":* Lochner, 130.
310 *"Like the supreme military genius":* Churchill, 536–537.
311 *"German troops were beaten":* Zhukov, *Marshal Zhukov's Greatest Battles,* 67.
311 *"It was cold":* Walter Kerr, *The Russian Army,* 49.
311 *"Stalin told me":* Axell, 87.

312   *"The Führer had no intention"*: Lochner, 136.
312   *"He wanted to be"*: Manstein, 283.
312   *"The bringing in of fresh"*: Eden, 341.
313   *"I found myself"* and *"But I knew"*: Schecter, 169.
313   *"All the anti-Nazi nations"*: Churchill, 537.
314   *"The arrival of Army Group Center"*: R. H. S. Stolfi, *Hitler's Panzers East*, 24.
314   *"By the magnitude of"*: Ibid., ix.
314   *"This was the"*: Lesueur, 86.
315   *"The battle for Moscow allowed"*: Overy, *Russia's War*, 122.

Sources

PUBLICATIONS

Ananko, V., A. Domank and N. Romanichev, *Za kazhduiu piad.* Lvov: Kommunar, 1981.

Andreyev, Catherine. *Vlasov and the Russian Liberation Movement: Soviet Reality and Émigré Theories.* Cambridge: Cambridge University Press, 1989.

Applebaum, Anne. *Gulag: A History.* New York: Doubleday, 2003.

Axell, Albert. *Marshal Zhukov: The Man Who Beat Hitler.* London: Pearson Longman, 2003.

Banac, Ivo, ed. *The Diary of Georgi Dimitrov 1933–1949.* New Haven: Yale University Press, 2003.

Beevor, Antony. *Stalingrad.* New York: Penguin Books, 1999.

Beevor, Antony, and Luba Vinogradova, eds. *A Writer at War: Vasily Grossman with the Red Army, 1941–1945.* New York: Pantheon Books, 2006.

Berezhkov, Valentin M. *At Stalin's Side: His Interpreter's Memoirs from the October Revolution to the Fall of the Dictator's Empire.* New York: Carol Publishing Group, 1994.

Beria, Sergo. *Beria, My Father: Inside Stalin's Kremlin.* London: Gerald Duckworth & Co., 2001.

Bock, Fedor von. Klaus Gerbet, ed. *The War Diary: 1939–1945.* Atglen, PA: Schiffer Military History, 1996.

Bohlen, Charles E. *Witness to History: 1929–1969.* New York: W. W. Norton & Company, 1973.

Browning, Christopher R. *Ordinary Men: Reserve Police Battalion 101 and the Final Solution in Poland.* New York: Harper Perennial, 1992.

Bullock, Alan. *Hitler and Stalin: Parallel Lives.* London: Fontana Press, 1998.

Burdick, Charles, and Hans-Adolf Jacobsen, eds. *The Halder War Diary: 1939–1942.* London: Greenhill Books, 1988.

Butler, Susan, ed. *My Dear Mr. Stalin: The Complete Correspondence Between Franklin D. Roosevelt and Joseph V. Stalin.* New Haven: Yale University Press, 2005.

Cassidy, Henry C. *Moscow Dateline: 1941–1943.* Boston: Houghton Mifflin Company, 1943.

Churchill, Winston S. *The Grand Alliance.* Boston: Houghton Mifflin Company, 1950.

Ciechanowski, Jan. *Defeat in Victory.* New York: Doubleday & Company, 1947.

Conquest, Robert. *The Dragons of Expectation: Reality and Delusion in the Course of History.* New York: W. W. Norton & Company, 2005.

Conquest, Robert. *The Great Terror: A Reassessment.* New York: Oxford University Press, 1990.

Curie, Eve. *Journey Among Warriors.* New York: Doubleday, Doran and Co., 1943.

Dallin, Alexander. *German Rule in Russia 1941–1945: A Study of Occupation Policies.* London: Macmillan & Co., 1957.

Davies, Joseph E. *Mission To Moscow.* New York: Simon & Schuster, 1941.

Davies, Norman. *Heart of Europe: A Short History of Poland.* Oxford: Clarendon Press, 1984.

Deutscher, Isaac. *Stalin: A Political Biography.* New York: Oxford University Press, 1972.

Druzhnikov, Yuri. *Passport to Yesterday.* London: Peter Owen Publishers, 2004.

Dunn, Dennis J. *Caught Between Roosevelt & Stalin: America's Ambassadors to Moscow.* Lexington: The University Press of Kentucky, 1998.

Eberle, Henrik, and Matthias Uhl, eds., *The Hitler Book: The Secret Dossier Prepared for Stalin from the Interrogations of Hitler's Personal Aides.* New York: Public Affairs, 2005.

Eden, Anthony. *The Reckoning.* Boston: Houghton Mifflin Company, 1965.

Filatov, V. P., and others. *Moskovskaia bitva v khronike faktov i sobytii.* Moscow: Voennoe Izdatelstvo, 2004.

Fischer, George. *Soviet Opposition to Stalin: A Case Study in World War II.* Cambridge: Harvard University Press, 1952.

Glantz, David M. *Colossus Reborn: The Red Army at War, 1941–1943*. Lawrence: University Press of Kansas, 2005.

Glantz, David M. *Zhukov's Greatest Defeat: The Red Army's Epic Disaster in Operation Mars, 1942*. Lawrence: University Press of Kansas, 1999.

Glantz, David M., and Jonathan M. House. *When Titans Clashed: How the Red Army Stopped Hitler*. Edinburgh: Birlinn Limited, 2000.

Goldensohn, Leon. Robert Gellately, ed. *The Nuremberg Interviews: An American Psychiatrist's Conversations with the Defendants and Witnesses*. New York: Alfred A. Knopf, 2004.

Gorinov, M. M., and others, eds. *Moskva Voennaia, 1941–1945: Memuary i arkhivnye dokumenty*. Moscow: Mosgorarkhiv, 1995.

Grigorenko, Petro G. *Memoirs*. New York: W. W. Norton and Company, 1982.

Gromyko, Andrei. *Memoirs*. New York: Doubleday, 1989.

Grossman, Vasily. *Life and Fate*. London: Collins Harvill, 1985.

Guderian, Heinz. *Panzer Leader*. London: Macdonald & Co., 1982.

Harriman, W. Averell, and Elie Abel. *Special Envoy to Churchill and Stalin 1941–1946*. New York: Random House, 1975.

Hasegawa, Tsuyoshi. *Racing the Enemy: Stalin, Truman and the Surrender of Japan*. Cambridge: The Belknap Press of Harvard University Press, 2005.

Hayman, Ronald. *Hitler + Geli*. London: Bloomsbury Publishing, 1998.

Herwarth, Hans von, with S. Frederick Starr, *Against Two Evils*. New York: Rawson, Wade Publishers, 1981.

Hitler, Adolf. *Mein Kampf*. Boston: Houghton Mifflin Company, 1971.

Hull, Cordell. *The Memoirs of Cordell Hull, Volume II*. New York: The Macmillan Company, 1948.

Irving, David. *Hitler's War*. New York: Avon Books, 1990.

Ivanov, V. K. *Moskovskaia zona oborony. Eë rol' v zashchite stolitsy. 1941–1942 gg*. Moscow: Gosudarstvennyi Muzei Oborony Moskvy, 2001.

Jones, Robert Huhn. *The Roads to Russia: United States Lend-Lease to the Soviet Union*. Norman: University of Oklahoma Press, 1969.

Jukes, Geoffrey. *The Defense of Moscow*. New York: Ballantine Books, 1970.

Kammerer, Y. Y., V. S. Karaulov, and S. E. Lapirov, *Moskve—vozdushnaia trevoga! Mestnaia PVO v gody voiny*. Moscow: Agar, 2000.

Kennan, George F. *Memoirs: 1925–1950*. Boston: Little, Brown and Company, 1967.

Kerr, Walter. *The Russian Army: Its Men, Its Leaders, and Its Battles*. New York: Alfred A. Knopf, 1944.

Kershaw, Ian. *Hitler 1889–1936: Hubris*. London: The Penguin Press, 1998.

Kershaw, Ian. *Hitler 1936–45: Nemesis*. New York: W. W. Norton & Company, 2000.

Khokhlov, Nikolai. *In the Name of Conscience: The Testament of a Soviet Secret Agent.* New York: David McKay Company, 1959.

Kohler, Phyllis Penn, ed. and trans. *Journey for Our Time: The Journals of the Marquis de Custine.* New York: Pellegrini & Cudahy, 1951.

Kondrat'ev, O., and L. Myl'nikov. *Eto bylo na Rzhevsko-Viazemskom platsdarme (kniga tret'ia).* Rzhev: Rzhevskii knizhnii klub, 2003.

Kumanev, Georgii. *Riadom so Stalinym: Otkrovennyye svidel'stva.* Moscow: Bylina, 1999.

Ladygin, I. Z., and N. Smirnov. *Na Rzhevskom rubezhe.* Rzhev: Zhurnalist, 1992.

Lesueur, Larry. *Twelve Months That Changed The World.* New York: Alfred A. Knopf, 1943.

Lih, Lars T., Oleg V. Naumov, and Oleg V. Khlevniuk, eds. *Stalin's Letters to Molotov 1925–1936.* New Haven: Yale University Press, 1995.

Lochner, Louis P., ed. *The Goebbels Diaries: 1942–1943.* New York: Doubleday, 1948.

Lucas, James. *War on the Eastern Front: The German Soldier in Russia 1941–1945.* London: Greenhill Books, Military Book Club edition, 1991.

Maisky, Ivan. *Memoirs of a Soviet Ambassador: The War 1939–1943.* London: Hutchinson, 1967.

Manstein, Erich von. *Lost Victories.* Chicago: Henry Regnery Company, 1958.

Meacham, Jon. *Franklin and Winston: An Intimate Portrait of an Epic Friendship.* New York: Random House, 2003.

Medvedev, Roy. *Let History Judge: The Origins and Consequences of Stalinism.* New York: Columbia University Press, 1989.

Merridale, Catherine. *Ivan's War: Life and Death in the Red Army, 1939–1945.* New York: Metropolitan Books, 2006.

Mikoyan, Anastas. *Tak bylo.* Moscow: Vagrius, 1999.

Mikoyan, Stepan Anastasovich. *Memoirs of Military Test-Flying and Life with the Kremlin's Elite.* Shrewsbury: Airlife, 1999.

Miner, Steven Merritt. *Stalin's Holy War: Religion, Nationalism, and Alliance Politics, 1941–1945.* Chapel Hill: The University of North Carolina Press, 2003.

Misiunas, Romuald J., and Rein Taagepera. *The Baltic States: Years of Dependence 1940–1980.* Berkeley: University of California Press, 1983.

Montefiore, Simon Sebag. *Stalin: The Court of the Red Tsar.* New York: Alfred A. Knopf, 2004.

Moskovskaia Bitva v Postanovleniiakh Gosudarstvennogo Komiteta oborony. Dokumenty i materialy 1941–1942. Moscow: Bol'shaiia Rossiiskaia Entsiklopediia i Gosudarstvennyj Muzei Oborony Moskvy, 2001.

Moskva Prifrontovaia 1941–1942. Arkhivnye dokumenty i materialy. Moscow: Mosgorarkhiv, AO Moskovskie uchebniki, 2001.

Murphy, David E. *What Stalin Knew: The Enigma of Barbarossa.* New Haven: Yale University Press, 2005.

Oreshkin, Boris. *Viaz'ma,* in *Al'manakh "Podvig,"* issue 38. Moscow: *Molodaia Gvardiia,* 1991.

Overy, Richard. *The Dictators: Hitler's Germany, Stalin's Russia.* New York: W. W. Norton & Company, 2004.

Overy, Richard. *Russia's War.* New York: Penguin Books, 1998.

Palmer, R. R., and Joel Colton. *A History of the Modern World.* New York: Alfred A. Knopf, 1965.

Pechenkin, Aleksandr. *Voennaia Elita SSSR v 1935–1939 gg.: Repressii i obnovlenie.* Moscow: VZFEI, 2003.

Pleshakov, Constantine. *Stalin's Folly: The Tragic First Ten Days of World War II on the Eastern Front.* Boston: Houghton Mifflin, 2005.

Rayfield, Donald. *Stalin and His Hangmen: The Tyrant and Those Who Killed for Him.* New York: Random House, 2004.

Resis, Albert, ed. *Molotov Remembers: Inside Kremlin Politics.* Chicago: Ivan R. Dee, 1993.

Reynolds, Quentin. *By Quentin Reynolds.* New York: McGraw-Hill Book Company, 1963.

Rybin, A. T. *Riadom so Stalinym.* Moscow: Veteran, 1992.

Schecter, Jerrold L., with Vyacheslav V. Luchkov, eds. *Khrushchev Remembers: The Glasnost Tapes.* Boston: Little Brown and Company, 1990.

Schlabrendorff, Fabian von. *The Secret War Against Hitler.* New York: Pitman Publishing Corporation, 1965.

Seaton, Albert. *The Battle for Moscow.* New York: Jove, 1985.

Service, Robert. *Stalin: A Biography.* Cambridge: The Belknap Press of Harvard University Press, 2005.

Seth, Ronald. *Operation Barbarossa: The Battle for Moscow.* London: World Distributors, 1965.

Shepherd, Ben. *War in the Wild East: The German Army and Soviet Partisans.* Cambridge: Harvard University Press, 2004.

Sherwood, Robert E. *Roosevelt and Hopkins: An Intimate History.* New York: Harper & Brothers, 1948.

Shirer, William L. *The Rise and Fall of the Third Reich: A History of Nazi Germany.* Greenwich, CT: Fawcett Publications, 1965.

Shnol, S. E. *Geroi i zlodei rossiiskoi nauki.* Moscow: Kron-press, 1997.

Shvetsova, L. I., and others. *Moskva i moskvichi—partizanskomu dvizheniiu Velikoi Otechestvennoi voiny.* Moscow: "Atlantida—XXI vek," 2000.

Simonov, Konstantin. *The Living and the Dead.* Moscow: Progress Publishers, 1975.

Stalin, Joseph. *The War of National Liberation.* New York: International Publishers, 1942.

Stolfi, R. H. S. *Hitler's Panzers East: World War II Reinterpreted.* Norman: University of Oklahoma Press, 1992.

Strasser, Otto. *Hitler and I*. Boston: Houghton Mifflin Company, 1940.

Talbott, Strobe, ed. *Khrushchev Remembers*. Boston: Little Brown and Company, 1970.

Taubman, William. *Stalin's American Policy: From Entente to Détente to Cold War*. New York: W. W. Norton & Company, 1982.

Taylor, Fred, ed. *The Goebbels Diaries: 1939–1941*. London: Sphere Books Limited, 1983.

Toptygyn, Alexei. *Lavrentii Beriia: Neizvestnyi marshal Gosbezopasnosti*. Moscow: EKSMO, 2005.

Trevor-Roper, H. R., ed. *Hitler's War Directives: 1939–1945*. London: Pan Books, 1966.

Tumarkin, Nina. *The Living & The Dead: The Rise and Fall of the Cult of World War II in Russia*. New York: Basic Books, 1994.

Ulam, Adam B. *Expansion and Coexistence: Soviet Foreign Policy, 1917–73, Second Edition*. New York: Praeger Publishers, 1974.

Vinogradov, V. K., and others. *Lubianka v dni bitvy za Moskvu*. Moscow: Zvonnitsa, 2002.

Volkogonov, Dmitri. *Stalin: Triumph and Tragedy*. Rocklin, CA: Prima Publishing, 1991.

Werth, Alexander. *Russia at War: 1941–1945*. New York: Avon Books, 1965.

Whymant, Robert. *Stalin's Spy: Richard Sorge and the Tokyo Espionage Ring*. New York: St. Martin's Press, 1998.

Yeaton, Ivan D. *Memoirs of Ivan D. Yeaton, USA (Ret.)*. Palo Alto: Unpublished manuscript donated to Hoover Institution on War, Revolution and Peace, 1976, copyright Stanford University.

Yeroshin, V. P., and others. *Organy gosudarstvennoi bezopasnosti SSSR v Velikoi Otechestvennoi voine. Sbornik Dokumentov*. Moscow: Rus, 2000.

Zamoyski, Adam. *Moscow 1812: Napoleon's Fatal March*. New York: HarperCollins Publishers, 2004.

Zbarsky, Ilya, and Samuel Hutchinson. *Lenin's Embalmers*. London: The Harvill Press, 1999.

Zhukov, Georgi K. *Marshal Zhukov's Greatest Battles*. New York: Pocket Books, 1970.

Zhukov, G. K. *Vospominaniia i razmyshleniia. V trekh tomah*. Moscow: Novosti, 1995.

INTERVIEWS

Anufriyev, Yevgeny
Bogolyubskaya, Irina
Braginskaya, Ella
Buchin, Aleksandr
Bylinina, Tamara

Chegrinets, Yegor
Chernyavsky, Viktor
Dolgov, Vyacheslav
Druzhnikov, Yuri
Dudkina, Olga
Edelman, Vladimir
Eremko, Slava
Geykhman, Mikhail
Godov, Boris
Gordon, Abram
Kagan, Boris
Kharlamov, Vyacheslav
Khokhlov, Nikolai
Koneva, Natalya
Kravchenko, Natalya
Kumanev, Georgy
Labas, Yuli
Maklyarsky, Boris
Mikoyan, Sergo
Mikoyan, Stepan
Myagkov, Mikhail
Nevzorov, Boris
Palatov, Andrei
Petrova, Tatyana
Pokarzhevsky, Dmitry
Prokhorova, Valeria
Romanitchev, Nikolai
Rzhevskaya, Elena
Sarnov, Benedikt
Safonov, Dmitry
Saprykin, Pavel
Shaidayev, Magomed-Ganifa
Shchors, Igor
Shchors, Natalya
Shevelev, Leonid
Sobolevskaya, Faina
Stepanova, Vera
Sudoplatov, Anatoly
Suslov, Maxim
Teleguyev, Yevgeny
Timokhin, Semyon
Tsessarskaya, Tatyana
Tsessarsky, Albert
Vidensky, Boris

Vinitsky, Ilya
Wernicke, Richard
Yakovlev, Nikolai
Zarubina, Zoya
Zbarsky, Ilya
Zevelev, Aleksandr
Zhukova, Ella

Acknowledgments

The prerequisites for a nonfiction book are obvious: a good idea, good research and good reporting. In the case of *The Greatest Battle*, my agent Robert Gottlieb first suggested the idea, insisting that the story of the battle for Moscow hasn't ever been done justice. He also assured me that his Trident research team in Moscow could provide me with all the assistance I'd need to make this work. Since I was traveling to Moscow regularly anyway, he urged me to ask his people there to line up a few preliminary interviews to see what I might discover that I hadn't heard before about this chapter of history and to get a sense of how I might go about learning more.

Those first interviews left no doubt in my mind that there was a remarkable story to tell here, and that Zamir Gotta and Irina Krivaya would know how to get to the people and the newly available sources, especially previously secret documents, that could bring it to life. Zamir and Irina proved to be incredibly hardworking, skillful and imaginative research partners, amassing huge amounts of materials and hunting down people who in many cases hadn't told their stories in decades, if at all. Along with the indefatigable Olga Nikiforova and Anna Zaitseva, who joined the effort later, they patiently fielded my steady stream of requests for more interviews, more transcripts, more information, more details about this or that episode. There is no way I could have written the book without this incredible team.

Many others volunteered suggestions for people to interview and helped me locate them. In some cases they suggested older family members or friends, and in others simply people they'd heard of who had lived through this period. Among those who put me in touch with people who appear in these pages are Vladimir Voinovich, Valery Bazarov, Sergei Severinov, Owen Matthews, Christian Wernicke and David Gonnerman. Cameron Sawyer, an American friend in Moscow with an impressive grasp of Russian and German history, not only introduced me to the searchers Yegor Chegrinets and Andrey Palatov, who took me to the killing fields of Vyazma, but also served as the organizer and driver of our expedition.

Then, of course, there are the veterans, civilians and sons and daughters of the military and political leaders who figure in this story. Their names appear in these pages and in the Sources section. I'd like to say more about so many of them, but I'll limit myself to one generalization. Maybe because they survived when so many others didn't and then went on to live long lives in a country with an appallingly low life expectancy, they are a formidable lot. By and large, they are tough, and they are willing to confront painful memories with an honesty that perhaps only comes with the passage of time and the recognition that the Soviet system is no more, even if many of its myths still persist. They also were gracious and hospitable, inviting me into their homes and sharing whatever memories or experiences I asked them about. I can't thank them enough.

I also owe a tremendous debt to the Hoover Institution, which is well known for its impressive collection of documentation about the Soviet Union in its archives. Dave Brady and Mandy MacCalla of the media fellows program, along with Dave's predecessor Tom Henriksen, provided me with generous invitations to spend time there on several occasions, and Carol Leadenham offered invaluable help in the archives, as did Molly Molloy in the library. The chapters on diplomacy and the foreign community in Moscow are largely a product of that research.

None of this would have mattered if I hadn't had the support and encouragement for this project from Alice Mayhew at Simon & Schuster. Along with her talented colleague Roger Labrie, she took to the idea of a book about the battle for Moscow right away, and as always, offered invaluable advice on how to structure the story and keep the most important themes in focus. Alice isn't just an incredibly skillful editor; she's an inspiration every step of the way. At Simon & Schuster, I also want to thank Serena Jones and Victoria Meyer, and everyone else who was involved in the various stages of this project.

A former *Newsweek* colleague, Steve Shabad, did his usual punctilious job of checking the transliterations of Russian names. I had learned to rely on him when I was filing stories from Moscow during my earlier stints there, and I was delighted when he agreed to help me out again. At *Newsweek,* many editors and colleagues offered occasional advice and frequent encouragement. Among them: Rick Smith, Jon Meacham, Fareed Zakaria, Ron Javers, Jeff Bartholet, Fred Guterl, Nisid Hajari, Jon Alter, and Susan Szeliga. I also want to thank James Price, Simon Barnett and Leah Latella for their help with photos.

Many friends have provided additional support. In particular, I want to mention David Satter, who helped me immensely in Moscow when I first arrived there in 1981, and Ardith and Steve Hodes, who have been the best friends anyone could wish for since we met three decades ago.

It's hardest to express my gratitude to my family. My parents, Marie and Zygmunt, diligently read every chapter as soon as I wrote it, providing their valuable critiques. All my children—Alex, Adam, Sonia, Eva and her irrespressible husband, Taylor—also served as readers, sounding boards and providers of suggestions. Above all, they kept my spirits high. A special mention in that category goes to Sonia's daughter, our granddaughter, Stella.

The most challenging task of all is to figure out what to say about my wife Christina, or Krysia as all of us call her. She's always been my first editor and critic, who pulls no punches. Since she grew up in Poland when Soviet propaganda films were common fare and then lived in Moscow with me in both Soviet and post-Soviet times, she was quick to question anything that didn't ring true. Often this meant I'd have to go back to my sources for what seemed like the umpteenth time, only to discover that, yes, there was something more that had to be nailed down or straightened out. But along with the tough questioning, she provides everything else that makes my life and work possible. Which says everything and not nearly enough.

Index

About the Author

Andrew Nagorski is a senior editor at Newsweek International. An award-winning foreign correspondent, he has served two tours as Moscow bureau chief. He has also reported from Warsaw, Rome, Hong Kong, Washington, Bonn and Berlin. He is the author of *Reluctant Farewell: An American Reporter's Candid Look Inside the Soviet Union* and *The Birth of Freedom: Shaping Lives and Societies in the New Eastern Europe*. His novel *Last Stop Vienna* was a *Washington Post* bestseller. He and his wife, Christina, who have four children, live in Pelham Manor, New York.

About the Author

Andrew Nagorski is a senior editor at Newsweek International. An award-winning foreign correspondent, he has served two tours as Moscow bureau chief. He has also reported from Warsaw, Rome, Hong Kong, Washington, Bonn and Berlin. He is the author of *Reluctant Farewell: An American Reporter's Candid Look Inside the Soviet Union* and *The Birth of Freedom: Shaping Lives and Societies in the New Eastern Europe*. His novel *Last Stop Vienna* was a *Washington Post* best-seller. He and his wife, Christina, who have four children, live in Pelham Manor, New York.